내신백신,

고등　기출문제집

Common English 1

오선영

❦ Preface ❦

Learning is not attained by chance,
It must be sought for with ardor
And attended with diligence.

배움은 우연히 얻어지는 것이 아니라
열성을 다해 갈구하고
부지런히 집중해야 얻을 수 있는 것입니다.

-Abigail Adams-

이 책의 **구성과 특징**

Words

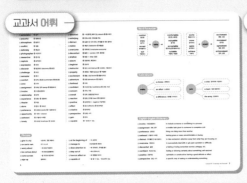

교과서 어휘

교과서 어휘 익히기

교과서에 제시된 주요 단어와 숙어를 정리하고, 기본 다지기와 실력 다지기 문제를 통해 어휘를 연습할 수 있습니다.

Functions

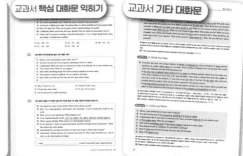

교과서 핵심 및 기타 대화문

교과서 핵심 대화문 익히기

교과서 대화문의 해석과 해설을 보며 익히고, 교과서 핵심 대화문 익히기를 통해 학습한 내용을 확인할 수 있습니다.

Grammar

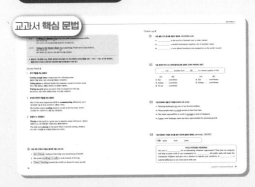
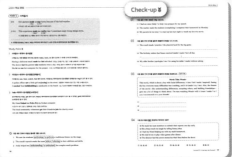

교과서 핵심 문법 Check-up

단원별 핵심 문법 사항을 정리하고, Check-up 문제를 통해 연습할 수 있습니다.

Reading

교과서 본문 분석

교과서 본문 외 지문 분석

교과서 본문 익히기

교과서 본문에 대한 첨삭식 해설을 통해 문장을 정확히 익히고, 빈칸 완성하기, 옳은 어법·어휘 고르기, 틀린 부분 고치기 등의 활동을 통해 연습할 수 있습니다.

내신 1등급 공략

내신 1등급 어휘 공략

내신 1등급 어법 공략

교과서 지문을 이용하여 수능 어휘와 어법 문제 유형을 집중 연습할 수 있도록 구성하였습니다.

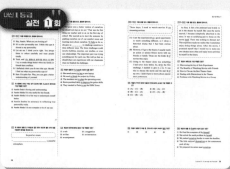

내신 1등급 실전 1회~3회

실제 학교 내신 기출 문제에서 엄선한 내신 기출 문제와 내신 시험에 나올 확률이 높은 문제들로 구성된 내신 1등급 실전 문제를 통해 풍부한 실전 경험을 쌓을 수 있습니다.

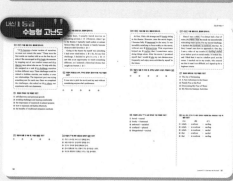

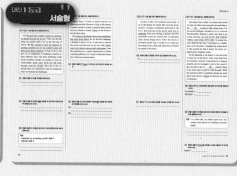

내신 1등급 수능형 고난도

내신 1등급 서술형

교과서 변형 지문을 활용하여 수능형 고난도 문제를 훈련하고, 다양한 서술형 문항도 대비할 수 있도록 구성하였습니다.

중간고사, 기말고사

중간고사

기말고사

최종 점검 중간고사와 기말고사를 통해 학교 내신 1등급에 완벽하게 대비할 수 있습니다.

이 책의 **차례**

01

—

A Journey into Yourself

Functions

▶ 능력 유무 표현하기
I'm good at creating a peaceful atmosphere.

▶ 관심 표현하기
I'm interested in seeking new opportunities to grow.

Grammar

▶ **Going to the theater alone** was something I had never done before.

▶ This experience **made** me **realize** that I sometimes enjoy doing things alone.

교과서 어휘

personality	명 성격	
peaceful	형 평화로운	
atmosphere	명 분위기	
conflict	명 갈등	
definitely	부 확실히	
photographer	명 사진작가	
researcher	명 연구원	
capture	동 포착하다	
expression	명 표정	
discover	동 발견하다 (discovery 명 발견)	
challenge	명 도전	
semester	명 학기	
comfort	명 안락, 편안함 (comfortable 형 편안한)	
zone	명 지역	
assignment	명 과제, 임무 (assign 동 할당하다)	
involve	동 수반[포함]하다	
relationship	명 관계	
experience	명 경험 동 경험하다	
theater	명 극장	
alone	부 혼자 형 외로운	
preference	명 선호(도) (prefer 동 더 좋아하다)	
opportunity	명 기회 (= chance)	
awkward	형 (기분이) 어색한	
lonely	형 외로운 (loneliness 명 외로움)	

absorbed	형 ~에 몰두한, 빠져 있는 (absorb 동 흡수하다)
satisfying	형 만족스러운, 만족감을 주는
distract	동 집중이 안 되게 하다, (주의를) 딴 데로 돌리다
realize	동 깨닫다 (realization 명 깨달음)
overcome	동 극복하다 (-overcame-overcome)
discomfort	명 불편 (↔ comfort, 안락, 편안함)
shallow	형 얕은 (↔ deep 깊은)
assure	동 장담하다, 확언하다
beginner	명 초보자
instructor	명 강사, 교사 (instruct 동 지시하다, 가르치다)
properly	부 제대로, 적절히 (proper 형 적절한)
excitement	명 흥분, 신남 (excite 동 흥분시키다)
adventure	명 모험 (adventurer 명 모험가)
forehead	명 이마
confident	형 자신감 있는 (confidence 명 신뢰, 자신)
concern	명 우려, 걱정
overall	부 전부, 종합[전반]적으로
reaction	명 반응, 반작용 (react 동 반응하다)
positive	형 긍정적인 (↔ negative 부정적인)
effect	명 효과 (effective 형 효과적인)
creative	형 창의적인
perspective	명 관점, 시각
gain	동 얻다
capable	형 ~을 할 수 있는

give it a try	시도하다, 한번 해보다
on one's own	자기 스스로
worry about	~에 대해 걱정하다
be curious about	~에 대해 궁금해하다
come across	~을 우연히 발견하다
sign up	등록하다

at the beginning of	~의 초반에
manage to	간신히[용케] 해내다
draw attention to	~에 주목하다, 주의를 끌다
step out of	~에서 벗어나다
have an effect on	~에 영향을 미치다
capable of	~을 할 수 있는, ~할 능력이 있는

Word Formation

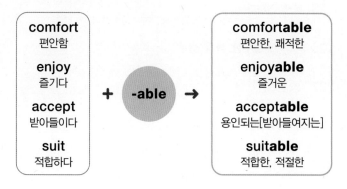

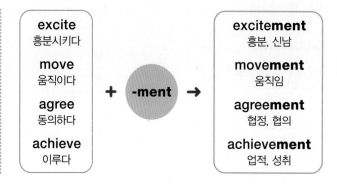

Collocations

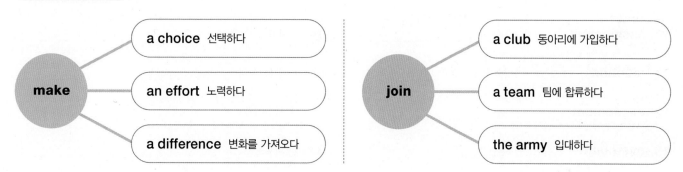

English-English Dictionary

□ **involve** 수반[포함]하다   to include someone or something in a process

□ **assignment** 과제, 임무   a smaller task given to someone to complete a job

□ **preference** 선호(도)   liking one thing more than another

□ **awkward** (기분이) 어색한   lacking grace or ease; uncomfortable or clumsy

□ **distract** (주의를) 딴 데로 돌리다   to take someone's attention away from what they are focusing on

□ **overcome** 극복하다   to successfully deal with or get past a problem or difficulty

□ **discomfort** 불편   a feeling of being somewhat worried, unhappy, etc.

□ **confident** 자신감 있는   feeling or showing certainty about something; self-assured

□ **positive** 긍정적인   optimistic or constructive; having a good attitude or effect

□ **perspective** 관점, 시각   a specific way of seeing or understanding something

교과서 어휘 익히기

❖ 다음 영어는 우리말로, 우리말은 영어로 쓰시오.

01	theater	명 _____	25	동 발견하다	_____
02	assure	동 _____	26	형 ~에 몰두한, 빠져 있는	_____
03	shallow	형 _____	27	명 관계	_____
04	personality	명 _____	28	형 긍정적인	_____
05	challenge	명 _____	29	명 불편	_____
06	atmosphere	명 _____	30	동 포함하다	_____
07	distract	동 _____	31	형 만족스러운	_____
08	gain	동 _____	32	형 자신감 있는	_____
09	comfort	명 _____	33	명 연구원	_____
10	assignment	명 _____	34	명 이마	_____
11	reaction	명 _____	35	명 관점, 시각	_____
12	excitement	명 _____	36	명 사진작가	_____
13	overcome	동 _____	37	형 외로운	_____
14	opportunity	명 _____	38	명 선호(도)	_____
15	experience	명 _____	39	부 확실히	_____
16	capture	동 _____	40	동 깨닫다	_____
17	awkward	형 _____	41	형 ~을 할 수 있는	_____
18	instructor	명 _____	42	부 제대로, 적절히	_____
19	give it a try	_____	43	~에 대해 궁금해하다	_____
20	on one's own	_____	44	~에 대해 걱정하다	_____
21	come across	_____	45	~에 주목하다, 주의를 끌다	_____
22	manage to	_____	46	등록하다	_____
23	have an effect on	_____	47	~에서 벗어나다	_____
24	at the beginning of	_____	48	~을 할 수 있는	_____

A 다음 괄호 안의 단어를 알맞은 형태로 고쳐 빈칸에 쓰시오.

01 It gave me such a rush of _____. (excite)

02 I have never enjoyed water activities or felt _____ while doing them. (comfort)

03 This program is _____ for children of all ages. (suit)

04 It is _____ to wear casual clothes to the event. (accept)

05 There was a general _____ among the team members to extend the deadline. (agree)

B 다음 빈칸에 들어갈 말로 알맞은 것을 보기에서 골라 쓰시오.

> 보기   make   take   joined   had

01 One of them tried new foods from different countries, while another _____ a creative writing club.

02 I promised myself that I would try to _____ my own choices more often and enjoy more activities by myself in the future.

C 다음 밑줄 친 부분의 영어 뜻풀이로 알맞은 것을 골라 기호를 쓰시오.

> ⓐ lacking grace or ease; uncomfortable or clumsy
> ⓑ a feeling of being somewhat worried, unhappy, etc.
> ⓒ a specific way of seeing or understanding something

01 For the second challenge, I decided to try to overcome this discomfort. (   )

02 We gained different perspectives on life and had a lot of fun, too! (   )

03 At first, it felt a bit awkward and lonely to sit in the theater by myself. (   )

교과서 핵심 대화문

능력 유무 표현하기

G Hey, Austin. What are you looking at?
　　　　　　　　　　　　　　look at: ~을 보다

B It's a color personality test. I think this type is closest to my personality.
　　　　　　　　　　　　　　　　　(that)　　　　　형용사 close(가까운)의 최상급

G Let me see. I think you're right. You always listen to others carefully and
　　　　　　　　　(that)　　　　　　　　　　VI　　　　　　등위접속사

treat people kindly.
V2

B Yeah, and **I'm good at creating a peaceful atmosphere**. I try to make
　　　　　　be good at+동명사: ~을 잘하다　　　　　　　　　　　　　~하려고 노력하다

things better when my family or friends have conflicts.
　　　　　접속사(~할 때)

G I definitely think you fit into this type. Should I find out
　　　　　　　　　　(that)

what my personality type is?
명사절(의문사+주어+동사)

B Sure. It's quite fun. Plus, you can gain a better understanding of yourself.
　　　　　　부사(꽤, 매우)

G: 안녕, Austin. 뭐 보고 있어?

B: 색깔 성격 테스트야. 이 타입이 내 성격에 가장 가까운 것 같아.

G: 어디 보자. 네 말이 맞는 것 같아. 너는 항상 다른 사람들 이야기를 잘 들어주고 친절하게 대하잖아.

B: 응, 그리고 나는 평화로운 분위기를 만드는 걸 잘해. 가족이나 친구들이 갈등이 있을 때 상황을 개선하려고 노력해.

G: 확실히 네가 이 타입에 맞는 것 같아. 나도 내 성격 타입을 알아볼까?

B: 물론이지. 꽤 재미있어. 게다가 너 자신에 대해 더 잘 이해할 수 있어.

Study Point ❧

I'm good at ~은 '~을 잘하다'라는 뜻으로 자신이 잘하는 것을 말할 때 사용하는 표현이다.

More Expressions ❧

잘하는 것을 말하는 표현들

I'm talented in ~(나는 ~에 재능이 있다), I'm accomplished in ~(나는 ~에 노련하다), I'm proficient in ~(나는 ~에 능숙하다), I specialize in ~(나는 ~을 전문으로 한다) 등도 잘하는 것을 말할 때 사용할 수 있는 표현이다.

I'm talented in learning new languages. 나는 새로운 언어를 배우는 데 재능이 있다.

I'm accomplished in art and design. 나는 예술과 디자인 분야에 능숙하다.

I'm proficient in musical composition. 나는 음악 작곡에 능숙하다.

I specialize in designing websites. 나는 웹사이트 디자인을 전문으로 한다.

Check-up ❧

다음 대화의 빈칸에 들어갈 말로 적절하지 <u>않은</u> 것은?

> **A** Are you preparing the food yourself?
>
> **B** Yes. _____ the art of cooking.

① I am good at
② I am talented in
③ I am proficient in
④ I specialize in
⑤ I have an interest in

Function 2 관심 표현하기

M Our guest for today is Janis Smith. Please tell us about yourself.
<u>tell A about B: A에게 B에 대해 말하다</u>

W Sure. I'm a photographer, travel guide, and researcher. I travel around the
세계 일주를 하다
world for my work.

M Wow, you're a true adventurer! What inspires you?
의문사 주어 단수동사

W I love experiencing the world. And **I'm interested in seeking new**
동명사(목적어 역할)   be interested in: ~에 관심이 있다
opportunities to grow.

M That's a great attitude. What makes your photography unique?

W In my pictures, I focus on capturing human emotions through facial
focus on: ~에 초점을 맞추다
expressions. I think that makes my work unique.
접속사가 아니라 think의 목적어 역할을 하는 명사절의 주어임.

M Interesting! Do you have any advice for those who want to follow their
those who: ~하는 사람들
dreams?

W Absolutely. Always pursue your dreams and look for what really interests
전치사의 목적어 역할(의문사 주어+동사+목적어)
you. Life is short, so do what makes you happy.
do의 목적어 역할(의문사 주어+동사+목적어+목적보어)

≪ M: 오늘의 게스트는 Janis Smith입니다. 자기소개를 부탁드립니다.

W: 네. 저는 사진작가이자 여행 가이드며, 연구원입니다. 제 일을 위해 전 세계를 여행합니다.

M: 와, 당신은 진정한 모험가이시군요! 무엇이 당신에게 영감을 주나요?

W: 저는 세상을 경험하는 것을 좋아합니다. 그리고 저는 성장할 수 있는 새로운 기회를 찾는 데 관심이 있습니다.

M: 멋진 태도네요. 무엇이 당신의 사진을 독특하게 만드나요?

W: 제 사진에서, 저는 얼굴 표정을 통해 인간의 감정을 포착하는 데 중점을 둡니다. 그게 제 작업을 독특하게 만든다고 생각해요.

M: 흥미롭네요! 자신의 꿈을 쫓고 싶은 사람들을 위해 해주실 조언이 있나요?

W: 물론이죠. 항상 꿈을 추구하고 진정으로 관심 있는 것을 찾으세요. 인생은 짧으니까, 당신을 행복하게 만드는 일을 하세요.

Study Point ❧

I'm interested in ~은 '~에 관심이 있다'라는 뜻으로 관심이 있는 것을 말할 때 사용하는 표현이다.

More Expressions ❧

관심을 표현하는 다른 표현들

I have an interest in ~(나는 ~에 관심이 있다), I'm drawn to ~(나는 ~에 끌린다), I'm fascinated by ~(나는 ~에 매료되었다) 등도 관심을 표현할 때 사용할 수 있는 표현이다.

I have an interest in environmental conservation. 나는 환경 보호에 관심이 있다.

I'm drawn to nature and doing outdoor activities. 나는 자연과 야외 활동 하는 것에 끌린다.

I'm fascinated by ancient history. 나는 고대 역사에 매료되어 있다.

Check-up ❧

다음 대화에서 밑줄 친 부분의 의도로 가장 적절한 것은?

> **A** What motivates you to travel so often?
> **B** I'm interested in exploring different cultures and languages.

① 바람 표현하기　　　　② 장래 희망 말하기　　　　③ 관심 표현하기

④ 능력 표현하기　　　　⑤ 좋아하는 것 말하기

교과서 기타 대화문

TOPIC 1 C. Listen and Interact

M ❶ Finding your strengths is an important part of self-discovery. And ❷ it's easy to do! Just grab a pen and write down the answers to a few simple questions. ❸ To start with, think about how you perceive yourself. ❹ What do you think your good qualities are? What are you better at than others? Next, consider ❺ how others see you. What are some things ❻ that others often praise you for? What are some strengths your family and friends think you have? ❼ Once you've answered all of these questions, go back and review your answers. Then circle words ❽ that stand out. What did you discover about yourself?

❶ 동명사가 주어 역할을 할 때는 단수 취급 ❷ 「가주어 it, 진주어 to부정사」 구문 ❸ To start with: 우선 ❹ Do you think?＋What are your good qualities? ❺ 동사 consider의 목적어 역할을 하는 간접의문문 ❻ 목적격 관계대명사 ❼ once: 일단 ~하면 ❽ words를 수식하는 주격 관계대명사절

Q1 You must answer questions about yourself to find your strengths. (T / F)

TOPIC 4 B. While You View

M Everyone has their own unique identity, ❶ which is composed of various elements. ❷ Some identity markers are visible, while others are invisible. These markers influence how you perceive the world. They also influence how the world perceives you.
❸ An easy way to identify these markers is ❹ to create an identity portrait. Here's how you make one. First, draw a picture of your face, neck, and shoulders. Then draw a vertical line down the middle of your face. Color in the features of your face on ❺ one side of the line. On the other side, add your invisible identity markers. They can be words or pictures. The choice is yours!
❻ Drawing identity portraits isn't just a fun and creative activity. It's a way to learn about yourself and others. It also reminds us that everyone's identity is ❼ as complex and beautiful as our own!

❶ 계속적 용법의 관계대명사 which / be composed of: ~로 구성되다 ❷ Some ~, while others ...: 몇 개는 ~이고, 반면에 다른 것들은 … ❸ 문장의 주어는 An easy way ~ markers이고, 동사는 is / to identify는 way를 수식하는 형용사적 용법의 to부정사 ❹ 보어 역할을 하는 명사적 용법의 to부정사 ❺ 둘 중 하나는 one, 다른 하나는 the other ❻ 동명사가 주어 역할을 할 때는 단수 취급 ❼ as＋원급＋as: ~만큼 …한

Q2 Identity markers influence both how you see the world and how the world sees you. (T / F)

Wrap Up A. Listen and Write

G Marco, your presentation is next week, ❶ isn't it?
B Yes, but I'm nervous. ❷ I'm not good at speaking ❸ in front of others.
G I understand. But if you want to overcome your fears, you must ❹ get out of your comfort zone.
B ❺ That makes sense. What do you suggest?
G Start with ❻ something small. ❼ How about asking a question in class today?
B That doesn't sound too difficult. Do you think it will help?
G Sure! ❽ After you take the first step, the next step will be easier.
B Okay. I'll ❾ give it a try.

❶ be동사의 부가의문문 ❷ be not good at: ~을 잘 못하다 ❸ in front of: ~ 앞에서 / others: other people ❹ get out of: ~에서 벗어나다 ❺ That makes sense.: 말 되네. ❻ -thing으로 끝나는 부정대명사는 형용사가 뒤에서 수식 ❼ How about v-ing?: ~하는 게 어때? ❽ 시간 접속사(~ 후에) ❾ give it a try: 시도하다, 한번 해보다

Q3 Marco feels confident about speaking in front of others. (T / F)

교과서 핵심 대화문 익히기

01 자연스러운 대화가 되도록 순서대로 바르게 배열한 것은?

> **G** Hey, Austin. What are you looking at?
> **B** It's a color personality test. I think this type is closest to my personality.
> **G** Let me see. I think you're right. You always listen to others carefully and treat people kindly.
> (A) Sure. It's quite fun. Plus, you can gain a better understanding of yourself.
> (B) I definitely think you fit into this type. Should I find out what my personality type is?
> (C) Yeah, and I'm good at creating a peaceful atmosphere. I try to make things better when my family or friends have conflicts.

① (A) – (B) – (C)   ② (A) – (C) – (B)   ③ (B) – (A) – (C)
④ (C) – (A) – (B)   ⑤ (C) – (B) – (A)

02 다음 대화의 빈칸에 들어갈 말로 가장 적절한 것은?

> **G** Marco, your presentation is next week, isn't it?
> **B** Yes, but I'm nervous. I'm not good at speaking in front of others.
> **G** I understand. But if you want to overcome your fears, you must get out of your comfort zone.
> **B** That makes sense. What do you suggest?
> **G** Start with something small. How about asking a question in class today?
> **B** That doesn't sound too difficult. Do you think it will help?
> **G** Sure! After you take the first step, the next step will be easier.
> **B** _____

① Okay. I'll give it a try.   ② I think I'll take a nap.
③ I'll just skip class today.   ④ No way. I'm too busy.
⑤ I'm already good at public speaking.

03 다음 대화의 밑줄 친 우리말과 같은 뜻이 되도록 괄호 안의 말을 사용하여 문장을 완성하시오.

> **M** Our guest for today is Janis Smith. Please tell us about yourself.
> **W** Sure. I'm a photographer, travel guide, and researcher. I travel around the world for my work.
> **M** Wow, you're a true adventurer! What inspires you?
> **W** I love experiencing the world. 그리고 저는 성장할 수 있는 새로운 기회를 찾는 데 관심이 있습니다.
> **M** That's a great attitude. What makes your photography unique?
> **W** In my pictures, I focus on capturing human emotions through facial expressions. I think that makes my work unique.
> **M** Interesting! Do you have any advice for those who want to follow their dreams?
> **W** Absolutely. Always pursue your dreams and look for what really interests you. Life is short, so do what makes you happy.

> → And _____ to grow. (interested, seek, opportunities)

교과서 핵심 문법

POINT 1 동명사

예제	**Writing in a journal** helps improve your communication skills. 　　동명사 주어(단수 취급)　　　동사 일기 쓰기는 너의 의사소통 능력을 향상시키는 데 도움이 된다.
교과서	**Going to the theater alone** was something I had never done before. 　　동명사 주어(단수 취급)　　　동사 혼자 극장에 가는 것은 내가 전에 해본 적이 없는 일이었다.

▶ 동명사는 「동사원형+ing」 형태로 문장에서 명사처럼 쓰여 주어, 목적어, 보어의 역할을 하며, '~하기', '~하는 것'으로 해석된다.
　동명사(구)가 주어로 쓰이면 단수 취급하여 뒤에 단수형 동사가 와야 한다.

Study Point 🐰

1 주어 역할을 하는 동명사

Getting enough sleep is important for relieving stress.
충분한 수면을 취하는 것은 스트레스를 완화하는 데 중요하다.

Taking photos is allowed inside the museum, except in certain areas.
특정 구역을 제외하고, 박물관 내부에서 사진 촬영이 허용된다.

Waking up early gives you more time to prepare for the day.
일찍 일어나는 것은 너에게 하루를 준비하는 데 더 많은 시간을 준다.

2 보어와 목적어 역할을 하는 동명사

One of the most important skills is **communicating** effectively. [보어]
가장 중요한 기술 중 하나는 효과적으로 소통하는 것이다.

My brother enjoys **reading** mystery novels in his free time. [목적어]
나의 형은 여가 시간에 추리 소설을 읽는 것을 즐긴다.

3 동명사 vs. 현재분사

Playing in the park is a great way to spend a sunny afternoon. [동명사]
공원에서 노는 것은 햇볕 좋은 오후를 보내는 훌륭한 방법이다.

The kids were **playing** in the park when it started raining. [현재분사]
비가 내리기 시작했을 때 아이들은 공원에서 놀고 있었다.

Q 다음 네모 안에서 어법상 올바른 것을 고르시오.

1 Eat / Eating a balanced diet helps you maintain good health.

2 She prefers walking / to walk to work instead of driving.

3 Travel / Traveling around the world is a dream for many people.

Check-up 🎙

01 다음 괄호 안의 동사를 알맞은 형태로 고쳐 빈칸에 쓰시오.

(1) _____ in the pool is a fantastic way to relax. (swim)

(2) _____ a musical instrument requires a lot of practice. (play)

(3) _____ to new places broadens your perspective on the world. (travel)

02 다음 문장의 빈칸 (A), (B)에 들어갈 말로 알맞은 것끼리 짝지어진 것은?

> _____(A)_____ healthy food _____(B)_____ to a better quality of life.

	(A)	(B)		(A)	(B)
①	Eat	⋯ contribute	②	Eat	⋯ contributes
③	Eating	⋯ contribute	④	Eating	⋯ contributes
⑤	To eat	⋯ contribute			

03 다음 문장에서 밑줄 친 부분을 바르게 고쳐 쓰시오.

(1) Painting landscapes <u>are</u> one of my favorite hobbies.

(2) Many people enjoy <u>to watch</u> movies in their free time.

(3) Her main responsibility at work is <u>manages</u> a team of designers.

(4) <u>Learn</u> a new language opens up many opportunities for personal growth.

04 다음 보기에서 적절한 동사를 골라 빈칸에 알맞은 형태로 고쳐 쓰시오. 교과서 23쪽

> 보기 make   look   paint

> **VOLUNTEERS NEEDED**
> Are you (1) _____ for an interesting volunteer opportunity? Then join our program and help us paint walls in our community! (2) _____ old public walls will make the community brighter and give you a chance to express your creativity. (3) _____ a colorful difference in our town starts with you!

POINT 2 사역동사

예제	Our parents **made** us **stay** home because of the bad weather. 사역동사 동사원형 부모님은 나쁜 날씨 때문에 우리를 집에 있도록 하셨다.
교과서	This experience **made** me **realize** that I sometimes enjoy doing things alone. 사역동사 동사원형 이 경험을 통해 나는 때때로 혼자서 무언가를 하는 것을 즐긴다는 것을 깨달았다.

▶ 사역동사(make, have, let)는 목적어와 목적격보어가 능동 관계일 때 목적격보어로 동사원형을 쓴다.

Study Point ♉

1 사역동사＋목적어＋동사원형

사역동사는 어떤 행동을 하게 하는 동사로 make, have, let 등이 있으며 '(~하게) 시키다'로 해석한다.

Having a delicious snack **made** her **feel** refreshed. 맛있는 간식을 먹는 것은 그녀를 상쾌하게 느끼도록 만들었다.

The doctor **had** the patient **take** medicine twice a day. 의사는 환자가 하루에 두 번 약을 복용하게 했다.

She **let** me **use** her computer for the project. 그녀는 프로젝트를 위해 내게 그녀의 컴퓨터를 사용하게 해주었다.

2 지각동사＋목적어＋동사원형[현재분사]

지각동사는 see, hear, watch, feel 등이 있으며, 지각동사는 목적격보어로 동사원형과 현재분사(v-ing)가 모두 올 수 있다.

A police officer **saw** a little girl **cry[crying]** on the street. 경찰관이 거리에서 울고 있는 작은 소녀를 보았다.

I **watched** Tom **build[building]** a sandcastle on the beach. 나는 Tom이 해변에서 모래성을 쌓는 것을 지켜보았다.

3 help＋목적어＋동사원형[to부정사]

준사역동사는 help, get 등이 있다. help는 목적격보어로 동사원형과 to부정사가 모두 올 수 있지만, get은 목적격보어로 to부정사만 올 수 있다.

My friend **helped** me **fix[to fix]** my broken computer.
내 친구가 내가 고장 난 컴퓨터를 고치는 것을 도와주었다.

The local community volunteers **got** their friends **to join** the charity event.
지역 사회 자원봉사자들은 자신들의 친구들이 자선 행사에 참여하도록 했다.

Q 다음 네모 안에서 어법상 올바른 것을 고르시오.

1 We saw the students performing / to perform a traditional dance on the stage.

2 The coach's speech made the team believe / believing in their abilities and skills.

3 Andy helped me understanding / to understand the complex math problem.

Check-up 🏅

01 다음 괄호 안에서 알맞은 것을 고르시오.

(1) I had my sister (help / to help) me prepare for my speech.

(2) The teacher made the students (completing / complete) their homework by Monday.

(3) My parents let me (stay / to stay) up late last night to watch my favorite movie.

02 다음 괄호 안의 단어를 알맞게 배열하여 문장을 다시 쓰시오.

(1) The coach (made / practice / the players) hard for the big game.

→ _____

(2) The birthday wishes that Susan received (smile / made / her) all day.

→ _____

(3) My older brother (apologize / me / for using his tablet / made) without asking.

→ _____

03 다음 괄호 안의 단어를 알맞게 배열하여 문장을 완성하시오. (교과서 23쪽)

> **Movie Title: *Wonder***
> This movie, which is about a boy with facial differences, (1) (me / feel / made / inspired). Seeing the boy overcome many difficulties was touching, and it (2) (made / cry / me). Also, the themes of the movie—like understanding differences, accepting others, and building friendships— gave me a lot of things to think about. I'm sure watching *Wonder* will (1) (want / make / to / you / recommend) it to your friends!

(1) _____

(2) _____

(3) _____

04 다음 중 어법상 틀린 문장끼리 짝지어진 것은?

> ⓐ He made his team members to submit their reports one day early.
> ⓑ She always made me laugh by telling funny jokes.
> ⓒ I had my friend helping me with my math homework.
> ⓓ My dad let me to play video games after dinner.
> ⓔ The director had the actors memorize their lines before the shoot.

① ⓐ, ⓑ, ⓓ   ② ⓐ, ⓒ, ⓓ   ③ ⓑ, ⓒ, ⓓ   ④ ⓒ, ⓓ, ⓔ   ⑤ ⓓ, ⓔ

교과서 본문 분석

Discovering Yourself through Challenges
도전을 통해 자신을 발견하기

01 "[To grow into a better version of ourselves], we should not stay as we are."
부사적 용법의 to부정사(목적) · ~해서는 안 된다 · 접속사(~대로)

"우리 자신의 더 나은 모습으로 성장하기 위해서, 우리는 지금 모습 그대로 머물러 있어서는 안 됩니다."

02 That was the first thing [our teacher said to us on the first day of school].
(that) · 목적격 관계대명사절

그것은 학교 첫날 우리 선생님이 우리에게 하신 첫 번째 말씀이었다.

03 She wanted us to start the semester by pushing ourselves out of our comfort zones and learning
want + 목적어 + to-v: ~가 …하기를 바라다 · by v-ing: ~함으로써 · pushing과 병렬 연결

more about ourselves.

그녀는 우리가 우리 자신을 우리의 안전지대 밖으로 밀어내고 우리 자신에 관해 더 많이 배움으로써 학기를 시작하기를 바라셨다.

04 부사적 용법의 to부정사(목적) · 간접목적어 · 직접목적어
[To help us do so], she gave us an assignment [to challenge ourselves in three different ways].
help + 목적어 + (to-)v: ~가 …하도록 돕다 · 형용사적 용법의 to부정사

우리가 그렇게 하는 것을 도와주기 위해서, 그녀는 우리에게 세 가지 다른 방식으로 우리 자신에게 도전할 과제를 주셨다.

05 The three challenges could involve hobbies, exercise, our studies, or even our relationships.
A, B, C, or D: 여러 개를 나열할 때 마지막에만 접속사를 붙임

그 세 가지 도전들은 취미, 운동, 우리의 학업, 혹은 심지어 우리의 관계까지도 수반할 수 있었다.

06 = challenge
The important part was trying something new for each one.
동명사(보어 역할) · -thing으로 끝나는 부정대명사는 형용사가 뒤에서 수식함

가장 중요한 부분은 각각의 것에 대해 새로운 무언가를 시도해 보는 것이었다.

07 She told us [that we should share our experiences with our classmates when we finished the challenges].
명사절(told의 직접목적어) · Share A with B: B와 A를 공유하다 · 접속사(~할 때)

그녀는 우리에게 우리가 도전들을 마치면 반 친구들에게 우리의 경험을 공유해야 한다고 말씀하셨다.

Challenge 1: Ticket for One
도전 1: 한 사람을 위한 티켓

08 These days, I tend to watch movies on streaming services.
tend to-v: ~하는 경향이 있다

요즘, 나는 스트리밍 서비스로 영화를 보는 경향이 있다.

09 However, if I go to the theater, I usually watch an action or science fiction movie with my friends
접속사(~한다면)
or family.

그런데, 만약 내가 영화관에 가면, 나는 보통 친구들이나 가족과 함께 액션이나 공상과학 영화를 본다.

10 = action or science fiction movies   목적격 관계대명사절
Those are the kinds of movies [they enjoy].
'종류'라는 의미의 명사 (that) = my friends or family

그것들은 그들이 즐기는 종류의 영화들이다.

11 Going to the theater alone was something [I had never done before].
S(동명사구)   V   (that) 과거완료(경험)

혼자 영화관에 가는 것은 내가 이전에 한 번도 해보지 않은 것이었다.

12 So, for the first challenge, I decided to give it a try.
decide to-v: ~하기로 결심하다

그래서, 첫 번째 도전으로, 나는 그것을 시도해 보기로 결심했다.

13 It was nice [to choose the movie and the seat on my own].
가주어   진주어   on one's own: 자기 스스로

스스로 영화와 좌석을 선택하는 것이 좋았다.

14 worry about: ~에 대해 걱정하다
I didn't have to worry about anyone else's preferences.
don't have to: ~할 필요가 없다

나는 다른 누군가의 선호에 관해 걱정하지 않아도 되었다.

15 형용사적 용법
I saw the experience as a good opportunity [to watch something different],
see A as B: A를 B로 보다[여기다]   과거완료(계속)   -thing으로 끝나는 부정대명사는 형용사가 뒤에서 수식함
so I chose a historical drama [that I had been curious about].
목적격 관계대명사절

나는 그 경험을 다른 것을 관람할 좋은 기회라고 보았으므로, 나는 내가 궁금해해왔던 사극을 골랐다.

16 가주어
At first, it felt a bit awkward and lonely [to sit in the theater by myself].
feel+형용사: ~하게 느끼다   진주어   by oneself: 홀로, 혼자서

처음에는, 혼자 극장 안에 앉아 있는 것이 다소 어색하고 외롭게 느껴졌다.

17 But once the movie started, I became completely absorbed in the story.
접속사(~하자마자)   become+형용사: ~(해)지다, ~하게 되다

하지만 영화가 시작하자마자, 나는 이야기에 완전히 몰두하게 되었다.

18 It was so satisfying [just to focus on the movie itself.]
가주어   진주어   focus on: ～에 집중하다   재귀대명사 〈강조 용법〉

그저 영화 자체에 집중하는 것이 매우 만족스러웠다.

19 There was nothing [to distract me]!
                   형용사적 용법

나를 산만하게 할 게 아무것도 없었다!

20 명사절(realize의 목적어)   동명사구(enjoy의 목적어)
This experience made me realize [that I sometimes enjoy {doing things alone}].
             make+목적어+동사원형: ～가 …하게 만들다   enjoy+동명사

이 경험은 내가 가끔 일을 혼자 하는 것을 즐긴다는 것을 깨닫게 했다.

21 명사절(promised의 목적어)
After the movie, I promised myself [that I would try to make my own choices more often
           병렬 연결   make a choice: 선택하다
and enjoy more activities by myself in the future].
    (would)

영화 후에, 나는 앞으로 더 자주 나만의 선택을 하도록 노력하고 혼자서 더 많은 활동들을 즐기겠다고 스스로 약속했다.

Challenge 2: Riding the Waves
도전 2: 파도타기

22 현재완료(계속)
Ever since I was a child, I've always been afraid of water.
접속사(～이후로 줄곧[계속])   be afraid of: ～을 두려워하다

어릴 때부터, 나는 항상 물을 두려워해 왔다.

23 have never   (I was)   = water activities
So I have never enjoyed water activities or felt comfortable while doing them.
    현재완료(경험)   병렬 연결   접속사(～하는 동안)

그래서 나는 물놀이를 즐기거나 그것을 하는 동안 편하게 느낀 적이 한 번도 없었다.

24 For the second challenge, I decided [to try to overcome this discomfort].
                     명사적 용법(decided의 목적어)

두 번째 도전으로, 나는 이 불편함을 극복하기 위해 노력하기로 결심했다.

25 However, I wasn't sure what to do at first.
            what to-v: 무엇을 ～할지

하지만 나는 처음에 무엇을 해야 할지 잘 몰랐다.

26 One day, I came across a video clip of my cousin [surfing at an indoor pool] on social media.
come across: ~을 우연히 발견하다   현재분사구

어느 날, 나는 소셜 미디어로 실내 수영장에서 서핑하는 사촌의 영상을 우연히 보았다.

27 It looked fun, and I liked the fact that it took place in a shallow pool, not in the ocean.
= 동격의 that절

그것은 재미있어 보였고, 나는 그것이 바다가 아닌 얕은 수영장에서 행해졌다는 사실이 마음에 들었다.

28 I messaged my cousin about it.
동사: 메시지를 보내다

나는 내 사촌에게 그것에 관해 메시지를 보냈다.

29 She assured me [that it wasn't too hard], so I signed up for a beginner course.
간접목적어   명사절(assured의 직접목적어)

그녀가 내게 그것이 아주 어렵지는 않았다고 장담해서, 나는 초보자 과정에 등록했다.

30 At the beginning of the lesson, it was hard [just to stand up on the board].
At the beginning of: ~의 초반에   가주어   진주어

강습 초반에는 그저 보드 위에서 일어나는 것이 어려웠다.

31 After some help from the instructor, however, I learned how to balance properly and even
V1   how to-v: ~하는 방법

managed to surf a few waves!
V2   a few+복수명사

그러나 강사로부터의 약간의 도움 후, 나는 제대로 균형을 잡는 법을 배웠고 심지어는 용케 약간의 파도를 탔다!

32 = to surf a few waves
It gave me such a rush of excitement.
「such(+a(n))(+형용사)+명사」의 어순

그것은 내게 솟아나는 흥분감을 주었다.

33 과거완료(대과거)
Being in the water wasn't as bad as I had thought.
S(동명사구)   V   as+형용사[부사]의 원급+as: …만큼 ~한[하게]

물속에 있는 것은 내가 생각했던 것만큼 나쁘지 않았다.

34 While the experience didn't completely change my mind about water sports,
접속사(~이긴 하지만)

it did help me discover my sense of adventure.
동사 강조   help+목적어+(to-)v: ~가 …하도록 돕다

그 경험이 수상 스포츠에 대한 내 생각을 완전히 변화시킨 것은 아니었지만, 그것은 내가 나의 모험심을 발견하는 데 정말로 도움이 되었다.

Challenge 3: A New Look
도전 3: 새로운 모습

35 Of all the challenges [I chose for myself], the third one made me the most nervous: changing my
(which[that])
~ 중에　　for oneself: 스스로　　make+목적어+목적격보어(형용사): ~가 …하게 만들다
hairstyle.

나 자신을 위해 선택한 모든 도전 중에서, 세 번째 것이 나를 가장 초조하게 했다. 내 머리 모양을 바꾸는 것이었다.

36 For many years, I had kept the same hairstyle because I had been worried about my forehead.
과거완료(계속)　　접속사(~ 때문에) 과거완료(계속)

수년간, 나는 내 이마가 걱정되었기 때문에 같은 머리 모양을 유지해 왔었다.

37 I had always thought it was large, and I didn't want to draw attention to it.
과거완료(계속)　= forehead　　　　　= my forehead

나는 그것이 넓다고 항상 생각해 왔고, 그것에 주의를 끌고 싶지 않았다.

38 Since I was feeling confident after the first two challenges, I went to a hair salon and talked to
접속사(~ 때문에)　　　　　　V1　　　　　V2
the stylist.

첫 두 가지 도전 후에 자신감을 느끼고 있었기 때문에, 나는 미용실에 가서 미용사에게 말을 건넸다.

39 He listened to my concerns and helped me find a shorter hairstyle [that suited me].
help+목적어+(to-)v: ~가 …하도록 돕다
V1　　　　　　V2　　　　　　주격 관계대명사절

그는 나의 우려를 듣고 내가 내게 어울리는 더 짧은 머리 모양을 찾도록 도와주었다.

40 The next day at school, my classmates were a bit surprised.
사람이 주어이므로 과거분사 형용사가 와야 함

다음 날 학교에서 나의 반 친구들은 약간 놀랐다.

41 But overall, the reactions were positive.

그러나 전반적으로는, 반응이 긍정적이었다.

42 I realized [that trying a different look wasn't as difficult as I thought it would be].
명사절(realized의 목적어)
S(동명사구)　　　V'　　as+원급+as: …만큼 ~한[하게]　= trying a different look

나는 다른 모습을 시도하는 것이 내가 그럴 거라고 생각했던 만큼 어렵지 않다는 것을 깨달았다.

43 In fact, it made me feel more confident about myself.
make(사역동사)+목적어+동사원형: ~가 …하게 만들다

사실, 그것은 내가 나 자신에 대해 더 자신감을 느끼게 했다.

44 I didn't expect [that stepping out of my comfort zone would have such a positive effect on
명사절(expect+의 목적어)   V′ (동명사구)   V′   such(+a(n))(+형용사)+명사: 그렇게 ~한 …

{how I felt about myself}].
의문사절(전치사 on의 목적어)

나는 나의 안전지대에서 나오는 것이 내가 나 자신에 대해 어떻게 생각하는지에 이렇게 긍정적인 영향을 미칠 거라고 예상하지 못했다.

45 = to challenge myself in three different ways
I learned a lot about myself through this assignment, and I found out [that my classmates did], too.
V1   V2   명사절(found out의 목적어)

나는 이번 과제를 통해 나 자신에 관해 많이 배웠고, 나의 반 친구들도 그러했다는 것을 알게 되었다.

46 One of them tried new foods from different countries, while another joined a creative writing club.
= my classmates   접속사(~인 반면에)

그들 중 한 명은 여러 나라의 새로운 음식들을 먹어 본 반면, 다른 친구는 문예 창작 동아리에 가입했다.

47 가주어   진주어
Through these experiences, we all realized [how important it is {to push ourselves to try new things}].
간접의문문(realized의 목적어): 「의문사+주어+동사」의 어순   부사적 용법(목적)

이 경험들을 통해, 우리 모두는 새로운 것들을 시도하기 위해 우리 자신을 밀어붙이는 것이 얼마나 중요한지 깨달았다.

48 We gained different perspectives on life and had a lot of fun, too!
V1   V2

우리는 삶에 대한 여러 시각을 얻었고 매우 즐거운 시간을 보내기도 했다!

49 My classmates and I even talked about [setting more challenges for ourselves].
동명사구(전치사 about의 목적어)

나의 반 친구들과 나는 심지어 우리 자신을 위해 더 많은 도전들을 정하는 것에 관해 이야기하기도 했다.

50 There are always more things [that we can discover about ourselves], and it's exciting
목적격 관계대명사절   가주어

[to keep learning and growing].
진주어   동명사구(keep의 목적어)

우리 자신에 관해 발견할 수 있는 더 많은 것들이 항상 있고, 계속해서 배우고 성장하는 것은 신이 나는 일이다.

51 접속사(~까지)
We never know [what we're capable of] until we try!
간접의문문(know의 목적어): 「의문사+주어+동사」의 어순

우리가 시도할 때까지 우리는 우리가 무엇을 할 수 있는지 전혀 모른다!

♣ 다음 우리말과 일치하도록 빈칸에 알맞은 말을 쓰시오.

01 "To grow into a better version of ourselves, we _____ as we are."
"우리 자신의 더 나은 모습으로 성장하기 위해서, 우리는 지금 모습 그대로 머물러 있어서는 안 됩니다."

02 She wanted us to start the semester _____ out of our comfort zones and learning more about ourselves.
그녀는 우리가 우리 자신을 우리의 안전지대 밖으로 밀어내고 우리 자신에 관해 더 많이 배움으로써 학기를 시작하기를 바라셨다.

03 To help us do so, she _____ to challenge ourselves in three different ways.
우리가 그렇게 하는 것을 도와주기 위해서, 그녀는 우리에게 세 가지 다른 방식으로 우리 자신에게 도전할 과제를 주었다.

04 The three challenges _____, exercise, our studies, or even our relationships.
그 세 가지 도전들은 취미, 운동, 우리의 학업, 혹은 심지어 우리의 관계까지도 수반할 수 있었다.

05 The important part was _____ for each one.
가장 중요한 부분은 각각의 것에 대해 새로운 무언가를 시도해 보는 것이었다.

06 She told us that we should _____ our classmates when we finished the challenges.
그녀는 우리에게 우리가 도전들을 마치면 반 친구들에게 우리의 경험을 공유해야 한다고 말씀하셨다.

07 These days, I _____ on streaming services.
요즘, 나는 스트리밍 서비스로 영화를 보는 경향이 있다.

08 However, if I go to the theater, I usually _____ with my friends or family.
그런데, 만약 내가 영화관에 가면, 나는 보통 친구들이나 가족과 함께 액션이나 공상과학 영화를 본다.

09 Those are _____ they enjoy.
그것들은 그들이 즐기는 종류의 영화들이다.

10 Going to the theater alone was something I _____.
혼자 영화관에 가는 것은 내가 이전에 한 번도 해보지 않은 것이었다.

11 So, for the first challenge, I decided to _____.
그래서, 첫 번째 도전으로, 나는 그것을 시도해 보기로 결심했다.

12 _____ the movie and the seat on my own.
스스로 영화와 좌석을 선택하는 것이 좋았다.

13 I didn't _____ anyone else's preferences.
나는 다른 누군가의 선호에 관해 걱정하지 않아도 되었다.

14 I saw the experience _____ to watch something different, so I chose a historical drama that I had been curious about.
나는 그 경험을 다른 것을 관람할 좋은 기회라고 보았으므로, 나는 내가 궁금해왔던 사극을 골랐다.

15 At first, it felt a bit _____ to sit in the theater by myself.

처음에는, 혼자 극장 안에 앉아 있는 것이 다소 어색하고 외롭게 느껴졌다.

16 But once the movie started, I _____ the story.

하지만 영화가 시작하자마자, 나는 이야기에 완전히 몰두하게 되었다.

17 There was _____ me!

나를 산만하게 할 게 아무것도 없었다!

18 This experience _____ that I sometimes enjoy doing things alone.

이 경험은 내가 가끔 일을 혼자 하는 것을 즐긴다는 것을 깨닫게 했다.

19 After the movie, I promised myself that I would try to _____ more often and enjoy more activities by myself in the future.

영화 후에, 나는 앞으로 더 자주 나만의 선택을 하도록 노력하고 혼자서 더 많은 활동들을 즐기겠다고 스스로 약속했다.

20 Ever since I was a child, I've always _____.

어릴 때부터, 나는 항상 물을 두려워해 왔다.

21 So I have never enjoyed water activities or _____ while doing them.

그래서 나는 물놀이를 즐기거나 그것을 하는 동안 편하게 느낀 적이 한 번도 없었다.

22 For the second challenge, I _____ this discomfort.

두 번째 도전으로, 나는 이 불편함을 극복하기 위해 노력하기로 결심했다.

23 One day, I _____ a video clip of my cousin surfing at an indoor pool on social media.

어느 날, 나는 소셜 미디어로 실내 수영장에서 서핑하는 사촌의 영상을 우연히 보았다.

24 It looked fun, and I liked the fact that _____ in a shallow pool, not in the ocean.

그것은 재미있어 보였고, 나는 그것이 바다가 아닌 얕은 수영장에서 행해졌다는 사실이 마음에 들었다.

25 She assured me that it wasn't too hard, so I _____ a beginner course.

그녀가 내게 그것이 아주 어렵지는 않았다고 장담해서, 나는 초보자 과정에 등록했다.

26 _____ the lesson, it was hard just to stand up on the board.

강습 초반에는 그저 보드 위에서 일어나는 것이 어려웠다.

27 After some help from the instructor, however, I learned how to balance properly and even _____!

그러나 강사로부터의 약간의 도움 후, 나는 제대로 균형을 잡는 법을 배웠고 심지어는 용케 약간의 파도를 탔다!

28 It gave me such _____.

그것은 내게 솟아나는 흥분감을 주었다.

29 _____ wasn't as bad as I had thought.

물속에 있는 것은 내가 생각했었던 것만큼 나쁘지 않았다.

30 While the experience didn't completely change my mind about water sports,

it _____ my sense of adventure.

그 경험이 수상 스포츠에 대한 내 생각을 완전히 변화시킨 것은 아니었지만, 그것은 내가 나의 모험심을 발견하는 데 정말로 도움이 되었다.

31 I had always thought it was large, and I didn't want to _____ it.

나는 그것이 넓다고 항상 생각해 왔고, 그것에 주의를 끌고 싶지 않았다.

32 He listened to my concerns and helped me find a shorter hairstyle _____.

그는 나의 우려를 듣고 내가 내게 어울리는 더 짧은 머리 모양을 찾도록 도와주었다.

33 I realized that trying a different look wasn't _____ I thought it would be.

나는 다른 모습을 시도하는 것이 내가 그럴 거라고 생각했던 만큼 어렵지 않다는 것을 깨달았다.

34 I didn't expect that stepping out of my comfort zone would _____

how I felt about myself.

나는 나의 안전지대에서 나오는 것이 내가 나 자신에 대해 어떻게 생각하는지에 이렇게 긍정적인 영향을 미칠 거라고 예상하지 못했다.

35 I learned a lot about myself _____, and I found out that my classmates did,

too.

나는 이번 과제를 통해 나 자신에 관해 많이 배웠고, 나의 반 친구들도 그러했다는 것을 알게 되었다.

36 One of them tried new foods from different countries, _____ a creative writing

club.

그들 중 한 명은 여러 나라의 새로운 음식들을 먹어 본 반면, 다른 친구는 문예 창작 동아리에 가입했다.

37 Through these experiences, we all realized how important it is to _____

new things.

이 경험들을 통해, 우리 모두는 새로운 것들을 시도하기 위해 우리 자신을 밀어붙이는 것이 얼마나 중요한지 깨달았다.

38 We _____ on life and had a lot of fun, too!

우리는 삶에 대한 여러 시각을 얻었고 매우 즐거운 시간을 보내기도 했다!

39 There are always more things that we can discover about ourselves, and it's exciting

_____.

우리 자신에 관해 발견할 수 있는 더 많은 것들이 항상 있고, 계속해서 배우고 성장하는 것은 신이 나는 일이다.

40 We never know _____ until we try!

우리가 시도할 때까지 우리는 우리가 무엇을 할 수 있는지 전혀 모른다!

교과서 본문 익히기 ❷ 옳은 어법·어휘 고르기

♣ 다음 네모 안에서 옳은 것을 고르시오.

01　"Growing / To grow into a better version of ourselves, we should not stay as we are."

02　That was the first thing our teacher said to us on the one / first day of school.

03　She wanted us start / to start the semester by pushing ourselves out of our comfort / discomfort zones and learning more about ourselves.

04　To help us do so, she gave us an assignment / experience to challenge ourselves in three different ways.

05　The important part was try / trying something new for each one.

06　She told us that we should share our experiences of / with our classmates when we finished the challenges.

07　However, if I go to the gallery / theater, I usually watch an action or science fiction movie with my friends or family.

08　Those are the kind / kinds of movies they enjoy.

09　Going to the theater alone was / were something I had never done before / ago.

10　So, for the first challenge, I decided giving / to give it a try.

11　It / That was nice to choose the movie and the seat on my own.

12　I didn't have to worry about anyone else's preferences / references.

13　I saw the experience as a good opportunity to watch something different / different something, so I chose a historical drama that I have been / had been curious about.

14　At first, it felt a bit awkward and lonely to sit in the theater by / for myself.

15   But once the movie started, I became completely absorbing / absorbed in the story.

16   There was anything / nothing to distract me!

17   This experience made me realize / to realize that I sometimes enjoy to do / doing things alone.

18   After the movie, I promised myself that I would try to make / take my own choices more often and enjoy more activities by myself in the future.

19   So I have never enjoyed water activities or feel / felt comfortable while doing them.

20   For the second challenge, I decided trying / to try to overcome this comfort / discomfort.

21   One day, I came across a video clip of my cousin surfing / surfed at an indoor pool on social media.

22   It looked fun / funny, and I liked the fact that it took place in a deep / shallow pool, not in the ocean.

23   She assured me that it wasn't too hard, so I signed up for a beginner / professional course.

24   At the beginning / end of the lesson, it was hard just to stand up on the board.

25   After some help from the instructor, however, I learned how to balance proper / properly and even managed to surf a few / a little waves!

26   It gave me such a rush of excite / excitement.

27   Be / Being in the water wasn't as bad as I had thought.

28   As / While the experience didn't completely change my mind about water sports, it did help me discover / discovering my sense of adventure.

29 Of all the challenges I chose for myself, the third one made me the | more / most | nervous: changing my hairstyle.

30 For many years, I had kept | the same / different | hairstyle because I had been worried about my forehead.

31 Since I was feeling | confident / confidently | after the first two challenges, I went to a hair salon and talked to the stylist.

32 He listened to my concerns and helped me | find / finding | a shorter hairstyle that suited me.

33 The next day at school, my classmates were a bit | surprised / surprising |.

34 I realized that trying a different look wasn't as difficult | as / than | I thought it would be.

35 In fact, it made me | feel / to feel | more confident about myself.

36 I didn't expect that | stepping / stepped | out of my comfort zone would have | so / such | a positive effect on how I felt about myself.

37 I learned a lot about | me / myself | through this assignment, and I found out that my classmates did, too.

38 One of them tried new foods from different countries, while | another / the other | joined a creative writing club.

39 Through these experiences, we all realized how important it is to | push / pull | ourselves to try new things.

40 We gained different perspectives on life and had a lot of | fun / funny |, too!

41 There are always more things that we can discover about | myself / ourselves |, and it's exciting to keep learning and growing.

42 We never know | what / that | we're capable of until we try!

♣ 다음 밑줄 친 부분을 바르게 고쳐 쓰시오.

01 "<u>Growing</u> into a better version of ourselves, we should not stay as we are."

02 She wanted us to start the semester by <u>push</u> ourselves out of our comfort zones and learning more about ourselves.

03 To help us do so, she gave us an assignment to challenge <u>herself</u> in three different ways.

04 The important part was trying <u>new something</u> for each one.

05 These days, I tend to <u>watching</u> movies on streaming services.

06 <u>To go</u> to the theater alone was something I had never done before.

07 So, for the first challenge, I decided <u>giving</u> it a try.

08 It was nice <u>choose</u> the movie and the seat on my own.

09 I didn't <u>must</u> worry about anyone else's preferences.

10 I saw the experience as a good opportunity to watch something different, so I chose a historical drama that I <u>have been</u> curious about.

11 But once the movie started, I became completely <u>absorbing</u> in the story.

12 It was so <u>satisfied</u> just to focus on the movie itself.

13 This experience made me <u>to realize</u> that I sometimes enjoy doing things alone.

14 After the movie, I promised myself that I would try <u>making</u> my own choices more often and enjoy more activities by myself in the future.

15 So I have never enjoyed water activities or <u>feel</u> comfortable while doing them.

16 One day, I came across a video clip of my cousin <u>surfed</u> at an indoor pool on social media.

17 It looked fun, and I liked the fact <u>if</u> it took place in a shallow pool, not in the ocean.

18 After some help from the instructor, however, I learned <u>what</u> to balance properly and even managed to surf a few waves!

19 It gave me such a rush of <u>excite</u>.

20 Being in the water wasn't as <u>badly</u> as I had thought.

21 While the experience didn't completely change my mind about water sports, it <u>does</u> help me discover my sense of adventure.

22 Of all the challenges I chose for myself, the third one made me the <u>more</u> nervous: changing my hairstyle.

23 For many years, I had kept the same hairstyle <u>so</u> I had been worried about my forehead.

24 I <u>have</u> always thought it was large, and I didn't want to draw attention to it.

25 He listened to my concerns and helped me <u>finding</u> a shorter hairstyle that suited me.

26 The next day at school, my classmates were a bit <u>surprising</u>.

27 I realized that <u>tried</u> a different look wasn't as difficult as I thought it would be.

28 In fact, it made me <u>to feel</u> more confident about myself.

29 I didn't expect that <u>stepped</u> out of my comfort zone would have such a positive effect on how I felt about myself.

30 I learned a lot about myself through this assignment, and I found out that my classmates <u>do</u>, too.

31 One of them tried new foods from different countries, while <u>other</u> joined a creative writing club.

32 Through these experiences, we all realized how important <u>is it</u> to push ourselves to try new things.

33 We gained different perspectives on life and had a lot of <u>funny</u>, too!

34 My classmates and I even talked about <u>set</u> more challenges for ourselves.

35 There are always more things that we can discover about ourselves, and it's exciting to keep learning and <u>to grow</u>.

36 We never know <u>that</u> we're capable of until we try!

교과서 본문 외 지문 분석

A. Preview

As a resolution for the new semester, I ❶ decided to develop better time-management skills. ❷ This is because good time-management skills will be very important ❸ during a busy semester. ❹ To keep my resolution, I will use a planner. ❺ Writing down my assignments and due dates will ❻ help me organize my schedule and complete tasks efficiently. Also, I'll use an app ❼ to limit my screen time. ❽ By removing distractions ❾ while studying or doing homework, I think I can focus better and use my time more effectively. I know ❿ keeping my resolution will require hard work, but I will ⓫ do my best ⓬ to achieve my goal.

❶ decide+to부정사: ~하기로 결심하다 ❷ This is because ~: 이것은 ~ 때문이다 ❸ during+시간의 시점: ~ 동안 ❹ 부사적 용법의 to부정사 (목적: ~하기 위해서) ❺ write down: ~을 기록하다 / Writing ~ dates는 주어 역할을 하는 동명사구(~하는 것) ❻ help+목적어+to부정사[동사 원형] ❼ 형용사적 용법의 to부정사 (명사 수식: ~하는, ~할) ❽ by+동명사: ~함으로써 ❾ studying, doing은 병렬구조임. ❿ 주어 역할을 하는 동 명사구 ⓫ do one's best: 최선을 다하다 ⓬ 부사적 용법의 to부정사 (목적: ~하기 위해서)

Q1 The writer will limit their screen time by using a planner. (T / F)

B. Read and Discuss

❶ Learning about yourself is very important. ❷ First of all, it ❸ helps you make better decisions. We often ❹ let others tell us ❺ what we should do. ❻ As a result, we work towards goals ❼ that won't make us happy. However, if you know yourself well, you can ❽ make decisions ❾ based on your true needs. Learning about yourself also ❿ makes you feel more confident. ⓫ Once you know your true self, you will ⓬ care less about ⓭ what others think of you. This ⓮ allows you to love yourself the way you are. So ⓯ why don't you start your journey of self-discovery today?

❶ 주어 역할을 하는 동명사구(~하는 것) / 동명사(구)가 주어인 경우 단수 취급하므로 동사는 is ❷ first of all: 무엇보다 먼저 ❸ help+목적어+to 부정사[동사원형] ❹ let+목적어+동사원형: 목적어로 하여금 ~하게 허락하다 ❺ what we should do = what to do ❻ as a result: 결과적으로 ❼ that: 명사 goals를 수식하는 주격 관계대명사 ❽ make decisions: 결정하다 ❾ based on: ~에 근거하여 ❿ make+목적어+동사원형: 목적어 로 하여금 ~하게 만들다 ⓫ once: 일단 ~하면 ⓬ care less about: ~에 대해 덜 신경을 쓰다 ⓭ what: 선행사를 포함하는 관계대명사(~하는 것) ⓮ allow A to B: A가 B 하는 것을 허락하다 ⓯ why don't you ~?: ~하는 게 어때?

Q2 Learning about yourself can help you make decisions that match with your true needs. (T / F)

다음 빈칸에 알맞은 말을 쓰시오.

01   As a resolution for the new semester, I _____ better time-management skills.

새 학기를 위한 다짐으로, 나는 더 나은 시간 관리 기술을 계발하기로 결심했다.

02   _____ good time-management skills will be very important during a busy semester.

이는 바쁜 학기 동안 좋은 시간 관리 기술이 매우 중요할 것이기 때문이다.

03   _____, I will use a planner. 내 다짐을 지키기 위해, 나는 플래너(일정 계획 수첩)를 사용할 것이다.

04   Writing down my assignments and due dates will _____ my schedule and complete tasks efficiently.

나의 과제들과 마감일들을 적어 두는 것은 내가 나의 일정을 정리하고 과업들을 능률적으로 완수하는 데 도움이 될 것이다.

05   Also, I'll use an app _____.

또한, 나는 나의 스크린 타임(전자 기기 사용 시간)을 제한해 줄 앱을 사용할 것이다.

06   _____ while studying or doing homework, I think I can focus better and use my time more effectively.

공부나 숙제를 하는 동안 집중을 방해하는 것들을 제거함으로써, 나는 내가 더 잘 집중하고 내 시간을 더 효과적으로 쓸 수 있다고 생각한다.

07   I know keeping my resolution will _____, but I will do my best to achieve my goal.

나는 내 다짐을 지키는 것이 힘든 일을 요할 것임을 알지만, 나는 내 목표를 달성하기 위해 최선을 다할 것이다.

08   _____ is very important. 당신 자신에 관해 배우는 것은 매우 중요하다.

09   First of all, it helps you _____.

무엇보다도, 그것은 당신이 더 나은 결정을 하는 것을 도와준다.

10   We often _____ us what we should do.

우리는 흔히 다른 사람들이 우리에게 우리가 해야 할 것을 말하게 한다.

11   As a result, we work towards goals that won't _____.

그 결과, 우리는 우리를 행복하게 해주지 않을 목표들을 위해 노력한다.

12   However, if you know yourself well, you can make decisions _____ your true needs.

하지만, 만약 당신이 당신 자신을 잘 알면, 당신은 당신의 진정한 요구에 기반하여 결정들을 할 수 있다.

13   Learning about yourself also makes you _____.

당신 자신에 관해 배우는 것은 또한 당신이 더 자신감을 느끼게 한다.

14   Once you know your true self, you will care less about _____.

일단 당신이 당신의 진정한 모습을 알면, 당신은 다른 이들이 당신에 대해 생각하는 것에 관해 신경을 덜 쓰게 될 것이다.

15   This _____ yourself the way you are.

이는 당신이 있는 그대로의 당신 자신을 사랑하게 해줄 것이다.

16   So _____ your journey of self-discovery today?

그러니 오늘 당신의 자기 발견 여정을 시작하는 게 어떨까?

01 (A), (B), (C)의 각 네모 안에서 문맥에 맞는 낱말로 가장 적절한 것은?

"To grow into a better version of ourselves, we should not stay as we are." That was the first thing our teacher said to us on the (A) first / last day of school. She wanted us to start the semester by (B) pulling / pushing ourselves out of our comfort zones and learning more about ourselves. To help us do so, she gave us an assignment to challenge ourselves in three different ways. The three challenges could involve hobbies, exercise, our studies, or even our relationships. The important part was trying something new for each one. She told us that we should share our experiences with our classmates when we (C) started / finished the challenges.

	(A)		(B)		(C)
①	first	⋯	pulling	⋯	started
②	first	⋯	pushing	⋯	started
③	first	⋯	pushing	⋯	finished
④	last	⋯	pulling	⋯	finished
⑤	last	⋯	pushing	⋯	started

02 다음 글의 밑줄 친 부분 중, 문맥상 낱말의 쓰임이 적절하지 않은 것은?

At the ① beginning of the lesson, it was ② hard just to stand up on the board. After some help from the instructor, however, I learned how to balance ③ properly and even managed to surf a few waves! It gave me such a rush of excitement. Being in the water wasn't as ④ good as I had thought. While the experience didn't completely change my mind about water sports, it did help me ⑤ discover my sense of adventure.

①   ②   ③   ④   ⑤

03 다음 글의 밑줄 친 부분 중, 문맥상 낱말의 쓰임이 적절하지 않은 것은?

These days, I tend to watch ① movies on streaming services. However, if I go to the theater, I usually watch an action or science fiction movie with my friends or family. Those are the kinds of movies they enjoy.

Going to the theater ② alone was something I had never done before. So, for the first ③ challenge, I decided to give it a try. It was nice to choose the movie and the seat on my own. I didn't have to worry about anyone else's ④ references. I saw the experience as a good ⑤ opportunity to watch something different, so I chose a historical drama that I had been curious about.

①   ②   ③   ④   ⑤

04 (A), (B), (C)의 각 네모 안에서 문맥에 맞는 낱말로 가장 적절한 것은?

At first, it felt a bit awkward and lonely to sit in the theater by myself. But once the movie started, I became completely absorbed in the story. It was so (A) satisfying / disappointing just to focus on the movie itself. There was (B) nothing / something to distract me! This experience made me realize that I sometimes enjoy doing things alone. After the movie, I promised myself that I would try to (C) take / make my own choices more often and enjoy more activities by myself in the future.

	(A)		(B)		(C)
①	satisfying	⋯	something	⋯	make
②	satisfying	⋯	nothing	⋯	make
③	satisfying	⋯	nothing	⋯	take
④	disappointing	⋯	something	⋯	take
⑤	disappointing	⋯	nothing	⋯	make

05 (A), (B), (C)의 각 네모 안에서 문맥에 맞는 낱말로 가장 적절한 것은?

Ever since I was a child, I've always been afraid of water. So I have never enjoyed water activities or felt (A) comfortable / uncomfortable while doing them. For the second challenge, I decided to try to overcome this (B) comfort / discomfort . However, I wasn't sure what to do at first. One day, I came across a video clip of my cousin surfing at an indoor pool on social media. It looked fun, and I liked the fact that it took place in a (C) deep / shallow pool, not in the ocean. I messaged my cousin about it. She assured me that it wasn't too hard, so I signed up for a beginner course.

	(A)	(B)	(C)
①	comfortable	⋯ comfort	⋯ deep
②	comfortable	⋯ comfort	⋯ shallow
③	comfortable	⋯ discomfort	⋯ shallow
④	uncomfortable	⋯ comfort	⋯ deep
⑤	uncomfortable	⋯ discomfort	⋯ shallow

06 (A), (B), (C)의 각 네모 안에서 문맥에 맞는 낱말로 가장 적절한 것은?

The next day at school, my classmates were a bit surprised. But overall, the reactions were (A) positive / negative . I realized that trying a different look wasn't as (B) easy / difficult as I thought it would be. In fact, it made me feel more confident about myself. I didn't expect that stepping out of my (C) comfort / discomfort zone would have such a positive effect on how I felt about myself.

	(A)	(B)	(C)
①	positive	⋯ easy	⋯ comfort
②	positive	⋯ easy	⋯ discomfort
③	positive	⋯ difficult	⋯ comfort
④	negative	⋯ easy	⋯ discomfort
⑤	negative	⋯ difficult	⋯ discomfort

07 다음 글의 밑줄 친 부분 중, 문맥상 낱말의 쓰임이 적절하지 않은 것은?

Of all the challenges I chose for myself, the third one made me the most ① nervous: changing my hairstyle. For many years, I had kept ② the same hairstyle because I had been worried about my forehead. I had always thought it was large, and I didn't want to draw attention to it. Since I was feeling ③ disappointed after the first two challenges, I went to a hair salon and talked to the stylist. He listened to my ④ concerns and helped me find a shorter hairstyle that ⑤ suited me.

①   ②   ③   ④   ⑤

08 (A), (B), (C)의 각 네모 안에서 문맥에 맞는 낱말로 가장 적절한 것은?

I learned a lot about myself through this assignment, and I found out that my classmates did, too. One of them tried new foods from (A) the same / different countries, while another joined a creative writing club. Through these experiences, we all realized how important it is to push ourselves to try new things. We gained different (B) perspectives / opportunities on life and had a lot of fun, too! My classmates and I even talked about setting more challenges for ourselves. There are always more things that we can discover about ourselves, and it's (C) boring / exciting to keep learning and growing. We never know what we're capable of until we try!

	(A)	(B)	(C)
①	the same	⋯ opportunities	⋯ boring
②	the same	⋯ perspectives	⋯ exciting
③	different	⋯ perspectives	⋯ boring
④	different	⋯ perspectives	⋯ exciting
⑤	different	⋯ opportunities	⋯ exciting

01 다음 글의 밑줄 친 부분 중, 어법상 <u>틀린</u> 것은?

"To grow into a better version of ourselves, we should not stay as we are." That was the first thing our teacher said to us on the first day of school. She wanted us ① to start the semester by pushing ourselves out of our comfort zones and ② to learn more about ourselves. To help us do so, she gave us an assignment to ③ challenge ourselves in three different ways. The three challenges could involve hobbies, exercise, our studies, or even our relationships. The important part was trying ④ something new for each one. She told us that we should share our experiences with our classmates ⑤ when we finished the challenges.

①   ②   ③   ④   ⑤

02 (A), (B), (C)의 각 네모 안에서 어법에 맞는 표현으로 가장 적절한 것은?

At first, it felt a bit awkward and lonely to sit in the theater (A) by myself / for myself. But once the movie started, I became completely absorbed in the story. It was so (B) satisfying / satisfied just to focus on the movie itself. There was nothing to distract me! This experience made me (C) realize / to realize that I sometimes enjoy doing things alone. After the movie, I promised myself that I would try to make my own choices more often and enjoy more activities by myself in the future.

	(A)		(B)		(C)
①	by myself	…	satisfied	…	realize
②	by myself	…	satisfying	…	realize
③	by myself	…	satisfying	…	to realize
④	for myself	…	satisfying	…	realize
⑤	for myself	…	satisfied	…	to realize

03 (A), (B), (C)의 각 네모 안에서 어법에 맞는 표현으로 가장 적절한 것은?

These days, I tend to watch movies on streaming services. However, if I go to the theater, I usually watch an action or science fiction movie with my friends or family. Those are the (A) kind / kinds of movies they enjoy.

Going to the theater alone was something I had never done before. So, for the first challenge, I decided to give it a try. It was nice (B) choose / to choose the movie and the seat on my own. I didn't have to worry about anyone else's preferences. I saw the experience as a good opportunity to watch something different, so I chose a historical drama that I (C) have been / had been curious about.

	(A)		(B)		(C)
①	kind	…	choose	…	have been
②	kind	…	to choose	…	had been
③	kinds	…	choose	…	have been
④	kinds	…	to choose	…	have been
⑤	kinds	…	to choose	…	had been

04 다음 글의 밑줄 친 부분 중, 어법상 <u>틀린</u> 것은?

At the beginning of the lesson, it was hard just ① to stand up on the board. After some help from the instructor, however, I learned ② how to balance properly and even managed to surf a few waves! It gave me such a rush of ③ excitement. Being in the water wasn't as bad as I had thought. ④ While the experience didn't completely change my mind about water sports, it ⑤ did helped me discover my sense of adventure.

①   ②   ③   ④   ⑤

05 (A), (B), (C)의 각 네모 안에서 어법에 맞는 표현으로 가장 적절한 것은?

Ever since I was a child, I've always been afraid of water. So I have (A) ever / never enjoyed water activities or felt comfortable while doing them. For the second challenge, I decided (B) trying / to try to overcome this discomfort. However, I wasn't sure what to do at first. One day, I came across a video clip of my cousin surfing at an indoor pool on social media. It looked fun, and I liked the fact (C) if / that it took place in a shallow pool, not in the ocean. I messaged my cousin about it. She assured me that it wasn't too hard, so I signed up for a beginner course.

	(A)		(B)		(C)
①	ever	⋯	trying	⋯	if
②	ever	⋯	to try	⋯	that
③	never	⋯	to try	⋯	that
④	never	⋯	to try	⋯	if
⑤	never	⋯	trying	⋯	that

06 (A), (B), (C)의 각 네모 안에서 어법에 맞는 표현으로 가장 적절한 것은?

Of all the challenges I chose for myself, the third one made me the most nervous: changing my hairstyle. (A) For / During many years, I had kept the same hairstyle because I had been worried about my forehead. I had always thought it was large, and I didn't want to draw attention to it. Since I was feeling (B) confident / confidently after the first two challenges, I went to a hair salon and talked to the stylist. He listened to my concerns and helped me (C) find / finding a shorter hairstyle that suited me.

	(A)		(B)		(C)
①	For	⋯	confidently	⋯	find
②	For	⋯	confident	⋯	finding
③	For	⋯	confident	⋯	find
④	During	⋯	confidently	⋯	find
⑤	During	⋯	confident	⋯	finding

07 (A), (B), (C)의 각 네모 안에서 어법에 맞는 표현으로 가장 적절한 것은?

The next day at school, my classmates were a bit (A) surprising / surprised. But overall, the reactions were positive. I realized that (B) try / trying a different look wasn't as difficult as I thought it would be. In fact, it made me (C) feel / to feel more confident about myself. I didn't expect that stepping out of my comfort zone would have such a positive effect on how I felt about myself.

	(A)		(B)		(C)
①	surprising	⋯	try	⋯	feel
②	surprising	⋯	trying	⋯	to feel
③	surprised	⋯	trying	⋯	feel
④	surprised	⋯	trying	⋯	to feel
⑤	surprised	⋯	try	⋯	feel

08 (A), (B), (C)의 각 네모 안에서 어법에 맞는 표현으로 가장 적절한 것은?

I learned a lot about myself through this assignment, and I found out that my classmates did, too. One of them tried new foods from different countries, while (A) another / the other joined a creative writing club. Through these experiences, we all realized how important it is to push ourselves to try new things. We gained different perspectives on life and had a lot of fun, too! My classmates and I even talked about (B) set / setting more challenges for ourselves. There are always more things that we can discover about ourselves, and it's exciting to keep learning and growing. We never know (C) what / that we're capable of until we try!

	(A)		(B)		(C)
①	another	⋯	set	⋯	that
②	another	⋯	setting	⋯	what
③	another	⋯	set	⋯	what
④	the other	⋯	setting	⋯	that
⑤	the other	⋯	setting	⋯	what

[03~04] 다음 글을 읽고, 물음에 답하시오.

"To grow into a better version of ourselves, we should not stay as we are." That was the first thing our teacher said to us on the first day of school. She wanted us to start the semester by pushing ourselves out of our comfort zones and learning more about ourselves. <u>To help</u> us do so, she gave us _____ to challenge ourselves in three different ways. The three challenges could involve hobbies, exercise, our studies, or even our relationships. The important part was trying something new for each one. She told us that we should share our experiences with our classmates when we finished the challenges.

03 윗글의 밑줄 친 To help와 쓰임이 다른 것은?

① She saved money <u>to buy</u> a new laptop.
② We need <u>to finish</u> the project by Friday.
③ The members met <u>to plan</u> the upcoming event.
④ Kevin practiced daily <u>to improve</u> his guitar skills.
⑤ They traveled to Paris <u>to see</u> the Eiffel Tower.

[01~02] 다음 대화를 읽고, 물음에 답하시오.

G Hey, Austin. What are you looking at?
B It's a color personality test. I think this type is closest to my personality.
G Let me see. I think you're right. You always listen to others carefully and treat people kindly.
B Yeah, and 나는 평화로운 분위기를 만드는 걸 잘해. I try to make things better when my family or friends have conflicts.
G I definitely think you fit into this type. Should I find out what my personality type is?
B Sure. It's quite fun. Plus, you can gain a better understanding of yourself.

01 위 대화에 나타난 색상 성격 검사에 대한 Austin의 생각으로 가장 적절한 것은?

① Austin finds it boring and uninteresting.
② Austin thinks it's only useful for his friends.
③ Austin thinks it is a fun way to understand oneself better.
④ Austin doubts its accuracy in reflecting true personality traits.
⑤ Austin thinks it is too complex to be of any use.

04 윗글의 빈칸에 들어갈 말로 가장 적절한 것은?

① a rule   ② a suggestion
③ an idea   ④ an instruction
⑤ an assignment

02 위 대화의 밑줄 친 우리말과 같은 뜻이 되도록 괄호 안의 말을 이용하여 문장을 완성하시오.

> be good at, create

→ _____ a peaceful atmosphere.

[05~06] 다음 글을 읽고, 물음에 답하시오.

These days, I tend to watch movies ① on streaming services.

(A) I saw the experience ② as a good opportunity to watch something different, so I chose a historical drama that I had been curious about.

(B) However, if I go to the theater, I usually watch an action or science fiction movie with my friends or family. Those are the kinds ③ of movies they enjoy.

(C) Going to the theater alone was something I had never done before. So, ④ for the first challenge, I decided to give it a try. It was nice to choose the movie and the seat ⑤ of my own. I didn't have to worry about anyone else's preferences.

05 윗글의 주어진 문장 다음에 이어질 글의 순서로 가장 적절한 것은?

① (A) – (C) – (B)
② (B) – (A) – (C)
③ (B) – (C) – (A)
④ (C) – (A) – (B)
⑤ (C) – (B) – (A)

06 윗글의 밑줄 친 부분 중, 전치사의 쓰임이 바르지 <u>않은</u> 것은?

①   ②   ③   ④   ⑤

[07~08] 다음 글을 읽고, 물음에 답하시오.

At first, it felt a bit awkward and lonely to sit in the theater by myself. But once the movie started, I became completely absorbed in the story. It was so satisfying just to focus on the movie <u>itself</u>. There was nothing to distract me! This experience made me realize that I sometimes enjoy doing things alone. After the movie, I promised myself that I would try to make my own choices more often and enjoy more activities by myself in the future.

07 윗글의 제목으로 가장 적절한 것은?

① Discovering the Joy of Solo Experiences
② The Benefits of Watching Movies with Friends
③ How to Choose the Best Theater Seats
④ Dealing with Distractions in the Theater
⑤ Problems with Watching Movies in a Group

08 윗글의 밑줄 친 itself와 쓰임이 같은 것은?

① He fixed the computer all by <u>himself</u>.
② She solved the math problem by <u>herself</u>.
③ We pushed <u>ourselves</u> harder to meet the deadline.
④ The kids enjoyed <u>themselves</u> at the amusement park all day.
⑤ We prepared the entire meal <u>ourselves</u>.

09 다음 글의 빈칸 (A), (B)에 들어갈 말이 바르게 짝지어진 것은?

Ever since I was a child, I've always been afraid of water. So I have never enjoyed water activities or felt comfortable while doing them. For the second challenge, I decided to try to overcome this discomfort. ___(A)___, I wasn't sure what to do at first. One day, I came across a video clip of my cousin surfing at an indoor pool on social media. It looked fun, and I liked the fact that it took place in a shallow pool, not in the ocean. I messaged my cousin about it. She assured me that it wasn't too hard, ___(B)___ I signed up for a beginner course.

	(A)		(B)
①	But	…	because
②	However	…	so
③	However	…	because
④	Therefore	…	so
⑤	Therefore	…	because

10 다음 글의 밑줄 친 우리말과 같은 뜻이 되도록 주어진 단어를 이용하여 조건에 맞게 문장을 완성하시오.

At the beginning of the lesson, it was hard just to stand up on the board. After some help from the instructor, however, I learned how to balance properly and even managed to surf a few waves! It gave me such a rush of excitement. 물속에 있는 것은 내가 생각했던 것만큼 나쁘지 않았다. While the experience didn't completely change my mind about water sports, it did help me discover my sense of adventure.

wasn't / be / as / in the water / as / bad

조건
• 「as+원급+as」 구문을 사용할 것
• 필요시 문맥과 어법에 맞게 어휘를 변형할 것

_____ I had thought.

[11~12] 다음 글을 읽고, 물음에 답하시오.

Of all the challenges I chose for myself, the third one made me the most nervous: changing my hairstyle. For many years, I had kept the same hairstyle because I had been worried about my forehead. I had always thought it was large, and I didn't want to draw attention to it. Since I was feeling confident after the first two challenges, I went to a hair salon and talked to the stylist. He listened to my concerns and helped me finding a shorter hairstyle that suited me.

The next day at school, my classmates were a bit surprised. But overall, the reactions were positive. I realized that trying a different look wasn't as difficult as I thought it would be. In fact, it made me feel more confident about myself. I didn't expect that stepping out of my comfort zone would have such a positive effect on how I felt about myself.

11 윗글의 밑줄 친 문장에서 틀린 부분을 찾아 문장을 다시 쓰시오.

→ _____

_____

12 윗글의 내용을 한 문장으로 요약할 때, 빈칸 (A), (B)에 들어갈 말로 가장 적절한 것은?

I ___(A)___ my nervousness about changing my hairstyle, ___(B)___ positive feedback, and felt more confident as a result.

	(A)		(B)
①	increased	…	received
②	increased	…	rejected
③	overcame	…	ignored
④	overcame	…	received
⑤	overcame	…	refused

I learned a lot about myself through this assignment, and I found out that my classmates did, too. One of them tried new foods from different countries, while _____ joined a creative writing club. Through these experiences, we all realized how important it is to push ourselves to try new things. We gained different perspectives on life and had a lot of fun, too! My classmates and I even talked about setting more challenges for ourselves. There are always more things that we can discover about ourselves, and it's exciting to keep learning and growing. We never know what we're capable of until we try!

13 윗글의 빈칸에 들어갈 말로 가장 적절한 것은?

① other
② another
③ others
④ some
⑤ the other

14 윗글의 밑줄 친 that과 쓰임이 다른 것은?

① He has a friend that lives in New York.
② I think that he is the most suitable for the job.
③ I know the man that you introduced to me.
④ The movie that I watched last night was really fun.
⑤ The book that I borrowed from the library is due today.

15 다음 대화의 밑줄 친 우리말과 같은 뜻이 되도록 보기의 단어들을 바르게 배열하여 쓰시오.

A Marco, your presentation is next week, isn't it?
B Yes, but I'm nervous. 나는 다른 사람들 앞에서 말하는 것을 잘하지 못해.
A I understand. But if you want to overcome your fears, you must get out of your comfort zone.
B That makes sense. What do you suggest?
A Start with something small. How about asking a question in class today?
B That doesn't sound too difficult. Do you think it will help?
A Sure! After you take the first step, the next step will be easier.
B Okay. I'll give it a try.

보기 I'm / good / others / speaking / not / at / in front of

→ _____

[01~02] 다음 대화를 읽고, 물음에 답하시오.

> G Marco, your presentation is next week, isn't it?
>
> B Yes, but I'm nervous. I'm not good at speaking in front of others.
>
> G I understand. But if you want to overcome your fears, you must get out of your comfort zone.
>
> B That makes sense. What do you suggest?
>
> G Start with something small. How about asking a question in class today?
>
> B That doesn't sound too difficult. Do you think it will help?
>
> G Sure! After you take the first step, the next step will be easier.
>
> B _____

01 위 대화의 빈칸에 들어갈 말로 가장 적절한 것은?

① No, I don't think that will help.
② Okay. I'll give it a try.
③ I don't like asking questions in class.
④ Maybe I should just skip the presentation.
⑤ I'll wait until the last minute to prepare.

02 위 대화에서 Marco가 받은 조언과 관련이 없는 것은?

① Start by asking a question in class.
② Take small steps to build confidence.
③ Practice speaking in front of a mirror.
④ Get out of your comfort zone.
⑤ Avoid public speaking.

[03~04] 다음 글을 읽고, 물음에 답하시오.

> "____(A)____ into a better version of ourselves, we should not stay as we are." ① That was the first thing our teacher said to us on the first day of school. ② She wanted us to start the semester by pushing ourselves out of our comfort zones and learning more about ourselves. ③ The classroom was brightly decorated with motivational posters. ④ To help us do so, she gave us an assignment to challenge ourselves in three different ways. ⑤ The three challenges could involve hobbies, exercise, our studies, or even our relationships. The important part was ____(B)____ something new for each one. She told us that we should share our experiences with our classmates when we finished the challenges.

03 윗글에서 전체 흐름과 관계 없는 문장은?

①   ②   ③   ④   ⑤

04 윗글의 빈칸 (A), (B)에 들어갈 말로 가장 적절한 것은?

	(A)	(B)
①	Growing	⋯ trying
②	Growing	⋯ to try
③	Growing	⋯ try
④	To grow	⋯ trying
⑤	To grow	⋯ try

[05~06] 다음 글을 읽고, 물음에 답하시오.

These days, I tend to watch movies on streaming services. However, if I go to the theater, I usually watch an action or science fiction movie with my friends or family. Those are the kinds of movies they enjoy.

Going to the theater alone was something I had never done before. So, for the first challenge, I decided to give it a try. <u>Choosing the movie and the seat on my own was nice.</u> I didn't have to worry about anyone else's preferences. I saw the experience <u>as</u> a good opportunity to watch something different, so I chose a historical drama that I had been curious about.

05 윗글의 밑줄 친 문장과 같은 뜻이 되도록 조건에 맞게 영작하시오.

> **조건**
> • 가주어 it과 진주어 to부정사를 이용할 것
> • 필요시 문맥과 어법에 맞게 어휘를 변형할 것

_____

_____

06 윗글의 밑줄 친 as와 쓰임이 같은 것은?

① He left early <u>as</u> he had an important meeting.
② She was nervous <u>as</u> she walked onto the stage to give her speech.
③ <u>As</u> the sun set, the sky turned a beautiful shade of orange.
④ She worked <u>as</u> a teacher before becoming a famous singer.
⑤ <u>As</u> it was very cold outside, she wore a coat.

[07~08] 다음 글을 읽고, 물음에 답하시오.

At first, it felt a bit (A) awkward / awkwardly and lonely to sit in the theater by myself. But once the movie started, I became completely (B) absorbing / absorbed in the story. It was so satisfied just to focus on the movie itself. There was nothing to distract me! This experience made me (C) realize / to realize that I sometimes enjoy doing things alone. After the movie, I promised myself that I would try to _____ my own choices more often and enjoy more activities by myself in the future.

07 (A), (B), (C)의 각 네모 안에서 어법에 맞는 표현으로 가장 적절한 것은?

	(A)	(B)	(C)
①	awkward	absorbing	to realize
②	awkward	absorbed	realize
③	awkward	absorbed	to realize
④	awkwardly	absorbing	realize
⑤	awkwardly	absorbed	realize

08 윗글의 빈칸에 들어갈 말로 가장 적절한 것은?

① join ② make ③ change ④ accept ⑤ ignore

09 다음 글의 밑줄 친 부분 중, 의미가 <u>잘못</u> 연결된 것은?

Ever since I was a child, I've always been afraid of water. So I have never enjoyed water activities or felt comfortable while doing them. For the second challenge, I decided to ⓐ <u>try to overcome</u> this discomfort. However, I wasn't sure what to do at first. One day, I ⓑ <u>came across</u> a video clip of my cousin surfing at an indoor pool on social media. It ⓒ <u>looked fun</u>, and I liked the fact that it ⓓ <u>took place</u> in a shallow pool, not in the ocean. I messaged my cousin about it. She assured me that it wasn't too hard, so I ⓔ <u>signed up</u> for a beginner course.

① ⓐ: 극복하기 위해 노력하다
② ⓑ: 우연히 보았다
③ ⓒ: 재미있어 보였다
④ ⓓ: 행해졌다
⑤ ⓔ: 서명했다

10 다음 글의 흐름으로 보아, 주어진 문장이 들어가기에 가장 적절한 곳은?

It gave me such a rush of excitement.

(①) At the beginning of the lesson, it was hard just to stand up on the board. (②) After some help from the instructor, however, I learned how to balance properly and even managed to surf a few waves! (③) Being in the water wasn't as bad as I had thought. (④) While the experience didn't completely change my mind about water sports, it did help me discover my sense of adventure. (⑤)

①   ②   ③   ④   ⑤

[11~12] 다음 글을 읽고, 물음에 답하시오.

Of all the ① <u>challenges</u> I chose for myself, the third one made me the most nervous: changing my hairstyle. For many years, I had kept the same hairstyle because I had been worried about my forehead. I had always thought it was large, and I didn't want to draw ② <u>attention</u> to it.

_____(A)_____ I was feeling confident after the first two challenges, I went to a hair salon and talked to the stylist. He listened to my ③ <u>jokes</u> and helped me find a shorter hairstyle that suited me.

The next day at school, my classmates were a bit surprised. But overall, the ④ <u>reactions</u> were positive. I realized that trying a different look wasn't as difficult as I thought it would be. _____(B)_____, it made me feel more confident about myself. I didn't expect that stepping out of my comfort zone would have such a positive ⑤ <u>effect</u> on how I felt about myself.

11 윗글의 밑줄 친 부분 중, 문맥상 낱말의 쓰임이 적절하지 <u>않은</u> 것은?

①   ②   ③   ④   ⑤

12 윗글의 빈칸 (A), (B)에 들어갈 말이 바르게 짝지어진 것은?

	(A)		(B)
①	As	…	Moreover
②	However	…	Therefore
③	Since	…	In fact
④	Unless	…	In fact
⑤	Although	…	Moreover

I learned a lot about myself through this assignment, and I found out ___(A)___ my classmates did, too. One of them tried new foods from different countries, ___(B)___ another joined a creative writing club. Through these experiences, we all realized how important it is to push ourselves to try new things. We gained different perspectives on life and had a lot of fun, too! My classmates and I even talked about setting more challenges for ourselves. There are always more things that we can discover about ourselves, and it's exciting to keep learning and growing. We never know what we're capable of ___(C)___ we try!

13 다음 영어 뜻풀이에 해당하는 단어를 윗글에서 찾아 쓰시오.

a specific way of seeing or understanding something

→ _____

14 윗글의 빈칸 (A), (B), (C)에 들어갈 말이 바르게 짝지어진 것은?

	(A)	(B)	(C)
①	if	while	until
②	if	when	while
③	that	so	that
④	that	while	until
⑤	that	when	while

15 다음 글을 읽고, 요약문의 빈칸에 알맞은 말을 본문에서 찾아 쓰시오.

Finding your strengths is an important part of self-discovery. And it's easy to do! Just grab a pen and write down answers to a few simple questions. To start with, think about how you perceive yourself. What do you think your good qualities are? What are you better at than others? Next, consider how others see you. What are some things that others often praise you for? What are some strengths your family and friends think you have? Once you've answered all of these questions, go back and review your answers. Then circle words that stand out. What did you discover about yourself?

We can identify and understand our personal _____ through self-reflection and feedback from others.

01 다음 중 Janis Smith에 대한 설명으로 알맞지 <u>않은</u> 것은?

M Our guest for today is Janis Smith. Please tell us about yourself.

W Sure. I'm a photographer, travel guide, and researcher. I travel around the world for my work.

M Wow, you're a true adventurer! What inspires you?

W I love experiencing the world. And I'm interested in seeking new opportunities to grow.

M That's a great attitude. What makes your photography unique?

W In my pictures, I focus on capturing human emotions through facial expressions. I think that makes my work unique.

M Interesting! Do you have any advice for those who want to follow their dreams?

W Absolutely. Always pursue your dreams and look for what really interests you. Life is short, so do what makes you happy.

① She has multiple jobs as a photographer, travel guide, and researcher.
② She travels around the world for her work.
③ She emphasizes depicting human emotions through facial expressions in her photography.
④ She advises people to pursue their dreams and do what makes them happy.
⑤ She primarily focuses on capturing landscapes and natural scenery.

[02~03] 다음 글을 읽고, 물음에 답하시오.

"ⓐ To grow into a better version of ourselves, we should not stay as we are." That was the first thing our teacher said to us on ⓑ the first day of school. <u>그녀는 우리가 우리 자신을 우리의 안전지대 밖으로 밀어내고 우리 자신에 관해 더 많이 배움으로써 학기를 시작하기를 바랐다.</u> To help us do so, she gave us an assignment to challenge ⓒ herself in three different ways. The three challenges could involve hobbies, exercise, our studies, or even our relationships. The important part was ⓓ trying something new for each one. She told us that we should share our experiences ⓔ of our classmates when we finished the challenges.

02 윗글의 밑줄 친 부분 중, 어법상 <u>틀린</u> 것을 <u>모두</u> 고른 것은?

① ⓐ, ⓒ
② ⓐ, ⓔ
③ ⓑ, ⓒ
④ ⓒ, ⓔ
⑤ ⓓ, ⓔ

03 윗글의 밑줄 친 우리말과 같은 뜻이 되도록 **보기**의 단어들을 바르게 배열하여 문장을 완성하시오.

보기 pushing / our comfort zones / ourselves / and / out of / more / learning / by / about ourselves

She wanted us to start the semester _____
_____
_____.

[04~05] 다음 글을 읽고, 물음에 답하시오.

These days, I tend to watch movies on streaming services. However, if I go to the theater, I usually watch an action or science fiction movie with my friends or family. Those are the kinds of movies they enjoy.

Going to the theater alone was something I had never done before. So, for the first challenge, I decided to give it a try. It was nice to choose the movie and the seat on my own. I didn't have to worry ____(A)____ anyone else's preferences. I saw the experience as a good opportunity to watch something different, so I chose a historical drama that I had been curious ____(B)____.

04 윗글을 쓴 필자의 심경으로 가장 적절한 것은?

① anxious   ② content
③ surprised   ④ frustrated
⑤ indifferent

05 윗글의 빈칸 (A), (B)에 공통으로 알맞은 전치사는?

① for   ② of   ③ from
④ about   ⑤ on

[06~07] 다음 글을 읽고, 물음에 답하시오.

At first, it felt a bit _____ to sit in the theater by myself. But once the movie started, I became completely absorbed in the story. It was so satisfying just to focus on the movie itself. There was nothing (A) distract me! This experience made me realize that I sometimes enjoy (B) do things alone. After the movie, I promised myself that I would try to make my own choices more often and enjoy more activities by myself in the future.

06 윗글의 빈칸에 들어갈 말로 가장 적절한 것은?

① familiar and warm
② exciting and thrilling
③ comfortable and enjoyable
④ awkward and lonely
⑤ disappointing and frustrating

07 윗글의 밑줄 친 (A), (B)를 어법에 맞는 형태로 바르게 고쳐 쓴 것은?

	(A)		(B)
①	distract	⋯	do
②	distract	⋯	doing
③	distracting	⋯	doing
④	to distract	⋯	to do
⑤	to distract	⋯	doing

[08~09] 다음 글을 읽고, 물음에 답하시오.

Ever since I was a child, I've always been afraid of water. So I have never enjoyed water activities or felt comfortable while doing them. For the second challenge, I decided to try to overcome this discomfort. However, I wasn't sure what to do at first. One day, I came across a video clip of my cousin surfing at an indoor pool on social media. It looked fun, and I liked the fact that it took place in a shallow pool, not in the ocean. I messaged my cousin about it. She assured me that it wasn't too hard, so I signed up for a beginner course.

08 윗글을 읽고, 다음 질문에 알맞은 대답을 고르면?

Q Why did the writer decide to sign up for a beginner course?

① To follow their cousin's advice
② To compete with friends
③ To overcome their fear of water
④ To enjoy swimming in the ocean
⑤ To improve their social media presence

09 다음 영어 뜻풀이에 해당하는 단어를 윗글에서 찾아 쓰시오.

to successfully deal with or get past a problem or difficulty

→ _____

10 다음 글의 밑줄 친 부분 중, 틀린 것을 찾아 기호를 쓰고 바르게 고쳐 쓰시오.

At the beginning of the lesson, it was ⓐ hard just to stand up on the board. After some help from the instructor, however, I learned how to balance ⓑ properly and even managed to surf a few waves! It gave me such a rush of ⓒ excite. Being in the water wasn't as ⓓ bad as I had thought. While the experience didn't ⓔ completely change my mind about water sports, it did help me discover my sense of adventure.

_____ → _____

11 다음 중 밑줄 친 단어의 쓰임이 어색한 것은?

① My sister is suitable of fixing broken things.
② Alex has a preference for sitting in the window seat when flying.
③ I was so absorbed in the book that I stayed up late.
④ A small act of kindness can make a big difference in someone's day.
⑤ According to the museum's rules, taking photos is not acceptable.

Of all the challenges I chose for myself, the third one made me the most nervous: changing my hairstyle. For many years, I had kept the same hairstyle because I had been worried about my forehead.

(A) I had always thought it was large, and I didn't want to draw attention to it. Since I was feeling confident after the first two challenges, I went to a hair salon and talked to the stylist. He listened to my concerns and helped me find a shorter hairstyle that suited me.

(B) In fact, it made me feel more confident about myself. I didn't expect that stepping out of my comfort zone would have such a positive effect on how I felt about myself.

(C) The next day at school, my classmates were a bit surprised. But overall, the reactions were positive. I realized that trying a different look wasn't as difficult as I thought it would be.

12 윗글의 주어진 문장 다음에 이어질 글의 순서로 가장 적절한 것은?

① (A) – (C) – (B) ② (B) – (A) – (C)
③ (B) – (C) – (A) ④ (C) – (A) – (B)
⑤ (C) – (B) – (A)

13 윗글의 밑줄 친 Since와 쓰임이 같은 것끼리 모은 것은?

ⓐ I have been living in this city since 2020.
ⓑ Since it was raining, we decided to stay indoors.
ⓒ He hasn't visited us since last summer.
ⓓ Since the concert was canceled, I got a refund for the ticket.

① ⓐ, ⓑ ② ⓐ, ⓒ
③ ⓑ, ⓒ ④ ⓑ, ⓓ
⑤ ⓑ, ⓒ, ⓓ

I learned a lot about myself through this assignment, and I found out that my classmates did, too. One of them tried new foods from different countries, while another joined a creative writing club. Through these experiences, we all realized how important is it to push ourselves to try new things. We gained different perspectives on life and had a lot of fun, too! My classmates and I even talked about ___(A)___ more challenges for ourselves. There are always more things that we can discover about ourselves, and it's exciting ___(B)___ learning and growing. We never know what we're capable of until we try!

14 윗글의 빈칸 (A), (B)에 들어갈 말이 바르게 짝지어진 것은?

　　　(A)　　　　(B)
① set　　…　keep
② setting　…　to keep
③ setting　…　keep
④ to set　…　keeping
⑤ to set　…　to keep

15 윗글의 밑줄 친 문장에서 틀린 부분을 찾아 바르게 고쳐 문장을 다시 쓰시오.

→ _____
_____

[01~02] 다음 글을 읽고, 물음에 답하시오.

"① To become a better version of ourselves, we must not remain the same." These were the first words our teacher told us on the first day of school. She encouraged us ② to begin the semester by stepping out of our comfort zones and ③ to discover more about who we are. To help with this, she assigned us a task ④ to challenge ourselves in three different ways. These challenges could be related to hobbies, exercise, our studies, or even our relationships. The important part was trying something new for each one. Once we completed the challenges, she asked us ⑤ to share our experiences with our classmates.

01 윗글의 주제로 가장 적절한 것은?

① self-discovery and personal growth
② avoiding challenges and staying comfortable
③ the importance of teamwork in school projects
④ how to maintain old habits effectively
⑤ the benefits of traditional education methods

02 윗글의 밑줄 친 부분 중, 어법상 틀린 것은?

①   ②   ③   ④   ⑤

[03~04] 다음 글을 읽고, 물음에 답하시오.

These days, I usually watch movies on streaming services. (①) However, when I go to the theater, I typically watch action or science fiction films with my friends or family because those are their favorites. (②)

Going to the theater by myself was something I had never tried before. (③) So, for my first challenge, I decided to give it a try. (④) I saw this as an opportunity to watch something different, so I selected a historical drama that caught my interest. (⑤)

03 윗글의 흐름으로 보아, 주어진 문장이 들어가기에 가장 적절한 곳은?

It was nice to pick the movie and my seat without considering anyone else's preferences.

①   ②   ③   ④   ⑤

04 윗글의 "I"에 관한 내용으로 알맞지 않은 것은?

① 주로 스트리밍 서비스로 영화를 본다.
② 보통 액션이나 공상과학 영화를 본다.
③ 친구나 가족과 함께 영화관에 간다.
④ 혼자 영화관에 가는 경험이 주는 즐거움을 느꼈다.
⑤ 자신의 취향대로 영화를 고르는 것을 좋아했다.

[05~06] 다음 글을 읽고, 물음에 답하시오.

At first, I felt a bit strange and ① <u>lonely</u> sitting in the theater. However, once the movie began, I became fully ② <u>immersed</u> in the story. It was incredibly satisfying to focus solely on the movie, without any ③ <u>distractions</u>. This experience helped me ④ <u>realize</u> that I sometimes enjoy doing things alone. After the movie, I promised myself that I would ⑤ <u>take</u> my own choices more frequently and enjoy more activities by myself in the future.

05 윗글의 밑줄 친 부분 중, 문맥상 낱말의 쓰임이 적절하지 <u>않은</u> 것은?

①　　　②　　　③　　　④　　　⑤

06 윗글에 나타난 "I"의 심경 변화로 가장 적절한 것은?

① bored → scared
② lonely → frustrated
③ awkward → satisfied
④ confused → pleased
⑤ disappointed → excited

[07~08] 다음 글을 읽고, 물음에 답하시오.

Since I was a child, I've always had a fear of water, (A) which / that has made me uncomfortable with doing water sports. For my second challenge, I decided (B) confront / to confront this fear. At first, I wasn't sure how to approach it. One day, I saw a video of my cousin (C) surfing / surfed at an indoor pool on social media. It looked fun, and I liked that it was in a shallow pool, not the ocean. I reached out to my cousin, who assured me that it wasn't too difficult, so I signed up for a beginner course.

07 윗글의 제목으로 가장 적절한 것은?

① The Joy of Swimming
② A New Adventure in the Ocean
③ Family Fun at the Pool
④ Overcoming My Fear of Water
⑤ My Favorite Summer Activities

08 (A), (B), (C)의 각 네모 안에서 어법에 맞는 표현으로 가장 적절한 것은?

	(A)	(B)	(C)
①	which	confront	surfing
②	which	to confront	surfing
③	which	to confront	surfed
④	that	confront	surfed
⑤	that	to confront	surfing

[09~10] 다음 글을 읽고, 물음에 답하시오.

(①) At the (A) beginning / end of the lesson, I struggled just standing on the board. (②) However, with the help of the (B) beginner / instructor , I learned to balance properly and even managed to surf a few waves! (③) Being in the water turned out to be less (C) scary / exciting than I thought. (④) While it didn't completely change my mind about water sports, it did help me discover my sense of adventure. (⑤)

09 윗글의 흐름으로 보아, 주어진 문장이 들어가기에 가장 적절한 곳은?

It was an exciting experience.

① ② ③ ④ ⑤

10 (A), (B), (C)의 각 네모 안에서 문맥에 맞는 낱말로 가장 적절한 것은?

	(A)	(B)	(C)
①	beginning	beginner	scary
②	beginning	instructor	scary
③	beginning	instructor	exciting
④	end	beginner	exciting
⑤	end	instructor	scary

[11~12] 다음 글을 읽고, 물음에 답하시오.

① Among all the ___(A)___ I chose for myself, the third one made me the most nervous: changing my hairstyle. For many years, I had kept the same hairstyle because I ② had been worried about my forehead. I always thought it was large, and I didn't want ③ to draw attention to it. ④ Felt confident after the first two ___(B)___, I decided to visit a hair salon and discuss my options with the stylist. He listened to my worries and helped me ⑤ choose a shorter hairstyle that suited me.

11 윗글의 빈칸 (A), (B)에 공통으로 들어갈 말로 알맞은 것은?

① tasks
② choices
③ activities
④ challenges
⑤ experiences

12 윗글의 밑줄 친 부분 중, 어법상 틀린 것은?

① ② ③ ④ ⑤

The next day at school, my classmates were a bit surprised, but their overall reactions were (A) positive / negative . I realized that trying out a new look wasn't as _____ as I had thought. In fact, it made me feel more (B) anxious / confident . I didn't expect that stepping out of my (C) comfort / discomfort zone would have such a positive effect on how I felt about myself.

13 (A), (B), (C)의 각 네모 안에서 문맥에 맞는 낱말로 가장 적절한 것은?

	(A)	(B)	(C)
①	positive …	anxious …	comfort
②	positive …	confident …	comfort
③	positive …	confident …	discomfort
④	negative …	anxious …	discomfort
⑤	negative …	confident …	comfort

14 윗글의 빈칸에 들어갈 말로 가장 적절한 것은?

① pleasant
② satisfying
③ comfortable
④ depressing
⑤ challenging

15 주어진 문장 다음에 이어질 글의 순서로 가장 적절한 것은?

I discovered a lot about myself through this assignment, and my classmates did as well.

(A) My classmates and I even discussed setting more challenges for ourselves. There are always more things that we can discover about ourselves, and it's thrilling to continue learning and growing.

(B) One of them tried food from various countries, while another joined a creative writing club. These experiences taught us the importance of pushing ourselves to try new things. We gained fresh perspectives on life and had a great time, too!

(C) We can't truly know our capabilities until we give it a try!

① (A) – (B) – (C)
② (A) – (C) – (B)
③ (B) – (A) – (C)
④ (B) – (C) – (A)
⑤ (C) – (A) – (B)

[01~03] 다음 글을 읽고, 물음에 답하시오.

"(A) To grow into a better version of ourselves, we should not stay as we are." That was the first thing our teacher said to us on the first day of school. (B) She wanted us start the semester by pushing ourselves out of our comfort zones and learn more about ourselves. To help us do so, she gave us an assignment to challenge ourselves in three different ways. The three challenges could involve hobbies, exercise, our studies, or even our relationships. 중요한 부분은 각각의 것에 대해 새로운 무언가를 시도해 보는 것이었다. She told us that we should share our experiences with our classmates when we finished the challenges.

01 윗글의 밑줄 친 (A)를 우리말로 해석하시오.

→ _____

02 윗글의 밑줄 친 (B)에서 틀린 부분을 두 군데 찾아 바르게 고친 후 문장을 다시 쓰시오.

→ _____

03 윗글의 밑줄 친 우리말과 같은 뜻이 되도록 조건에 맞게 바르게 영작하시오.

> **조건**
> • important, try, something, each를 사용할 것
> • 동명사를 사용할 것

→ _____

[04~05] 다음 글을 읽고, 물음에 답하시오.

These days, I tend to watch movies on streaming services. However, if I go to the theater, I usually watch an action or science fiction movie with my friends or family. Those are the kinds of movies they enjoy.

(A) Going to the theater alone were something I had never done before. So, for the first challenge, I decided to give it a try. It was nice to choose the movie and the seat on my own. (B) I didn't must worry about anyone else's preferences. I saw the experience as a good opportunity to watch something different, so I chose a historical drama that I had been curious about.

04 윗글의 밑줄 친 Those가 가리키는 것이 무엇인지 영어로 쓰시오.

→ _____

05 윗글의 밑줄 친 (A)와 (B)에서 어법상 틀린 부분을 찾아 바르게 고쳐 문장을 다시 쓰시오.

(A) _____

_____

(B) _____

_____

[06~07] 다음 글을 읽고, 물음에 답하시오.

At first, it felt a bit awkward and lonely to sit in the theater by myself. But once the movie started, I became completely absorbed in the story. Just to focus on the movie itself was so satisfying. There was nothing to distract me! This experience made me realize that I sometimes enjoy doing things alone. After the movie, I promised myself that I would try to make my own choices more often and enjoy more activities by myself in the future.

06 윗글의 밑줄 친 문장을 가주어 It을 사용하여 바꿔 쓰시오.

→ It _____

_____ .

07 윗글의 "I"가 느낀 감정의 변화를 나타내는 단어를 찾아 쓰시오.

_____ → _____

[08~10] 다음 글을 읽고, 물음에 답하시오.

Ever since I was a child, I've always been afraid of water. So I have never enjoyed water activities or felt _____(A)_____ (comfort) while doing them. For the second challenge, I decided to try to overcome this discomfort. However, I wasn't sure what to do at first. One day, 나는 소셜 미디어로 실내 수영장에서 서핑하는 사촌의 영상을 우연히 보았다. It looked fun, and I liked the fact that it took place in a shallow pool, not in the ocean. I messaged my cousin about it. She assured me that it wasn't too hard, so I signed up for a beginner course.

At the beginning of the lesson, it was hard just to stand up on the board. After some help from the instructor, however, I learned how to balance properly and even managed to surf a few waves! It gave me such a rush of _____(B)_____ (excite). Being in the water wasn't as bad as I had thought. While the experience didn't completely change my mind about water sports, it helped me discover my sense of adventure.

08 윗글의 빈칸 (A), (B)에 알맞은 말을 괄호 안의 단어를 변형하여 쓰시오.

(A) comfort → _____

(B) excite → _____

09 윗글의 밑줄 친 우리말과 같은 뜻이 되도록 보기의 단어들을 바르게 배열하여 쓰시오.

> 보기 I / a video clip / an indoor pool / at / my cousin / came across / of / surfing / on social media

→ _____

_____

10 윗글의 밑줄 친 helped를 강조동사 do를 사용하여 두 단어로 바꿔 쓰시오.

helped → _____

[11~12] 다음 글을 읽고, 물음에 답하시오.

Of all the challenges I chose for myself, the third one made me the most nervous: changing my hairstyle. For many years, I had kept the same hairstyle because I had worried about my forehead. I had been always thought it was large, and I didn't want to draw attention to it. Since I was feeling _____ⓐ_____ after the first two challenges, I went to a hair salon and talked to the stylist. He listened to my concerns and helped me find a shorter hairstyle that suited me.

(A) The next day at school, my classmates were a bit surprising. But overall, the reactions were _____ⓑ_____. (B) I realized that trying a different look wasn't as difficult than I thought it would be. (C) In fact, it made me to feel more confident about myself. I didn't expect that stepping out of my comfort zone would have such a positive effect on how I felt about myself.

11 윗글의 빈칸 ⓐ, ⓑ에 들어갈 말을 다음 영어 뜻풀이를 참고해 주어진 철자로 시작하여 쓰시오.

ⓐ feeling or showing certainty about something; self-assured

ⓑ optimistic or constructive; having a good attitude or effect

ⓐ c_____ ⓑ p_____

12 윗글의 밑줄 친 (A)~(C)에서 어법상 틀린 부분을 찾아 바르게 고쳐 문장을 다시 쓰시오.

(A) _____

_____

(B) _____

_____

(C) _____

_____

[13~14] 다음 글을 읽고, 물음에 답하시오.

I learned a lot about myself through this assignment, and I found out that my classmates did, too. 그들 중 한 명은 여러 나라의 새로운 음식들을 먹어 본 반면, 다른 친구는 문예 창작 동아리에 가입했다. Through these experiences, we all realized how important it is to push ourselves to try new things. We gained different perspectives on life and had a lot of fun, too! My classmates and I even talked about setting more challenges for ourselves. There are always more things that we can discover about ourselves, and it's exciting to keep learning and growing. We never know what we're capable of until we try!

13 윗글의 밑줄 친 우리말과 같은 뜻이 되도록 조건 에 맞게 빈칸에 알맞은 말을 넣어 문장을 완성하시오.

조건
• another와 the other 중 하나를 골라서 사용할 것
• 접속사와 a creative writing club을 사용할 것

→ One of them tried new foods from different countries,

_____ .

14 윗글의 요약문을 본문에 있는 단어를 사용하여 완성하시오. (필요시 형태를 바꿀 것)

Through this (1) _____ , we realized the (2) _____ of trying new things. We discovered new (3) _____ on life and are (4) _____ to keep learning and growing.

02

— Health Matters!

Functions

▶ 충고하기
I think you should try to go for a walk after you eat.

▶ 희망, 기대 표현하기
I hope these tips help you enjoy your favorite shows in a healthy way.

Structures

▶ I needed to find a way **to bring** psychiatry into the community.

▶ **It** is such a rewarding experience **to help** people make positive changes in their lives.

교과서 어휘

Words

□ friendship	몡 우정
□ guest	몡 손님
□ welcome	동 환영하다
□ founder	몡 창립자, 설립자 (found 동 설립하다)
□ inspire	동 영감을 주다 (inspiration 몡 영감)
□ psychiatrist	몡 정신과 의사
□ patient	몡 환자
□ severely	부 심하게, 극심하게 (severe 형 극심한)
□ depressed	형 우울한; 우울증을 앓는
□ afford	동 (~을 할) 여유[형편]가 되다
□ transportation	몡 교통 (기관); 수송, 운송
□ receive	동 받다
□ medical	형 의학의
□ treatment	몡 치료 (treat 동 치료하다)
□ furthermore	부 게다가
□ lack	몡 부족 (= shortage)
□ population	몡 인구
□ beginning	몡 시작 (↔ end 끝)
□ explain	동 설명하다 (explanation 몡 설명)
□ accessible	형 접근 가능한 (access 몡 접근)
□ therapy	몡 치료, 요법
□ depression	몡 우울증
□ anxiety	몡 불안(감), 염려 (anxious 형 불안해하는)

□ respected	형 존경받는 (respect 동 존경하다)
□ elderly	형 연세가 드신
□ volunteer	동 자원하다, 자원 봉사로 하다 몡 자원봉사자
□ emotional	형 감정의, 감정적인 (emotion 몡 감정)
□ counselor	몡 상담가
□ empathy	몡 공감, 감정이입
□ ability	몡 능력 (able 형 ~할 수 있는)
□ meaningful	형 의미 있는 (meaning 몡 의미)
□ reliable	형 믿을[신뢰할] 수 있는 (rely 동 의지하다)
□ effort	몡 노력
□ train	동 훈련하다
□ struggle	몡 투쟁, 분투; 힘든 일
□ incredibly	부 믿을 수 없을 정도로, 엄청나게
□ successful	형 성공적인 (success 몡 성공)
□ face-to-face	형 마주 보는, 대면하는
□ available	형 구할[이용할] 수 있는
□ region	몡 지방, 지역
□ vision	몡 시력, 비전
□ distance	몡 거리 (distant 형 먼)
□ expand	동 확대[확장]하다, 확대[확장]시키다
□ wounded	형 부상을 입은, 다친; (마음이) 상한
□ recovery	몡 회복 (recover 동 회복하다)
□ rewarding	형 보람된

Phrases

□ be unable to	~할 수 없다
□ deal with	~을 다루다
□ such as	~와 같은
□ be connected to	~와 연결[연관]되다
□ thousands of	수천 명의
□ be encouraged to	~하도록 장려되다

□ relate to	~을 이해하다, ~에 공감하다
□ struggle with	~로 고심하다
□ make a difference	변화를 가져오다
□ go through	~을 겪다
□ pass away	돌아가시다
□ back on track	(실수·실패 뒤에) 다시 정상 궤도에 들어선

come up with ~을 생각하다, 생각을 떠올리다	The leaders held a meeting to **come up with** solutions to their problems. 그 지도자들은 그들의 문제에 대한 해결책을 떠올리기 위해 회의를 개최했다.
engage in ~에 관여[참여]하다	It is important to **engage in** regular exercise to maintain a healthy lifestyle. 건강한 생활방식을 유지하기 위해서는 규칙적인 운동에 참여하는 것이 중요하다.
be ashamed of ~을 부끄러워하다	He should **be ashamed of** himself for telling such a lie. 그는 그런 거짓말을 하는 것에 대해 스스로에게 부끄러워해야 한다.

Collocations

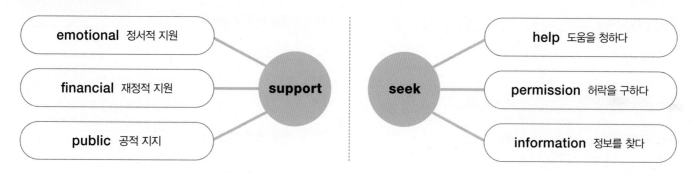

emotional 정서적 지원

financial 재정적 지원

public 공적 지지

support

seek

help 도움을 청하다

permission 허락을 구하다

information 정보를 찾다

English-English Dictionary

☐ **inspire** 영감을 주다   to give someone the desire or motivation to do something creative or positive

☐ **depressed** 우울한   feeling extremely sad or hopeless

☐ **transportation** 수송, 운송   the system or means of moving people or goods from one place to another

☐ **population** 인구   the total number of people living in a specific area or region

☐ **accessible** 접근 가능한   easy to approach, enter, or use

☐ **therapy** 치료   treatment aimed at relieving or healing a medical or mental health problem

☐ **anxiety** 불안(감), 염려   a feeling of worry or fear about future events or situations

☐ **volunteer** 자원하다   to offer to do something without being paid

☐ **empathy** 공감, 감정이입   understanding and sharing someone else's emotions

☐ **struggle** 투쟁, 분투; 힘든 일   a difficult task or challenge; an effort to overcome obstacles

☐ **incredibly** 믿을 수 없을 정도로   to an astonishing or unbelievable degree; extremely

☐ **expand** 확대[확장]하다   to increase in size, volume, or scope; to spread out or grow larger

☐ **wounded** 다친; (마음이) 상한   injured physically or emotionally

☐ **recovery** 회복   returning to a normal state after a period of illness or injury

교과서 어휘 익히기

♣ 다음 영어는 우리말로, 우리말은 영어로 쓰시오.

01	vision	명 _____	25	명 우정 _____
02	afford	동 _____	26	명 치료, 요법 _____
03	wounded	형 _____	27	형 우울한; 우울증을 앓는 _____
04	inspire	동 _____	28	명 노력 _____
05	founder	명 _____	29	명 교통 (기관); 수송, 운송 _____
06	available	형 _____	30	형 믿을[신뢰할] 수 있는 _____
07	medical	형 _____	31	명 회복 _____
08	severely	부 _____	32	부 믿을 수 없을 정도로 _____
09	lack	명 _____	33	명 지방, 지역 _____
10	accessible	형 _____	34	동 자원하다 _____
11	expand	동 _____	35	명 투쟁, 분투; 힘든 일 _____
12	furthermore	부 _____	36	형 감정의, 감정적인 _____
13	meaningful	형 _____	37	형 마주 보는, 대면하는 _____
14	counselor	명 _____	38	명 능력 _____
15	depression	명 _____	39	명 회복 _____
16	empathy	명 _____	40	명 환자 _____
17	anxiety	명 _____	41	명 정신과 의사 _____
18	elderly	형 _____	42	명 인구 _____
19	treatment	명 _____	43	~에 관여[참여]하다 _____
20	come up with	_____	44	돌아가시다 _____
21	be ashamed of	_____	45	~하도록 장려되다 _____
22	such as	_____	46	~을 다루다 _____
23	go through	_____	47	~와 연결[연관]되다 _____
24	struggle with	_____	48	~을 이해하다, ~에 공감하다 _____

A 다음 우리말과 일치하도록 보기에서 알맞은 말을 골라 빈칸에 쓰시오.

> 보기 go through   come up with   engage in   relate to   be ashamed of

01 You should _____ spreading rumors about your classmates.
너는 학급 친구들에 대한 소문을 퍼뜨린 것에 대해 부끄러워해야 한다.

02 Can you tell us what inspired you to _____ the program?
무엇이 당신으로 하여금 그 프로그램을 떠올리도록 영감을 주었는지 우리에게 말씀해 주시겠어요?

03 They decided to _____ a group discussion about the project.
그들은 프로젝트에 대한 그룹 토론에 참여하기로 결정했다.

04 She had to _____ hardship before she found success.
그녀는 성공을 찾기 전에 고난을 겪어야 했다.

05 He can't _____ their problems because he's never experienced them.
그는 그들의 문제를 결코 경험해본 적이 없기 때문에 그것들에 공감할 수 없다.

B 다음 우리말과 일치하도록 괄호 안에서 알맞은 말을 고르시오.

01 These women volunteer to sit with patients at the benches, listen to their stories, and provide them with emotional (support / struggle).
이 여성들은 환자들과 함께 벤치에 앉는 것을 자원하고, 그들의 이야기를 듣고, 그들에게 정서적 지원을 제공한다.

02 (Avoiding / Seeking) help for mental health problems is nothing to be ashamed of.
정신 건강 문제에 대한 도움을 구하는 것은 부끄러워할 일이 아니다.

C 다음 밑줄 친 부분의 영어 뜻풀이로 알맞은 것을 골라 기호를 쓰시오.

> ⓐ to offer to do something without being paid
> ⓑ a feeling of worry or fear about future events or situations
> ⓒ the system or means of moving people or goods from one place to another

01 It offers talk therapy sessions to people dealing with issues such as depression or anxiety.
(   )

02 Now let's hear from one of the grandmothers who volunteers for the program. (   )

03 It is difficult for many people in Zimbabwe to pay for transportation and receive medical treatment. (   )

Function 1 충고하기

B Hey, Lisa! Why didn't you come to our math club meeting yesterday?

G I had a stomachache after lunch, so I went home early.
　　　have a stomachache: 배가 아프다

B Oh, that's too bad. What do you think caused it?
　　유감을 표현할 때 쓰는 표현　　　　　　　　　　= stomachache

G I'm not sure. These days, I often have an upset stomach when I'm in the
　　　　　　　　　　　　　　　　　　　　　　　～할 때 〈접속사〉
library after lunch.

B Maybe that's the problem. Sitting right after a meal can be bad for your
　　　　　　　　(that)　　　　동명사 주어　　　　　　～에 나쁘다
health. **I think you should try to go for a walk after you eat.**
　　　　　　　～하려고 노력하다 산책하다　　～한 후에 〈접속사〉
　　　　　　　　　　　　　　더 자주
G You're right. I should do that more often.
　　　　　　　　　　　= going for a walk

《 B: 안녕, Lisa! 어제 우리 수학 동아리 모임에 왜 안 왔어?

G: 점심 식사 후에 배가 아파서 집에 일찍 갔어.

B: 아, 안됐구나. 무엇 때문이라고 생각해?

G: 잘 모르겠어. 요즘 점심 식사 후 도서관에 있으면 자주 배가 불편해.

B: 아마 그게 문제인 것 같아. 식사 후 바로 앉아 있는 것은 건강에 좋지 않을 수 있어. 나는 네가 식사 후에 산책을 해보는 게 좋다고 생각해.

G: 네 말이 맞아. 그렇게 더 자주 해 봐야겠어.

Study Point ☙

I think you should ～는 '나는 네가 ～해야 한다고 생각해'라는 뜻으로 상대방에게 충고를 할 때 자신의 의견을 부드럽게 전달할 수 있는 표현이다.

More Expressions ☙

충고하는 표현들

Why don't you ～?(～하는 것이 어때?), It could be helpful to ～(～하는 것이 도움이 될 수 있다), In my opinion, you ought to ～(내 의견으로는, 너는 ～해야 한다) 등도 충고할 때 사용할 수 있는 표현이다.

Why don't you take a break and relax for a while? 잠깐 쉬면서 휴식을 취하는 것이 어때?

It could be helpful to join a study group if you need to improve your grades.
성적을 올릴 필요가 있다면 스터디 그룹에 참여하는 것이 도움이 될 수 있다.

In my opinion, you ought to exercise regularly to maintain good health.
내 의견으로는, 너는 건강을 유지하기 위해 규칙적으로 운동해야 한다.

Check-up ☙

다음 문장의 밑줄 친 부분과 바꿔 쓸 수 있는 것은?

> <u>I think you should</u> save some money for your future.
> (너의 미래를 위해 돈을 좀 저축해야 한다고 생각해.)

① I know you must
② I feel you have to
③ I wish you would
④ I don't believe you can
⑤ In my opinion, you ought to

Function 2 희망, 기대 표현하기

W Thanks to streaming platforms, you can watch your favorite shows
~덕분에
anytime. You can even watch a whole series without stopping! This is
전치사+동명사
called binge-watching. It sounds fun, but binge-watching isn't good for
수동태   sound+형용사: ~처럼 들리다   ~에 좋지 않다
you. It can cause sleep problems and lead to reduced physical activity.
V1   V2
So, how can you prevent binge-watching from affecting your health?
prevent A from B: A가 B 하지 못하게 하다
First, decide how long you are going to watch a show before you start,
간접의문문(decide의 목적어 역할)
and set an alarm. When the alarm goes off, it's important to stop watching
(알람 등이) 울리다   가주어   진주어
even if you are in the middle of the show. Second, watch shows only
비록 ~일지라도   ~의 도중에
while doing a productive activity, such as exercising or organizing your
접속사(you are)   ~와 같은
desk. When you finish the activity, turn off the show. **I hope these tips**
~할 때 〈접속사〉   ~을 끄다 (↔ turn on)   (that)
help you enjoy your favorite shows in a healthy way.
help+목적어+동사원형: 목적어가 ~하는 것을 돕다

≪ W: 스트리밍 플랫폼 덕분에 좋아하는 프로그램을 언제든지 볼 수 있습니다. 심지어 멈춤 없이 전체 시리즈를 시청할 수도 있죠! 이것을 '폭식 시청(binge-watching)'이라고 합니다. 재미있게 들리지만, 폭식 시청은 건강에 좋지 않습니다. 수면 문제를 일으킬 수 있고 신체 활동이 줄어들게 할 수 있습니다. 그렇다면 어떻게 폭식 시청이 건강에 영향을 미치지 않도록 예방할 수 있을까요? 첫째, 프로그램을 보기 시작하기 전에 얼마나 오랫동안 볼 것인지 결정하고 알람을 설정하세요. 알람이 울리면, 프로그램의 중간이라도 시청을 중단하는 것이 중요합니다. 둘째, 운동이나 책상 정리 같은 생산적인 활동을 하는 동안만 프로그램을 보세요. 활동이 끝나면 프로그램을 끄세요. 이 팁들이 여러분이 좋아하는 프로그램을 건강하게 즐기는 데 도움이 되길 바랍니다.

Study Point ♉

I hope (that) ~은 '~하기를 바라다'라는 뜻으로 희망이나 기대를 표현할 때 사용한다.

More Expressions ♉

희망이나 기대를 말하는 표현들

I expect ~(나는 ~을 기대한다), I look forward to ~(나는 ~을 고대한다) 등도 희망이나 기대를 말할 때 사용할 수 있는 표현이다.

I expect that the new movie will be a big hit. 나는 새 영화가 큰 성공을 거둘 것이라고 기대한다.

I look forward to hearing from you soon. 나는 곧 너의 소식을 듣기를 고대한다.

Check-up ♉

다음 우리말과 같은 뜻이 되도록 빈칸에 알맞은 말을 쓰시오.

A How can you improve your digital well-being?
B I'm going to try to focus on my hobbies more.
A Good idea! _____ that brings you a healthier digital life.
   (좋은 생각이야! 나는 그것이 너에게 더 건강한 디지털 생활을 가져오길 바라.)

교고서 기타 대화문

TOPIC 1 C. Listen and Interact

B I think I've ❶ <u>gained some weight</u>. This shirt feels tight.

G Oh, what do you think ❷ <u>made you gain</u> weight?

B I think I eat snacks too often, especially at night.

G That's a bad habit. Let's look up ways to ❸ <u>help you break</u> it.

B Okay. Oh, this website suggests ❹ <u>drinking more water</u>. It says people often mistake being thirsty for being hungry.

G Right. And here it says ❺ <u>not to skip</u> meals during the day. That just makes you hungrier at night. Also, if you ❻ <u>do need</u> a snack, you should have fruit or nuts.

B Those are good tips. I think I should try them.

G Yes, ❼ <u>it's important to take</u> care of your health.

❶ gain weight: 살이 찌다 (↔ lose weight) ❷ 사역동사+목적어+동사원형 ❸ help+목적어+(to+)동사원형: 목적어가 ~하도록 돕다 ❹ 목적어 역할을 하는 동명사구 ❺ not+to부정사: to부정사의 부정 ❻ 강조동사 do+동사원형 ❼ 「가주어 it, 진주어 to부정사」 구문 / take care of: ~을 돌보다

Q1 The girl suggests drinking more water will help with weight loss. (T / F)

TOPIC 4 B. While You View

M Think about the last time you were about to take an exam. If you were anxious, did your hands get sweaty? Maybe you felt more relaxed ❶ <u>after</u> a classmate ❷ <u>made you laugh</u>. Similarly, you might sometimes ❸ <u>feel your mood improve</u> ❹ <u>after</u> having a healthy meal. These situations reflect the mind-body connection.

❺ <u>According to</u> this concept, our minds and bodies can influence each other. For example, constant worry can ❻ <u>result in</u> stomach problems. Therefore, you should look after ❼ <u>both your mental and physical well-being</u>. When you're feeling down, focus on the breath in and out. This is an effective strategy to ❽ <u>cope with</u> your negative thoughts or emotions. If you're feeling stressed, go walking or jogging outdoors. When you're losing focus, take a break or stretch. That way, you can ❾ <u>reconnect your body with your mind</u>. Take care of your mind-body connection ❿ <u>to be</u> healthy inside and out.

❶ after: 부사절 접속사 ❷ make(사역동사)+목적어+동사원형 ❸ feel(지각동사)+목적어+동사원형 ❹ after(전치사)+동명사 ❺ according to: ~에 따르면 ❻ result in: 그 결과 ~가 되다 ❼ both A and B: A와 B 둘 다 ❽ cope with: ~을 다루다 ❾ reconnect A with B: A와 B를 다시 연결하다 ❿ 부사적 용법의 to부정사(목적)

Q2 According to the mind-body connection concept, our minds and bodies do not influence each other. (T / F)

Wrap Up A. Listen and Post

G What's that, Jake?

B It's my meal plan. It shows ❶ <u>what I'll eat</u> for each meal. ❷ <u>Thinking about it in advance helps</u> me maintain a healthy diet.

G Great idea! I often ❸ <u>end up having</u> unhealthy fast food ❹ <u>because</u> I can't decide ❺ <u>what to eat</u>.

B Really? Then I think you should make a meal plan, too.

G Can you explain ❻ <u>how you make</u> each meal healthy?

B Sure. I make sure there's the right balance of grains, protein, and vegetables. And I ❼ <u>try to eat</u> ❽ <u>a variety of</u> foods.

G Okay. I'll try that!

❶ 간접의문문(의문사+주어+동사) ❷ 동명사 주어+단수 동사 ❸ end up v-ing: 결국 ~하게 되다 ❹ 이유를 나타내는 부사절 접속사 ❺ 의문사+to부정사: 명사구 ❻ 간접의문문(의문사+주어+동사) ❼ try+to부정사: ~하려고 애쓰다, 노력하다 ❽ a variety of: 다양한

Q3 Jake believes that planning his meals in advance helps him maintain a healthy diet. (T / F)

교과서 핵심 대화문 익히기

01 다음 대화의 흐름으로 보아, 주어진 문장이 들어가기에 가장 적절한 곳은?

> I think you should try to go for a walk after you eat.

> B Hey, Lisa! Why didn't you come to our math club meeting yesterday?
> G I had a stomachache after lunch, so I went home early. (①)
> B Oh, that's too bad. What do you think caused it? (②)
> G I'm not sure. These days, I often have an upset stomach when I'm in the library after lunch. (③)
> B Maybe that's the problem. Sitting right after a meal can be bad for your health. (④)
> G You're right. I should do that more often. (⑤)

02 밑줄 친 우리말과 같은 뜻이 되도록 괄호 안에 주어진 단어들을 바르게 배열하시오.

> W Thanks to streaming platforms, you can watch your favorite shows anytime. You can even watch a whole series without stopping! This is called binge-watching. It sounds fun, but binge-watching isn't good for you. It can cause sleep problems and lead to reduced physical activity. So, how can you prevent binge-watching from affecting your health? First, decide how long you are going to watch a show before you start, and set an alarm. When the alarm goes off, it's important to stop watching even if you are in the middle of the show. Second, watch shows only while doing a productive activity, such as exercising or organizing your desk. When you finish the activity, turn off the show. 이 팁들이 여러분이 좋아하는 프로그램을 건강하게 즐기는 데 도움이 되길 바랍니다.

→ _____

(these tips / you / enjoy / I hope / in a healthy way / your favorite shows / help)

03 다음 대화의 주제로 가장 적절한 것은?

> G What's that, Jake?
> B It's my meal plan. It shows what I'll eat for each meal. Thinking about it in advance helps me maintain a healthy diet.
> G Great idea! I often end up having unhealthy fast food because I can't decide what to eat.
> B Really? Then I think you should make a meal plan, too.
> G Can you explain how you make each meal healthy?
> B Sure. I make sure there's the right balance of grains, protein, and vegetables. And I try to eat a variety of foods.
> G Okay. I'll try that!

① Exercise routines for weight loss
② The benefits of fast food
③ Stress management techniques
④ Tips for studying effectively
⑤ Meal planning and healthy eating

교과서 핵심 문법

POINT 1 to부정사의 형용사적 용법

예제   There are many tasks **to complete** before the deadline.
└─────┘ 형용사적 용법의 to부정사(앞의 명사 tasks 수식)

마감일 전에 완료해야 할 많은 작업들이 있다.

교과서   I needed to find a way **to bring** psychiatry into the community.
└─────┘ 형용사적 용법의 to부정사(앞의 명사 a way 수식)

나는 정신의학을 지역 사회에 도입할 방법을 찾아야 했다.

▶ to부정사는 (대)명사 뒤에서 형용사처럼 (대)명사를 수식할 수 있다. 수식 받는 (대)명사가 부정사구 안에 있는 전치사의 목적어가 되는 경우 전치사를 빠뜨리지 않도록 주의한다.

Study Point ❦

1 to부정사의 형용사적 용법

The best way **to learn** a new language is to practice speaking it every day.

새로운 언어를 배우는 가장 좋은 방법은 매일 그 언어를 말하는 연습을 하는 것이다.

The news article has enough information **to understand** the current situation.

그 뉴스 기사는 현재 상황을 이해하기에 충분한 정보를 가지고 있다.

There is nothing **to be** afraid of in this situation. 이 상황에서 두려워할 것이 아무것도 없다.

2 to부정사의 명사적 용법

To achieve success in life requires hard work and a positive mindset. [주어 역할]
인생에서 성공을 이루기 위해서는 노력과 긍정적인 사고방식이 필요하다.

She plans **to move** to another city for a fresh start. [목적어 역할]
그녀는 새로운 시작을 위해 다른 도시로 이사할 계획이다.

My dream is **to write** a novel that inspires people all around the world. [보어 역할]
내 꿈은 전 세계 사람들에게 영감을 주는 소설을 쓰는 것이다.

3 to부정사의 부사적 용법

He is taking a cooking class **to learn** new recipes. (목적: ~하기 위해서)
그는 새로운 요리법을 배우기 위해 요리 수업을 듣고 있다.

I was surprised **to see** my old friend at the cafe. (원인: ~해서)
나는 카페에서 옛 친구를 보게 되어 놀랐다.

Q 다음 네모 안에서 어법상 올바른 것을 고르시오.

1 We like play / to play online games with our friends on the weekends.

2 David studied all night preparing / to prepare for the exam the next day.

3 I don't understand your decision to skip / skipping school for a concert.

Check-up 🍏

01 다음 문장에서 밑줄 친 부분을 바르게 고쳐 쓰시오.

(1) The players need a new coach <u>improve</u> their skills.

(2) This is a great movie <u>watching</u> with friends.

(3) Everyone makes mistakes, so there is nothing <u>to be ashamed</u>.

02 자연스러운 흐름이 되도록 빈칸에 알맞은 말이 바르게 짝지어진 것은?

> _____(A)_____ fun with friends, you should plan activities _____(B)_____ together.
> I love _____(C)_____ to the park or watch a movie.

	(A)	(B)	(C)			(A)	(B)	(C)
①	To have	enjoying	to go		②	To have	to enjoy	go
③	To have	to enjoy	to go		④	Having	to enjoy	to go
⑤	Having	to enjoy	going					

03 우리말과 같은 뜻이 되도록 괄호 안의 단어를 사용하여 문장을 완성하시오.

(1) Sarah는 내년 여름에 유럽으로 여행하기를 희망한다. (hope, travel)
→ Sarah _____ to Europe next summer.

(2) Peter는 휴가 동안 읽을 책을 찾고 있다. (read, book)
→ Peter is looking for _____ during his vacation.

(3) 그들은 콘서트에 가는 길에 교통 체증을 피하기 위해 일찍 떠났다. (avoid, traffic)
→ They left early _____ on their way to the concert.

04 다음 보기에서 적절한 동사를 골라 빈칸에 알맞은 형태로 고쳐 쓰시오. (교과서 45쪽)

> 보기   check   share   be   keep

> Welcome aboard Flight 123 to New York City. For your safety, we would like to
> (1) _____ some important information. Please make sure your seatbelt is fastened,
> as this is the best way (2) _____ you safe during the flight. Also, please
> (3) _____ the location of the nearest emergency exit. We are glad to have the
> opportunity (4) _____ a part of your travel experience.

POINT 2 가주어 it

예제	**It** is very important **to manage** your time effectively to succeed.

<u>It</u>(가주어) ... <u>to manage</u>(진주어)

성공하기 위해 너의 시간을 효과적으로 관리하는 것이 매우 중요하다.

교과서	**It** is such a rewarding experience **to help** people make positive changes in their lives.

It(가주어) ... to help(진주어)

사람들이 그들의 삶에 긍정적인 변화를 가져오도록 돕는 것은 정말 보람된 경험이다.

▶ 가주어 it은 뒤에 오는 명사구나 명사절을 대신하여 형식상의 주어로 쓰일 수 있다. to부정사(구)나 종속접속사 that이 이끄는 절이 문장에서 주어 역할을 하는 경우, 그 자리에 가주어 it을 쓰고 to부정사(구)나 that절은 문장 뒤로 보낸다.

Study Point 🍅

1 가주어 it, 진주어 to부정사

It is important **to set** goals for your future.
당신의 미래를 위해 목표를 설정하는 것이 매우 중요하다.

It was a great honor **to receive** the award for my volunteer work.
나의 자원봉사 활동으로 상을 받게 되어 큰 영광이었다.

cf. to부정사의 의미상의 주어

> **It** was difficult for her **to balance** work and school effectively.
> 그녀가 일과 학교를 효과적으로 병행하는 것은 어려웠다.

> **It** is hard for us **to make** decisions when we have too many options.
> 너무 많은 선택지가 있을 때 우리가 결정을 내리는 것은 어렵다.

2 가주어 it, 진주어 that절

It is surprising **that** she won the competition.
그녀가 대회에서 우승했다는 것이 놀랍다.

It is important **that** everyone participates in the discussion.
모든 사람이 토론에 참여하는 것이 중요하다.

It is necessary **that** you complete your assignments on time.
당신이 과제를 제때에 완료하는 것이 필요하다.

Q 다음 네모 안에서 어법상 올바른 것을 고르시오.

1 It is fun | go / to go | hiking and explore nature on a sunny day.

2 | It / That | is inspiring to hear stories of people overcoming great challenges.

3 It is a fact | to / that | climate change is affecting weather patterns worldwide.

4 It is crucial | for you / of you | to review your notes before the exam.

Check-up ❦

01 다음 괄호 안에서 알맞은 것을 고르시오.

(1) It is a fact (that / if) the earth revolves around the sun.

(2) It is very important (maintain / to maintain) a balanced diet for good health.

(3) (It / That) is enjoyable to bake cookies and decorate them with chocolate chips.

02 다음 문장을 가주어 it을 사용하여 다시 쓰시오.

(1) To go camping with friends during the summer is fun.

→ _____

(2) That regular exercise improves both physical and mental health is a fact.

→ _____

03 다음 괄호 안의 단어를 알맞게 배열하여 문장을 완성하시오. (교과서 45쪽)

> Dear Nicky,
> We want to thank you for joining us at the charity event. (1) (was / it / to / nice / have) your support. Your presence made a real difference, and (2) (it / truly / wonderful / to / was / see) everyone come together for such a great purpose. (3) (hard / was / to / it / for us / thank) you personally at the event, but we are grateful for your kindness and support.
>
> Yours sincerely,
> The Hope Charity

(1) _____

(2) _____

(3) _____

04 다음 중 어법상 틀린 문장끼리 짝지어진 것은?

> ⓐ It is exciting to travel to new places and meet new people.
> ⓑ She needs a friend helping her with her homework.
> ⓒ It is important students to study regularly for good grades.
> ⓓ It is fun attend concerts and enjoy live music.
> ⓔ I want to learn how to play the piano during the vacation.

① ⓐ, ⓑ, ⓒ   ② ⓐ, ⓒ, ⓓ   ③ ⓑ, ⓒ, ⓓ   ④ ⓑ, ⓓ, ⓔ   ⑤ ⓒ, ⓓ, ⓔ

교과서 본문 분석

Talk It Out, Help Is Here
말해 보세요, 도움이 여기 있습니다

01 **Host** On today's show, we are going to learn about special park benches in Zimbabwe [called
be going to-v: ~할 예정이다 과거분사구
Friendship Benches].

진행자: 오늘 방송에서는 우정 벤치라고 불리는 짐바브웨의 특별한 공원 벤치에 대해 알아보겠습니다.

02 We have two special guests.

두 분의 특별한 손님들이 있습니다.

03 First, please welcome the founder [of the Friendship Bench program], Dr. Dixon Chibanda.
동격
전치사구

먼저 우정 벤치 프로그램의 창시자인 Dixon Chibanda 박사님을 환영해 주세요.

04 간접의문문(tell의 직접목적어): 「의문사(주어)+동사」의 어순
Can you tell us [what inspired you to come up with the program]?
inspire+목적어+to-v: ~를 자극하여 …할 마음을 품게 하다

무엇이 박사님으로 하여금 그 프로그램을 떠올리도록 영감을 주었는지 저희에게 말씀해 주시겠어요?

05 **Dr. Chibanda** Sure. The idea came from an experience [I had as a psychiatrist].
(which[that]) ~로서(전치사)
목적격 관계대명사절

Chibanda 박사: 네. 그 아이디어는 제가 정신과 의사로서 겪었던 경험에서 나왔습니다.

06 One of my patients had become severely depressed.
과거완료

제 환자 중 한 명이 심하게 우울증을 앓게 되었습니다.

07 However, she couldn't get help because she was unable to afford the bus ride to the hospital.
be unable to-v: ~할 수 없다

하지만 그녀는 병원까지 가는 버스비를 감당할 여유가 없어 도움을 받을 수 없었습니다.

08 접속사(~이기 때문에)
This shocked me, as I had never considered such a problem before.
앞 문장 내용 과거완료(경험) 「such(+a)(+형용사)+명사」 어순

이것은 저에게 충격을 주었는데, 제가 전에는 한 번도 그런 문제를 생각해 본 적이 없었기 때문입니다.

09 (to)
In fact, it is difficult for many people in Zimbabwe [to pay for transportation and receive medical
가주어 의미상 주어(for+목적격) 진주어 병렬 연결
treatment].

실제로, 짐바브웨에서는 많은 사람들이 교통비를 내고 의학적 치료를 받는 것이 어렵습니다.

10 Furthermore, there has been a lack of psychiatrists in the country for many years.
　　　　　　　　　　현재완료(계속)　　　　　　　　　　　　　　　　　　　　　　~동안(전치사)

게다가 그 나라에서는 수년 동안 정신과 의사가 부족했습니다.

11 When the Friendship Bench program started in 2006, there were only eleven psychiatrists [serving
　　　현재분사구

Zimbabwe's population of over twelve million people].

2006년에 우정 벤치 프로그램이 시작되었을 때, 1,200만 명이 넘는 짐바브웨의 인구를 위해 일하는 정신과 의사는 11명뿐이었습니다.

12 I needed to find a way [to bring psychiatry into the community].
　　명사적 용법(needed의 목적어)　　　　형용사적 용법

저는 정신의학을 지역 사회에 도입할 방법을 찾아야 했습니다.

13 **Host** Oh, so that was the beginning of it.
　　　　　　　　　　　　　　= the Friendship Bench program

진행자: 아, 그러니까 그게 그것의 시작이었군요.

14 Could you explain to us [how the Friendship Bench program works]?
　　　　　　　　간접의문문(explain의 직접목적어): 「의문사+주어+동사」의 어순

우정 벤치 프로그램이 어떻게 운영되는지 저희에게 설명해 주시겠어요?

15 **Dr. Chibanda** Certainly. The program was created as a way [to provide accessible mental health
　　　　　　　　　　　　　　　　　수동태(be+p.p.)　　　　　　형용사적 용법
services].

Chibanda 박사: 물론이죠. 그 프로그램은 접근하기 쉬운 정신 건강 서비스를 제공할 하나의 방법으로 만들어졌습니다.

16 It offers talk therapy sessions to people [dealing with issues such as depression or anxiety].
　　　　　　　　　　　　　　　　　　　　현재분사구　　　　　~와 같은

그것은 우울증이나 불안과 같은 문제를 겪고 있는 사람들에게 대화 치료 세션을 제공합니다.

17 The sessions are free and are provided by respected elderly women [from the community].
　　　　S　　VI　　　　V2(수동태)　　　　　　　　　　　전치사구

그 세션은 무료이며 지역 사회의 존경받는 노인 여성들에 의해 제공됩니다.

18 These women, [called "grandmothers,"] volunteer to sit with patients at the benches, listen to
　　　　S　　　　　　　　　　　　　VI　　명사적 용법(volunteer의 목적어)　　　　　V2
their stories, and provide them with emotional support.
　　　　V3 (provide A with B: A에게 B를 제공하다)

'할머니들'이라고 불리는 이 여성들은 환자들과 함께 벤치에 앉는 것을 자원하고, 그들의 이야기를 듣고, 그들에게 정서적 지원을 제공합니다.

19 **Host** What a wonderful idea! How did these amazing grandmothers become a part of your
감탄문: 「What+a(n)+형용사+명사+(주어)+(동사)!」
program?

진행자: 정말 멋진 아이디어군요! 이 놀라운 할머니들이 어떻게 당신의 프로그램의 일부가 되었나요?

20 **Dr. Chibanda** Grandmothers were chosen for our program because they are deeply connected to
수동태   be connected to: ~와 연결[연관]되다
the community.

Chibanda 박사: 할머니들은 지역 사회와 깊이 연결되어 있기 때문에 저희 프로그램에 선정되었습니다.

21 Moreover, they have all the qualities of a counselor, such as excellent listening skills, empathy,
~와 같은
and the ability [to engage in meaningful discussions].
형용사적 용법

또한 그들은 뛰어난 경청 기술, 공감, 그리고 의미 있는 토론에 참여할 수 있는 능력과 같은, 상담가로서의 모든 자질을 갖추고 있습니다.

22 They are also very reliable, [which is important for our efforts {to support mental health}].
계속적 용법의 주격 관계대명사절(선행사는 앞 절 내용)   형용사적 용법

그들은 또한 매우 믿음직한데, 이는 정신 건강을 지원하려는 우리의 노력에 중요합니다.

23 At the beginning, we started with only fourteen volunteer grandmothers.

처음에, 저희는 겨우 14명의 자원봉사자 할머니들과 함께 시작했습니다.

24 But today, there are thousands of grandmothers [who have been trained {to provide Friendship
현재완료 수동태: have been p.p.   부사적 용법(목적)
Bench therapy}] in Zimbabwe.

하지만 오늘날 짐바브웨에는 우정 벤치 치료를 제공하도록 교육받은 수천 명의 할머니가 있습니다.

25 **Host** That's interesting! What happens after patients complete their sessions with the
접속사(~한 후에)
grandmothers?

진행자: 흥미롭네요! 환자들이 할머니들과의 세션을 마친 후에는 무슨 일이 일어나나요?

26 **Dr. Chibanda** When the sessions with the grandmothers are over, patients are encouraged to join
be over: 끝나다   be encouraged to-v: ~하도록 장려되다
a community support group [made up of former patients of the program].
과거분사구(~로 구성된)

Chibanda 박사: 할머니들과의 세션이 끝나면, 환자들은 프로그램의 이전 환자들로 구성된 커뮤니티 지원 그룹에 참여하도록 권장됩니다.

27 The members of these groups can easily relate to and support one another.
                                              (can)
S   V1   V2   서로

이 그룹의 구성원들은 서로 쉽게 공감하고 지지할 수 있습니다.

28 This is because most of them come from the same community and have experienced similar
S'1　　　V'1　　　　　　　　　　　　　　　　　　　　　V'2 현재완료(경험)
struggles.

이것은 그들 대부분이 같은 지역 사회 출신이고 비슷한 어려움을 겪은 적이 있기 때문입니다.

29 **Host** That sounds like a great way [to continue the support and build a sense of community].
　　　　　　　　　　　　　　　　　　　　　　병렬 연결
　　　　　　　　　　↑_____| 형용사적 용법　　　　(to)

진행자: 지원을 지속하고 공동체 의식을 키울 수 있는 좋은 방법인 것 같네요.

30 And the program has been incredibly successful, right?
　　　　　　　　　현재완료(계속)

그리고 그 프로그램은 매우 성공적이었습니다, 그렇죠?

31 **Dr. Chibanda** That's correct. In 2022, we provided face-to-face counseling to about 90,000
patients in Zimbabwe.　　　　= we provided about 90,000 patients in Zimbabwe with face-to-face counseling

Chibanda 박사: 맞습니다. 2022년에, 저희는 짐바브웨에서 약 9만 명의 환자들에게 대면 상담을 제공했습니다.

32 Now, Friendship Benches are available in more than twenty different regions around the country.
　　　　　　　　　　　　　　　　　　　　　　~ 이상

현재, 우정 벤치는 전국의 20곳이 넘는 지역에서 이용 가능합니다.

33 Our vision is for everyone [to have a Friendship Bench within walking distance], and we are working
　　　　　　　　의미상 주어(for+목적격)　명사적 용법(주격 보어)
hard [to make it happen].
　　　부사적 용법(목적) make+목적어+동사원형: ~가 …하게 만들다

저희의 비전은 모두가 걸어서 갈 수 있는 거리에 우정 벤치를 갖는 것이고, 저희는 그것을 실현하기 위해 열심히 일하고 있습니다.

34 We've also started expanding the program, and we now offer online counseling through an app.
　　└ 현재완료 ┘　　동명사(started의 목적어)

저희는 또한 그 프로그램을 확장하기 시작했고, 이제는 앱을 통해 온라인 상담을 제공합니다.

35 　　　　　help+목적어+(to-)v: ~가 …하도록 돕다
This has helped us reach even more people.
　　　현재완료　　　　　　└___↑ 비교급 수식 부사(훨씬)

이것은 저희가 훨씬 더 많은 사람들에게 다가갈 수 있게 도와주었죠.

36 **Host** That's really amazing! Thank you for your time, Dr. Chibanda.

진행자: 정말 놀랍군요! 시간 내 주셔서 감사합니다, Chibanda 박사님.

37 Now let's hear from one of the grandmothers [who volunteers for the program].
　　　　　　　　　　　　　　　　　↑_____| 주격 관계대명사절

이제 그 프로그램에서 자원봉사를 하시는 할머니들 중 한 분의 이야기를 들어보겠습니다.

38 Can you introduce yourself and tell us [how you got involved with the Friendship Bench
program]?

간접의문문(+tell의 직접목적어): 「의문사+주어+동사」의 어순

자기소개를 해 주시고 저희에게 어떻게 우정 벤치 프로그램에 참여하게 되셨는지 말씀해 주시겠어요?

39 **Grandma Moyo** Hello, my name is Judith Moyo, but people call me Grandma Moyo.

call+목적어+목적격보어: ~을 …라고 부르다

Moyo 할머니: 안녕하세요, 제 이름은 Judith Moyo이지만, 사람들은 저를 Moyo 할머니라고 부릅니다.

40 I'm 76 years old, and I have been volunteering for the Friendship Bench program for about eight
years.

현재완료진행: have been v-ing   대략, 약~

저는 76세이고, 우정 벤치 프로그램에서 약 8년 동안 자원봉사를 해왔습니다.

41 I joined the program because many people in my community struggle with mental health problems,
and I wanted to do something about it.

S1 V1   S'1   V'1 ~로 고심하다
S2 V2   명사적 용법(wanted의 목적어)

저는 지역 사회에서 많은 사람들이 정신 건강 문제로 고심하고 있고, 제가 그것에 대해 무언가를 하고 싶었기 때문에 그 프로그램에 합류했습니다.

42 I knew [that I could help heal their wounded hearts by supporting them].

help+(to-)v: ~하는 것을 돕다
명사절(knew의 목적어)   by v-ing: ~함으로써

저는 그들을 지원함으로써 그들의 상처받은 마음을 치유하는 데 도움을 줄 수 있다는 것을 알았죠.

43 **Host** That's very kind of you. Can you tell us about your experience as a grandmother for the
Friendship Bench program?

전치사(~로서)

진행자: 정말 다정하시네요. 우정 벤치 프로그램을 위한 할머니로서 당신의 경험에 관해 저희에게 말씀해 주실 수 있을까요?

44 **Grandma Moyo** It's been wonderful. Seeking help for mental health problems is nothing [to be
ashamed of].

= has been
현재완료(계속)   S(동명사구)   V   형용사적 용법

Moyo 할머니: 정말 좋았습니다. 정신 건강 문제에 대한 도움을 구하는 것은 부끄러워할 일이 아닙니다.

45 I've seen [how it can make a difference in people's lives].

변화를 가져오다, 영향을 주다
간접의문문(have seen의 목적어): 「의문사+주어+동사」의 어순

저는 그것이 사람들의 삶에 어떻게 변화를 가져올 수 있는지 보았습니다.

46 One patient of mine, a nineteen-year old girl, was going through a difficult time after her mom passed away.

접속사(~한 후에)
S 동격 V S'
V'

제 환자 중 한 명인 열아홉 살의 소녀는 그녀의 엄마가 돌아가신 후 힘든 시간을 보내고 있었습니다.

47 I counseled her and helped her begin her recovery journey.

help+목적어+(to-)v: ~가 …하도록 돕다

저는 그녀를 상담했고 그녀가 회복의 여정을 시작할 수 있도록 도왔습니다.

48 Now her life is back on track, and she has even started her own business!

다시 정상 궤도에 들어선

이제 그녀의 삶은 다시 정상 궤도에 올랐고, 그녀는 심지어 자신의 사업도 시작했습니다!

49 Cases like this make me so proud to be part of the program.

make+목적어+목적격보어(형용사): ~가 …하게 만들다
S V

이와 같은 사례들은 제가 그 프로그램의 일부가 된 것을 매우 자랑스러워하게 합니다.

50 It is such a rewarding experience [to help people make positive changes in their lives].

가주어 진주어
Such+a(n)+형용사+명사: 그렇게 ~한 … help+목적어+(to-)v: ~가 …하도록 돕다

사람들이 그들의 삶에 긍정적인 변화를 가져오도록 돕는 것은 정말 보람된 경험입니다.

51 **Host** Thanks for sharing your experiences with us today, Grandma Moyo.

전치사+동명사

진행자: 오늘 저희에게 당신의 경험을 공유해 주셔서 감사합니다. Moyo 할머니.

52 It's truly inspiring [to see the influence {that the Friendship Bench program has had}].

가주어 가주어 목적격 관계대명사절 현재완료

우정 벤치 프로그램이 미친 영향력을 보는 것은 정말 고무적입니다.

53 And it's all thanks to the hard work of people like you and Dr. Chibanda.

~덕분에 전치사(~와 같은)

그리고 그것은 모두 당신과 Chibanda 박사님 같은 분들의 노고 덕분입니다.

♣ 다음 빈칸에 알맞은 말을 쓰시오.

01 First, please welcome _____ the Friendship Bench program, Dr. Dixon Chibanda.
먼저 우정 벤치 프로그램의 창시자인 Dixon Chibanda 박사님을 환영해 주세요.

02 Can you tell us what _____ the program?
무엇이 박사님으로 하여금 그 프로그램을 떠올리도록 영감을 주었는지 저희에게 말씀해 주시겠어요?

03 The idea _____ I had as a psychiatrist.
그 아이디어는 제가 정신과 의사로서 겪었던 경험에서 나왔습니다.

04 One of my patients _____ severely _____ .
제 환자 중 한 명이 심하게 우울증을 앓게 되었습니다.

05 However, she couldn't get help because she _____ the bus ride to the hospital.
하지만 그녀는 병원까지 가는 버스비를 감당할 여유가 없어 도움을 받을 수 없었습니다.

06 This shocked me, as I had never _____ before.
이것은 저에게 충격을 주었는데, 제가 전에는 한 번도 그런 문제를 생각해 본 적이 없었기 때문입니다.

07 In fact, it is difficult for many people in Zimbabwe _____ and receive medical treatment.
실제로, 짐바브웨에서는 많은 사람들이 교통비를 내고 의학적 치료를 받는 것이 어렵습니다.

08 When the Friendship Bench program started in 2006, there were only _____ Zimbabwe's population of over twelve million people.
2006년에 우정 벤치 프로그램이 시작되었을 때, 1,200만 명이 넘는 짐바브웨의 인구를 위해 일하는 정신과 의사는 11명뿐이었습니다.

09 I needed to find a way to _____ psychiatry _____ .
저는 정신의학을 지역 사회에 도입할 방법을 찾아야 했습니다.

10 The program was created _____ accessible mental health services.
그 프로그램은 접근하기 쉬운 정신 건강 서비스를 제공할 하나의 방법으로 만들어졌습니다.

11 It offers talk therapy sessions to _____ such as depression or anxiety.
그것은 우울증이나 불안과 같은 문제를 겪고 있는 사람들에게 대화 치료 세션을 제공합니다.

12 The sessions are free and are provided by _____ from the community.
그 세션은 무료이며 지역 사회의 존경받는 노인여성들에 의해 제공됩니다.

13 These women, called "grandmothers," volunteer to sit with patients at the benches, listen to their stories, and _____ .
'할머니들'이라고 불리는 이 여성들은 환자들과 함께 벤치에 앉는 것을 자원하고, 그들의 이야기를 듣고, 그들에게 정서적 지원을 제공합니다.

14 Grandmothers were chosen for our program because they _____ the community.

할머니들은 지역 사회와 깊이 연결되어 있기 때문에 저희 프로그램에 선정되었습니다.

15 Moreover, they have all the qualities of a counselor, such as excellent listening skills, empathy, and _____ meaningful discussions.

또한 그들은 뛰어난 경청 기술, 공감, 그리고 의미 있는 토론에 참여할 수 있는 능력과 같은, 상담가로서의 모든 자질을 갖추고 있습니다.

16 They are also very reliable, which is important for our efforts _____.

그들은 또한 매우 믿음직한데, 이는 정신 건강을 지원하려는 우리의 노력에 중요합니다.

17 But today, there are thousands of grandmothers _____ to provide Friendship Bench therapy in Zimbabwe.

하지만 오늘날 짐바브웨에는 우정 벤치 치료를 제공하도록 교육받은 수천 명의 할머니가 있습니다.

18 When the sessions with the grandmothers are over, patients _____ a community support group _____ former patients of the program.

할머니들과의 세션이 끝나면, 환자들은 프로그램의 이전 환자들로 구성된 커뮤니티 지원 그룹에 참여하도록 권장됩니다.

19 The members of these groups _____ and support one another.

이 그룹의 구성원들은 서로 쉽게 공감하고 지지할 수 있습니다.

20 That sounds like a great way to continue the support and _____.

지원을 지속하고 공동체 의식을 키울 수 있는 좋은 방법인 것 같네요.

21 And the program has been _____, right?

그리고 그 프로그램은 매우 성공적이었습니다, 그렇죠?

22 In 2022, we provided _____ to about 90,000 patients in Zimbabwe.

2022년에, 저희는 짐바브웨에서 약 9만 명의 환자들에게 대면 상담을 제공했습니다.

23 Now, Friendship Benches are _____ twenty different regions around the country.

현재, 우정 벤치는 전국의 20곳이 넘는 지역에서 이용 가능합니다.

24 Our vision is for everyone to have a Friendship Bench _____, and we are working hard to make it happen.

저희의 비전은 모두가 걸어서 갈 수 있는 거리에 우정 벤치를 갖는 것이고, 저희는 그것을 실현하기 위해 열심히 일하고 있습니다.

25 We've also _____ the program, and we now offer online counseling through an app.

저희는 또한 그 프로그램을 확장하기 시작했고, 이제는 앱을 통해 온라인 상담을 제공합니다.

26 This has helped us _____.

이것은 저희가 훨씬 더 많은 사람들에게 다가갈 수 있게 도와주었죠.

27 Can you introduce yourself and tell us _____ the Friendship Bench program?

자기소개를 해 주시고 저희에게 어떻게 우정 벤치 프로그램에 참여하게 되셨는지 말씀해 주시겠요?

28   I'm 76 years old, and I _____ the Friendship Bench program for about eight years.

저는 76세이고, 우정 벤치 프로그램에서 약 8년 동안 자원봉사를 해왔습니다.

29   I joined the program because many people in my community _____ mental

health problems, and I wanted to do something about it.

저는 지역 사회에서 많은 사람들이 정신 건강 문제로 고심하고 있고, 제가 그것에 대해 무언가를 하고 싶었기 때문에 그 프로그램에 합류했습니다.

30   I knew that I could help _____ by supporting them.

저는 그들을 지원함으로써 그들의 상처받은 마음을 치유하는 데 도움을 줄 수 있다는 것을 알았죠.

31   That's very kind of you. Can you tell us _____ as a grandmother for the

Friendship Bench program?

정말 다정하시네요. 우정 벤치 프로그램을 위한 할머니로서 당신의 경험에 관해 저희에게 말씀해 주실 수 있을까요?

32   It's been wonderful. Seeking help for mental health problems is _____.

정말 좋았습니다. 정신 건강 문제에 대한 도움을 구하는 것은 부끄러워할 일이 아닙니다.

33   I've seen how it can _____ in people's lives.

저는 그것이 사람들의 삶에 어떻게 변화를 가져올 수 있는지 보았습니다.

34   One patient of mine, a nineteen-year old girl, was _____ a difficult time after her

mom passed away.

제 환자 중 한 명인 열아홉 살의 소녀는 그녀의 엄마가 돌아가신 후 힘든 시간을 보내고 있었습니다.

35   I counseled her and helped her _____.

저는 그녀를 상담했고 그녀가 회복의 여정을 시작할 수 있도록 도왔습니다.

36   Now her life _____, and she has even started her own business!

이제 그녀의 삶은 다시 정상 궤도에 올랐고, 그녀는 심지어 자신의 사업도 시작했습니다!

37   Cases like this _____ to be part of the program.

이와 같은 사례들은 제가 그 프로그램의 일부가 된 것을 매우 자랑스러워하게 합니다.

38   It is _____ to help people make positive changes in their lives.

사람들이 그들의 삶에 긍정적인 변화를 가져오도록 돕는 것은 정말 보람된 경험입니다.

39   Thanks for _____ us today, Grandma Moyo.

오늘 저희에게 당신의 경험을 공유해 주셔서 감사합니다, Moyo 할머니.

40   _____ the influence that the Friendship Bench program has had.

우정 벤치 프로그램이 미친 영향력을 보는 것은 정말 고무적입니다.

41   And it's all _____ the hard work of people like you and Dr. Chibanda.

그리고 그것은 모두 당신과 Chibanda 박사님 같은 분들의 노고 덕분입니다.

교과서 본문 익히기 ❷ 옳은 어법·어휘 고르기

♣ 다음 네모 안에서 옳은 것을 고르시오.

01 On today's show, we are going to learn about special park benches in Zimbabwe ☐called / calling☐ Friendship Benches.

02 First, please welcome the ☐finder / founder☐ of the Friendship Bench program, Dr. Dixon Chibanda.

03 Can you tell us what inspired you ☐come / to come☐ up with the program?

04 The idea came from an experience I had as a ☐dentist / psychiatrist☐.

05 One of my patients had become severely ☐depressing / depressed☐.

06 However, she couldn't get help because she was unable to ☐afford / affording☐ the bus ride to the hospital.

07 This shocked me, as I had never considered ☐so / such☐ a problem before.

08 In fact, it is difficult for many people in Zimbabwe ☐pay / to pay☐ for transportation and receive medical treatment.

09 Furthermore, there has been a lack of psychiatrists in the country ☐during / for☐ many years.

10 When the Friendship Bench program started in 2006, there were only eleven psychiatrists ☐serving / served☐ Zimbabwe's population of over twelve million people.

11 I needed ☐finding / to find☐ a way to bring psychiatry into the community.

12 Oh, so that was the ☐end / beginning☐ of it. Could you explain ☐for / to☐ us how the Friendship Bench program works?

13 The program ☐created / was created☐ as a way to provide accessible mental health services.

14 It offers talk therapy sessions to people ☐dealing / dealt☐ with issues such as depression or anxiety.

15 The sessions are free and are provided by respected ☐young / elderly☐ women from the community.

16 These women, called "grandmothers," volunteer to sit with patients at the benches, listen to their stories, and ☐provide / providing☐ them with emotional support.

17　How / What a wonderful idea! How did these amazing grandmothers become a part of your program?

18　Grandmothers chose / were chosen for our program because they are deeply connected to the community.

19　Moreover, they have all the qualities of a counselor, such as excellent listening skills, empathy, and the ability engage / to engage in meaningful discussions.

20　They are also very reliable, which / that is important for our efforts to support mental health.

21　At the beginning, we started from / with only fourteen volunteer grandmothers.

22　But today, there are thousands of grandmothers who have been trained / have trained to provide Friendship Bench therapy in Zimbabwe.

23　That's interesting! What happens before / after patients complete their sessions with the grandmothers?

24　When the sessions with the grandmothers are over, patients are encouraged join / to join a community support group made up of former patients of the program.

25　The members of these groups can easily relate to and support one other / another.

26　This is because most of them come from the same community and have experienced similar / different struggles.

27　That sounds like a great way to continue the support and build / break a sense of community.

28　In 2022, we provided face-to-face counseling to / with about 90,000 patients in Zimbabwe.

29　Now, Friendship Benches are available in more than / less than twenty different regions around the country.

30　Our vision is for everyone to have a Friendship Bench within walking distance, and we are working hard to make it to happen / happen.

31　We've also started expanding / expanded the program, and we now offer online counseling through an app.

32　This has helped us reach very / even more people.

33 Now let's hear from one of the ⟨grandmother / grandmothers⟩ who volunteers for the program.

34 Can you introduce yourself and tell us ⟨how you got / how did you get⟩ involved with the Friendship Bench program?

35 I'm 76 years old, and I have been ⟨volunteering / volunteered⟩ for the Friendship Bench program for about eight years.

36 I joined the program because many people in my community struggle with mental health problems, and I wanted to do ⟨anything / something⟩ about it.

37 I knew that I could help ⟨heal / healing⟩ their wounded hearts by supporting them.

38 Can you tell us about your experience ⟨like / as⟩ a grandmother for the Friendship Bench program?

39 ⟨Seek / Seeking⟩ help for mental health problems is nothing to be ashamed of.

40 I've seen how it can ⟨take / make⟩ a difference in people's lives.

41 One patient of ⟨mine / my⟩, a nineteen-year old girl, was going through a difficult time after her mom passed away.

42 I counseled her and helped her begin her ⟨recover / recovery⟩ journey.

43 Cases like this ⟨make / makes⟩ me so proud to be part of the program.

44 It is such a rewarding experience to help people make ⟨positive / negative⟩ changes in their lives.

45 Thanks for ⟨share / sharing⟩ your experiences with us today, Grandma Moyo.

46 It's ⟨true / truly⟩ inspiring to see the influence that the Friendship Bench program has had.

♣ 다음 밑줄 친 부분을 바르게 고쳐 쓰시오.

01   On today's show, we are going to learn about special park benches in Zimbabwe <u>calling</u> Friendship Benches.

02   Can you tell us what inspired you <u>coming</u> up with the program?

03   The idea came from an experience I <u>have</u> as a psychiatrist.

04   One of my patients had <u>became</u> severely depressed.

05   This shocked me, as I had <u>ever</u> considered such a problem before.

06   In fact, it is difficult <u>of</u> many people in Zimbabwe to pay for transportation and receive medical treatment.

07   Furthermore, there has been a lack of psychiatrists in the country <u>during</u> many years.

08   When the Friendship Bench program started in 2006, there were only eleven psychiatrists <u>served</u> Zimbabwe's population of over twelve million people.

09   I needed to find a way <u>bring</u> psychiatry into the community.

10   Could you explain to us how the Friendship Bench program <u>work</u>?

11   The program was <u>creating</u> as a way to provide accessible mental health services.

12   It offers talk therapy sessions <u>for</u> people dealing with issues such as depression or anxiety.

13   The sessions are free and are <u>providing</u> by respected elderly women from the community.

14   These women, <u>calling</u> "grandmothers," volunteer to sit with patients at the benches, listen to their stories, and provide them with emotional support.

15   <u>How</u> a wonderful idea! How did these amazing grandmothers become a part of your program?

16   Grandmothers were chosen for our program <u>so</u> they are deeply connected to the community.

17   Moreover, they have all the qualities of a counselor, such as excellent listening skills, empathy, and the <u>able</u> to engage in meaningful discussions.

18   They are also very reliable, <u>that</u> is important for our efforts to support mental health.

19   When the sessions with the grandmothers are over, patients are encouraged to join a community support group <u>make</u> up of former patients of the program.

20 The members of these groups can easily relate to and support <u>one other</u>.

21 This is <u>so</u> most of them come from the same community and have experienced similar struggles.

22 In 2022, we provided face-to-face counseling <u>with</u> about 90,000 patients in Zimbabwe.

23 Now, Friendship Benches are available in <u>most</u> than twenty different regions around the country.

24 Our vision is for everyone to have a Friendship Bench within <u>walk</u> distance, and we are working hard to make it happen.

25 We've also started <u>expand</u> the program, and we now offer online counseling through an app.

26 This has helped us reach <u>very</u> more people.

27 That's really <u>amazed</u>! Thank you for your time, Dr. Chibanda.

28 Now let's hear from one of the grandmothers <u>which</u> volunteers for the program.

29 Can you introduce <u>you</u> and tell us how you got involved with the Friendship Bench program?

30 I'm 76 years old, and I have been <u>volunteered</u> for the Friendship Bench program for about eight years.

31 I joined the program because many people in my community struggle with mental health problems, and I wanted <u>doing</u> something about it.

32 I knew that I could help heal their <u>wounding</u> hearts by supporting them.

33 <u>Seek</u> help for mental health problems is nothing to be ashamed of.

34 I've seen how <u>can it</u> make a difference in people's lives.

35 I counseled her and helped her <u>beginning</u> her recovery journey.

36 Cases like this <u>makes</u> me so proud to be part of the program.

37 It is <u>so</u> a rewarding experience to help people make positive changes in their lives.

38 Thanks for <u>share</u> your experiences with us today, Grandma Moyo.

39 It's truly inspiring <u>see</u> the influence that the Friendship Bench program has had.

40 And it's all thanks <u>for</u> the hard work of people like you and Dr. Chibanda.

TOPIC 5 A. Preview

What ❶ made me feel that way

I ❷ had to ❸ give a presentation in English class today. I had practiced hard, so I ❹ felt confident at first. However, when I stood ❺ in front of the class, my mind went blank. I forgot ❻ what to say and ruined my presentation. I felt so disappointed in myself.

How I ❼ dealt with my feelings

After I got home, I ❽ spent some time working on my model airplane. As I ❾ put the parts together, the frustration of the day ❿ faded away, and I ⓫ was able to forget the disappointment I had felt in myself.

What I learned from the experience

Anyone can ⓬ mess up. Also, I shouldn't ⓭ worry too much about something that already happened. ⓮ I'm sure I can do better next time.

❶ make(사역동사)+목적어+동사원형 ❷ had to+동사원형: ~해야 했다(have to의 과거형) ❸ give a presentation: 프레젠테이션하다 ❹ feel+형용사: ~하게 느끼다 ❺ in front of: ~ 앞에 ❻ 의문사+to부정사: 무슨 말을 해야 할지 ❼ deal with: ~을 다루다 ❽ spend+시간+v-ing on: ~하는 데 시간을 쓰다 ❾ put ~ together: 조립하다 ❿ fade away: 차츰 사라지다 ⓫ be able to: ~할 수 있다(= can) ⓬ mess up: ~을 엉망으로 만들다[망치다] ⓭ worry about: ~에 대해 걱정하다 ⓮ I'm sure ~: ~을 확신하다

Q1 The speaker felt proud of their performance after the presentation. (T / F)

Wrap Up B. Read and Discuss

Surprisingly, your posture can ❶ influence your mind and your emotions. ❷ In fact, the relationship ❸ between mind and body is ❹ so powerful that your body position ❺ plays a large role in ❻ how you think, feel, and act. For example, ❼ sitting and standing up straight will ❽ increase your confidence and decrease your stress. ❾ Try walking ❿ with your chest out and your chin raised. Don't you feel more confident in this position? Also, research has shown ⓫ that good posture can be highly beneficial for students. ⓬ If students have good posture, ⓭ it is easier for them to concentrate and stay in a good mood.

❶ influence: 영향을 미치다 ❷ In fact: 사실상, 실제로 ❸ between A and B: A와 B 사이에 ❹ so ~ that ...: 너무 ~해서 …하다 ❺ play a ~ role: ~한 역할을 하다 ❻ 의문사+주어+동사: 간접의문문 ❼ 주어 역할을 하는 동명사 ❽ increase 증가시키다 (↔ decrease 감소시키다) ❾ try+동명사: 한번 ~해보다 ❿ with+명사+과거분사: 명사를 ~한 채로 ⓫ that: 명사절을 이끄는 접속사(목적어 역할) ⓬ If: 조건을 나타내는 접속사 ⓭ it is ~ for+목적격+to부정사: 가주어·진주어 구문

Q2 Good posture has no impact on a person's emotions or ability to concentrate. (T / F)

🐚 다음 빈칸에 알맞은 말을 쓰시오.

01 I had to _____ in English class today. 나는 오늘 영어 수업 중에 발표를 해야 했다.

02 I had practiced hard, so I _____ at first.
나는 열심히 연습했었으므로, 처음에는 자신감을 느꼈다.

03 However, when I stood in front of the class, my mind _____.
하지만, 내가 학생들 앞에 서자, 머릿속이 하얘졌다.

04 I forgot what to say and _____. 나는 무엇을 말할지 잊어버리고 나의 발표를 망쳤다.

05 I _____ in myself. 나는 스스로에게 매우 실망했다.

06 After I got home, I _____ on my model airplane.
집에 온 후에, 나는 내 모형 비행기를 작업하는 데 약간의 시간을 보냈다.

07 As I put the parts together, the frustration of the day _____, and I was able to forget the disappointment I had felt in myself.
내가 부품들을 조립하는 동안, 그날의 좌절감이 사라졌고, 나 자신에게 느낀 실망감을 잊을 수 있었다.

08 Anyone can _____. 누구나 망칠 수 있다.

09 Also, I _____ too much _____ something that already happened.
또한, 나는 이미 일어난 일에 관해 너무 많이 걱정하지 말아야 한다.

10 I'm sure I _____ next time. 나는 내가 다음번에 더 잘할 수 있다고 확신한다.

11 Surprisingly, _____ your mind and your emotions.
놀랍게도, 당신의 자세가 당신의 마음과 감정에 영향을 줄 수 있다.

12 In fact, the relationship between mind and body is so powerful that your body position _____ in how you think, feel, and act.
사실, 마음과 신체 사이의 관계는 너무 강력해서 당신의 신체 자세가 당신이 생각하고, 느끼고, 행동하는 방식에 큰 역할을 한다.

13 For example, sitting and standing up straight will increase your confidence and _____.
예를 들어, 똑바로 앉고 서는 것은 당신의 자신감을 높이고 당신의 스트레스를 낮출 것이다.

14 Try _____ your chest out and your chin _____.
당신의 가슴을 내밀고 당신의 턱을 든 채로 한번 걸어 보라.

15 _____ more confident in this position? 이 자세에서 더 자신감을 느끼지 않는가?

16 Also, research has shown that good posture can be _____ for students.
또한, 연구는 좋은 자세가 학생들에게 매우 이로울 수 있다는 것을 보여 주었다.

17 If students have good posture, it is _____ and stay in a good mood.
만약 학생들이 좋은 자세를 지니고 있다면, 그들이 집중하고 좋은 기분으로 있기가 더 쉽다.

01 (A), (B), (C)의 각 네모 안에서 문맥에 맞는 낱말로 가장 적절한 것은?

Dr. Chibanda The idea came from an experience I had as a psychiatrist. One of my patients had become severely depressed. However, she couldn't get help because she was (A) able / unable to afford the bus ride to the hospital. This shocked me, as I had never considered such a problem before. In fact, it is difficult for many people in Zimbabwe to pay for transportation and receive medical treatment. Furthermore, there has been a (B) lack / plenty of psychiatrists in the country for many years. When the Friendship Bench program started in 2006, there were only eleven psychiatrists serving Zimbabwe's (C) civilization / population of over twelve million people. I needed to find a way to bring psychiatry into the community.

	(A)		(B)		(C)
①	able	···	lack	···	civilization
②	able	···	plenty	···	population
③	unable	···	lack	···	population
④	unable	···	lack	···	civilization
⑤	unable	···	plenty	···	population

02 다음 글의 밑줄 친 부분 중, 문맥상 낱말의 쓰임이 적절하지 않은 것은?

Dr. Chibanda The program was ① created as a way to provide accessible mental health services. It offers talk ② therapy sessions to people dealing with issues such as depression or anxiety. The sessions are free and are provided by respected ③ young women from the community. These women, called "grandmothers," volunteer to sit with ④ patients at the benches, listen to their stories, and provide them with ⑤ emotional support.

①   ②   ③   ④   ⑤

03 다음 글의 밑줄 친 부분 중, 문맥상 낱말의 쓰임이 적절하지 않은 것은?

Host What a wonderful idea! How did these ① amazing grandmothers become a part of your program?

Dr. Chibanda Grandmothers were chosen for our program because they are deeply connected to the ② community. Moreover, they have all the qualities of a counselor, such as excellent listening skills, empathy, and the ③ ability to engage in meaningful discussions. They are also very reliable, which is important for our efforts to support ④ physical health. At the beginning, we started with only fourteen volunteer grandmothers. But today, there are thousands of grandmothers who have been ⑤ trained to provide Friendship Bench therapy in Zimbabwe.

①   ②   ③   ④   ⑤

04 (A), (B), (C)의 각 네모 안에서 문맥에 맞는 낱말로 가장 적절한 것은?

Host That's interesting! What happens after (A) patients / psychiatrists complete their sessions with the grandmothers?

Grandma Moyo When the sessions with the grandmothers are over, patients are (B) discouraged / encouraged to join a community support group made up of former patients of the program. The members of these groups can easily relate to and support one another. This is because most of them come from the same community and have experienced (C) similar / different struggles.

	(A)		(B)		(C)
①	patients	···	encouraged	···	different
②	patients	···	encouraged	···	similar
③	patients	···	discouraged	···	different
④	psychiatrists	···	encouraged	···	similar
⑤	psychiatrists	···	discouraged	···	similar

05 (A), (B), (C)의 각 네모 안에서 문맥에 맞는 낱말로 가장 적절한 것은?

> **Host** That sounds like a great way to continue the support and build a sense of community. And the program has been incredibly successful, right?
> **Dr. Chibanda** That's (A) correct / wrong . In 2022, we provided face-to-face counseling to about 90,000 patients in Zimbabwe. Now, Friendship Benches are (B) available / reliable in more than twenty different regions around the country. Our vision is for everyone to have a Friendship Bench within walking distance, and we are working hard to make it happen. We've also started expanding the program, and we now offer (C) online / offline counseling through an app. This has helped us reach even more people.

	(A)	(B)	(C)
①	correct	⋯ available	⋯ offline
②	correct	⋯ available	⋯ online
③	correct	⋯ reliable	⋯ offline
④	wrong	⋯ available	⋯ online
⑤	wrong	⋯ reliable	⋯ offline

06 다음 글의 밑줄 친 부분 중, 문맥상 낱말의 쓰임이 적절하지 않은 것은?

> **Host** That's really amazing! Thank you for your time, Dr. Chibanda. Now let's hear from one of the grandmothers who ① volunteers for the program. Can you introduce yourself and tell us how you got ② involved with the Friendship Bench program?
> **Grandma Moyo** Hello, my name is Judith Moyo, but people call me Grandma Moyo. I'm 76 years old, and I have been volunteering for the Friendship Bench program for about eight years. I ③ joined the program because many people in my community struggle with ④ mental health problems, and I wanted to do something about it. I knew that I could help heal their ⑤ healthy hearts by supporting them.

①   ②   ③   ④   ⑤

[07~08] 다음 글을 읽고, 물음에 답하시오.

> **Host** That's very kind of you. Can you tell us about your experience as a grandmother for the Friendship Bench program?
> **Grandma Moyo** It's been wonderful. Seeking help for mental health problems is nothing to be (A) afraid / ashamed of. I've seen how it can make a difference in people's lives. One patient of mine, a nineteen-year old girl, was going through a (B) comfortable / difficult time after her mom passed away. I counseled her and helped her begin her recovery journey. Now her life is back on track, and she has even started her own business! Cases like this make me so proud to be part of the program. It is such a rewarding experience to help people make (C) positive / negative changes in their lives.
> **Host** Thanks for sharing your experiences with us today, Grandma Moyo. It's truly inspiring to see the influence that the Friendship Bench program has had. And it's all thanks to the hard work of people like you and Dr. Chibanda.

07 (A), (B), (C)의 각 네모 안에서 문맥에 맞는 낱말로 가장 적절한 것은?

	(A)	(B)	(C)
①	afraid	⋯ comfortable	⋯ positive
②	afraid	⋯ difficult	⋯ positive
③	ashamed	⋯ comfortable	⋯ negative
④	ashamed	⋯ difficult	⋯ positive
⑤	ashamed	⋯ difficult	⋯ negative

08 다음 영어 뜻풀이에 해당하는 단어를 윗글에서 찾아 쓰시오.

> returning to a normal state after a period of illness or injury

→ _____

01 (A), (B), (C)의 각 네모 안에서 어법에 맞는 표현으로 가장 적절한 것은?

Dr. Chibanda The idea came from an experience I had as a psychiatrist. One of my patients had become severely (A) depressing / depressed . However, she couldn't get help because she was unable to afford the bus ride to the hospital. This shocked me, as I had never considered such a problem before. In fact, it is difficult (B) for / of many people in Zimbabwe to pay for transportation and receive medical treatment. Furthermore, there has been a lack of psychiatrists in the country for many years. When the Friendship Bench program started in 2006, there were only eleven psychiatrists serving Zimbabwe's population of over twelve million people. I needed to find a way (C) bring / to bring psychiatry into the community.

	(A)	(B)	(C)
①	depressing	⋯ for ⋯	bring
②	depressing	⋯ of ⋯	to bring
③	depressed	⋯ for ⋯	to bring
④	depressed	⋯ for ⋯	bring
⑤	depressed	⋯ of ⋯	to bring

02 다음 글의 밑줄 친 부분 중, 어법상 틀린 것은?

Dr. Chibanda The program was created ①as a way to provide accessible mental health services. It offers talk therapy sessions to people ②dealing with issues such as depression or anxiety. The sessions are free and are ③provided by respected elderly women from the community. These women, ④calling "grandmothers," volunteer to sit with patients at the benches, listen to their stories, and ⑤provide them with emotional support.

①   ②   ③   ④   ⑤

03 다음 글의 밑줄 친 부분 중, 어법상 틀린 것은?

Host ①What a wonderful idea! How did these amazing grandmothers become a part of your program?

Dr. Chibanda Grandmothers were ②chosen for our program because they are deeply connected to the community. Moreover, they have all the qualities of a counselor, such as excellent listening skills, empathy, and the ability ③to engage in meaningful discussions. They are also very reliable, ④which is important for our efforts to support mental health. At the beginning, we started with only fourteen volunteer grandmothers. But today, there are thousands of grandmothers ⑤which have been trained to provide Friendship Bench therapy in Zimbabwe.

①   ②   ③   ④   ⑤

04 (A), (B), (C)의 각 네모 안에서 어법에 맞는 표현으로 가장 적절한 것은?

Host That's interesting! What happens after patients complete their sessions with the grandmothers?

Dr. Chibanda When the sessions with the grandmothers are over, patients are encouraged (A) joining / to join a community support group made up of former patients of the program. The members of these groups can (B) easy / easily relate to and support one another. This is (C) so / because most of them come from the same community and have experienced similar struggles.

	(A)	(B)	(C)
①	joining	⋯ easy ⋯	because
②	joining	⋯ easily ⋯	because
③	to join	⋯ easy ⋯	so
④	to join	⋯ easily ⋯	so
⑤	to join	⋯ easily ⋯	because

05 다음 글의 밑줄 친 부분 중, 어법상 틀린 것은?

> **Host** That sounds like a great way to continue the support and build a sense of community. And the program has been incredibly successful, right?
> **Dr. Chibanda** That's correct. In 2022, we provided face-to-face counseling ① with about 90,000 patients in Zimbabwe. Now, Friendship Benches are available in ② more than twenty different regions around the country. Our vision is for everyone to have a Friendship Bench within walking distance, and we are working hard to make it ③ happen. We've also started ④ expanding the program, and we now offer online counseling through an app. This has helped us ⑤ reach even more people.

①   ②   ③   ④   ⑤

06 (A), (B), (C)의 각 네모 안에서 어법에 맞는 표현으로 가장 적절한 것은?

> **Host** That's really amazing! Thank you for your time, Dr. Chibanda. Now let's hear from one of the grandmothers (A) who / which volunteers for the program. Can you introduce yourself and tell us how you got involved with the Friendship Bench program?
> **Dr. Chibanda** Hello, my name is Judith Moyo, but people call me Grandma Moyo. I'm 76 years old, and I have been (B) volunteering / volunteered for the Friendship Bench program for about eight years. I joined the program because many people in my community struggle with mental health problems, and I wanted to do something about it. I knew that I could help heal their wounded hearts by (C) supporting / supported them.

	(A)	(B)	(C)
①	who	volunteering	supported
②	who	volunteering	supporting
③	who	volunteered	supporting
④	which	volunteering	supporting
⑤	which	volunteered	supported

[07~08] 다음 글을 읽고, 물음에 답하시오.

> **Host** That's very kind of you. Can you tell us about your experience as a grandmother for the Friendship Bench program?
> **Dr. Chibanda** It's been wonderful. (A) Seek / Seeking help for mental health problems is nothing to be ashamed of. I've seen how (B) it can / can it make a difference in people's lives. One patient of mine, a nineteen-year old girl, was going through a difficult time after her mom passed away. I counseled her and helped her begin her recovery journey. Now her life is back on track, and she has even started her own business! Cases like this make me so proud to be part of the program. It is (C) so / such a rewarding experience to help people make positive changes in their lives.
> **Host** Thanks for sharing your experiences with us today, Grandma Moyo. To see the influence that the Friendship Bench program has had is truly inspiring. And it's all thanks to the hard work of people like you and Dr. Chibanda.

07 (A), (B), (C)의 각 네모 안에서 어법에 맞는 표현으로 가장 적절한 것은?

	(A)	(B)	(C)
①	Seek	it can	such
②	Seek	can it	so
③	Seeking	it can	such
④	Seeking	it can	so
⑤	Seeking	can it	such

08 윗글의 밑줄 친 문장을 가주어 It으로 시작하여 문장을 다시 쓰시오.

→ _____

_____

01 다음 중 남자아이가 Lisa에게 제안한 것으로 가장 적절한 것은?

> B Hey, Lisa! Why didn't you come to our math club meeting yesterday?
>
> G I had a stomachache after lunch, so I went home early.
>
> B Oh, that's too bad. What do you think caused it?
>
> G I'm not sure. These days, I often have an upset stomach when I'm in the library after lunch.
>
> B Maybe that's the problem. Sitting right after a meal can be bad for your health. I think you should try to go for a walk after you eat.
>
> G You're right. I should do that more often.

① Skip lunch
② Eat lighter meals
③ Avoid the library
④ Join a different club
⑤ Go for a walk after eating

02 다음 글의 밑줄 친 우리말과 같은 뜻이 되도록 괄호 안의 말을 이용하여 문장을 완성하시오.

> **Host** On today's show, we are going to learn about special park benches in Zimbabwe called Friendship Benches. We have two special guests. First, please welcome the founder of the Friendship Bench program, Dr. Dixon Chibanda. 무엇이 당신으로 하여금 그 프로그램을 떠올리도록 영감을 주었는지 저희에게 말씀해 주시겠어요?

→ Can you tell us _____
_____?

(inspire, come up with)

[03~04] 다음 글을 읽고, 물음에 답하시오.

> **Dr. Chibanda** The idea came from an experience I had (A) as a psychiatrist. One of my patients had become severely depressed. (①) However, she couldn't get help because she was unable to afford the bus ride to the hospital. This shocked me, (B) as I had never considered such a problem before. (②) In fact, it is difficult for many people in Zimbabwe to pay for transportation and receive medical treatment. (③) When the Friendship Bench program started in 2006, there were only eleven psychiatrists serving Zimbabwe's population of over twelve million people. (④) I needed to find a way to bring psychiatry into the community. (⑤)

03 윗글에서 주어진 문장이 들어가기에 가장 적절한 곳은?

> Furthermore, there has been a lack of psychiatrists in the country for many years.

①   ②   ③   ④   ⑤

04 윗글의 밑줄 친 (A), (B)에 쓰인 as의 쓰임과 같은 것을 보기에서 골라 기호를 쓰시오.

> 보기
>
> ⓐ She works as a teacher at a high school.
> ⓑ As the sun set, the temperature began to drop.
> ⓒ He smiled as he remembered the happy moment.
> ⓓ They used the old box as a table for their picnic.

(A) _____   (B) _____

[05~06] 다음 글을 읽고, 물음에 답하시오.

Host _____

Dr. Chibanda Certainly. The program was created as a way to provide accessible mental health services. It offers talk therapy sessions to people dealing with issues such as depression or anxiety. The sessions are free and are provided by respected elderly women from the community. These women, called "grandmothers," volunteer to sit with patients at the benches, listen to their stories, and provide them with emotional support.

05 윗글의 빈칸에 들어갈 질문으로 가장 적절한 것은?

① What inspired you to become a psychiatrist?
② How many people can use the Friendship Bench program?
③ Could you explain to us how the Friendship Bench program works?
④ What do the grandmothers do in the program?
⑤ How do you select and train the "grandmothers" for the program?

06 다음 영어 뜻풀이에 해당하는 단어를 윗글에서 찾아 쓰시오.

a feeling of worry or fear about future events or situations

→ _____

[07~08] 다음 글을 읽고, 물음에 답하시오.

Host How did these amazing grandmothers become a part ① of your program?

Dr. Chibanda Grandmothers were chosen ② from our program because they are deeply connected to the community. Moreover, they have all the qualities of a counselor, such as excellent listening skills, empathy, and the ability to engage ③ in meaningful discussions. They are also very reliable, which is important for our efforts to support mental health. ④ At the beginning, we started ⑤ with only fourteen volunteer grandmothers. But today, there are thousands of grandmothers who have been trained to provide Friendship Bench therapy in Zimbabwe.

07 윗글의 밑줄 친 부분 중, 전치사의 쓰임이 바르지 않은 것은?

①   ②   ③   ④   ⑤

08 윗글의 내용과 일치하지 않는 것은?

① Grandmothers were chosen for their community connections.
② The grandmothers have good listening skills and empathy.
③ The program started with fourteen volunteer grandmothers.
④ Now, thousands of grandmothers are trained to provide therapy.
⑤ The grandmothers are paid professionals with experience.

09 다음 글의 빈칸 (A), (B)에 들어갈 말이 바르게 짝지어진 것은?

> Host That's interesting! What happens after patients complete their sessions with the grandmothers?
>
> **Dr. Chibanda** ___(A)___ the sessions with the grandmothers are over, patients are encouraged to join a community support group made up of former patients of the program. The members of these groups can easily relate to and support one another. This is ___(B)___ most of them come from the same community and have experienced similar struggles.

     (A)   (B)

① After ⋯ since
② When ⋯ because
③ While ⋯ although
④ Before ⋯ unless
⑤ Until ⋯ despite

10 다음 글의 밑줄 친 말과 같은 뜻이 되도록 조건에 맞게 문장을 다시 쓰시오.

> **Dr. Chibanda** That's correct. In 2022, <u>we provided face-to-face counseling to about 90,000 patients in Zimbabwe.</u> Now, Friendship Benches are available in more than twenty different regions around the country. Our vision is for everyone to have a Friendship Bench within walking distance, and we are working hard to make it happen. We've also started expanding the program, and we now offer online counseling through an app. This has helped us reach even more people.

조건
- 전치사 to 대신 with를 사용할 것
- 문장의 단어 수는 동일하게 할 것

_____

_____

[11~12] 다음 글을 읽고, 물음에 답하시오.

> Host That's really amazing! Thank you for your time, Dr. Chibanda. Now let's hear from one of the grandmothers _____ volunteers for the program. Can you introduce yourself and tell us how you got involved with the Friendship Bench program?
>
> **Dr. Chibanda** Hello, my name is Judith Moyo, but people call me Grandma Moyo. I'm 76 years old, and I have been volunteering for the Friendship Bench program <u>for</u> about eight years. I joined the program because many people in my community struggle with mental health problems, and I wanted to do something about it. I knew that I could help heal their wounded hearts by supporting them.

11 윗글의 빈칸에 들어갈 말로 가장 적절한 것은?

① who   ② which
③ what   ④ where
⑤ when

12 윗글의 밑줄 친 for와 쓰임이 다른 것은?

① We drove on the highway <u>for</u> three hours.
② I donated some money <u>for</u> a poor child.
③ She has lived in New York <u>for</u> ten years.
④ The music festival lasted <u>for</u> five days.
⑤ We traveled around Europe <u>for</u> a few months.

Host Can you tell us about your experience as a grandmother for the Friendship Bench program?
Grandma Moyo It's been wonderful. ① Seek help for mental health problems is nothing to be ashamed of. ② I've seen how it can make a difference in people's lives. ③ One patient of mine, a nineteen-year old girl, was going through a difficult time after her mom passed away. ④ I counseled her and helped her begin her recovery journey. ⑤ Now her life is back on track, and she has even started her own business! Cases like this make me so proud to be part of the program. 사람들이 그들의 삶에 긍정적인 변화를 가져오도록 돕는 것은 정말 보람된 경험입니다.
Host Thanks for sharing your _____s with us today, Grandma Moyo. It's truly inspiring to see the influence that the Friendship Bench program has had. And it's all thanks to the hard work of people like you and Dr. Chibanda.

13 윗글의 ①~⑤ 중, 어법상 틀린 문장은?

①   ②   ③   ④   ⑤

14 윗글의 밑줄 친 우리말과 같은 뜻이 되도록 조건에 맞게 영작하시오.

조건
• 가주어 it과 진주어 to부정사를 사용할 것
• such, rewarding, positive를 포함할 것
• 빈칸에 총 12단어를 넣을 것

→ _____

_____ in their lives.

15 윗글의 빈칸에 들어갈 말을 본문에서 찾아 쓰시오.

→ _____

[01~02] 다음 담화를 읽고, 물음에 답하시오.

W Thanks to streaming platforms, you can watch your favorite shows anytime. You can even watch a whole series without stopping! This is called binge-watching. It sounds fun, but binge-watching isn't good for you. It can cause sleep problems and lead to reduced physical activity. So, how can you prevent binge-watching from affecting your health? First, decide how long you are going to watch a show before you start, and set an alarm. When the alarm goes off, it's important to stop watching even if you are in the middle of the show. Second, watch shows only while doing a productive activity, such as exercising or organizing your desk. When you finish the activity, turn off the show. I hope these tips help you enjoy your favorite shows in a healthy way.

01 위 담화의 주제로 가장 적절한 것은?

① The benefits of streaming platforms
② The popularity of TV series
③ The importance of physical activity
④ How to choose the best streaming service
⑤ The dangers of binge-watching and how to avoid them

02 위 담화에서 빈지 워칭을 예방하기 위한 제안으로 언급되지 않은 것은?

① 시청을 시작하기 전에 알람을 설정한다.
② 알람이 울리면 시청을 중단한다.
③ 생산적인 활동을 하면서 프로그램을 시청한다.
④ 계획한 시간이 끝나도 프로그램을 끝까지 시청한다.
⑤ 생산적인 활동을 마치면 프로그램을 끈다.

[03~04] 다음 글을 읽고, 물음에 답하시오.

Dr. Chibanda The idea came from an experience I had ___(A)___ a psychiatrist. One of my patients had become severely depressed. However, she couldn't get help because she was unable to afford the bus ride to the hospital. ① This shocked me, as I had never considered such a problem before. ② In fact, it is difficult for many people in Zimbabwe to pay for transportation and receive medical treatment. ③ Many people in Zimbabwe enjoy traditional music and dance. ④ Furthermore, there has been a lack of psychiatrists in the country ___(B)___ many years. ⑤ When the Friendship Bench program started in 2006, there were only eleven psychiatrists serving Zimbabwe's population of over twelve million people. I needed to find a way to bring psychiatry ___(C)___ the community.

03 윗글의 ①~⑤ 중, 전체 흐름과 관계 <u>없는</u> 문장은?

①   ②   ③   ④   ⑤

04 윗글의 빈칸 (A), (B), (C)에 들어갈 전치사로 가장 적절한 것을 보기 에서 찾아 쓰시오.

보기 of   for   in   from   as   into   with

(A) _____ (B) _____ (C) _____

[05~06] 다음 글을 읽고, 물음에 답하시오.

Host Oh, so that was the beginning of it. 우정 벤치 프로그램이 어떻게 운영되는지 저희에게 설명해 주시겠어요?

Dr. Chibanda Certainly. The program was created as a way to provide accessible ① mental health services. It offers ② talk therapy sessions to people dealing with issues such as depression or anxiety. The sessions are ③ paid and are provided by respected elderly women from the ④ community. These women, called "grandmothers," ⑤ volunteer to sit with patients at the benches, listen to their stories, and provide them with emotional support.

05 윗글의 밑줄 친 우리말과 같은 뜻이 되도록 보기의 단어를 알맞게 배열하시오.

보기 you / could / the Friendship Bench program / explain / us / to / how / works

_____

_____

06 윗글의 밑줄 친 부분 중, 낱말의 쓰임이 어색한 것을 찾아 번호를 쓰고 바르게 고쳐 쓴 후 이유를 쓰시오.

_____ : _____ → _____

이유: _____

_____

_____

[07~08] 다음 글을 읽고, 물음에 답하시오.

Host What a wonderful idea! How did these amazing grandmothers become a part of your program?

Dr. Chibanda Grandmothers were chosen for our program ____(A)____ they are deeply connected to the community. ____(B)____, they have all the qualities of a counselor, such as excellent listening skills, empathy, and the ability to engage in meaningful discussions. They are also very reliable, that is important for our efforts to support mental health. At the beginning, we started with only fourteen volunteer grandmothers. ____(C)____ today, there are thousands of grandmothers who have been trained to provide Friendship Bench therapy in Zimbabwe.

07 윗글의 반칸 (A), (B), (C)에 알맞은 것이 바르게 짝지어진 것은?

	(A)	(B)	(C)
①	since	In fact	As a result
②	because	Moreover	But
③	as	In addition	Finally
④	for	Besides	Although
⑤	due to	Additionally	Nevertheless

08 윗글의 밑줄 친 문장에서 어법상 틀린 부분을 찾아 바르게 고쳐 쓰시오.

_____ → _____

[09~10] 다음 글을 읽고, 물음에 답하시오.

> **Host** That's interesting! What happens after patients complete their sessions with the grandmothers?
>
> **Dr. Chibanda** When the sessions with the grandmothers are over, patients are encouraged to join a community support group (A) made / making up of former patients of the program. The members of these groups can (B) easy / easily relate to and support one another. This is because most of them come from the same community and (C) experienced / have experienced similar struggles.

09 (A), (B), (C)의 각 네모 안에서 어법에 맞는 표현으로 가장 적절한 것은?

	(A)	(B)	(C)
①	made	… easy	… experienced
②	made	… easy	… have experienced
③	made	… easily	… have experienced
④	making	… easily	… experienced
⑤	making	… easy	… have experienced

10 윗글의 내용과 일치하지 <u>않는</u> 것은?

① 할머니들과의 세션이 끝난 후 환자들은 지역 사회 지원 그룹에 참여하도록 권장된다.
② 지역 사회 지원 그룹은 프로그램의 이전 환자들로 구성되어 있다.
③ 그룹 구성원들은 서로를 쉽게 이해하고 지원할 수 있다.
④ 대부분의 그룹 구성원들은 같은 지역 사회 출신이다.
⑤ 그룹 구성원들은 각기 다양한 어려움을 경험했다.

[11~12] 다음 글을 읽고, 물음에 답하시오.

> **Host**
> 지원을 지속하고 공동체 의식을 키울 수 있는 좋은 방법인 것 같네요. And the program has been incredibly successful, right?

> **Dr. Chibanda**
> (A) Now, Friendship Benches are available in more than twenty different regions around the country. Our vision is for everyone to have a Friendship Bench within walking distance, and we are working hard to make it happen.
> (B) We've also started expanding the program, and we now offer online counseling through an app. This has helped us reach even more people.
> (C) That's correct. In 2022, we provided face-to-face counseling to about 90,000 patients in Zimbabwe.

11 윗글의 밑줄 친 우리말과 같은 뜻이 되도록 **보기**의 단어를 이용하여 영작하시오. (필요시 단어를 추가할 것)

> **보기** way / continue / great / support / sense / build / community

→ That sounds like _____

_____.

12 윗글의 (A), (B), (C)를 올바른 순서로 배열한 것은?

① (A) – (B) – (C) 　　② (A) – (C) – (B)
③ (B) – (A) – (C) 　　④ (C) – (A) – (B)
⑤ (C) – (B) – (A)

[13~14] 다음 글을 읽고, 물음에 답하시오.

Host That's really amazing! Thank you for your time, Dr. Chibanda. Now let's hear from one of the grandmothers who volunteers for the program. _____

Grandma Moyo Hello, my name is Judith Moyo, but people call me Grandma Moyo. I'm 76 years old, and I have been volunteering for the Friendship Bench program for about eight years. I joined the program because many people in my community struggle with mental health problems, and I wanted to do something about it. I knew that I could help heal their wounded hearts by supporting them.

13 다음 두 문장을 한 문장으로 만들어 빈칸에 들어갈 말을 쓰시오.

• Can you introduce yourself and tell us?
• How did you get involved with the Friendship Bench program?

→ _____
_____

14 Moyo 할머니에 관한 윗글의 내용과 일치하지 않는 것은?

① 그녀의 본명은 Judith Moyo이다.
② 그녀의 나이는 76세이다.
③ 우정 벤치 프로그램에서 약 8년 동안 자원봉사를 해왔다.
④ 지역 사회의 정신 건강 문제를 돕기 위해 프로그램에 참여했다.
⑤ 정신과 의사로서 전문적인 치료를 제공한다.

15 다음 글의 밑줄 친 부분의 의미가 잘못된 것은?

Host That's very kind of you. Can you tell us about your experience as a grandmother for the Friendship Bench program?

Grandma Moyo It's been wonderful. Seeking help for mental health problems is nothing to ① be ashamed of. I've seen how it can ② make a difference in people's lives. One patient of mine, a nineteen-year old girl, was ③ going through a difficult time after her mom ④ passed away. I counseled her and helped her begin her recovery journey. Now her life is ⑤ back on track, and she has even started her own business! Cases like this make me so proud to be part of the program. It is such a rewarding experience to help people make positive changes in their lives.

Host Thanks for sharing your experiences with us today, Grandma Moyo. It's truly inspiring to see the influence that the Friendship Bench program has had. And it's all thanks to the hard work of people like you and Dr. Chibanda.

① be ashamed of: ~을 부끄러워하다
② make a difference: 변화를 일으키다
③ go through: ~을 겪다, 경험하다
④ pass away: 지나가다
⑤ back on track: 다시 정상 궤도에 들어선

[01~02] 다음 대화를 읽고, 물음에 답하시오.

> G What's that, Jake?
>
> B It's my meal plan. It shows what I'll eat for each meal. Thinking about it in advance ① helps me maintain a healthy diet.
>
> G Great idea! I often end up ② having unhealthy fast food because I can't decide what to eat.
>
> B Really? Then I think you ③ will make a meal plan, too.
>
> G Can you explain how you make each meal ④ healthy?
>
> B Sure. I make sure there's the right balance of grains, protein, and vegetables. And I try ⑤ to eat a variety of foods.
>
> G _____

01 위 대화의 빈칸에 들어갈 말로 알맞은 것은?

① That sounds too complicated for me.
② Okay. I'll try that!
③ I prefer to eat whatever I want.
④ Can you make a meal plan for me instead?
⑤ I don't think balanced meals are important.

02 위 대화의 밑줄 친 부분 중, 어법상 틀린 것은?

①   ②   ③   ④   ⑤

[03~04] 다음 글을 읽고, 물음에 답하시오.

> **Host** On today's show, we are going to learn about special park benches in Zimbabwe called Friendship Benches. We have two special guests. First, please welcome the founder of the Friendship Bench program, Dr. Dixon Chibanda. Can you tell us what inspired you to come up with the program?
>
> **Dr. Chibanda** Sure. The idea came from an experience I had as a psychiatrist. One of my patients had become severely depressed. _____(A)_____, she couldn't get help because she was unable to afford the bus ride to the hospital. This shocked me, as I had never considered such a problem before. _____(B)_____, it is difficult for many people in Zimbabwe to pay for transportation and receive medical treatment. _____(C)_____, there has been a lack of psychiatrists in the country for many years. When the Friendship Bench program started in 2006, there were only eleven psychiatrists serving Zimbabwe's population of over twelve million people. I needed to find a way to bring psychiatry into the community.

03 윗글의 (A), (B), (C)에 알맞은 접속사가 바르게 짝지어진 것은?

	(A)	(B)	(C)
①	Therefore	Moreover	Additionally
②	Although	Besides	Nevertheless
③	Meanwhile	Indeed	Consequently
④	However	In fact	Furthermore
⑤	Despite	Thus	Meanwhile

04 윗글에 나타난 Chibanda 박사의 환자에 대한 태도로 가장 적절한 것은?

① critical   ② indifferent
③ empathetic   ④ professional
⑤ objective

[05~06] 다음 글을 읽고, 물음에 답하시오.

> **Host** Oh, so that was the beginning of it. Could you explain to us how the Friendship Bench program works?
>
> **Dr. Chibanda** Certainly. The program was created as a way to provide accessible mental health services. It offers talk therapy sessions to people dealing with issues such as depression or anxiety. The sessions are free and are provided by respected elderly women from the community. These women, called "grandmothers," volunteer to sit with patients at the benches, listen to their stories, and <u>provide emotional support to them.</u>

05 Chibanda 박사가 설명한 우정 벤치 프로그램의 주요 특징으로 알맞은 것은?

① 환자들에게 비싼 정신과 약물을 제공한다.
② 전문 치료사가 이끄는 무료 대화 치료 세션을 제공한다.
③ 지역사회 어르신들이 무료 대화 치료를 제공한다.
④ 아주 심각한 정신 질환 치료에만 집중한다.
⑤ 젊은 대학생 자원봉사자들이 온라인으로 상담 서비스를 제공한다.

06 윗글의 밑줄 친 부분과 같은 뜻이 되도록 할 때 빈칸에 알맞은 것은?

> provide them _____ emotional support

① on   ② of   ③ for
④ with   ⑤ from

[07~08] 다음 글을 읽고, 물음에 답하시오.

> **Host** What a wonderful idea! How did these amazing grandmothers become a part of your program?
>
> **Dr. Chibanda** Grandmothers were chosen for our program because they are deeply connected to the community. Moreover, they have all the qualities of a counselor, such as excellent listening skills, empathy, and the ability to engage in meaningful discussions. They are also very reliable, ___(A)___ is important for our efforts to support mental health. At the beginning, we started with only fourteen volunteer grandmothers. But today, there are thousands of grandmothers ___(B)___ have been trained <u>to provide</u> Friendship Bench therapy in Zimbabwe.

07 윗글의 빈칸 (A), (B)에 들어갈 말로 가장 적절한 것은?

  (A)   (B)
① who   ⋯ which
② which ⋯ who
③ who   ⋯ who
④ which ⋯ which
⑤ which ⋯ what

08 윗글의 밑줄 친 to provide와 쓰임이 같은 것은?

① Katie wants <u>to travel</u> around the world.
② I need a book <u>to read</u> during my vacation.
③ My brother plans <u>to study</u> engineering at university.
④ We agreed <u>to participate</u> in the project.
⑤ Lucy studies hard <u>to improve</u> her grades.

[09~10] 다음 글을 읽고, 물음에 답하시오.

Surprisingly, your posture can influence your mind and your emotions. In fact, the relationship between mind and body is so ① powerful that your body position plays a large role in how you think, feel, and act. For example, sitting and standing up straight will increase your ② nervousness and decrease your stress. Try walking with your chest out and your chin ③ raised. Don't you feel more ④ confident in this position? Also, research has shown that good posture can be highly ⑤ beneficial for students. If students have good posture, it is easier for them to concentrate and stay in a good mood.

09 윗글의 주제로 가장 적절한 것은?

① 신체 건강을 위한 바른 자세의 중요성
② 자세가 마음과 감정에 미치는 영향
③ 신체 언어를 연구하는 방법
④ 학생들의 집중력을 향상시키는 기술
⑤ 자신감과 학업 성공 사이의 관계

10 윗글의 밑줄 친 부분 중, 문맥상 낱말의 쓰임이 적절하지 <u>않은</u> 것은?

①   ②   ③   ④   ⑤

11 주어진 영어 뜻풀이에 해당하는 단어를 알맞은 형태로 바꿔 빈칸에 쓰시오.

Host That sounds like a great way to continue the support and build a sense of community. And the program has been incredibly successful, right?
Dr. Chibanda That's correct. In 2022, we provided face-to-face counseling to about 90,000 patients in Zimbabwe. Now, Friendship Benches are available in more than twenty different regions around the country. Our vision is for everyone to have a Friendship Bench within walking distance, and we are working hard to make it happen. We've also started _____ the program, and we now offer online counseling through an app. This has helped us reach even more people.

to increase in size, volume, or scope; to spread out or grow larger

→ _____

12 다음 글의 밑줄 친 문장에서 틀린 곳을 두 군데 찾아 바르게 고쳐 쓰시오.

Host That's interesting! What happens after patients complete their sessions with the grandmothers?
Dr. Chibanda <u>When the sessions with the grandmothers are over, patients are encouraging to join a community support group making up of former patients of the program.</u> The members of these groups can easily relate to and support one another. This is because most of them come from the same community and have experienced similar struggles.

(1) _____ → _____

(2) _____ → _____

Host That's really amazing! Thank you for your time, Dr. Chibanda. Now let's hear from one of the grandmothers who (A) volunteer / volunteers for the program. Can you introduce yourself and tell us how you got involved with the Friendship Bench program?

Dr. Chibanda Hello, my name is Judith Moyo, but people call me Grandma Moyo. I'm 76 years old, and I have been (B) volunteered / volunteering for the Friendship Bench program for about eight years. I joined the program because many people in my community struggle with mental health problems, and I wanted to do something about it. I knew that I could help heal their (C) wounded / wounding hearts by supporting them.

13 윗글을 통해 Moyo 할머니에 대해 알 수 없는 것을 모두 고르면?

① 나이
② 가족 관계
③ 프로그램에 참여한 이유
④ 프로그램을 알게 된 시점
⑤ 프로그램에서 자원봉사를 한 기간

14 (A), (B), (C)의 각 네모 안에서 어법에 맞는 표현으로 가장 적절한 것은?

	(A)	(B)	(C)
①	volunteer	volunteered	wounding
②	volunteer	volunteering	wounded
③	volunteers	volunteering	wounded
④	volunteers	volunteered	wounded
⑤	volunteers	volunteering	wounding

15 다음 글의 밑줄 친 문장에서 **틀린** 부분을 찾아 바르게 고치고 **틀린** 이유를 쓰시오.

Host Can you tell us about your experience as a grandmother for the Friendship Bench program?

Grandma Moyo It's been wonderful. <u>Seeking help for mental health problems are nothing to be ashamed of.</u> I've seen how it can make a difference in people's lives. One patient of mine, a nineteen-year old girl, was going through a difficult time after her mom passed away. I counseled her and helped her begin her recovery journey. Now her life is back on track, and she has even started her own business! Cases like this make me so proud to be part of the program. It is such a rewarding experience to help people make positive changes in their lives.

Host Thanks for sharing your experiences with us today, Grandma Moyo. It's truly inspiring to see the influence that the Friendship Bench program has had. And it's all thanks to the hard work of people like you and Dr. Chibanda.

(1) 틀린 부분: _____ → _____

(2) 틀린 이유: _____

_____

[01~02] 다음 글을 읽고, 물음에 답하시오.

Host On today's show, we're going to explore special park benches in Zimbabwe ① knowing as Friendship Benches. We have two distinguished guests with us. First, please welcome Dr. Dixon Chibanda, the founder of the Friendship Bench program. Can you share what inspired you ② to create this program?

Dr. Chibanda Of course. The idea originated from my experience as a psychiatrist. One of my patients became severely ③ depressed but was unable to seek help because she couldn't afford the bus fare to the hospital. This realization shocked me, as I ④ had never considered such an issue before. Many people in Zimbabwe struggle to pay for transportation and receive medical care. Additionally, there has been a long-standing shortage of psychiatrists in the country. When the Friendship Bench program was launched in 2006, there were only eleven psychiatrists available to serve Zimbabwe's population of over twelve million. I knew I needed ⑤ to find a way to bring psychiatric care into the community.

01 윗글의 밑줄 친 부분 중, 어법상 틀린 것은?

①   ②   ③   ④   ⑤

02 Chibanda 박사가 우정 벤치 프로그램을 시작한 목적으로 가장 적절한 것은?

① 짐바브웨의 교통 문제를 해결하기 위해
② 정신 건강 치료의 접근성을 높이기 위해
③ 새로운 공원 벤치를 디자인하기 위해
④ 지역 사회의 경제를 활성화하기 위해
⑤ 정신과 의사 수를 줄이기 위해

[03~04] 다음 글을 읽고, 물음에 답하시오.

Host So that's how it all started. Could you tell us how the Friendship Bench program operates?

Dr. Chibanda Of course. The program was designed to offer accessible mental health care. It provides ＿＿＿＿＿＿＿＿＿＿ for people struggling with conditions like depression or anxiety. These sessions are led by respected elderly women from the community, known as "grandmothers," who volunteer to sit with patients at the benches, listen to their stories, and give them emotional support.

03 윗글의 주제로 가장 적절한 것은?

① The role of elderly women in African communities
② A cost-effective mental health intervention in Zimbabwe
③ Challenges in providing mental health care in developing countries
④ The importance of professional therapy for depression
⑤ Cultural differences in treating mental illness

04 윗글의 빈칸에 들어갈 말로 가장 적절한 것은?

① medication and clinical treatments
② financial assistance and job training
③ free talk therapy sessions
④ physical exercise and nutrition advice
⑤ religious counseling and spiritual guidance

[05~06] 다음 글을 읽고, 물음에 답하시오.

> **Host** What a fantastic idea! How did these remarkable grandmothers get (A) involving / involved in your program?
>
> **Dr. Chibanda** ① Grandmothers were selected for our program because they have strong ties to the community. They possess essential qualities of a counselor, including great listening skills, empathy, and the ability to engage in meaningful discussions. ② Many grandmothers enjoy gardening in their free time, which helps them relax. ③ They are also very reliable, (B) which / that is important for our efforts to support mental health. ④ Initially, we began with just fourteen volunteers. ⑤ But now we have thousands of grandmothers who (C) have trained / have been trained to offer Friendship Bench therapy across Zimbabwe.

05 윗글의 ①~⑤ 중, 전체 흐름과 관계 <u>없는</u> 문장은?

①   ②   ③   ④   ⑤

06 (A), (B), (C)의 각 네모 안에서 어법에 맞는 표현으로 가장 적절한 것은?

	(A)	(B)	(C)
①	involving	which	have been trained
②	involving	that	have trained
③	involved	which	have been trained
④	involved	which	have trained
⑤	involved	that	have been trained

[07~08] 다음 글을 읽고, 물음에 답하시오.

> **Host** That's interesting! What happens after patients (A) start / finish their sessions with the grandmothers?
>
> **Dr. Chibanda** After the sessions with the grandmothers end, (B) patients / grandmothers are encouraged to join a community support group composed of former program participants. The members of these groups can easily connect with and support one another, as they typically come from the same community and have experienced (C) similar / different challenges.

07 (A), (B), (C)의 각 네모 안에서 문맥에 맞는 낱말로 가장 적절한 것은?

	(A)	(B)	(C)
①	start	patients	similar
②	start	grandmothers	different
③	finish	patients	different
④	finish	patients	similar
⑤	finish	grandmothers	similar

08 윗글의 Chibanda 박사의 말과 일치하도록 빈칸 (A), (B), (C)에 들어갈 말로 가장 적절한 것은?

>   (A)   the sessions with the grandmothers are over, patients are encouraged to join a community support group of former participants   (B)   share similar struggles and the same community backgrounds,   (C)   them to easily connect and support one another.

	(A)	(B)	(C)
①	Since	which	allowing
②	When	who	enabling
③	If	which	helping
④	As	who	allowing
⑤	While	which	enabling

[09~10] 다음 글을 읽고, 물음에 답하시오.

Host That sounds ① <u>like</u> an excellent way to sustain support and foster a sense of community. The program has been extremely successful, ② <u>hasn't it</u>?

Dr. Chibanda Absolutely. In 2022, we provided in-person counseling to approximately 90,000 patients in Zimbabwe. Currently, Friendship Benches ③ <u>are located</u> in over twenty different regions throughout the country. Our goal is for everyone to have a Friendship Bench within walking distance, and we are diligently working towards that. We've also begun ④ <u>expanding</u> the program and now offer online counseling through an app, which has allowed us ⑤ <u>reach</u> even more individuals.

09 윗글의 밑줄 친 부분 중, 어법상 틀린 것은?

①   ②   ③   ④   ⑤

10 윗글의 내용과 일치하지 <u>않는</u> 것은?

① 2022년에 약 90,000명의 환자에게 대면 상담을 제공했다.
② 우정 벤치는 짐바브웨의 20개 미만의 지역에 위치해 있다.
③ 모든 사람이 도보 거리 내에서 우정 벤치 프로그램을 이용할 수 있게 하는 것이 목표이다.
④ 우정 벤치 프로그램은 성공적이었다.
⑤ 프로그램을 확장하여 앱을 통해 온라인 상담 서비스를 제공하고 있다.

[11~12] 다음 글을 읽고, 물음에 답하시오.

Host That's truly remarkable! Thank you for your time, Dr. Chibanda. Now, let's hear from one of the grandmothers who volunteers for the program. Could you _____ and share how you became involved with the Friendship Bench program?

Grandma Moyo Hello, my name is Judith Moyo, but everyone calls me Grandma Moyo. I'm 76 years old, and I've been volunteering for the Friendship Bench program for about eight years. I joined the program because many people in my community face mental health challenges, and I wanted to take action. I felt that I could help heal their wounded hearts by providing support.

11 윗글의 빈칸에 들어갈 말로 가장 적절한 것은?

① tell us your story
② explain your role
③ describe your experience
④ introduce yourself
⑤ describe your background

12 윗글에서 Moyo 할머니가 한 말의 내용과 일치하는 것은?

① Grandma Moyo joined the Friendship Bench program to address mental health issues in her community.
② The Friendship Bench program only accepts volunteers who are over 70 years old.
③ Grandma Moyo has been a professional therapist for eight years.
④ The Friendship Bench program pays its volunteers a high salary.
⑤ Grandma Moyo joined the program to learn new skills for her personal development.

Host That's very kind of you. Could you share your experience as a grandmother involved in the Friendship Bench program?

Grandma Moyo It's been ⓐ <u>amazing</u>. There's no shame in seeking help for mental health issues. (①) I've ⓑ <u>witnessed</u> the positive impact it can have on people's lives. (②) One of my patients, a nineteen-year-old girl, faced a tough time after her mother ⓒ <u>was born</u>. (③) Now, her life is back on track, and she has even ⓓ <u>launched</u> her own business! (④) Stories like this fill me with pride for being a part of the program. (⑤) It is such a rewarding experience to help people make positive changes in their lives.

Host Thank you for sharing your _____ with us today, Grandma Moyo. It's truly inspiring to see the ⓔ <u>impact</u> that the Friendship Bench program has had. And it's all thanks to the hard work of people like you and Dr. Chibanda.

13 윗글의 흐름으로 보아, 주어진 문장이 들어가기에 가장 적절한 곳은?

I counseled her and helped her start her journey to recovery

①   ②   ③   ④   ⑤

14 윗글의 밑줄 친 부분 중 낱말의 쓰임이 적절하지 <u>않은</u> 것은?

① ⓐ   ② ⓑ   ③ ⓒ   ④ ⓓ   ⑤ ⓔ

15 윗글의 빈칸에 들어갈 말로 가장 적절한 것은?

① feelings   ② thoughts
③ opinions   ④ experiences
⑤ knowledge

01 괄호 안의 단어를 이용하여 다음 질문에 대한 답을 조건에 맞게 완성하시오.

> 조건
> • 주어진 단어들을 모두 사용할 것
> • 필요시 문맥과 어법에 맞게 어휘를 변형할 것

> Q: What was your main goal in developing the Friendship Bench program?
> A: I _____
>   (find, a way, need, bring)
> psychiatry into the community.

02 다음 영어 뜻풀이에 해당하는 단어를 윗글에서 찾아 쓰시오.

(1) feeling extremely sad or hopeless

→ _____

(2) the total number of people living in a specific area or region

→ _____

03 윗글의 밑줄 친 우리말과 같은 뜻이 되도록 조건에 맞게 문장을 완성하시오.

> 조건
> • 「It is ~ to부정사 ...」 구문을 사용할 것
> • receive, pay for, transportation, medical treatment 를 사용할 것

→ In fact, _____ for many people in Zimbabwe

_____ .

[02~04] 다음 글을 읽고, 물음에 답하시오.

Dr. Chibanda The idea came from an experience I had as a psychiatrist. One of my patients had become severely depressed. However, she couldn't get help because she was unable to afford the bus ride to the hospital. This shocked me, as I had never considered such a problem before. In fact, 짐바브웨에서는 많은 사람들이 교통비를 내고 의학적 치료를 받는 것이 어렵습니다. Furthermore, there has been a lack of psychiatrists in the country for many years. When the Friendship Bench program started in 2006, there were only eleven psychiatrists serving Zimbabwe's population of over twelve million people. I needed to find a way to bring psychiatry into the community.

04 윗글의 내용을 한 문장으로 요약할 때, 빈칸에 들어갈 말을 찾아 쓰시오.

> Dr. Chibanda started the Friendship Bench program after witnessing a patient unable to seek _____ for severe depression due to _____ costs and the _____ of psychiatrists in Zimbabwe.

05 다음 글의 밑줄 친 문장에서 **틀린** 부분을 바르게 고쳐 문장을 다시 쓰시오.

> **Host** Oh, so that was the beginning of it. <u>Could you explain to us how does the Friendship Bench program work?</u>
> **Dr. Chibanda** Certainly. The program was created as a way to provide accessible mental health services. It offers talk therapy sessions to people dealing with issues such as depression or anxiety. The sessions are free and are provided by respected elderly women from the community. These women, called "grandmothers," volunteer to sit with patients at the benches, listen to their stories, and provide them with emotional support.

→ _____

_____

06 다음 빈칸에 들어갈 말을 〈보기〉에서 골라 알맞은 형태로 바꿔 쓰시오.

> **Dr. Chibanda** That's correct. In 2022, we provided face-to-face counseling to about 90,000 patients in Zimbabwe. Now, Friendship Benches are available in more than twenty different regions around the country. Our vision is for everyone to have a Friendship Bench within walking distance, and we are working hard to make it ___(A)___ . We've also started ___(B)___ the program, and we now offer online counseling through an app. This has helped us ___(C)___ even more people.

> 〈보기〉 expand   reach   happen

(A) _____
(B) _____
(C) _____

[07~08] 다음 글을 읽고, 물음에 답하시오.

> **Host** ⓐ <u>What</u> a wonderful idea! How did these amazing grandmothers become a part of your program?
> **Dr. Chibanda** Grandmothers ⓑ <u>chose</u> for our program because they are deeply connected to the community. Moreover, they have all the qualities of a counselor, such as excellent listening skills, empathy, and the ability ⓒ <u>to engage</u> in meaningful discussions. They are also very reliable, which is important for our efforts ⓓ <u>to support</u> mental health. At the beginning, we started with only fourteen volunteer grandmothers. But today, there are thousands of grandmothers ⓔ <u>which</u> have been trained to provide Friendship Bench therapy in Zimbabwe.

07 윗글의 밑줄 친 ⓐ~ⓔ 중, 어법상 틀린 것을 두 개 찾아 바르게 고쳐 쓰고 수정해야 하는 이유를 쓰시오.

번호	기호	고친 것	이유
(1)			
(2)			

08 주어진 영어 뜻풀이에 해당하는 단어를 윗글에서 찾아 쓰시오.

> treatment aimed at relieving or healing a medical or mental health problem

→ _____

[09~10] 다음 글을 읽고, 물음에 답하시오.

Host That's really amazing! Thank you for your time, Dr. Chibanda. 이제 그 프로그램에서 자원봉사를 하시는 할머니들 중 한 분의 이야기를 들어보겠습니다. Can you introduce yourself and tell us how you got involved with the Friendship Bench program?

Grandma Moyo Hello, my name is Judith Moyo, but people call me Grandma Moyo. I'm 76 years old, and I have been volunteering for the Friendship Bench program for about eight years. I joined the program because many people in my community struggle with mental health problems, and I wanted to do something about it. I knew that I could help heal their wounded hearts by supporting them.

09 윗글의 밑줄 친 우리말과 같은 뜻이 되도록 빈칸에 알맞은 말을 쓰시오.

Now let's hear from one of the grandmothers _____ _____ _____ the program.

10 윗글의 내용과 일치하도록 Moyo 할머니에 관한 정보를 빈칸에 쓰시오.

(1) 이름: _____

(2) 나이: _____

(3) 봉사기간: _____

(4) 가입 이유: _____

_____

[11~12] 다음 글을 읽고, 물음에 답하시오.

Host That's very kind of you. Can you tell us about your experience as a grandmother for the Friendship Bench program?

Grandma Moyo It's been wonderful. 정신 건강 문제에 대한 도움을 구하는 것은 부끄러워할 일이 아닙니다. I've seen how it can make a difference in people's lives. One patient of mine, a nineteen-year old girl, was going through a difficult time after her mom passed away. I counseled her and helped her begin her recovery journey. Now her life is back on track, and she has even started her own business! Cases ____(A)____ this make me so proud to be part of the program. It is such a rewarding experience to help people make positive changes in their lives.

Host Thanks for sharing your experiences with us today, Grandma Moyo. It's truly inspiring to see the influence that the Friendship Bench program has had. And it's all thanks to the hard work of people ____(B)____ you and Dr. Chibanda.

11 윗글의 밑줄 친 우리말과 같은 뜻이 되도록 다음 빈칸에 알맞은 단어를 쓰시오.

→ _____ help for mental health problems _____ nothing to be ashamed _____.

12 윗글의 빈칸 (A), (B)에 공통으로 들어갈 한 단어를 쓰시오.

_____

01 다음 영어 뜻풀이에 해당하는 표현이 쓰인 문장은?

> to successfully deal with or get past a problem or difficulty

① She assured me that it wasn't too hard.
② I decided to try to overcome this discomfort.
③ There was nothing to distract me!
④ We gained different perspectives on life.
⑤ She was unable to afford the bus ride to the hospital.

02 다음 담화의 주제로 가장 적절한 것은?

W Thanks to streaming platforms, you can watch your favorite shows anytime. You can even watch a whole series without stopping! This is called binge-watching. It sounds fun, but binge-watching isn't good for you. It can cause sleep problems and lead to reduced physical activity. So, how can you prevent binge-watching from affecting your health? First, decide how long you are going to watch a show before you start, and set an alarm. When the alarm goes off, it's important to stop watching even if you are in the middle of the show. Second, watch shows only while doing a productive activity, such as exercising or organizing your desk. When you finish the activity, turn off the show. I hope these tips help you enjoy your favorite shows in a healthy way.

① 인기 있는 TV 시리즈 추천
② 운동하면서 TV 시청하는 방법
③ 스트리밍 플랫폼의 장단점 비교
④ 스트리밍 서비스 구독료 절약 팁
⑤ 과도한 연속 시청의 부작용과 예방법

[03~04] 다음 글을 읽고, 물음에 답하시오.

"①To grow into a better version of ourselves, we should not stay as we are." That was ②the first thing our teacher said to us on the first day of school. 그녀는 우리가 우리 자신을 우리의 안전지대 밖으로 밀어내고 우리 자신에 관해 더 많이 배움으로써 학기를 시작하기를 바라셨다. To help us do so, she gave us an assignment to challenge ③ourselves in three different ways. The three challenges could involve hobbies, exercise, our studies, or even our relationships. The important part was ④try something new for each one. She told us that we should share our experiences with our classmates ⑤when we finished the challenges.

03 윗글의 밑줄 친 부분 중, 어법상 틀린 것은?

①　　　　②　　　　③　　　　④　　　　⑤

04 윗글의 밑줄 친 우리말과 같은 뜻이 되도록 보기 의 단어를 배열하여 문장을 완성하시오. (필요시 어형을 변화시킬 것)

> 보기 by / more / ourselves / to / about ourselves / the semester / our comfort zones / and / learn / start / push / out of

→ She wanted us _____
_____
_____.

[05~06] 다음 글을 읽고, 물음에 답하시오.

These days, I tend to watch movies on streaming services. However, if I go to the theater, I usually watch an action or science fiction movie with my friends or family. Those are the kinds of movies they enjoy.

(A) Go / Going to the theater alone was something I had never done before. So, for the first challenge, I decided to give it a try. It was nice to choose the movie and the seat on my own. I didn't have to worry about anyone else's preferences. I saw the experience as a good opportunity to watch something different, so I chose a historical drama (B) that / what I had been curious about.

At first, it felt a bit _____ to sit in the theater by myself. But once the movie started, I became completely absorbed in the story. It was so satisfying just to focus on the movie itself. There was nothing to distract me! This experience made me (C) realize / to realize that I sometimes enjoy doing things alone. After the movie, I promised myself that I would try to make my own choices more often and enjoy more activities by myself in the future.

05 윗글의 빈칸에 들어갈 말로 가장 적절한 것은?

① exciting and thrilling
② awkward and lonely
③ familiar and boring
④ comfortable and relaxing
⑤ disappointing and frustrating

06 (A), (B), (C)의 각 네모 안에서 어법에 맞는 것으로 짝지어진 것은?

	(A)	(B)	(C)
①	Go	... that	... realize
②	Go	... what	... realize
③	Going	... that	... realize
④	Going	... that	... to realize
⑤	Going	... what	... to realize

[07~09] 다음 글을 읽고, 물음에 답하시오.

Ever since I was a child, I've always been afraid of water. So I have never enjoyed water activities or felt (A) comfort while doing them. For the second challenge, I decided to ⓐtry to overcome this discomfort. However, I wasn't sure what to do at first. One day, I ⓑcame across a video clip of my cousin surfing at an indoor pool on social media. It looked fun, and I liked the fact that it ⓒtook place in a shallow pool, not in the ocean. I messaged my cousin about it. She assured me that it wasn't too hard, so I ⓓsigned up for a beginner course.

At the beginning of the lesson, it was hard just to stand up on the board. After some help from the instructor, however, I learned how to balance properly and even ⓔmanaged to surf a few waves! It gave me such a rush of (B) excite. 물속에 있는 것은 내가 생각했었던 것만큼 나쁘지 않았다. While the experience didn't completely change my mind about water sports, it did help me discover my sense of adventure.

07 윗글의 밑줄 친 ⓐ~ⓔ의 뜻이 잘못 연결된 것은?

① ⓐ: ~하려고 노력하다
② ⓑ: 지나쳤다
③ ⓒ: 행해졌다
④ ⓓ: 등록했다
⑤ ⓔ: 간신히 해냈다

08 윗글의 밑줄 친 (A), (B)를 알맞은 형태로 바꿔 쓰시오.

(A) comfort → _____
(B) excite → _____

09 윗글의 밑줄 친 우리말과 같은 뜻이 되도록 조건에 맞게 쓰시오.

조건
• 「as+원급+as」 구문을 이용할 것
• be, water, bad를 이용할 것
• 시제에 주의하고 필요시 어휘를 변형시킬 것

→ _____ I had thought.

[10~12] 다음 글을 읽고, 물음에 답하시오.

Of all the challenges I chose for myself, the third one made me the most nervous: changing my hairstyle. For many years, I had kept the same hairstyle because I had been worried about my forehead. I had always thought it was large, and I didn't want to draw ⓐattention to it. Since I was feeling confident after the first two challenges, I went to a hair salon and talked to the stylist. He listened to my concerns and helped me find a shorter hairstyle that suited me.

The next day at school, my classmates were a bit surprised. But overall, the reactions were ⓑpositive. I realized that trying a different look wasn't as difficult as I thought it would be. In fact, it made me feel more confident about myself. I didn't expect that stepping out of my ⓒdiscomfort zone would have such a positive effect on how I felt about myself.

I learned a lot about myself through this ⓓassignment, and I found out that my classmates did, too. One of them tried new foods from different countries, while another joined a creative writing club. Through these experiences, we all realized how important it is to push ourselves to try new things. We gained different perspectives on life and had a lot of fun, too! My classmates and I even talked about setting more ⓔchallenges for ourselves. There are always more things that we can discover about ourselves, and it's exciting to keep learning and growing. We never know what we're capable of until we try!

10 윗글을 쓴 필자의 심경으로 가장 적절한 것은?

① angry
② frustrated
③ content
④ indifferent
⑤ disappointed

11 윗글의 밑줄 친 부분 중, 문맥상 낱말의 쓰임이 적절하지 않은 것은?

① ⓐ ② ⓑ ③ ⓒ ④ ⓓ ⑤ ⓔ

12 윗글의 내용과 일치하지 않는 것은?

① 세 번째 도전으로 헤어스타일을 바꾸기로 했다.
② 오랫동안 같은 헤어스타일을 유지해왔다.
③ 급우들은 새로운 헤어스타일에 부정적인 반응을 보였다.
④ 이 경험을 통해 자신에 대해 더 자신감을 갖게 되었다.
⑤ 급우들도 각자 새로운 도전을 시도했다.

[13~14] 다음 글을 읽고, 물음에 답하시오.

Host On today's show, we are going to learn about special park benches in Zimbabwe called Friendship Benches. We have two special guests. First, please welcome the founder of the Friendship Bench program, Dr. Dixon Chibanda. Can you tell us what inspired you to come up with the program?

Dr. Chibanda Sure. The idea came from an experience I had as a psychiatrist. One of my patients had become severely depressed. ___(A)___, she couldn't get help because she was unable to afford the bus ride to the hospital. This shocked me, as I had never considered such a problem before. ___(B)___, it is difficult for many people in Zimbabwe to pay for transportation and receive medical treatment. ___(C)___, there has been a lack of psychiatrists in the country for many years. When the Friendship Bench program started in 2006, there were only eleven psychiatrists serving Zimbabwe's population of over twelve million people. I needed to find a way to bring psychiatry into the community.

13 윗글의 빈칸 (A), (B), (C)에 알맞은 접속사가 바르게 짝지어진 것은?

	(A)	(B)	(C)
①	Therefore	… Indeed	… Besides
②	However	… In fact	… Furthermore
③	Although	… Actually	… In addition
④	Unfortunately	… Moreover	… However
⑤	Nevertheless	… Additionally	… Consequently

14 윗글의 내용을 한 문장으로 요약할 때, 빈칸에 알맞은 말을 보기 에서 골라 쓰시오.

보기 transportation depression mental shortage

Dr. Chibanda started the Friendship Bench program after seeing a patient with severe _____ who couldn't get help because she couldn't afford _____. He also recognized the _____ of psychiatrists in Zimbabwe, which motivated him to create a more accessible _____ health support system.

15 다음 중 어법상 틀린 문장을 2개 골라 고쳐 쓰고 틀린 이유를 쓰시오.

ⓐ Painting old public walls will make the community brighter.

ⓑ To grow into a better version of ourselves, we should not stay as we are.

ⓒ *Wonder* will make you wanting to recommend it to your friends!

ⓓ This is the best way to keep you safe during the flight.

ⓔ It was hard for us thanking you personally at the event.

(1) _____ : _____ → _____
틀린 이유: _____

(2) _____ : _____ → _____
틀린 이유: _____

[16~17] 다음 글을 읽고, 물음에 답하시오.

Host Oh, so that was the beginning of it. Could you explain to us how the Friendship Bench program works?

Dr. Chibanda Certainly. The program was created as a way to provide accessible mental health services. (①) It offers talk therapy sessions to people dealing with issues such as depression or anxiety. The sessions are free and are provided by respected elderly women from the community. (②) These women, called "grandmothers," volunteer to sit with patients at the benches, listen to their stories, and provide them with emotional support. (③)

Host What a wonderful idea! How did these amazing grandmothers become a part of your program?

Dr. Chibanda Grandmothers were chosen for our program because they are deeply connected to the community. Moreover, they have all the qualities of a counselor, such as excellent listening skills, empathy, and the ability to engage in meaningful discussions. (④) At the beginning, we started with only fourteen volunteer grandmothers. (⑤) But today, there are thousands of grandmothers who have been trained to provide Friendship Bench therapy in Zimbabwe.

16 윗글의 흐름으로 보아, 주어진 문장이 들어가기에 가장 적절한 곳은?

They are also very reliable, which is important for our efforts to support mental health.

①   ②   ③   ④   ⑤

17 윗글의 밑줄 친 idea가 나타내는 것을 우리말로 쓰시오.

_____

_____

Host That's interesting! What happens after patients complete their sessions with the grandmothers?

Dr. Chibanda When the sessions with the grandmothers are over, patients are encouraged to join a _____ support group made up of former patients of the program. The members of these groups can easily relate to and support one another. This is because most of them come from the same _____ and have experienced similar struggles.

Host That sounds like a great way to continue the support and build a sense of _____. And the program has been incredibly successful, right?

Dr. Chibanda

(A) Now, Friendship Benches are available in more than twenty different regions around the country. Our vision is for everyone to have a Friendship Bench within walking distance, and we are working hard to make it happen.

(B) That's correct. In 2022, we provided face-to-face counseling to about 90,000 patients in Zimbabwe.

(C) We've also started expanding the program, and we now offer online counseling through an app. This has helped us reach even more people.

18 윗글의 빈칸에 공통으로 들어갈 말로 알맞은 것은?

① peer
② community
③ belonging
④ therapy
⑤ grandmothers

19 자연스러운 순서가 되도록 바르게 배열한 것은?

① (A) – (B) – (C)
② (A) – (C) – (B)
③ (B) – (A) – (C)
④ (B) – (C) – (A)
⑤ (C) – (A) – (B)

20 윗글의 내용과 일치하는 것은?

① 우정 벤치 프로그램은 2022년에 약 90,000명의 환자에게 대면 상담을 제공했다.
② 프로그램 참가자들은 세션 완료 후 전문 상담사와의 추가 상담을 받는다.
③ 우정 벤치는 현재 짐바브웨 전역의 10개 지역에서 이용 가능하다.
④ 온라인 상담 앱의 도입으로 프로그램의 접근성이 감소했다.
⑤ 지원 그룹의 구성원들은 대부분 서로 다른 배경과 경험을 가지고 있다.

21 다음 대화의 빈칸에 들어갈 말로 알맞은 것은?

G Marco, your presentation is next week, isn't it?

B Yes, but I'm nervous. I'm not good at speaking in front of others.

G I understand. But if you want to overcome your fears, you must get out of your comfort zone.

B That makes sense. What do you suggest?

G Start with something small. How about asking a question in class today?

B That doesn't sound too difficult. Do you think it will help?

G Sure! After you take the first step, the next step will be easier.

B _____

① Okay. I'll give it a try.
② I don't think I can do it.
③ I'm not sure if that will work for me.
④ I'd rather just skip the presentation.
⑤ That sounds like a waste of time.

[22~23] 다음 글을 읽고, 물음에 답하시오.

Host That's really amazing! Thank you for your time, Dr. Chibanda. Now let's hear from one of the grandmothers (A) who / which volunteers for the program. _____

_____

Grandma Moyo Hello, my name is Judith Moyo, but people call me Grandma Moyo. I'm 76 years old, and I have been (B) volunteered / volunteering for the Friendship Bench program for about eight years. I joined the program because many people in my community struggle with mental health problems, and I wanted (C) doing / to do something about it. I knew that I could help heal their wounded hearts by supporting them.

22 (A), (B), (C)의 각 네모 안에서 어법에 맞는 것으로 짝지어진 것은?

	(A)		(B)		(C)
①	who	...	volunteered	...	to do
②	who	...	volunteering	...	to do
③	who	...	volunteering	...	doing
④	which	...	volunteered	...	doing
⑤	which	...	volunteering	...	to do

23 다음 두 문장을 한 문장으로 만들어 윗글의 빈칸에 들어갈 말을 쓰시오.

Can you introduce yourself and tell us?
+
How did you get involved with the Friendship Bench program?

→ _____

[24~25] 다음 글을 읽고, 물음에 답하시오.

Host That's very kind of you. Can you tell us about your experience as a grandmother for the Friendship Bench program?
Grandma Moyo It's been wonderful. (A) Seeking help for mental health problems are nothing to be ashamed of. I've seen how it can make a difference in people's lives. One patient of mine, a nineteen-year old girl, was going through a difficult time after her mom passed away. I counseled her and helped her begin her recovery journey. Now her life is back on track, and she has even started her own business! Cases like this make me so proud to be part of the program. (B) 사람들이 그들의 삶에 긍정적인 변화를 가져오도록 돕는 것은 정말 보람된 경험입니다.
Host Thanks for sharing your experiences with us today, Grandma Moyo. It's truly inspiring to see the influence that the Friendship Bench program has had. And it's all thanks to the hard work of people like you and Dr. Chibanda.

24 윗글의 밑줄 친 문장 (A)에서 틀린 부분을 찾아 바르게 고쳐 쓰시오.

_____ → _____

25 윗글의 밑줄 친 (B)의 우리말과 같은 뜻이 되도록 조건에 맞게 문장을 완성하시오.

조건
• 가주어 it과 진주어 to부정사를 사용할 것
• such, rewarding, experience, positive를 반드시 포함할 것
• 빈칸에 총 12단어를 넣어 문장을 완성할 것

→ _____

_____ in their lives.

03

Nature & Us

Functions

▶ 동의나 이의 여부 묻기
Don't you agree?

▶ 확실성 정도 표현하기
I'm sure that we can make the world a better place.

Grammar

▶ **Without** you and all your friends, we humans **wouldn't be** able to get enough oxygen.

▶ I noticed **that** a family of birds has made a nest in your branches.

교과서 어휘

Words

☐ appreciate	동 진가를 알아보다; 고마워하다
☐ oxygen	명 산소
☐ produce	동 생산하다; 만들어 내다
☐ nest	명 (새의) 둥지
☐ branch	명 나뭇가지
☐ environment	명 환경
☐ urban	형 도시의 (↔ rural 시골의)
☐ strategy	명 전략
☐ millennium	명 천 년
☐ drought	명 가뭄
☐ decline	동 거절하다; (힘이) 쇠하다
☐ furthermore	부 게다가
☐ decrease	동 감소하다 (↔ increase 증가하다)
☐ amount	명 총액, 양
☐ threat	명 협박, 위협
☐ resident	명 거주자, 주민 (residence 명 거주)
☐ consumption	명 소비[소모](량) (consume 동 소모하다)
☐ greenhouse gas	온실 가스
☐ emission	명 배출; 배출물, 배기가스
☐ loss	명 손실 (lose 동 잃어버리다, 잃다)
☐ ambitious	형 야심 있는; 야심적인 (ambition 명 야망)
☐ plant	동 심다 명 식물
☐ involve	동 포함하다
☐ interactive	형 상호적인; 대화형의

☐ symbol	명 상징(물); 부호, 기호
☐ indicate	동 나타내다, 보여 주다 (indication 명 암시)
☐ species	명 종(種)
☐ function	명 기능
☐ specific	형 특정한
☐ purpose	명 목적
☐ council	명 의회
☐ damage	동 손상시키다 명 손상
☐ unexpected	형 예기치 않은, 예상 밖의
☐ phenomenon	명 현상
☐ spread	동 퍼지다 (spread-spread)
☐ separate	동 분리하다, 나누다
☐ planet	명 행성
☐ popularity	명 인기 (popular 형 인기 있는)
☐ sustainable	형 지속 가능한
☐ collective	형 집단의, 단체의
☐ generation	명 세대
☐ locally	부 지역적으로 (local 형 지역적인)
☐ environmentally friendly	형 환경친화적인
☐ measure	동 측정하다, 재다 (measurement 명 측정)
☐ monitor	동 추적 관찰하다
☐ meanwhile	부 한편
☐ remain	동 계속 ~이다
☐ predict	동 예측하다 (prediction 명 예측)

Phrases

☐ in front of	~의 앞에
☐ take a deep breath	깊은 숨을 쉬다
☐ by the way	그런데
☐ provide A with B	A에게 B를 제공하다
☐ believe it or not	믿기 힘들겠지만
☐ by the time	~할 때까지
☐ as a result	그 결과

☐ lead to	~로 이어지다
☐ set a goal	목표를 설정하다
☐ step out of	~에서 벗어나다
☐ have little hope of	~할 희망이 거의 없다
☐ on track	(원하는 결과를 향해) 착착 나아가는[진행 중인]
☐ interact with	~와 상호작용하다

Word Formation

danger 위험		dangerous 위험한
humor 유머		humorous 재미있는, 유머러스한
courage 용기	**+** **-ous** **→**	courageous 용감한
nerve 긴장, 불안		nervous 불안해[초조해]하는

expected 예상되는		unexpected 예기치 않은, 예상 밖의
usual 흔히 하는[있는]		unusual 특이한, 흔치 않은
un- **+**		fair 타당한, 공평한 **→** unfair 부당한, 불공평한
believable 그럴듯한		unbelievable 믿을 수 없는

Collocations

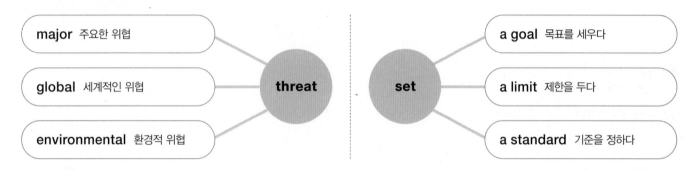

major 주요한 위협		
global 세계적인 위협	**threat**	
environmental 환경적 위협		

		a goal 목표를 세우다
	set	**a limit** 제한을 두다
		a standard 기준을 정하다

English-English Dictionary

□ **appreciate** 고마워하다 — to be grateful for something

□ **produce** 생산하다; 만들어 내다 — to create, make, or manufacture something

□ **nest** (새의) 둥지 — a structure built by birds to lay eggs and raise their young

□ **urban** 도시의 — having characteristics of a town or city

□ **drought** 가뭄 — a long period of time with very little or no rain

□ **threat** 협박, 위협 — a statement or situation that suggests harm or danger

□ **resident** 거주자, 주민 — a person who lives in a particular place

□ **consumption** 소비[소모](량) — the act of using up a resource, or the amount used

□ **emission** 배출 — the act of releasing gas, heat, light, etc., into the air

□ **ambitious** 야심 있는 — having a strong desire to achieve success or a specific goal

□ **interactive** 상호적인 — involving communication or action between two or more things or people

□ **phenomenon** 현상 — an observable event or fact, especially one that is unusual or remarkable

□ **sustainable** 지속 가능한 — able to be maintained over time without harming the environment or depleting resources

교과서 어휘 익히기

✤ 다음 영어는 우리말로, 우리말은 영어로 쓰시오.

01 branch ⑲ _____

02 urban ⑱ _____

03 strategy ⑲ _____

04 threat ⑲ _____

05 appreciate ⑤ _____

06 emission ⑲ _____

07 involve ⑤ _____

08 interactive ⑱ _____

09 purpose ⑲ _____

10 phenomenon ⑲ _____

11 unexpected ⑱ _____

12 function ⑲ _____

13 popularity ⑲ _____

14 furthermore ⑯ _____

15 amount ⑲ _____

16 council ⑲ _____

17 spread ⑲ _____

18 locally ⑯ _____

19 monitor ⑤ _____

20 provide A with B _____

21 as a result _____

22 step out of _____

23 interact with _____

24 have little hope of _____

25 ⑲ (새의) 둥지 _____

26 ⑤ 생산하다; 만들어 내다 _____

27 ⑲ 환경 _____

28 ⑱ 가뭄 _____

29 ⑲ 소비[소모](량) _____

30 ⑤ 거절하다; (힘이) 쇠하다 _____

31 ⑱ 야심 있는; 야심적인 _____

32 ⑲ 종(種) _____

33 ⑤ 나타내다, 보여 주다 _____

34 ⑱ 특정한 _____

35 ⑤ 손상시키다 _____

36 ⑤ 분리하다, 나누다 _____

37 ⑱ 지속 가능한 _____

38 ⑱ 집단의, 단체의 _____

39 ⑲ 천 년 _____

40 ⑲ 산소 _____

41 ⑤ 예측하다 _____

42 ⑤ 측정하다, 재다 _____

43 ⑯ 한편 _____

44 온실 가스 _____

45 깊은 숨을 쉬다 _____

46 믿기 힘들겠지만 _____

47 ~로 이어지다 _____

48 목표를 설정하다 _____

A 다음 괄호 안의 단어를 알맞은 형태로 고쳐 쓰시오.

01 My sister was _____ enough to climb the mountain. (courage)

02 He was _____ about speaking in front of the crowd. (nerve)

03 The comedian told a _____ story that made everyone laugh. (humor)

04 Traveling can sometimes come with _____ surprises. (expected)

05 It was _____ to see snow in summer, so everyone was surprised. (usual)

B 다음 우리말과 같은 뜻이 되도록 빈칸에 알맞은 말을 보기에서 골라 쓰시오.

> 보기   limit   set   put   threat

01 The loss of canopy cover is a major _____ to urban environments because it raises temperatures.

임관 피복도의 줄어듦은 기온을 상승시키기 때문에 도시 환경에 주요한 위협이다.

02 It _____ the ambitious goal of planting more than 3,000 trees every year for the next twenty years.

그것은 다음 20년 동안 매년 3,000그루가 넘는 나무들을 심는 야심찬 목표를 설정했다.

C 다음 밑줄 친 부분의 영어 뜻풀이로 알맞은 것을 골라 기호를 쓰시오.

> ⓐ the act of using up a resource, or the amount used
> ⓑ involving communication or action between two or more things or people
> ⓒ able to be maintained over time without harming the environment or depleting resources

01 We are all connected to nature, and we are all involved in building a more sustainable world.
(   )

02 This speeds up climate change by increasing energy consumption and greenhouse gas emissions. (   )

03 This interactive map shows the location of every single tree in the city's parks and along its roads. (   )

교과서 핵심 대화문

Function 1 동의나 이의 여부 묻기

B Look at the bees on the flowers. Even the smallest things help to
~을 보다   심지어 ~조차도   동의 여부를 묻는 표현

keep nature balanced. **Don't you agree?**
keep+목적어+과거분사: 목적어를 ~한 상태로 유지하다

동의할 때 쓰는 표현

G Absolutely. It is amazing [that some insects help plants produce fruit and
가주어   진주어   help+목적어+(to-)v

seeds].

B Right. By the way, I recently came across an interesting fact about insects.
그런데   come across: ~을 우연히 발견하다

G Oh, what is it?

B There are about one million insect species. But only 0.5 percent of them
대략   = one million insect species

cause damage to crops. Most insects can help crops grow better by feeding
help+목적어+(to-)v   전치사+동명사

on weeds and pests.

G Oh, I didn't know that!

≪ B: 꽃 위의 벌들을 봐. 가장 작은 것들
조차도 자연의 균형을 유지하는 데
도움을 주지. 동의하지 않니?

G: 물론이지. 일부 곤충들이 식물이 열
매와 씨앗을 만들도록 돕는다는 게
놀라워.

B: 맞아. 그런데, 나는 최근에 곤충에
대한 흥미로운 사실을 알게 됐어.

G: 오, 뭔데?

B: 약 백만 종의 곤충이 있어. 하지만
그중 오직 0.5퍼센트만이 농작물에
피해를 줘. 대부분의 곤충들은 잡초
와 해충을 먹어치움으로써 농작물
이 더 잘 자라도록 도울 수 있어.

G: 오, 그건 몰랐어!

Study Point ❦

Don't you agree?는 '동의하지 않니?'라는 뜻으로 상대방의 동의를 구하거나 확인할 때 사용하는 표현이다.

More Expressions ❦

동의 여부를 묻는 표현들

Isn't it true ~?(~가 사실이지 않니?), Don't you think ~?(~라고 생각하지 않니?), Are we on the same page?
(우리는 같은 생각을 하고 있는 거지?) 등이 있다.

Isn't it true that exercise is good for your health? 운동이 건강에 좋다는 게 사실이지 않나요?

Don't you think it's important to help the environment by recycling?

재활용을 통해 환경을 돕는 것이 중요하다고 생각하지 않나요?

We should arrive at the airport two hours before the flight. **Are we on the same page?**

우리는 비행기 출발 2시간 전에 공항에 도착해야 해. 우리 의견이 일치하니?

Check-up ❦

다음 대화의 빈칸에 들어갈 말로 가장 적절한 것은?

> **A** I think dumping waste carelessly really harms the environment. _____
> **B** Yes, I do. It leads to many kinds of problems, including soil pollution.

① How about you?   ② Don't you agree?   ③ What do you mean?

④ Is that so?   ⑤ Can you explain more?

Function 2 확실성 정도 표현하기

W Would you like to contribute to research and make a difference in the
~하고 싶니?　　　　　　　　　~에 기여하다　　　　　　　　변화를 만들다
world? Join Eco Trackers to participate in environmental citizen science
　　　　　　　　　　부사적 용법(목적) / participate in: ~에 참여하다
projects! Scientists need data, but it's hard for them to collect the
　　　(that)　　　　　　　　　　　가주어　　의미상의 주어　진주어
information they need alone. Our website allows people [from around the
　　　　　　　　allow A to B: A가 B 하도록 허락하다　　　　　전치사구
world] to collect data while they work together on research projects. Do
　　　　　　　　　접속사　　　함께 일하다　　~에 관한(= about)
you enjoy hiking? Help scientists study air quality by taking photographs
enjoy+동명사　　help+목적어+(to-)v　　　전치사+동명사 / take photographs: 사진을 찍다
from the tops of mountains. How about gardening? Try growing crops
　　　　　　　　　　　　How about+v-ing?: ~하는 게 어때? V1 (try+동명사: 한번 해보다)
in your community garden and check your area's soil quality. You can
　　　　　　　　　종속접속사　병렬 연결　V2
even help scientists while looking at the stars! Just record light pollution
　　　　　　　　　　(you are)
by reporting how visible stars are. Come and join Eco Trackers today!
전치사+동명사　　　간접의문문(reporting의 목적어 역할)
I'm sure that we can make the world a better place.
확실성을 말하는 표현(that은 명사절을 이끄는 종속접속사로 생략 가능)

W: 연구에 기여하고 세상에 변화를 만들고 싶으신가요? 환경 시민 과학 프로젝트에 참여하기 위해 Eco Trackers에 가입하세요! 과학자들은 데이터가 필요하지만, 혼자서 필요한 정보를 수집하기는 어렵습니다. 우리 웹사이트는 전 세계 사람들이 연구 프로젝트에 함께 참여하며 데이터를 수집할 수 있게 해줍니다. 등산을 즐기시나요? 산 정상에서 사진을 찍어 과학자들의 대기질 연구를 도와주세요. 정원 가꾸기는 어떠세요? 커뮤니티 정원에서 작물을 재배하고 지역의 토양 품질을 확인해보세요. 별을 보면서도 과학자들을 도울 수 있어요! 별이 얼마나 잘 보이는지 보고하여 빛 공해를 기록하세요. 오늘 Eco Trackers에 가입하세요! 우리가 함께 세상을 더 나은 곳으로 만들 수 있다고 확신합니다.

Study Point 🏅

I'm sure that ~은 '~라고 확신한다'라는 뜻으로 어떤 사실이나 상황에 대해 강한 확신을 가지고 있음을 나타낼 때 사용한다.
that 뒤에는 완전한 문장이 오며 that은 종종 생략되기도 한다.

More Expressions 🏅

확신을 말하는 표현

I'm certain[confident / convinced] that ~(나는 ~라고 확신한다)은 확신을 말할 때 사용하는 표현이다.

I'm certain that we'll find a solution if we work together. 우리가 함께 일한다면 해결책을 찾을 수 있을 거라고 확신한다.

I'm confident that our team will win the championship this year. 우리 팀이 올해 우승할 것이라고 확신한다.

I'm convinced that climate change is the biggest challenge of our generation.

기후 변화가 우리 세대의 가장 큰 도전이라고 확신한다.

Check-up 🏅

다음 대화의 빈칸에 들어갈 말로 적절하지 <u>않은</u> 것은?

A That sounds really interesting!
B I agree! I'm _____ that the project will help scientists better understand and protect birds.

① sure　　　　　　　② confident　　　　　　③ certain
④ doubtful　　　　　⑤ convinced

교과서 기타 대화문

TOPIC 1 **C. Listen and Interact**

W Everything in nature ❶ is connected, and we're a part of nature. Therefore, our actions can ❷ have a direct influence on the environment around us. Then how can we help protect our planet? There are many simple ways ❸ to help, ❹ such as recycling, planting trees, and using ❺ less electricity. ❻ Buying fewer products can also be a very effective way to help the environment. ❼ This is because a lot of water is needed ❽ to make products. ❾ Not only that, but greenhouse gases ❿ are released during their production. Furthermore, you will produce a lot of household waste ⓫ if you buy too many products. So the next time you shop, consider ⓬ whether you really need an item ⓭ before buying it. ⓮ After all, ⓯ protecting the planet starts with you!

❶ 수동태(be p.p.) ❷ have an influence on: ~에 영향을 미치다 ❸ ways를 수식하는 형용사적 용법의 to부정사 ❹ such as: ~와 같은 ❺ less: little의 비교급 ❻ 동명사 주어 ❼ This is because ~: 이것은 ~ 때문이다 ❽ 부사적 용법의 to부정사(목적) ❾ not only A but (also) B: A뿐만 아니라 B도 ❿ 수동태 ⓫ if: 조건 접속사 ⓬ whether: ~인지 ⓭ 전치사+동명사 ⓮ after all: 결국 ⓯ 동명사 주어+단수 동사

Q1 According to the passage, buying more products is an effective way to help the environment. (T / F)

TOPIC 4 **B. While You View**

M In 1979, a young Indian man ❶ named Jadav Payeng ❷ came across some sandy land near his hometown. It ❸ used to be full of trees and wildlife. However, because the forest had been destroyed and there had been a serious flood, the land was beginning to turn barren. Payeng knew ❹ that he had to do something.
So, he ❺ started planting one tree a day. At first, the land changed very slowly. However, he continued his efforts, and the trees soon started reproducing ❻ by themselves. Now, over 40 years later, the once sandy land ❼ has become a dense forest. In fact, it is almost ❽ twice as large as New York's Central Park. Payeng ❾ is now known as the "Forest Man of India." People call the forest "Molai," ❿ which is one of Jadav's nicknames.
Molai Forest is now home to various plant and animal species. The Forest Man ⓫ plans to continue planting trees.

❶ man을 수식하는 과거분사 ❷ come across: 우연히 발견하다 ❸ used to+동사원형: 과거에 ~였다 ❹ 명사절을 이끄는 접속사(생략 가능) ❺ start+동명사: ~하기를 시작하다 ❻ by themselves: 스스로, 자연적으로 ❼ 현재완료(결과) ❽ 배수사+as+원급+as: ···배만큼 ~한 ❾ be known as: ~로 알려지다 ❿ which: 계속적 용법의 관계대명사 ⓫ plan+to부정사: ~하기를 계획하다

Q2 According to the passage, Jadav Payeng is known as the "Forest Man of India." (T / F)

Wrap Up **A. Listen and Post**

M The weather has been really strange ❶ lately. ❷ Don't you agree?
W Yes, I do. ❸ I heard that Venice is ❹ suffering from floods ❺ because sea levels are rising.
M That's too bad. Is it ❻ due to climate change?
W Yes, it is. Everything on Earth is connected. So ❼ when polar ice melts, cities with low sea levels ❽ like Venice can get flooded.
M ❾ I'm worried that other cities ❿ that are near the coast might also have floods.
W ⓫ So am I. This is a global problem ⓬ that affects everyone. So we all ⓭ need to deal with it together.

❶ lately: 최근에 ❷ 동의 여부를 묻는 표현 ❸ I heard that ~: ~을 들었다 ❹ suffer from: ~으로 고생하다 ❺ because: 이유를 나타내는 부사절 접속사 ❻ due to: ~ 때문에 ❼ when: 부사절 접속사 ❽ like: ~같은(전치사) ❾ I'm worried that ~: ~이 걱정스럽다 ❿ 주격 관계대명사절 ⓫ 나도 그래. (상대방의 말에 대해 동의하는 표현) ⓬ 주격 관계대명사 ⓭ need+to부정사: ~할 필요가 있다 / deal with: ~을 다루다

Q3 The impacts of climate change require global cooperation to address effectively. (T / F)

교과서 핵심 대화문 익히기

01 다음 대화의 빈칸에 들어갈 말로 가장 적절한 것은?

> **B** Look at the bees on the flowers. Even the smallest things help to keep nature balanced.
>
> _____
>
> **G** Absolutely. It is amazing that some insects help plants produce fruit and seeds.
> **B** Right. By the way, I recently came across an interesting fact about insects.
> **G** Oh, what is it?
> **B** There are about one million insect species. But only 0.5 percent of them cause damage to crops. Most insects can help crops grow better by feeding on weeds and pests.
> **G** Oh, I didn't know that!

① Don't you agree?　　　　② What do you think?　　　　③ How about you?

④ Is that so?　　　　⑤ Can you explain more?

02 자연스러운 대화가 되도록 순서대로 바르게 배열한 것은?

> **M** The weather has been really strange lately. Don't you agree?
> **W** Yes, I do. I heard that Venice is suffering from floods because sea levels are rising.
> **M** That's too bad. Is it due to climate change?
> (A) I'm worried that other cities that are near the coast might also have floods.
> (B) So am I. This is a global problem that affects everyone. So we all need to deal with it together.
> (C) Yes, it is. Everything on Earth is connected. So when polar ice melts, cities with low sea levels like Venice can get flooded.

① (A) – (B) – (C)　　　　② (A) – (C) – (B)　　　　③ (B) – (A) – (C)

④ (C) – (A) – (B)　　　　⑤ (C) – (B) – (A)

03 다음 밑줄 친 우리말과 같은 뜻이 되도록 괄호 안의 말을 배열하여 문장을 쓰시오.

> **W** Would you like to contribute to research and make a difference in the world? Join Eco Trackers to participate in environmental citizen science projects! Scientists need data, but it's hard for them to collect the information they need alone. Our website allows people from around the world to collect data while they work together on research projects. Do you enjoy hiking? Help scientists study air quality by taking photographs from the tops of mountains. How about gardening? Try growing crops in your community garden and check your area's soil quality. You can even help scientists while looking at the stars! Just record light pollution by reporting how visible stars are. Come and join Eco Trackers today! 나는 우리가 세상을 더 나은 곳으로 만들 수 있다고 확신한다.

> I'm / can / that / we / a better place / make the world / sure

→ _____

교과서 핵심 문법

(POINT 1) Without 가정법

> 예제
> **Without** the internet, our lives **would be** very different today.
> ~이 없다면 　　　　　　　　　　　　　　 가정법 과거
> 인터넷이 없다면, 오늘날 우리의 삶은 매우 다를 것이다.
>
> 교과서
> **Without** you and all your friends, we humans **wouldn't be** able to get enough oxygen.
> ~이 없다면 　　　　　　　　　　　　　　　　　　　　 가정법 과거
> 너와 네 모든 친구들이 없다면, 우리 인간들은 충분한 산소를 얻을 수 없을 거야.
>
> ▶ 「Without ~+가정법 과거/과거완료」는 '(현재) ~이 없다면/(과거에) ~이 없었더라면, ~할 텐데[했을 텐데]'라는 의미이다.

Study Point ✿

1 Without ~+가정법 과거

현재 사실에 대한 가정이며 「If it were not for[But for] ~+가정법 과거」로 바꿔 쓸 수 있다.

Without your help, I **would miss** good opportunities.
당신의 도움이 없다면, 나는 좋은 기회들을 놓칠 것이다.

Without proper preparation, the project **would fail** next month.
적절한 준비가 없다면, 그 프로젝트는 다음 달에 실패할 것이다.

2 Without ~+가정법 과거완료

과거 사실에 대한 가정이며 「If it had not been for[But for] ~+가정법 과거완료」로 바꿔 쓸 수 있다.

Without the map, we **would have gotten** lost in the city.
지도가 없었다면, 우리는 도시에서 길을 잃었을 것이다.

Without her car, we **couldn't have arrived** in time.
그녀의 차가 없었다면, 우리는 제시간에 도착할 수 없었을 것이다.

Q 다음 네모 안에서 어법상 올바른 것을 고르시오.

1 Without your help, I would [fail / have failed] the exam.
당신의 도움이 없다면, 나는 시험에 떨어질 것이다.

2 Without practice, she wouldn't [win / have won] the competition.
연습이 없었다면, 그녀는 그 대회에서 우승하지 못했을 것이다.

3 [With / Without] your support, I couldn't prepare for the presentation.
당신의 지원이 없다면, 나는 발표 준비를 할 수 없을 것이다.

4 If it [were not / had not been] for the traffic, we would arrive at the airport earlier.
교통 체증만 없다면, 우리는 공항에 더 일찍 도착할 수 있을 것이다.

Check-up

01 다음 밑줄 친 단어를 If로 시작하여 다시 쓰시오.

(1) <u>Without</u> water, all living things on Earth would die.

→ _____ water, all living things on Earth would die.

(2) <u>Without</u> modern technology, life would be much harder.

→ _____ modern technology, life would be much harder.

(3) <u>Without</u> the GPS, we would have gotten lost on the trip.

→ _____ the GPS, we would have gotten lost on the trip.

02 다음 문장의 의미가 모두 같도록 빈칸에 알맞은 말을 쓰시오.

> Without the evidence, they would doubt the whole thing.
>
> (1) _____ _____ the evidence, they would doubt the whole thing.
>
> (2) _____ _____ _____ _____ _____ the evidence, they would doubt the whole thing.
>
> (증거가 없다면, 그들은 전체를 의심할 것이다.)

03 우리말과 같은 뜻이 되도록 괄호 안의 단어를 이용하여 빈칸에 알맞은 말을 쓰시오.

(1) Without his help, we _____ the job. (could, complete)
(그의 도움이 없다면, 우리는 그 일을 완성할 수 없을 것이다.)

(2) Without your advice, I _____ a big mistake. (would, make)
(너의 조언이 없었다면, 나는 큰 실수를 했을 것이다.)

04 다음 글을 읽고, 물음에 답하시오. (교과서 69쪽)

> ### 5th Fall Novel Fair / October 25-28
>
> <u>If it were not for</u> fun and inspiring stories, life would be rather unexciting. It's true that we can experience stories through TV and movies. However, nothing can replace the impact novels have on our minds and spirits. <u>소설이 없다면, 세상은 확실히 상상력이 덜한 곳일 것이다.</u> So, this month, remember to pick up a novel!

(1) 윗글의 밑줄 친 If it were not for를 한 단어로 고쳐 쓰시오. _____

(2) 윗글의 우리말과 같은 뜻이 되도록 빈칸에 알맞은 동사를 쓰시오.

→ Without novels, the world _____ certainly _____ a less imaginative place.

POINT 2) 명사절을 이끄는 접속사 that

예제	I hope [**that** you achieve all your goals this year]. <small>명사절을 이끄는 접속사</small> 나는 네가 올해 모든 목표를 이루기를 바란다.
교과서	I noticed [**that** a family of birds has made a nest in your branches]. <small>명사절을 이끄는 접속사</small> 나는 한 새 가족이 너의 가지에 둥지를 튼 것을 알아챘다.

▶ 명사절을 이끄는 접속사 that은 문장에서 주어, 목적어, 보어 역할을 하는 명사절을 이끈다.

Study Point 🍅

1 목적어 역할을 하는 접속사 that

that절이 목적어로 쓰이는 경우 접속사 that은 생략할 수 있다. that절은 주로 '말하다, 생각하다, 믿다' 등의 동사와 함께 사용된다.

I think **(that)** the movie was better than the book. 나는 영화가 책보다 더 좋았다고 생각한다.

Jessica said **(that)** she would be late for the meeting. Jessica는 회의에 늦을 거라고 말했다.

2 주어 역할을 하는 접속사 that

that절이 주어 역할을 하는 경우, 보통 주어 자리에 가주어 it을 쓰고 that절을 뒤로 보낸다.

It is clear **that** they are working hard. 그들이 열심히 일하고 있다는 것은 분명하다.

It is likely **that** the concert will be canceled. 콘서트가 취소될 가능성이 높다.

3 보어 역할을 하는 접속사 that

that절이 보어 역할을 하는 경우, 주어와 보어를 연결해주는 동사(주로 be동사)가 필요하다.

The problem is **that** we don't have enough time. 문제는 우리가 시간이 충분하지 않다는 것이다.

The truth is **that** he didn't know what to do. 진실은 그가 무엇을 해야 할지 몰랐다는 것이다.

Q 밑줄 친 that절의 역할을 골라 동그라미 하시오.

1 Lisa said that she would not be late for the movie. (주어 / 보어 / 목적어)

2 It is surprising that she won the gold medal at the Olympics. (주어 / 보어 / 목적어)

3 I think that you should take a break to recharge your energy. (주어 / 보어 / 목적어)

4 I noticed that the store is having a big sale this weekend. (주어 / 보어 / 목적어)

5 The fact is that many people struggle with mental health issues. (주어 / 보어 / 목적어)

Check-up

01 다음 중 밑줄 친 부분의 쓰임이 <u>다른</u> 것은?

> 보기 I hope <u>that</u> our team wins the final match.

① I hope <u>that</u> the weather will be nice tomorrow.
② It is important <u>that</u> we protect the environment.
③ I think <u>that</u> this book is more interesting than that one.
④ He showed me the photos <u>that</u> he took during his trip.
⑤ We believe <u>that</u> everyone should be treated with respect.

02 우리말과 같은 뜻이 되도록 괄호 안의 단어를 알맞게 배열하여 문장을 쓰시오.

(1) 나는 열심히 일하는 것이 성공으로 이어진다고 믿는다.
(believe / I / success / leads to / that / hard work)

→ _____

(2) 기후 변화가 우리 지구에 영향을 미치고 있다는 것이 분명하다.
(clear / that / is / climate change / it / our planet / is affecting)

→ _____

03 다음 중 밑줄 친 that절이 목적어 역할을 하는 문장을 모두 고르면?

> ⓐ I believe <u>that we can finish this project on time.</u>
> ⓑ It is clear <u>that he is not telling the truth.</u>
> ⓒ She mentioned <u>that she would join us later.</u>
> ⓓ The problem is <u>that he doesn't listen to others' opinions.</u>
> ⓔ It is important <u>that they have already made their decision.</u>

① ⓐ, ⓑ   ② ⓐ, ⓒ   ③ ⓑ, ⓒ   ④ ⓒ, ⓔ   ⑤ ⓓ, ⓔ

04 다음 글의 빈칸에 공통으로 알맞은 접속사를 쓰시오. (교과서 69쪽)

> Welcome to the Royal Hotel, and thank you for choosing us! We offer free Wi-Fi access, a business center, an indoor pool, and more. We believe _____ we have everything you need for an enjoyable stay. Our staff is ready to help you at any time, so please let us know what we can do. We hope _____ you have a great experience here!
> Sincerely,
> *Mark Richard,*
> General Manager

Letters to Nature
자연에게 보내는 편지

01
복합관계부사(~할 때는 언제든지, ~할 때마다)
Dear Tree, [Whenever I walk past you], your beautiful leaves bring a smile to my face.
복합관계부사절   bring A to B: A를 B에게 가져오다

나무에게, 내가 너를 지나쳐 갈 때마다, 너의 아름다운 이파리들이 내 얼굴에 미소를 띠게 해.

02
깊은 숨을 쉬다
[Whenever I stop in front of you and take a deep breath of fresh air], I appreciate the oxygen [that
복합관계부사절   V1   V2   목적격 관계대명사절
you produce].

내가 네 앞에 서서 신선한 공기를 깊이 들이마실 때마다 나는 네가 만들어 내는 산소에 감사해.

03
= If it were not for ~, But for ~
Without you and all your friends, we humans wouldn't be able to get enough oxygen.
가정법 과거 「Without ~, 주어+조동사의 과거형+동사원형 …」: ~이 없다면, …할 텐데

너와 네 모든 친구들이 없다면, 우리 인간들은 충분한 산소를 얻을 수 없을 거야.

04
명사절(noticed의 목적어)
By the way, I noticed [that a family of birds has made a nest in your branches].
                              S'   V'   O'

그건 그렇고, 나는 한 새 가족이 너의 가지에 둥지를 튼 것을 알아챘어.

05
의미상 주어(of+목적격)
It's so kind of you [to provide them with a home].
가주어   진주어   = provide a home for them

네가 그들에게 집을 제공해 주는 것은 정말 친절해.

06
명사절(hope의 목적어)
I hope [that more people realize {how important you and all the other trees are to the
              S'   V'   간접의문문(realize의 목적어): 「의문사 + 주어 + 동사」의 어순
environment}]. Have a nice day!

나는 더 많은 사람들이 너와 다른 모든 나무들이 환경에 얼마나 중요한지 깨닫기를 바라. 좋은 하루 보내!

07
믿기 힘들겠지만 (이것은 사실이다)
Believe it or not, trees [in Melbourne, Australia] receive emails like this all the time.
                    S   전치사구   V   전치사(~처럼)

믿기 힘들겠지만, 호주 멜버른의 나무들은 이와 같은 이메일들을 항상 받는다.

08
How is it possible [that trees have email addresses]?
          가주어   진주어

나무들이 이메일 주소를 갖고 있는 것이 어떻게 가능할까?

09 And why are people sending them messages?
= trees

그리고 사람들은 왜 그들에게 메시지들을 보내고 있는 걸까?

10 The story [behind these emails] begins with Melbourne's Urban Forest Strategy plan, a response
S　　전치사구　　V　　　　　　　　　　　　　　　　　　　　　동격
to Australia's millennium drought.

이런 이메일들 뒤의 이야기는 호주의 밀레니엄 가뭄에 대한 대응인, 멜버른의 도시숲 전략 계획으로 시작한다.

11 This drought lasted from the late 1990s to 2010.
계속되었다

이 가뭄은 1990년대 후반부터 2010년까지 계속되었다.

12 By the time it ended, 40 percent of the city's 77,000 trees were in a state of declining health.
접속사(~할 때까지)　= this drought　　　　S(복수)　　　　V

그것이 끝날 때쯤, 도시의 77,000그루의 나무들 중 40퍼센트가 나빠지는 건강 상태에 있었다.

13 Furthermore, the overall number of trees was decreasing.
the number of: ~의 수(단수)
S(단수)　　　　V

게다가, 나무들의 전반적인 숫자도 감소하고 있었다.

14 As a result, the amount of shade [{provided by trees within the city}, also known as canopy
S　　　　　과거분사구　　　　　　　(which is)　삽입어구
cover], decreased.
V

그 결과, 임관 피복도라고도 알려져 있는, 도시 내에서 나무에 의해 제공되는 그늘의 양이 감소했다.

15 The loss [of canopy cover] is a major threat to urban environments [because it raises
S　　전치사구　　V　　　　　　　　　　　= the loss of canopy cover
temperatures].　　　　　　　　　　　　　　　이유의 부사절

임관 피복도의 줄어듦은 기온을 상승시키기 때문에 도시 환경에 주요한 위협이다.

16 Higher temperatures in cities can be dangerous for residents, as they increase the risk of heat
S　　　　　V　　　　　　　= higher temperatures
exhaustion.　　　　　　　접속사(~ 때문에)

도시 내에서의 보다 높은 기온은 주민들에게 위험할 수 있는데, 이는 그것들(= 보다 높은 기온)이 열사병의 위험을 높이기 때문이다.

17 = higher temperatures
They also lead to a rise in the use of air-conditioning.
~로 이어지다

그것들은 또한 에어컨 장치의 사용에 있어서의 증가로 이어진다.

18 This speeds up climate change by increasing energy consumption and greenhouse gas emissions.
= a rise in the use of air-conditioning   by v-ing: ~함으로써

이는 에너지 소비와 온실가스 배출물을 증가시킴으로써 기후변화를 가속화한다.

19 to부정사의 수동태: to be p.p.
Something had to be done [to deal with the loss of Melbourne's trees].
과거의 필요·의무(~해야 했다)   부사적 용법(목적)

무언가가 멜버른 나무들의 줄어듦에 대처하기 위해서 행해져야 했다.

20 In 2012, the city government announced its Urban Forest Strategy plan.

2012년에, 시 정부는 도시숲 전략 계획을 발표했다.

21 It set the ambitious goal of planting more than 3,000 trees every year for the next twenty years.
= the city government   └ 동격 ┘

그것은 다음 20년 동안 매년 3,000그루가 넘는 나무들을 심는 야심찬 목표를 설정했다.

22 The plan also involved the creation of an online map [called the Urban Forest Visual].
↑_____| 과거분사구

그 계획은 또한 도시숲 시각 자료라고 불리는 온라인 지도 제작을 포함했다.

23 전치사구
This interactive map shows the location [of every single tree {in the city's parks and along its
↑_____| 각자의, 하나하나의   전치사구   = the city's
roads}].

이 대화형 지도는 도시 내의 공원과 그것의 도로를 따라 나무 하나하나의 위치를 보여준다.

24 It uses colors and symbols [to indicate each tree's age and genus].
= This interactive map   부사적 용법(목적)

그것은 각 나무의 나이와 속(屬)을 나타내는 데 색상과 기호를 사용한다.

25 ┌──── 병렬 연결 ────┐
                              (to)
Also, users can click on a tree [to find out its species and even send it an email].
부사적 용법(목적)   = a tree

또한, 사용자들은 그것(= 나무)의 종을 알아내고 심지어는 그것에게 이메일을 보내기 위해 나무를 클릭할 수 있다.

26

At first, the "Email this tree" function had a specific purpose.
처음에

처음에는, '이 나무에게 이메일 보내기' 기능이 특정한 목적을 가지고 있었다.

27

수동태   부사적 용법(목적)

It was designed [to allow people to easily inform council workers about trees {that were damaged
= the "Email this tree" function   allow + 목적어 + to-v: ~가 …하도록 해주다   주격 관계대명사절
or in poor health}].

그것은 사람들이 의회에서 일하는 사람들에게 손상되거나 건강이 좋지 않은 나무들에 관해 쉽게 알려주도록 해주기 위해 고안되었다.

28

─thing으로 끝나는 부정대명사는 형용사가 뒤에서 수식함

After the map was posted online, something unexpected happened.
접속사(~한 후에)   수동태

지도가 온라인에 게재된 후, 예상 밖의 일이 일어났다.

29

The trees started receiving thousands of emails, but many of them were not reports about
동명사(started의 목적어) = to receive   = emails
damage or poor health.

나무들이 수천 개의 이메일들을 받기 시작했지만, 그것들 중 많은 것이 손상이나 좋지 않은 건강에 관한 보고가 아니었다.

30

Instead, they were love letters, poems, greetings, and messages [expressing appreciation for the
                                                                     현재분사구
trees].

대신에, 그것들은 연애편지, 시, 인사말, 그리고 나무들에 대한 고마움을 표현하는 메시지들이었다.

31

관계부사절

One person wrote, "I love [the way {the light shines on your leaves}] and [how your branches
                          관계부사절(the way와 how 중 하나는 반드시 생략)
hang so low].

한 사람은 '나는 빛이 네 잎들 위에 비치는 방식과 네 가지들이 그렇게 낮게 매달려 있는 방식을 정말 좋아해.

32

It is almost like you are trying to hug me."
            접속사(마치 ~인 것처럼)   명사적 용법(are trying의 목적어)

그것은 거의 네가 나를 껴안으려고 하는 것 같아.'라고 썼다.

33

The tree mail phenomenon quickly spread, and people [all over the world] started sending
                        S1   V1   S2   전치사구   V2   동명사(started의 목적어) = to send
messages.

나무 이메일 현상은 빠르게 퍼졌고, 전 세계의 사람들이 메시지들을 보내기 시작했다.

34

주격 관계대명사절

A message [that was sent all the way from Russia] said, "When I read about this wonderful
              수동태   접속사(~할 때)

project, I was inspired to write to you, even though I live thousands of miles away.
      수동태   접속사(비록 ~이지만, ~에도 불구하고)

멀리 러시아에서 전송된 한 메시지는 '내가 이 멋진 프로젝트에 관해 읽었을 때, 나는 수천 마일 떨어져 사는데도 불구하고 너에게 (메시지를) 쓰도록 고무되었어.

35

Although we are separated by a great distance, we share the same planet and the same
접속사(~이긴 하지만)   수동태

environment.

비록 우리가 엄청난 거리로 따로 떨어져 있기는 하지만, 우리는 같은 지구와 같은 환경을 공유해.

36

(that)

Perhaps one day we will meet. Until then, I hope [you can stay healthy and strong]."
                                          명사절(hope의 목적어)

아마 언젠가 우리는 만나게 될 거야. 그때까지, 나는 네가 건강하고 튼튼하게 지내길 바라.'라고 쓰여 있었다.

37

명사절(reminds의 직접목적어)

The global popularity [of the tree mail phenomenon] reminds us [that we are all connected to
            S   전치사구   V   간접목적어   수동태

nature, and we are all involved in {building a more sustainable world}].
     (that)   동명사구(전치사 in의 목적어)

나무 이메일 현상의 세계적인 인기는 우리에게 우리가 모두 자연에 연결되어 있고, 우리는 모두 보다 지속 가능한 세상을 만드는 것에 관련되어 있다는 것을 일깨워 준다.

38

= If it were not for ~, But for ~

Without collective action from people across the globe, we would have little hope of [saving our
가정법 과거 「Without ~, 주어+조동사의 과거형+동사원형 …」: ~이 없다면, …할 텐데   거의 없는   동명사구(전치사 of의 목적어)

planet for future generations].

전 세계 사람들로부터의 집단적인 행동이 없다면, 우리는 미래의 세대들을 위해 우리의 지구를 구할 희망을 거의 갖지 못할 것이다.

39

현재완료

Locally, the tree mail phenomenon has inspired many Melbourne residents to offer their own
                                     inspire + 목적어 + to-v: ~가 …하도록 고무하다

ideas about [building an environmentally friendly urban environment].
               동명사구(전치사 about의 목적어)

지역적으로, 나무 이메일 현상은 많은 멜버른 주민들이 환경친화적인 도시 환경을 조성하는 것에 관한 그들만의 생각들을 제안하도록 고무했다.

40

병렬 연결

Some have even volunteered [to measure trees and monitor animals] for nature programs in the
          현재완료   (to)

city.

일부는 심지어 도시 내의 자연 프로그램을 위해 나무들을 측정하고 동물들을 추적 관찰하는 일을 자원하기까지 했다.

41
Meanwhile, the Urban Forest Strategy's tree planting project has remained on track, and canopy
한편   현재완료(계속)
cover is predicted to increase from 23 percent in 2012 to 40 percent by the year 2040.
수동태   └─── from A to B: A에서 B까지 ───┘

한편, 도시숲 전략의 나무 심기 프로젝트는 계속 진행 중이며, 임관 피복도는 2012년에서의 23퍼센트에서 2040년까지 40퍼센트로 늘어날 것으로
예상된다.

42
                                         help+(to-)v: ~하는 것을 돕다
Melbourne's urban forest strategy will help keep the city cool.
                                                   O   OC

멜버른의 도시숲 전략은 도시를 시원하게 유지하는 데 도움이 될 것이다.

43
              allow + 목적어 + to-v: ~가 …하도록 해주다   (to)
It will also allow residents to interact with nature and engage in outdoor activities every day.
              └────────── 병렬 연결 ──────────┘   ~에 참여하다

그것은 또한 주민들이 매일 자연과 소통하고 야외 활동들에 참여하게 해줄 것이다.

44
As a result, residents will be happier and healthier as they move toward a greener future.
                                  비교급   접속사(~하는 동안)

결과적으로, 주민들은 그들이 더 환경 친화적인 미래를 향해 나아가는 동안 더 행복하고 건강해질 것이다.

♣ 다음 빈칸에 알맞은 말을 쓰시오.

01 Whenever I stop in front of you and _____ of fresh air, I appreciate the oxygen that you produce.

내가 네 앞에 서서 신선한 공기를 깊이 들이마실 때마다 나는 네가 만들어 내는 산소에 감사해.

02 Without you and all your friends, we humans _____ enough oxygen.

너와 네 모든 친구들이 없다면, 우리 인간들은 충분한 산소를 얻을 수 없을 거야.

03 By the way, _____ a family of birds has made a nest in your branches.

그건 그렇고, 나는 한 새 가족이 너의 가지에 둥지를 튼 것을 알아챘어.

04 I hope that more people realize how important you and all the other trees are _____.

나는 더 많은 사람들이 너와 다른 모든 나무들이 환경에 얼마나 중요한지 깨닫기를 바라.

05 _____, trees in Melbourne, Australia receive emails like this all the time.

믿기 힘들겠지만, 호주 멜버른의 나무들은 이와 같은 이메일들을 항상 받는다.

06 The story behind these emails begins with Melbourne's Urban Forest Strategy plan, _____ Australia's millennium drought.

이런 이메일들 뒤의 이야기는 호주의 밀레니엄 가뭄에 대한 대응인, 멜버른의 도시숲 전략 계획으로 시작한다.

07 _____ from the late 1990s to 2010.

이 가뭄은 1990년대 후반부터 2010년까지 계속되었다.

08 By the time it ended, 40 percent of the city's 77,000 trees were in _____.

그것이 끝날 때쯤, 도시의 77,000그루의 나무들 중 40퍼센트가 나빠지는 건강 상태에 있었다.

09 Furthermore, the overall number of trees _____.

게다가, 나무들의 전반적인 숫자도 감소하고 있었다.

10 As a result, the amount of shade provided by trees within the city, _____ canopy cover, decreased.

그 결과, 임관 피복도라고도 알려져 있는, 도시 내에서 나무에 의해 제공되는 그늘의 양이 감소했다.

11 The loss of canopy cover is a major threat to _____ because it raises temperatures.

임관 피복도의 줄어듦은 기온을 상승시키기 때문에 도시 환경에 주요한 위협이다.

12 _____ in cities can be dangerous for residents, as they increase the risk of heat exhaustion.

도시 내에서의 보다 높은 기온은 주민들에게 위험할 수 있는데, 이는 그것들(= 보다 높은 기온)이 열사병의 위험을 높이기 때문이다.

13 They also _____ in the use of air-conditioning.

그것들은 또한 에어컨 장치의 사용에 있어서의 증가로 이어진다.

14 This speeds up climate change by increasing _____ and greenhouse gas emissions.

이는 에너지 소비와 온실가스 배출물을 증가시킴으로써 기후변화를 가속화한다.

15 Something had to be done to _____ of Melbourne's trees.
무언가가 멜버른 나무들의 줄어듦에 대처하기 위해서 행해져야 했다.

16 In 2012, _____ announced its Urban Forest Strategy plan.
2012년에, 시 정부는 도시숲 전략 계획을 발표했다.

17 It _____ of planting more than 3,000 trees every year for the next twenty years.
그것은 다음 20년 동안 매년 3,000그루가 넘는 나무들을 심는 야심찬 목표를 설정했다.

18 The plan also _____ an online map called the Urban Forest Visual.
그 계획은 또한 도시숲 시각 자료라고 불리는 온라인 지도 제작을 포함했다.

19 This _____ the location of every single tree in the city's parks and along its roads.
이 대화형 지도는 도시 내의 공원과 그것의 도로를 따라 나무 하나하나의 위치를 보여준다.

20 At first, the "mail this tree" function _____.
처음에는, '이 나무에게 이메일 보내기' 기능이 특정한 목적을 가지고 있었다.

21 It was designed to allow people to easily _____ about trees that were damaged or in poor health.
그것은 사람들이 의회에서 일하는 사람들에게 손상되거나 건강이 좋지 않은 나무들에 관해 쉽게 알려주도록 해주기 위해 고안되었다.

22 After the map was posted online, _____ happened.
지도가 온라인에 게재된 후, 예상 밖의 일이 일어났다.

23 The trees _____ thousands of emails, but many of them were not reports about damage or poor health.
나무들이 수천 개의 이메일들을 받기 시작했지만, 그것들 중 많은 것이 손상이나 좋지 않은 건강에 관한 보고가 아니었다.

24 Instead, they were love letters, poems, greetings, and messages _____ for the trees.
대신에, 그것들은 연애편지, 시, 인사말, 그리고 나무들에 대한 고마움을 표현하는 메시지들이었다.

25 One person wrote, "I love the way the light shines on your leaves and _____ so low. It is almost like you are trying to hug me."
한 사람은 '나는 빛이 네 잎들 위에 비치는 방식과 네 가지들이 그렇게 낮게 매달려 있는 방식을 정말 좋아해. 그것은 거의 네가 나를 꺼안으려고 하는 것 같아.'라고 썼다.

26 The tree mail phenomenon quickly spread, and people all over the world _____.
나무 이메일 현상은 빠르게 퍼졌고, 전 세계의 사람들이 메시지들을 보내기 시작했다.

27 A message that was sent all the way from Russia said, "When I read about this wonderful project, I _____ to you, even though I live thousands of miles away.
멀리 러시아에서 전송된 한 메시지는 '내가 이 멋진 프로젝트에 관해 읽었을 때, 나는 수천 마일 떨어져 사는데도 불구하고 너에게 (메시지를) 쓰도록 고무되었어.

28 Although we are separated _____, we share the same planet and the same environment.
비록 우리가 엄청난 거리로 따로 떨어져 있기는 하지만, 우리는 같은 지구와 같은 환경을 공유해.

29   Perhaps one day we will meet. Until then, I hope you can _____."

아마 언젠가 우리는 만나게 될 거야. 그때까지, 나는 네가 건강하고 튼튼하게 지내길 바라.'라고 쓰여 있었다.

30   The global popularity of the tree mail phenomenon _____ we are all
connected to nature, and we are all involved in building a more sustainable world.

나무 이메일 현상의 세계적인 인기는 우리에게 우리가 모두 자연에 연결되어 있고, 우리는 모두 보다 지속 가능한 세상을 만드는
것에 관련되어 있다는 것을 일깨워 준다.

31   _____ collective action from people across the globe, we _____
little hope of saving our planet for future generations.

전 세계 사람들로부터의 집단적인 행동이 없다면, 우리는 미래의 세대들을 위해 우리의 지구를 구할 희망을 거의 갖지 못할 것이다.

32   Locally, the tree mail phenomenon has inspired many Melbourne residents to offer their own ideas about
_____ urban environment.

지역적으로, 나무 이메일 현상은 많은 멜버른 주민들이 환경친화적인 도시 환경을 조성하는 것에 관한 그들만의 생각들을 제안하도
록 고무했다.

33   Some have even _____ trees and monitor animals for nature programs in the city.

일부는 심지어 도시 내의 자연 프로그램을 위해 나무들을 측정하고 동물들을 추적 관찰하는 일을 자원하기까지 했다.

34   Meanwhile, the Urban Forest Strategy's tree planting project _____, and
canopy cover is predicted to increase from 23 percent in 2012 to 40 percent by the year 2040.

한편, 도시숲 전략의 나무 심기 프로젝트는 계속 진행 중이며, 임관 피복도는 2012년에서의 23퍼센트에서 2040년까지 40퍼센트
로 늘어날 것으로 예상된다.

35   It will also allow residents to interact with nature and _____ every day.

그것은 또한 주민들이 매일 자연과 소통하고 야외 활동들에 참여하게 해줄 것이다.

36   As a result, residents will be _____ as they move toward a greener future.

결과적으로, 주민들은 그들이 더 환경 친화적인 미래를 향해 나아가는 동안 더 행복하고 건강해질 것이다.

교과서 본문 익히기 ❷ 옳은 어법·어휘 고르기

♣ 다음 네모 안에서 옳은 것을 고르시오.

01 | However / Whenever | I walk past you, your beautiful leaves bring a smile to my face.

02   Whenever I stop in front of you and take a deep breath of fresh | air / water |, I appreciate the oxygen that you produce.

03 | With / Without | you and all your friends, we humans wouldn't be able to get enough oxygen.

04   By the way, I noticed | that / what | a family of birds has made a nest in your branches.

05   It's so kind | of / for | you to provide them with a home.

06   I hope | if / that | more people realize how important you and all the other trees are to the environment.

07   Believe it or not, trees in Melbourne, Australia | receive / send | emails like this all the time.

08   How is it | possible / impossible | that trees have email addresses?

09   And why are people | sending / receiving | them messages?

10   The story behind these emails | begin / begins | with Melbourne's Urban Forest Strategy plan, a response to Australia's millennium drought.

11   This drought | lasts / lasted | from the late 1990s to 2010.

12   By the time it ended, 40 percent of the city's 77,000 trees were in a state of | decline / declining | health.

13   Furthermore, the overall number of trees | was / were | decreasing.

14   As a result, the amount of shade | providing / provided | by trees within the city, also known as canopy cover, decreased.

15   The loss of canopy cover is a major threat to urban environments | so / because | it raises temperatures.

16 Lower / Higher temperatures in cities can be dangerous for residents, as they increase the risk of heat exhaustion.

17 They also lead to a rise / fall in the use of air-conditioning.

18 This speeds up climate change by increasing / increase energy consumption and greenhouse gas emissions.

19 Something had to do / be done to deal with the loss of Melbourne's trees.

20 In 2012, the city government announced its / it's Urban Forest Strategy plan.

21 It set the ambitious goal of planting more than / less than 3,000 trees every year for the next twenty years.

22 The plan also involved the creation of an offline / online map called the Urban Forest Visual.

23 This interactive map shows the location of every / all single tree in the city's parks and along its roads.

24 It uses colors and symbols indicating / to indicate each tree's age and genus.

25 Also, users can click on a tree to find out its / their species and even send it an email.

26 At first, the "mail this tree" function had a general / specific purpose.

27 It was designed to allow people to easily inform council workers about trees that were damaged or in poor / good health.

28 After the map was posted online, unexpected something / something unexpected happened.

29 The trees started receiving thousands of emails, but many / more of them were not reports about damage or poor health.

30 Instead, they were love letters, poems, greetings, and messages expressing / expressed appreciation for the trees.

정답 및 해설 p. 24

31   One person wrote, "I love the way the light shines on your leaves and how your branches hang so
       low / high . It is almost like you are trying to hug me."

32   The tree mail phenomenon quick / quickly spread, and people all over the world started sending messages.

33   A message that was sent all the way from Russia said, "When I read about this wonderful project, I was
       inspired / inspiring to write to you, even though I live thousands of miles away.

34   Although / While we are separated by a great distance, we share the same planet and the same
       environment.

35   Perhaps one day we will meet. Until then, I hope you can stay health / healthy and strong."

36   The global popularity of the tree mail phenomenon reminds us that we are all connected to nature, and we
       are all involved in build / building a more sustainable world.

37   Without / With collective action from people across the globe, we would have little hope of saving our
       planet for future generations.

38   Locally, the tree mail phenomenon has inspired many Melbourne residents to offer their own ideas about
       building an environmentally / environmental friendly urban environment.

39   Some have even volunteered to measure trees and monitoring / monitor animals for nature programs in
       the city.

40   Meanwhile, the Urban Forest Strategy's tree planting project has remained on track, and canopy cover is
       predicted to increase / decrease from 23 percent in 2012 to 40 percent by the year 2040.

41   Melbourne's urban forest strategy will help keeping / keep the city cool.

42   It will also allow residents interacting / to interact with nature and engage in outdoor activities every day.

43   As a result, residents will be happy / happier and healthier as they move toward a greener future.

Lesson 03 Nature & Us **139**

♣ 다음 밑줄 친 부분을 바르게 고쳐 쓰시오.

01   <u>Whatever</u> I walk past you, your beautiful leaves bring a smile to my face.

02   Whenever I stop in front of you and take a deep breath of fresh air, I appreciate the oxygen <u>what</u> you
      produce.

03   Without you and all your friends, we humans <u>would</u> be able to get enough oxygen.

04   It's so kind of you to provide them <u>to</u> a home.

05   Believe it <u>and</u> not, trees in Melbourne, Australia receive emails like this all the time.

06   The story behind these emails <u>begin</u> with Melbourne's Urban Forest Strategy plan, a response to Australia's
      millennium drought.

07   This drought lasted from the late 1990s <u>in</u> 2010.

08   By the time it ended, 40 <u>percents</u> of the city's 77,000 trees were in a state of declining health.

09   Furthermore, the overall number of trees <u>were</u> decreasing.

10   As a result, the amount of shade provided by trees within the city, also <u>knew</u> as canopy cover, decreased.

11   The <u>lose</u> of canopy cover is a major threat to urban environments because it raises temperatures.

12   Higher temperatures in cities can be dangerous for residents, <u>if</u> they increase the risk of heat exhaustion.

13   They <u>too</u> lead to a rise in the use of air-conditioning.

14   This speeds up climate change by <u>increase</u> energy consumption and greenhouse gas emissions.

15   Something had to <u>do</u> to deal with the loss of Melbourne's trees.

16   In 2012, the city government announced <u>it's</u> Urban Forest Strategy plan.

17   It set the ambitious goal of planting <u>many</u> than 3,000 trees every year for the next twenty years.

18   The plan also involved the creation of an online map <u>calling</u> the Urban Forest Visual.

19 This interactive map shows the <u>locate</u> of every single tree in the city's parks and along its roads.

20 It uses colors and symbols <u>indicating</u> each tree's age and genus.

21 Also, users can click on a tree to find out its species and even <u>sends</u> it an email.

22 It was designed to allow people to easily inform council workers about trees that <u>damaged</u> or in poor health.

23 After the map was posted online, <u>unexpected something</u> happened.

24 The trees started receiving thousands of emails, but <u>much</u> of them were not reports about damage or poor health.

25 Instead, they were love letters, poems, greetings, and messages <u>express</u> appreciation for the trees.

26 One person wrote, "I love the way the light shines on your leaves and how your branches hang so low. It is almost like you are trying <u>hugging</u> me."

27 The tree mail phenomenon <u>quick</u> spread, and people all over the world started sending messages.

28 Although we <u>separated</u> by a great distance, we share the same planet and the same environment.

29 The global popularity of the tree mail phenomenon reminds us <u>if</u> we are all connected to nature, and we are all involved in building a more sustainable world.

30 <u>With</u> collective action from people across the globe, we would have little hope of saving our planet for future generations.

31 Locally, the tree mail phenomenon has inspired many Melbourne residents to offer their own ideas about <u>build</u> an environmentally friendly urban environment.

32 Meanwhile, the Urban Forest Strategy's tree planting project has remained on track, and canopy cover is predicted to increase from 23 percent in 2012 to 40 percent <u>in</u> the year 2040.

33 Melbourne's urban forest strategy will help <u>keeping</u> the city cool.

34 It will also allow residents <u>interacting</u> with nature and engage in outdoor activities every day.

35 As a result, residents will be happier and <u>healthy</u> as they move toward a greener future.

교과서 본문 외 지문 분석

TOPIC 5 A. Preview

The above graph shows the eight most common items ❶ that pollute the world's oceans. Plastic bags are ❷ the most common waste item and make up about fourteen percent of ocean waste. Plastic bottles make up ❸ more than ten percent of ocean waste and are the second most common waste item. Wrappers are ❹ nearly ❺ as common in the world's oceans as food containers. Fishing items make up over seven percent of ocean waste, ❻ a little more than plastic caps and glass bottles. Drink cans are ❼ the least common of the listed items. From this graph, we can see that ❽ a wide variety of man-made items are polluting our oceans.

❶ 주격 관계대명사 ❷ common의 최상급 ❸ more than: ~ 이상 ❹ nearly: 거의 (= almost) ❺ as+원급+as: ~만큼 …한 ❻ a little: 비교급 수식 부사 ❼ the least common: 가장 덜 흔한 (↔ the most common) ❽ a wide variety of: 다양한 종류의, 광범위한 종류의

Q1 Plastic bags are the most common waste item in the world's oceans. (T / F)

Wrap Up B. Read and Present

Green walls are vertical structures ❶ on which plants are grown. You might think ❷ that they are just pleasant to look at. However, they offer many other benefits. First, green walls help save energy ❸ by reducing the need for air conditioning. Because plants absorb and reflect ❹ large amounts of sunlight, they help ❺ keep surrounding areas cool. Green walls also ❻ contribute to healthier living environments by producing more oxygen. They even ❼ provide shelter and food for small animals! Finally, green walls ❽ remind us of our connection to nature. Let's enjoy the benefits of green walls and remember ❾ that we ❿ must protect nature.

❶ 전치사+관계대명사 ❷ 명사절을 이끄는 접속사 ❸ 전치사+동명사 ❹ large amounts of: 많은 양의 ❺ keep+목적어+보어(형용사): 목적어를 ~한 상태로 유지하다 ❻ contribute to: ~에 기여하다 ❼ provide A for B: B에게 A를 제공하다 ❽ remind A of B: A에게 B를 상기시키다 ❾ remember의 목적어 역할을 하는 명사절을 이끄는 접속사 ❿ must+동사원형: ~해야 한다

Q2 Green walls contribute to healthier living environments by producing more carbon dioxide. (T / F)

❀ **다음 빈칸에 알맞은 말을 쓰시오.**

01 The above graph shows the eight _____ that pollute the world's oceans.
위 그래프는 세계의 해양을 오염시키는 여덟 가지의 가장 흔한 품목들을 보여 준다.

02 Plastic bags are the most common waste item and _____ about fourteen percent of
ocean waste. 비닐봉지가 가장 흔한 폐기물 품목이며 해양 쓰레기의 약 14퍼센트를 차지한다.

03 Plastic bottles make up _____ ten percent of ocean waste and are the second most
common waste item.
플라스틱병은 해양 쓰레기의 10퍼센트를 넘게 차지하며 두 번째로 가장 흔한 폐기물 품목이다.

04 Wrappers are nearly _____ in the world's oceans _____ food containers.
포장지는 세계의 해양에서 거의 식품 용기만큼 흔하다.

05 Fishing items make up over _____, a little more than plastic caps and glass bottles.
낚시용품은 플라스틱 뚜껑과 유리병보다 약간 더 많은, 해양 쓰레기의 7퍼센트를 넘게 차지한다.

06 Drink cans are _____ of the listed items.
음료수 캔은 열거된 품목들 중에서 가장 덜 흔하다.

07 From this graph, we can see that _____ man-made items are polluting our oceans.
이 그래프로부터, 우리는 인간이 만든 매우 다양한 품목들이 우리의 해양을 오염시키고 있음을 알 수 있다.

08 Green walls are vertical structures on which _____.
그린월은 그 위에 식물들이 자라는 수직 구조물이다.

09 You might think that they are just _____.
당신은 그것들이 그저 보기 좋다고 생각할지도 모른다.

10 However, they offer _____. 하지만, 그것들은 많은 다른 이점들을 제공한다.

11 First, green walls help save energy _____ the need for air conditioning.
첫 번째로, 그린월은 에어컨의 필요성을 줄임으로써 에너지를 절약하는 데 도움을 준다.

12 Because plants absorb and reflect large amounts of sunlight, they help _____.
식물들이 햇빛의 많은 양을 흡수하고 반사하기 때문에, 그것들은 주변 지역을 시원하게 유지하는 데 도움을 준다.

13 Green walls also _____ healthier living environments by producing more oxygen.
그린월은 또한 더 많은 산소를 만들어 냄으로써 더 건강한 생활 환경에 기여한다.

14 They even _____ for small animals!
그것들은 심지어 작은 동물들에게 살 곳과 먹이를 제공한다!

15 Finally, green walls _____ to nature.
마지막으로, 그린월은 우리에게 자연과 우리의 연관성을 일깨워 준다.

16 Let's enjoy the benefits of green walls and remember that _____.
그린월의 이점들을 즐기고 우리가 자연을 보호해야 한다는 것을 기억하자.

01 (A), (B), (C)의 각 네모 안에서 문맥에 맞는 낱말로 가장 적절한 것은?

Dear Tree,

Whenever I walk past you, your beautiful leaves bring a smile to my face. Whenever I stop in front of you and take a (A) deep / shallow breath of fresh air, I appreciate the oxygen that you produce. Without you and all your friends, we humans wouldn't be able to get enough oxygen. By the way, I noticed that a family of (B) fishes / birds has made a nest in your branches. It's so (C) kind / rude of you to provide them with a home. I hope that more people realize how important you and all the other trees are to the environment. Have a nice day!

	(A)		(B)		(C)
①	deep	···	fishes	···	kind
②	deep	···	birds	···	rude
③	deep	···	birds	···	kind
④	shallow	···	birds	···	kind
⑤	shallow	···	fishes	···	rude

02 다음 글의 밑줄 친 부분 중, 문맥상 낱말의 쓰임이 적절하지 않은 것은?

Believe it or not, trees in Melbourne, Australia ①receive emails like this all the time. How is it ②possible that trees have email addresses? And why are people sending them messages?

The story behind these emails begins with Melbourne's Urban Forest Strategy plan, a ③response to Australia's millennium drought. This drought ④lasted from the late 1990s to 2010. By the time it ended, 40 percent of the city's 77,000 trees were in a state of declining health. Furthermore, the overall number of trees was ⑤increasing.

① ② ③ ④ ⑤

03 (A), (B), (C)의 각 네모 안에서 문맥에 맞는 낱말로 가장 적절한 것은?

As a result, the (A) amount / number of shade provided by trees within the city, also known as canopy cover, decreased. The loss of canopy cover is a major threat to urban environments because it (B) lowers / raises temperatures. Higher temperatures in cities can be (C) safe / dangerous for residents, as they increase the risk of heat exhaustion. They also lead to a rise in the use of air-conditioning. This speeds up climate change by increasing energy consumption and greenhouse gas emissions.

	(A)		(B)		(C)
①	amount	···	lowers	···	dangerous
②	amount	···	raises	···	dangerous
③	amount	···	raises	···	safe
④	number	···	lowers	···	safe
⑤	number	···	raises	···	dangerous

04 다음 글의 밑줄 친 부분 중, 문맥상 낱말의 쓰임이 적절하지 않은 것은?

Something had to be done to deal with the ①loss of Melbourne's trees. In 2012, the city government announced its Urban Forest Strategy plan. It set the ambitious goal of planting more than 3,000 trees every year for the next twenty years. The plan also involved the creation of an ②online map called the Urban Forest Visual.

This ③interactive map shows the location of every single tree in the city's parks and along its roads. It uses colors and symbols to indicate each tree's age and genus. Also, users can click on a tree to find out its ④species and even send it an email. At first, the "mail this tree" function had a specific purpose. It was designed to allow people to easily ⑤reform council workers about trees that were damaged or in poor health.

① ② ③ ④ ⑤

05 (A), (B), (C)의 각 네모 안에서 문맥에 맞는 낱말로 가장 적절한 것은?

After the map was posted online, something (A) expected / unexpected happened. The trees started receiving thousands of emails, but many of them were not reports about damage or (B) poor / good health. Instead, they were love letters, poems, greetings, and messages expressing appreciation for the trees. One person wrote, "I love the way the light shines on your leaves and how your branches hang so low. It is almost like you are trying to hug me." The tree mail phenomenon (C) quickly / slowly spread, and people all over the world started sending messages.

	(A)		(B)		(C)
①	expected	⋯	poor	⋯	quickly
②	expected	⋯	good	⋯	slowly
③	unexpected	⋯	poor	⋯	quickly
④	unexpected	⋯	poor	⋯	slowly
⑤	unexpected	⋯	good	⋯	quickly

06 다음 글의 밑줄 친 부분 중, 문맥상 낱말의 쓰임이 적절하지 <u>않은</u> 것은?

A message that was sent all the way from Russia said, "When I read about this wonderful project, I was ①inspired to write to you, even though I live thousands of miles away. Although we are separated by a great distance, we ②share the same planet and the same environment. Perhaps one day we will meet. Until then, I hope you can stay healthy and strong."

The global ③popularity of the tree mail phenomenon reminds us that we are all connected to nature, and we are all involved in building a more ④unsustainable world. Without collective action from people across the globe, we would have ⑤little hope of saving our planet for future generations.

①   ②   ③   ④   ⑤

[07~08] 다음 글을 읽고, 물음에 답하시오.

Locally, the tree mail phenomenon has inspired many Melbourne residents to offer their own ideas about building an environmentally friendly (A) urban / rural environment. Some have even volunteered to measure trees and monitor animals for nature programs in the city.

Meanwhile, the Urban Forest Strategy's tree planting project has remained on track, and canopy cover is predicted to (B) decrease / increase from 23 percent in 2012 to 40 percent by the year 2040. Melbourne's urban forest strategy will help keep the city cool. It will also allow (C) residents / presidents to interact with nature and engage in outdoor activities every day. As a result, residents will be happier and healthier as they move toward a greener future.

07 (A), (B), (C)의 각 네모 안에서 문맥에 맞는 낱말로 가장 적절한 것은?

	(A)		(B)		(C)
①	urban	⋯	increase	⋯	presidents
②	urban	⋯	increase	⋯	residents
③	urban	⋯	decrease	⋯	residents
④	rural	⋯	increase	⋯	residents
⑤	rural	⋯	decrease	⋯	presidents

08 다음 영어 뜻풀이에 해당하는 단어를 윗글에서 찾아 쓰시오.

an observable event or fact, especially one that is unusual or remarkable

내신 1등급 어법 공략

01 (A), (B), (C)의 각 네모 안에서 어법에 맞는 표현으로 가장 적절한 것은?

> Dear Tree,
>
> Whenever I walk past you, your beautiful leaves bring a smile to my face. (A) However / Whenever I stop in front of you and take a deep breath of fresh air, I appreciate the oxygen that you produce. (B) Without / With you and all your friends, we humans wouldn't be able to get enough oxygen. By the way, I noticed that a family of birds (C) have / has made a nest in your branches. It's so kind of you to provide them with a home. I hope that more people realize how important you and all the other trees are to the environment. Have a nice day!

	(A)	(B)	(C)
①	However	⋯ With	⋯ have
②	However	⋯ Without	⋯ has
③	Whenever	⋯ Without	⋯ have
④	Whenever	⋯ Without	⋯ has
⑤	Whenever	⋯ With	⋯ has

02 (A), (B), (C)의 각 네모 안에서 어법에 맞는 표현으로 가장 적절한 것은?

> Believe it or not, trees in Melbourne, Australia receive emails like this all the time. How is it possible that trees have email addresses? And why are people sending them messages?
>
> The story behind these emails (A) begin / begins with Melbourne's Urban Forest Strategy plan, a response to Australia's millennium drought. This drought lasted from the (B) late / lately 1990s to 2010. By the time it ended, 40 percent of the city's 77,000 trees were in a state of (C) decline / declining health. Furthermore, the overall number of trees was decreasing.

	(A)	(B)	(C)
①	begin	⋯ late	⋯ declining
②	begin	⋯ lately	⋯ declining
③	begins	⋯ late	⋯ declined
④	begins	⋯ lately	⋯ declined
⑤	begins	⋯ late	⋯ declining

03 다음 글의 밑줄 친 부분 중, 어법상 틀린 것은?

> As a result, the amount of shade ① providing by trees within the city, also ② known as canopy cover, decreased. The loss of canopy cover is a major threat to urban environments ③ because it raises temperatures. ④ Higher temperatures in cities can be dangerous for residents, as they increase the risk of heat exhaustion. They also lead to a rise in the use of air-conditioning. This speeds up climate change by ⑤ increasing energy consumption and greenhouse gas emissions.

①   ②   ③   ④   ⑤

04 (A), (B), (C)의 각 네모 안에서 어법에 맞는 표현으로 가장 적절한 것은?

> Something had to (A) do / be done to deal with the loss of Melbourne's trees. In 2012, the city government announced its Urban Forest Strategy plan. It set the ambitious goal of planting more than 3,000 trees every year (B) for / during the next twenty years. The plan also involved the creation of an online map (C) calling / called the Urban Forest Visual.

	(A)	(B)	(C)
①	do	⋯ for	⋯ called
②	do	⋯ during	⋯ calling
③	be done	⋯ for	⋯ called
④	be done	⋯ for	⋯ calling
⑤	be done	⋯ during	⋯ called

05 (A), (B), (C)의 각 네모 안에서 어법에 맞는 표현으로 가장 적절한 것은?

This interactive map shows the location of every single tree in the city's parks and along its roads. It uses colors and symbols (A) indicate / to indicate each tree's age and genus. Also, users can click on a tree to find out its species and even (B) send / sending it an email. At first, the "mail this tree" function had a specific purpose. It was designed to allow people to easily inform council workers about trees (C) what / that were damaged or in poor health.

	(A)	(B)	(C)
①	indicate	… sending …	what
②	indicate	… send …	that
③	to indicate	… sending …	that
④	to indicate	… send …	that
⑤	to indicate	… send …	what

06 (A), (B), (C)의 각 네모 안에서 어법에 맞는 표현으로 가장 적절한 것은?

After the map was posted online, (A) something unexpected / unexpected something happened. The trees started receiving thousands of emails, but many of them were not reports about damage or poor health. Instead, they were love letters, poems, greetings, and messages (B) expressing / expressed appreciation for the trees. One person wrote, "I love the way the light shines on your leaves and how your branches hang so low. It is (C) most / almost like you are trying to hug me." The tree mail phenomenon quickly spread, and people all over the world started sending messages.

	(A)	(B)	(C)
①	something unexpected	… expressing …	most
②	something unexpected	… expressed …	almos
③	something unexpected	… expressing …	almost
④	unexpected something	… expressed …	almost
⑤	unexpected something	… expressed …	almost

07 다음 글의 밑줄 친 부분 중, 어법상 틀린 것은?

A message that ①was sent all the way from Russia said, "When I read about this wonderful project, I was inspired ②to write to you, even though I live thousands of miles away. Although we are separated by a great distance, we share the same planet and the same environment. Perhaps one day we will meet. Until then, I hope you can stay ③healthy and strong."

The global popularity of the tree mail phenomenon reminds us ④that we are all connected to nature, and we are all involved in building a more sustainable world. Without collective action from people across the globe, we ⑤would have had little hope of saving our planet for future generations.

①   ②   ③   ④   ⑤

08 다음 글의 밑줄 친 부분 중, 어법상 틀린 것은?

Locally, the tree mail phenomenon ①has inspired many Melbourne residents to offer their own ideas about building an environmentally friendly urban environment. Some have even volunteered to measure trees and ②monitor animals for nature programs in the city.

Meanwhile, the Urban Forest Strategy's tree planting project has remained on track, and canopy cover is predicted ③to increase from 23 percent in 2012 to 40 percent by the year 2040. Melbourne's urban forest strategy will help ④keeping the city cool. It will also allow residents to interact with nature and engage in outdoor activities every day. As a result, residents will be happier and ⑤healthier as they move toward a greener future.

①   ②   ③   ④   ⑤

[01~02] 다음 대화를 읽고, 물음에 답하시오.

> B Look at the bees on the flowers. Even the smallest things help to keep nature balanced. Don't you agree?
>
> (A) Oh, what is it?
>
> (B) Absolutely. It is amazing that some insects help plants produce fruit and seeds.
>
> (C) There are about one million insect species. But only 0.5 percent of them cause damage to crops. Most insects can help crops grow better by feeding on weeds and pests.
>
> (D) Right. By the way, I recently came across an interesting fact about insects.
>
> G Oh, I didn't know that!

01 자연스러운 대화가 되도록 바르게 배열한 것은?

① (A) – (B) – (C) – (D)

② (B) – (A) – (C) – (D)

③ (B) – (C) – (A) – (D)

④ (B) – (D) – (A) – (C)

⑤ (C) – (D) – (A) – (B)

02 위 대화의 내용과 일치하지 <u>않는</u> 것은?

① 작은 생물들도 자연의 균형을 유지하는 데 도움을 준다.

② 일부 곤충들은 식물이 과일과 씨앗을 생산하는 데 도움을 준다.

③ 전 세계에는 약 10만 종의 곤충이 있다.

④ 대부분의 곤충은 잡초와 해충을 먹어 작물이 더 잘 자라도록 돕는다.

⑤ 모든 곤충 종의 0.5%가 작물에 피해를 준다.

[03~05] 다음 글을 읽고, 물음에 답하시오.

> Dear Tree,
>
> Whenever I walk past you, your beautiful leaves bring a smile to my face. ___(A)___ I stop in front of you and take a deep breath of fresh air, I appreciate the oxygen that ⓐyou produce. ___(B)___ you and all your friends, we humans wouldn't be able to get enough oxygen. By the way, I noticed that a family of birds has made a nest in your branches. It's so kind ___(C)___ to provide ⓑthem with a home. I hope that more people realize how important you and all the other trees are to the environment. Have a nice day!

03 윗글에 드러난 필자의 심경으로 가장 적절한 것은?

① relieved   ② excited

③ anxious   ④ grateful

⑤ disappointed

04 윗글의 밑줄 친 ⓐ, ⓑ가 가리키는 것이 무엇인지 쓰시오.

ⓐ _____

ⓑ _____

05 (A), (B), (C)의 빈칸에 들어갈 말로 바르게 짝지어진 것은?

	(A)		(B)		(C)
①	However	···	With	···	of you
②	However	···	Without	···	of you
③	Whenever	···	Without	···	of you
④	Whenever	···	Without	···	for you
⑤	Wherever	···	With	···	for you

[06~07] 다음 글을 읽고, 물음에 답하시오.

The story behind these emails ①begin with Melbourne's Urban Forest Strategy plan, a response to Australia's millennium drought. This drought lasted from the ②late 1990s to 2010. By the time it ended, 40 percent of the city's 77,000 trees were in a state of ③declining health. ___(A)___, the overall number of trees was decreasing.

___(B)___, the amount of shade provided by trees within the city, also known as canopy cover, decreased. The loss of canopy cover is a major threat to urban environments ④because it raises temperatures. Higher temperatures in cities can be dangerous for residents, as they increase the risk of heat exhaustion. They also lead to a rise in the use of air-conditioning. This speeds up climate change by ⑤increasing energy consumption and greenhouse gas emissions.

06 윗글의 밑줄 친 부분 중, 어법상 틀린 것은?

①   ②   ③   ④   ⑤

07 윗글의 빈칸 (A), (B)에 들어갈 말로 가장 적절한 것은?

	(A)	(B)
①	However	… Nevertheless
②	Furthermore	… As a result
③	Therefore	… Moreover
④	Consequently	… In addition
⑤	Moreover	… However

[08~09] 다음 글을 읽고, 물음에 답하시오.

Something had to be done to deal with the loss of Melbourne's trees. In 2012, the city government announced its Urban Forest Strategy plan. It (A) set / took the ambitious goal of planting more than 3,000 trees every year for the next twenty years. The plan also involved the creation of an online map called the Urban Forest Visual.

This interactive map shows the location of every single tree in the city's parks and along its roads. It uses colors and symbols to (B) indicate / hide each tree's age and genus. Also, users can click on a tree to find out its species and even send it an email. At first, the "mail this tree" function had a specific purpose. It was designed to allow people to easily inform council workers about trees that were damaged or in (C) good / poor health.

08 다음 영어 뜻풀이에 해당하는 단어를 윗글에서 찾아 쓰시오.

_____ : involving communication or action between two or more things or people

09 (A), (B), (C)의 각 네모 안에서 문맥에 맞는 낱말로 가장 적절한 것은?

	(A)	(B)	(C)
①	set	… indicate	… good
②	set	… indicate	… poor
③	set	… hide	… poor
④	took	… indicate	… poor
⑤	took	… hide	… good

10 다음 글의 ①~⑤ 중, 전체 흐름상 어색한 문장은?

After the map was posted online, something unexpected happened. ① The trees started receiving thousands of emails, but many of them were not reports about damage or poor health. ② Instead, they were love letters, poems, greetings, and messages expressing appreciation for the trees. ③ The city government decided to increase the budget for park maintenance and tree planting. ④ One person wrote, "I love the way the light shines on your leaves and how your branches hang so low. It is almost like you are trying to hug me." ⑤ The tree mail phenomenon quickly spread, and people all over the world started sending messages.

①   ②   ③   ④   ⑤

11 다음 대화의 흐름으로 보아, 주어진 문장이 들어가기에 알맞은 곳은?

Everything on Earth is connected.

M: The weather has been really strange lately. Don't you agree?
W: Yes, I do. I heard that Venice is suffering from floods because sea levels are rising. (①)
M: That's too bad. Is it due to climate change?
W: Yes, it is. (②) So when polar ice melts, cities with low sea levels like Venice can get flooded. (③)
M: I'm worried that other cities that are near the coast might also have floods. (④)
W: So am I. This is a global problem that affects everyone. So we all need to deal with it together. (⑤)

①   ②   ③   ④   ⑤

[12~13] 다음 글을 읽고, 물음에 답하시오.

A message that was sent all the way from Russia said, "When I read about this wonderful project, I was inspired to write to you, even though I live thousands of miles away. ___(A)___ we are separated by a great distance, we share the same planet and the same environment. Perhaps one day we will meet. ___(B)___ then, I hope you can stay healthy and strong."

The global popularity of the tree mail phenomenon reminds us ___(C)___ we are all connected to nature, and we are all involved in building a more sustainable world. Without collective action from people across the globe, we would have little hope of saving our planet for future generations.

12 (A), (B), (C)의 빈칸에 들어갈 말로 바르게 짝지어진 것은?

	(A)		(B)		(C)
①	Despite	⋯	Before	⋯	how
②	While	⋯	After	⋯	which
③	Although	⋯	Until	⋯	that
④	Because	⋯	During	⋯	what
⑤	Since	⋯	Unless	⋯	where

13 윗글의 내용과 일치하지 <u>않는</u> 것은?

① 러시아에서 보낸 메시지에 관한 내용이다.
② 메시지 발신자는 나무와 물리적으로 멀리 떨어져 있다.
③ 트리 메일 현상은 전 세계적으로 인기를 얻었다.
④ 발신자는 나무와 직접 만날 계획을 세웠다.
⑤ 지구를 구하기 위해서는 전 세계 사람들의 집단 행동이 필요하다.

Locally, the tree mail phenomenon has inspired many Melbourne residents to offer their own ideas about ⓐbuilding an environmentally friendly urban environment. Some have even volunteered to measure trees and ⓑmonitored animals for nature programs in the city.

Meanwhile, the Urban Forest Strategy's tree planting project has ⓒremained on track, and canopy cover is predicted to increase from 23 percent in 2012 to 40 percent by the year 2040. Melbourne's urban forest strategy will help keep the city cool. It will also allow residents ⓓto interact with nature and engage in outdoor activities every day. As a result, residents will be happier and healthier ⓔas they move toward a greener future.

14 윗글의 요지로 가장 적절한 것은?

① 멜버른의 트리 메일 현상과 도시숲 전략이 도시 환경을 개선하여 삶의 질 향상에 기여하고 있다.

② 멜버른 시의 나무 심기 프로젝트가 도시의 미관을 개선하고 관광객 유치에 큰 도움이 되고 있다.

③ 트리 메일 현상으로 인해 멜버른 시의 행정 업무가 증가하여 도시 관리에 어려움을 겪고 있다.

④ 멜버른 시민들의 환경 의식이 높아져 개인 정원 가꾸기가 새로운 트렌드로 자리잡고 있다.

⑤ 도시숲 전략으로 인한 나무의 증가가 도시 인프라 관리에 부정적인 영향을 미치고 있다.

15 윗글의 밑줄 친 부분에 대한 설명 중, 올바른 것을 모두 고른 것은?

ⓐ 전치사 about의 목적어로 쓰인 동명사이다.

ⓑ monitored는 앞에 있는 volunteered와 병렬 구조를 이룬다.

ⓒ remain on track은 '계속 진행되고 있다'라는 뜻이다.

ⓓ 「allow + 목적어 + to부정사」 구문으로 '목적어로 하여금 ~하는 것을 허락하다'라는 의미이다.

ⓔ as는 이유를 나타내는 부사절을 이끄는 접속사이다.

① ⓐ, ⓑ, ⓒ

② ⓐ, ⓒ, ⓓ

③ ⓑ, ⓒ, ⓓ

④ ⓑ, ⓓ, ⓔ

⑤ ⓒ, ⓓ, ⓔ

[01~03] 다음 글을 읽고, 물음에 답하시오.

Dear Tree,

Whenever I walk past you, your beautiful leaves bring a ①smile to my face. Whenever I stop in front of you and take a deep ②breath of fresh air, I appreciate the oxygen that you produce. 너와 네 모든 친구들이 없다면, 우리 인간들은 충분한 산소를 얻을 수 없을 거야. By the way, I noticed that a family of birds has made a ③nest in your branches. It's so ④cruel of you to provide them with a home. I hope that more people realize how important you and all the other trees are to the ⑤environment. Have a nice day!

01 윗글의 밑줄 친 부분 중, 문맥상 낱말의 쓰임이 적절하지 <u>않은</u> 것은?

①   ②   ③   ④   ⑤

02 윗글의 밑줄 친 우리말과 같은 뜻이 되도록 다음 (보기)의 단어를 이용하여 문장을 완성하시오.

(보기) wouldn't / able / be / get / without / to / enough oxygen

→ _____ you and all your friends, we humans _____.

03 윗글의 밑줄 친 that과 쓰임이 <u>다른</u> 것은?

① Officials announced that the concert had been canceled.
② She's the girl that won the singing competition last year.
③ I hope that the weather will be nice for our camping trip tomorrow.
④ Many people believe that everyone deserves equal opportunities.
⑤ I think that climate change is a serious problem.

[04~06] 다음 글을 읽고, 물음에 답하시오.

The story behind these emails begins with Melbourne's Urban Forest Strategy plan, a ①response to Australia's millennium drought. This drought lasted from the late 1990s to 2010. By the time it ended, 40 percent of the city's 77,000 trees were in a state of declining health. Furthermore, the overall number of trees were decreasing.

As a result, the amount of ②light provided by trees within the city, also known as canopy cover, decreased. The loss of canopy cover is a ③major threat to urban environments because it raises temperatures. Higher temperatures in cities can be dangerous for residents, as they increase the ④risk of heat exhaustion. They also lead to a rise in the use of air-conditioning. This speeds up climate change by increasing energy ⑤consumption and greenhouse gas emissions.

04 윗글의 밑줄 친 부분 중, 문맥상 낱말의 쓰임이 적절하지 <u>않은</u> 것은?

①   ②   ③   ④   ⑤

05 윗글의 밑줄 친 문장에서 <u>틀린</u> 부분을 찾아 바르게 고쳐 쓰시오.

틀린 부분	고친 것

06 윗글의 내용과 일치하지 <u>않는</u> 것은?

① 멜버른의 도시숲 전략은 호주의 밀레니엄 가뭄에 대응하기 위해 시작되었다.

② 가뭄이 끝났을 때 도시 나무의 40%가 건강이 악화된 상태였다.

③ 나무로 인한 그늘의 양이 증가하여 도시 온도가 낮아졌다.

④ 도시의 높은 온도는 주민들에게 위험할 수 있다.

⑤ 에어컨 사용의 증가는 기후 변화를 가속화시킨다.

07 다음 대화의 빈칸 (A), (B), (C)에 들어갈 말을 보기에서 골라 기호를 쓰시오.

M The weather has been really strange lately.
_____(A)_____

W Yes, I do. I heard that Venice is suffering from floods because sea levels are rising.

M _____(B)_____ Is it due to climate change?

W Yes, it is. Everything on Earth is connected. So when polar ice melts, cities with low sea levels like Venice can get flooded.

M I'm worried that other cities that are near the coast might also have floods.

W _____(C)_____ This is a global problem that affects everyone. So we all need to deal with it together.

보기 ⓐ That's too bad.
　　　ⓑ Don't you agree?
　　　ⓒ So am I.

(A) _____ (B) _____ (C) _____

[08~09] 다음 글을 읽고, 물음에 답하시오.

Something had to be done to deal with the loss of Melbourne's trees. In 2012, the city government announced its Urban Forest Strategy plan. (①) It set the ambitious goal of planting more than 3,000 trees every year for the next twenty years. (②)

This interactive map shows the location of every single tree in the city's parks and along its roads. (③) It uses colors and symbols to indicate each tree's age and genus. Also, users can click on a tree to find out its species and even send it an email. (④) At first, the "mail this tree" function had a specific purpose. (⑤) It was designed to allow people to easily inform council workers about trees that were damaged or in poor health.

---

08 윗글의 흐름으로 보아, 주어진 문장이 들어가기에 가장 적절한 곳은?

The plan also involved the creation of an online map called the Urban Forest Visual.

---

①　　　　②　　　　③　　　　④　　　　⑤

09 윗글의 밑줄 친 This interactive map에 관한 내용과 일치하지 <u>않는</u> 것은?

① 도시의 공원과 도로에 있는 모든 나무의 위치를 보여준다.

② 나무의 나이와 속(genus)을 색상과 기호로 표시한다.

③ 사용자가 나무를 클릭하여 그 종(species)을 알아볼 수 있다.

④ 나무에 이메일을 보내는 기능이 있다.

⑤ 처음에는 건강한 나무를 찾기 위해 만들어졌다.

[10~11] 다음 글을 읽고, 물음에 답하시오.

After the map was posted online, something (A) expected / unexpected happened. The trees _____, but many of them were not reports about damage or poor health. Instead, they were love letters, poems, greetings, and messages (B) expressing / hiding appreciation for the trees. One person wrote, "I love the way the light shines on your leaves and how your branches hang so low. It is (C) almost / hardly like you are trying to hug me." The tree mail phenomenon quickly spread, and people all over the world started sending messages.

10 윗글의 빈칸에 들어갈 말로 가장 적절한 것은?

① began to grow faster
② were cut down
③ were relocated to different areas
④ became more resistant to diseases
⑤ started receiving thousands of emails

11 (A), (B), (C)의 각 네모 안에서 문맥에 맞는 낱말로 가장 적절한 것은?

	(A)		(B)		(C)
①	expected	⋯	expressing	⋯	almost
②	expected	⋯	hiding	⋯	hardly
③	unexpected	⋯	expressing	⋯	almost
④	unexpected	⋯	hiding	⋯	almost
⑤	unexpected	⋯	expressing	⋯	hardly

[12~13] 다음 글을 읽고, 물음에 답하시오.

A message that ① was sent all the way from Russia said, "When I read about this wonderful project, I ② was inspired to write to you, even though I live thousands of miles away. Although we are separated by a great distance, we ③ are shared the same planet and the same environment. Perhaps one day we will meet. Until then, I hope you can stay healthy and strong."

The global popularity of the tree mail phenomenon reminds us that we ④ are connected to nature, and we ⑤ are involved in building a more sustainable world. Without collective action from people across the globe, we would have little hope of saving our planet for future generations.

12 윗글의 밑줄 친 부분 중, 어법상 틀린 것은?

① ② ③ ④ ⑤

13 윗글의 밑줄 친 sustainable의 영어 뜻풀이로 알맞은 것은?

① having characteristics of a town or city
② having a strong desire to achieve success or a specific goal
③ involving communication or action between two or more things or people
④ able to be maintained over time without harming the environment or depleting resources
⑤ to create, make, or manufacture something

[14~15] 다음 글을 읽고, 물음에 답하시오.

Locally, the tree mail phenomenon has inspired many Melbourne residents to offer their own ideas about _____(A)_____ an environmentally friendly urban environment. Some have even volunteered to measure trees and monitor animals for nature programs in the city.

Meanwhile, the Urban Forest Strategy's tree planting project has remained on track, and canopy cover is _____(B)_____ to increase from 23 percent in 2012 to 40 percent by the year 2040. Melbourne's urban forest strategy will help keep the city cool. It will also allow residents _____(C)_____ with nature and engage in outdoor activities every day. As a result, _____

_____

as they move toward a greener future.

14 윗글의 빈칸에 들어갈 말로 가장 적절한 것은?

① the city will become a popular tourist destination
② trees will grow faster and stronger
③ residents will be happier and healthier
④ air pollution will decrease dramatically
⑤ property values in the area will increase significantly

15 윗글의 밑줄 친 (A), (B), (C)를 어법에 맞는 형태로 고쳐 쓰시오.

(A) build → _____

(B) predict → _____

(C) interact → _____

[01~02] 다음 담화를 읽고, 물음에 답하시오.

W Would you like to contribute to research and make a ①difference in the world? Join Eco Trackers to participate in environmental citizen science projects! Scientists need data, but it's hard for them to collect the information they need alone. Our website allows people from around the world to collect data while they work ②together on research projects. Do you enjoy hiking? Help scientists study air quality by taking ③photographs from the tops of mountains. How about gardening? Try growing crops in your community garden and check your area's soil quality. You can even help scientists while looking at the stars! Just record light ④pollution by reporting how visible stars are. Come and join Eco Trackers today! I'm sure that we can make the world a ⑤worse place.

01 위 담화의 목적으로 알맞은 것은?

① To recruit volunteers for environmental citizen science projects
② To advertise a new hiking app for mountain climbers
③ To sell gardening equipment for community gardens
④ To promote a stargazing event for astronomy enthusiasts
⑤ To raise funds for scientific research equipment

02 위 담화의 밑줄 친 부분 중, 문맥상 어색한 단어를 골라 바르게 고쳐 쓰시오.

_____ : _____ → _____

[03~04] 다음 글을 읽고, 물음에 답하시오.

Dear Tree,

_____(A)_____ I walk past you, your beautiful leaves bring a smile to my face. _____(B)_____ I stop in front of you and take a deep breath of fresh air, I ①appreciate the oxygen that you ②produce. Without you and all your friends, we humans wouldn't be able to get enough oxygen. By the way, I ③noticed that a family of birds has made a nest in your branches. It's so kind of you to ④provide them with a home. I hope that more people ⑤realize how important you and all the other trees are to the environment. Have a nice day!

03 윗글의 밑줄 친 ①~⑤ 중, 다음 영어 뜻풀이에 해당하는 단어로 가장 적절한 것은?

to recognize the value of something or to be grateful for something

①　　　　②　　　　③　　　　④　　　　⑤

04 윗글의 빈칸 (A), (B)에 공통으로 들어갈 말로 가장 적절한 것은?

① However　　　　② Wherever
③ Whenever　　　　④ Whatever
⑤ Whoever

[05~06] 다음 글을 읽고, 물음에 답하시오.

Believe it or not, trees in Melbourne, Australia receive emails like this all the time. How is it possible that trees have email addresses? And why are people sending them messages?

(A) They also lead to a rise in the use of air-conditioning. This speeds up climate change by increasing energy consumption and greenhouse gas emissions.

(B) The story behind these emails begins with Melbourne's Urban Forest Strategy plan, a response to Australia's millennium drought. This drought lasted from the late 1990s to 2010. By the time it ended, 40 percent of the city's 77,000 trees were in a state of declining health. Furthermore, the overall number of trees was decreasing.

(C) As a result, the amount of shade provided by trees within the city, also known as canopy cover, decreased. The loss of canopy cover is a major threat to urban environments because it raises temperatures. Higher temperatures in cities can be dangerous for residents, as they increase the risk of heat exhaustion.

05 윗글의 제목으로 가장 적절한 것은?

① Melbourne's Unique Tree Email System
② The Effects of Drought on Urban Trees
③ Climate Change and Urban Heat Islands
④ The Importance of Canopy Cover in Cities
⑤ Air Conditioning and Greenhouse Gas Emissions

06 주어진 글 다음에 이어질 글의 순서로 가장 적절한 것은?

① (A) – (C) – (B)   ② (B) – (A) – (C)
③ (B) – (C) – (A)   ④ (C) – (A) – (B)
⑤ (C) – (B) – (A)

[07~08] 다음 글을 읽고, 물음에 답하시오.

Something had to be done ① to deal with the loss of Melbourne's trees. In 2012, the city government announced its Urban Forest Strategy plan. It set the ambitious goal of planting more than 3,000 trees every year for the next twenty years. The plan also involved the creation of an online map ② to call the Urban Forest Visual.

This interactive map shows the location of every single tree in the city's parks and along its roads. It uses colors and symbols ③ to indicate each tree's age and genus. Also, users can click on a tree ④ to find out its species and even send it an email. At first, the "mail this tree" function had a specific purpose. It was designed ⑤ to allow people to easily inform council workers about trees that were _____ or in poor health.

07 윗글의 밑줄 친 ①~⑤ 중, 어법상 틀린 것은?

①   ②   ③   ④   ⑤

08 윗글의 빈칸에 들어갈 말로 가장 적절한 것은?

① planted   ② watered
③ damaged   ④ protected
⑤ identified

[09~10] 다음 글을 읽고, 물음에 답하시오.

_____(A)_____ the map was ①posting online, something unexpected happened. The trees started receiving ②thousands of emails, but many of them were not reports about damage or poor health. _____(B)_____, they were love letters, poems, greetings, and messages ③expressing appreciation for the trees. One person wrote, "I love the way the light shines on your leaves and how your branches hang so low. It is almost _____(C)_____ you are trying ④to hug me." The tree mail phenomenon quickly spread, and people all over the world started ⑤sending messages.

09 윗글의 빈칸 (A), (B), (C)에 들어갈 말로 가장 적절한 것은?

(A)	(B)	(C)
① Before	… However	… like
② When	… Therefore	… that
③ While	… Moreover	… as
④ After	… Instead	… like
⑤ Since	… Although	… as

10 윗글의 밑줄 친 부분 중, 어법상 틀린 것을 찾아 바르게 고쳐 쓰시오.

_____ : _____ → _____

[11~12] 다음 글을 읽고, 물음에 답하시오.

A message that was sent all the way from Russia said, "When I read about this wonderful project, I was inspired to write to you, even though I live thousands of miles away. Although we are separated by a great distance, we share the same planet and the same environment. Perhaps one day we will meet. Until then, I hope you can stay healthy and strong."

The global _____(A)_____ of the tree mail phenomenon reminds us that we are all connected to nature, and we are all involved in building a more sustainable world. Without _____(B)_____ action from people across the globe, we would have little hope of saving our planet for future generations.

11 윗글의 밑줄 친 that과 쓰임이 다른 것은?

① The song that he wrote became a big hit.
② I believe that honesty is the best policy.
③ The house that they built last year is beautiful.
④ The movie that we watched last night was boring.
⑤ The book that I bought yesterday is very interesting.

12 윗글의 빈칸 (A), (B)에 들어갈 말을 알맞은 형태로 고쳐 쓰시오.

(A) popular → _____

(B) collect → _____

13 다음 글의 빈칸 (A), (B)에 공통으로 들어갈 말로 가장 적절한 것은?

Welcome to the Royal Hotel, and thank you for choosing us! We offer free Wi-Fi access, a business center, an indoor pool, and more. We believe ____(A)____ we have everything you need for an enjoyable stay. Our staff is ready to help you at any time, so please let us know what we can do. We hope ____(B)____ you have a great experience here!

Sincerely,

Mark Richard,

General Manager

① if   ② as   ③ when
④ that   ⑤ because

14 다음 글의 밑줄 친 문장과 같은 뜻이 되도록 조건에 맞게 문장을 완성하시오.

5th Fall Novel Fair / October 25-28

Without fun and inspiring stories, life would be rather unexciting. It's true that we can experience stories through TV and movies. However, nothing can replace the impact novels have on our minds and spirits. <u>Without novels, the world would certainly be a less imaginative place.</u> So, this month, remember to pick up a novel!

조건

• if와 be동사를 사용할 것
• 필요시 어법에 맞게 어형을 바꿔 쓸 것

→ _____ novels, the world would certainly be a less imaginative place.

15 자연스러운 흐름이 되도록 바르게 배열한 것은?

(A) Meanwhile, the Urban Forest Strategy's tree planting project has remained on track, and canopy cover is predicted to increase from 23 percent in 2012 to 40 percent by the year 2040. Melbourne's urban forest strategy will help keep the city cool. It will also allow residents to interact with nature and engage in outdoor activities every day.

(B) As a result, residents will be happier and healthier as they move toward a greener future.

(C) Locally, the tree mail phenomenon has inspired many Melbourne residents to offer their own ideas about building an environmentally friendly urban environment. Some have even volunteered to measure trees and monitor animals for nature programs in the city.

① (A) – (C) – (B)   ② (B) – (A) – (C)
③ (B) – (C) – (A)   ④ (C) – (A) – (B)
⑤ (C) – (B) – (A)

[01~02] 다음 글을 읽고, 물음에 답하시오.

Dear Tree,

Every time I pass by you, your beautiful leaves make me smile. When I stop in front of you and take a deep (A) breath / breathe of fresh air, I am grateful for the oxygen you produce. Without you and your fellow trees, we humans wouldn't have enough oxygen to breathe. Also, I noticed (B) that / what a family of birds has built a nest in your branches. It's very generous (C) for / of you to offer them a home. I hope that more people understand how vital you and all other trees are for our environment. Wishing you a wonderful day!

01 윗글을 쓴 목적으로 가장 적절한 것은?

① 나무에 대한 감사와 중요성을 표현하기 위해
② 나무의 생태적 역할을 설명하기 위해
③ 자연의 아름다움을 묘사하기 위해
④ 나무와 사람의 관계를 서술하기 위해
⑤ 나무의 생리학적 특성을 분석하기 위해

02 (A), (B), (C)의 각 네모 안에서 어법에 맞는 낱말로 가장 적절한 것은?

	(A)		(B)		(C)
①	breathe	…	what	…	for
②	breathe	…	what	…	of
③	breath	…	that	…	for
④	breath	…	that	…	of
⑤	breath	…	what	…	of

[03~04] 다음 글을 읽고, 물음에 답하시오.

Surprisingly, trees in Melbourne, Australia receive emails. (①) You might wonder how trees could have email addresses and why people would send messages to them. (②)

The origin of this unique communication system can be traced back to Melbourne's Urban Forest Strategy plan. (③) When the drought finally ended, it was discovered that 40 percent of Melbourne's 77,000 trees were suffering from poor health. (④) Moreover, the total number of trees in the city was decreasing. (⑤)

03 윗글의 흐름으로 보아, 주어진 문장이 들어가기에 가장 적절한 곳은?

It was developed in response to the severe millennium drought that affected Australia from the late 1990s to 2010.

①　　　②　　　③　　　④　　　⑤

04 윗글의 내용과 일치하지 않는 것은?

① 호주 멜버른에 있는 나무들은 이메일을 받는다.
② 도시숲 전략 계획은 가뭄에 대응하기 위해 개발되었다.
③ 가뭄이 끝난 후 멜버른 나무의 40%가 건강 상태가 좋지 않았다.
④ 나무에 이메일 주소를 부여한 목적은 시민들의 개인적인 메시지를 받기 위해서였다.
⑤ 사람들은 나무에게 개인적인 메시지와 연애편지를 보내기 시작했다.

[05~06] 다음 글을 읽고, 물음에 답하시오.

ⓐConsequently, the tree canopy cover, which refers to the shade provided by trees in urban areas, diminished. This reduction in canopy cover poses a ⓑsignificant risk to city environments as it leads to increased temperatures. Higher temperatures in urban areas can be ⓒhazardous for residents, elevating the likelihood of heat-related illnesses. ⓓAdditionally, these warmer conditions result in greater use of air-conditioning systems. This increased reliance on cooling technology accelerates climate change by boosting energy usage and the ⓔrelease of greenhouse gases into the atmosphere.

05 윗글의 주제로 가장 적절한 것은?

① The importance of tree canopy cover in urban areas
② The health risks associated with the tree canopy cover
③ The relationship between air-conditioning and climate change
④ The negative consequences of reduced urban tree canopy cover
⑤ Methods to increase tree canopy cover in cities

06 윗글의 밑줄 친 부분과 바꿔 쓸 수 있는 것으로 바르지 <u>않은</u> 것은?

① ⓐ → As a result
② ⓑ → important
③ ⓒ → dangerous
④ ⓓ → Also
⑤ ⓔ → consumption

[07~08] 다음 글을 읽고, 물음에 답하시오.

Action was necessary to address the decline of trees in Melbourne. In 2012, the city government introduced the Urban Forest Strategy, ①aiming to plant over 3,000 trees annually for the next twenty years. This plan also included the development of an interactive online map ②called the Urban Forest Visual.

This map provides a comprehensive view of every tree in Melbourne's parks and streets. It employs a system of colors and symbols ③to represent each tree's age and genus. Additionally, users can interact with the map by ④clicking on individual trees to learn about their species and even send electronic messages to them. Initially, the "mail this tree" function was intended as a practical tool, allowing citizens to easily report ⑤damaging or unhealthy trees to city officials.

07 윗글의 제목으로 가장 적절한 것은?

① The History of Melbourne's Parks and Gardens
② Climate Change Effects on Australian Cities
③ Public Participation in Urban Planning
④ Melbourne's Innovative Urban Forest Plan
⑤ Technology in Modern Landscape Architecture

08 윗글의 밑줄 친 부분 중, 어법상 틀린 것은?

①   ②   ③   ④   ⑤

[09~10] 다음 글을 읽고, 물음에 답하시오.

After the map was posted online, something (A) expected / unexpected happened. ① The trees began receiving numerous emails, but surprisingly, many of them weren't reports of damage or health issues. ② Instead, people sent love letters, poems, greetings, and messages of gratitude to the trees. ③ The city also hosts an annual food festival that attracts many visitors. One individual wrote, "I love the way the light shines on your leaves and how your (B) roots / branches hang so low. ④ It almost feels as if you're reaching out to embrace me." ⑤ This tree communication trend rapidly gained (C) popularity / criticism, and people all over the world started sending messages to the trees.

09 윗글의 전체 흐름으로 보아, 관계 없는 문장은?

①   ②   ③   ④   ⑤

10 (A), (B), (C)의 각 네모 안에서 문맥에 맞는 낱말로 가장 적절한 것은?

	(A)	(B)	(C)
①	expected	⋯ roots	⋯ criticism
②	expected	⋯ branches	⋯ popularity
③	unexpected	⋯ roots	⋯ popularity
④	unexpected	⋯ branches	⋯ criticism
⑤	unexpected	⋯ branches	⋯ popularity

[11~12] 다음 글을 읽고, 물음에 답하시오.

A Russian wrote to a Melbourne tree, saying, "Learning about this wonderful project inspired me to send a message, even though I live thousands of miles away. Although we're far apart geographically, we inhabit the same planet and share a common environment. I hope we can meet someday. (A) Until / By then, I hope you can stay healthy and strong."

The widespread popularity of the email project serves (B) as / for a reminder of our universal connection to nature and our shared responsibility in _____. The preservation of our planet for future generations relies heavily (C) on / from global collaborative efforts; without such united action, our chances of success would be slim.

11 윗글의 빈칸에 들어갈 말로 가장 적절한 것은?

① promoting international tourism
② developing advanced technology
③ increasing economic growth
④ creating a more sustainable world
⑤ expanding urban development

12 (A), (B), (C)의 각 네모 안에서 어법에 맞는 낱말로 가장 적절한 것은?

	(A)	(B)	(C)
①	Until	⋯ for	⋯ on
②	Until	⋯ as	⋯ from
③	Until	⋯ as	⋯ on
④	By	⋯ as	⋯ on
⑤	By	⋯ for	⋯ from

[13~15] 다음 글을 읽고, 물음에 답하시오.

Locally, the tree mail phenomenon has inspired many Melbourne residents to offer their own ideas about building an environmentally friendly urban environment. Some enthusiastic residents have even offered to assist with tree measurements and wildlife monitoring for urban nature programs.

Meanwhile, the Urban Forest Strategy's tree planting project continues to progress as planned. The city anticipates an expansion of its canopy cover from 23 percent in 2012 to 40 percent by 2040. This urban forest plan is designed to maintain lower temperatures in Melbourne. Additionally, it will provide daily opportunities for residents to connect with nature and participate in outdoor activities. Consequently, as the city becomes greener, its residents will be happier and healthier.

13 윗글의 주제로 가장 적절한 것은?

① The unexpected success of the tree email project in Melbourne
② The importance of urban forests in combating climate change
③ The positive impacts of Melbourne's Urban Forest Strategy
④ The role of citizen participation in urban environmental programs
⑤ The health benefits of increased green spaces in cities

14 윗글의 내용을 한 문장으로 요약할 때 빈칸에 들어갈 말로 가장 적절한 것은?

The Urban Forest Strategy in Melbourne not only aims to increase the city's green cover but also provides _____ for residents.

① financial incentives
② job opportunities
③ educational programs
④ daily nature connections
⑤ urban farming spaces

15 윗글의 내용과 일치하지 <u>않는</u> 것은?

① 일부 주민들은 나무 측정과 야생동물 모니터링을 돕겠다고 제안했다.
② 도시숲 계획은 계획대로 진행되고 있다.
③ 멜버른 시는 2040년까지 캐노피 커버를 40%로 확대할 계획이다.
④ 도시숲 계획은 멜버른의 기온을 높이기 위해 설계되었다.
⑤ 도시가 더 푸르러지면 주민들의 행복과 건강이 증진될 것으로 예상된다.

[01~02] 다음 글을 읽고, 물음에 답하시오.

Dear Tree,

Whenever I walk past you, your beautiful leaves bring a smile to my face. ① Whenever I stop in front of you and take a deep breath of fresh air, I appreciate the oxygen that you produce. ② With you and all your friends, we humans wouldn't be able to get enough oxygen. ③ By the way, I noticed that a family of birds has made a nest in your branches. ④ It's so kind of you to provide them with a home. ⑤ I hope that more people realize how important you and all the other trees are to the environment. Have a nice day!

01 윗글의 내용을 한 문장으로 요약할 때 빈칸 (A), (B)에 들어갈 말로 가장 적절한 것은?

This letter expresses gratitude to the ____(A)____ for providing oxygen and shelter for birds, while emphasizing the importance of trees to the ____(B)____.

(A) _____ (B) _____

02 윗글의 ①~⑤ 중, 어법상 틀린 문장을 찾아 번호를 쓰고 문장을 다시 쓰시오.

번호	고친 문장

[03~04] 다음 글을 읽고, 물음에 답하시오.

The story behind these emails begins with Melbourne's Urban Forest Strategy plan, a ⓐ respond to Australia's millennium drought. This drought lasted from the late 1990s to 2010. By the time it ended, 40 percent of the city's 77,000 trees were in a state of declining health. Furthermore, the overall number of trees were decreasing.

As a result, the amount of shade provided by trees within the city, also known as canopy cover, decreased. 임관 피복도의 줄어듦은 기온을 상승시키기 때문에 도시 환경에 주요한 위협이다. Higher temperatures in cities can be dangerous for residents, as they increase the risk of heat exhaustion. They also lead to a rise in the use of air-conditioning. This speeds up climate change by increasing energy ⓑ consume and greenhouse gas emissions.

03 윗글의 밑줄 친 우리말과 같은 뜻이 되도록 다음 **보기** 안의 단어를 바르게 배열하시오.

보기 is / a / threat / environments / raises / to / urban / because / it / major / temperatures

The loss of canopy cover _____
_____.

04 윗글의 밑줄 친 ⓐ, ⓑ를 알맞은 형태로 바꿔 쓰시오.

ⓐ: _____ ⓑ: _____

[05~06] 다음 글을 읽고, 물음에 답하시오.

Something had to be done to deal with the loss of Melbourne's trees. In 2012, the city government announced its Urban Forest Strategy plan. 그것은 다음 20년 동안 매년 3,000그루가 넘는 나무들을 심는 야심찬 목표를 설정했다. The plan also involved the creation of an online map called the Urban Forest Visual.

This interactive map shows the location of every single tree in the city's parks and along its roads. ⓐIt uses colors and symbols to indicate each tree's age and genus. Also, users can click on a tree to find out its species and even send it an email. At first, the "mail this tree" function had a specific purpose. ⓑIt was designed to allow people to easily inform council workers about trees that were damaged or in poor health.

05 윗글의 밑줄 친 우리말과 같은 뜻이 되도록 빈칸에 알맞은 말을 쓰시오.

It _____ the ambitious _____ of planting _____ _____ 3,000 trees every year _____ the next twenty years.

06 윗글의 밑줄 친 ⓐ, ⓑ가 가리키는 것을 찾아 쓰시오.

ⓐ: _____

ⓑ: _____

07 다음 글의 밑줄 친 우리말과 같은 뜻이 되도록 괄호 안에 주어진 단어를 알맞게 배열하시오.

After the map was posted online, (1) 예상 밖의 일이 일어났다. The trees started receiving thousands of emails, but many of them were not reports about damage or poor health. Instead, they were love letters, poems, greetings, and messages expressing appreciation for the trees. One person wrote, "I love the way the light shines on your leaves and (2) 네 가지들이 그렇게 낮게 매달려 있는 방식. It is almost like you are trying to hug me." The tree mail phenomenon quickly spread, and people all over the world started sending messages.

(1) _____

(unexpected / something / happened)

(2) _____

(your branches / how / so low / hang)

08 다음 빈칸에 알맞은 말을 보기에서 골라 쓰시오.

보기 courageous   dangerous   nervous
      unfair   unusual   unexpected

(1) Poor air quality is especially _____ for young children.

(2) It is _____ for Sally to walk to school, as she rides her bike on most days.

(3) Although his friends were there to encourage him, he was still _____ about the test.

(4) The team's _____ victory in the championship shocked all the fans.

[09~10] 다음 글을 읽고, 물음에 답하시오.

A message that ①sent all the way from Russia said, "When I read about this wonderful project, I was inspired to write to you, ②even though I live thousands of miles away. Although we are separated by a great distance, we share the same planet and the same environment. Perhaps one day we will meet. Until then, I hope you can stay ③healthy and strong."

The global popularity of the tree mail phenomenon reminds us ④what we are all connected to nature, and we are all involved in ⑤building a more sustainable world. Without collective action from people across the globe, we would have little hope of saving our planet for future generations.

09 윗글의 밑줄 친 ①~⑤ 중, 어법상 틀린 것을 찾아 번호를 쓰고 틀린 것을 바르게 고쳐 쓰시오.

번호	틀린 것	고친 것

10 윗글의 밑줄 친 문장과 같은 뜻이 되도록 빈칸에 알맞은 말을 쓰시오.

(1) _____ _____ collective action from people across the globe, we would have little hope of saving our planet for future generations.

(2) _____ _____ _____ _____ _____ collective action from people across the globe, we would have little hope of saving our planet for future generations.

[11~12] 다음 글을 읽고, 물음에 답하시오.

Locally, the tree mail phenomenon has inspired many Melbourne residents ①to offer their own ideas about building an environmentally friendly urban environment. Some have even volunteered to measure trees and ②monitoring animals for nature programs in the city.

Meanwhile, the Urban Forest Strategy's tree planting project has remained on track, and canopy cover ③is predicted to increase from 23 percent in 2012 to 40 percent by the year 2040. Melbourne's urban forest strategy will help ④keep the city cool. 그것은 또한 주민들이 매일 자연과 소통하고 야외 활동들에 참여하게 해줄 것이다. As a result, residents will be happier and ⑤healthier as they move toward a greener future.

11 윗글의 밑줄 친 ①~⑤ 중, 어법상 틀린 것을 찾아 번호를 쓰고 바르게 고친 후 틀린 이유를 쓰시오.

번호	
고친 것	
틀린 이유	

12 윗글의 밑줄 친 우리말과 같은 뜻이 되도록 다음 보기 안의 단어를 바르게 배열하시오.

보기 allow / it / outdoor activities / to interact with / will / engage in / residents / every day / nature / also / and

_____

LESSON ✔

04

—

The Winds of Change

Functions

▶ 정의하기

This means we can learn new things more easily than ever before.

▶ 선호 표현하기

Which do you prefer?

Structures

▶ The article featured a shocking photograph of flames and smoke **rising from the river**.

▶ But this was not a photograph of the 1969 fire, **which** was put out so quickly that nobody took a picture of it.

교과서 어휘

Words

☐ capture	⑧ 정확히 포착하다, 담아내다	☐ anger	⑲ 화, 분노 (angry ⑱ 성난, 화가 난)
☐ emotion	⑲ 감정	☐ awareness	⑲ 의식, 관심
☐ convey	⑧ (생각·감정 등을) 전달하다	☐ standard	⑲ 수준, 기준
☐ complex	⑱ 복잡한 (↔ simple 단순한)	☐ establish	⑧ 설립[설정]하다; 수립하다
☐ photograph	⑲ 사진	☐ passage	⑲ 통로; (법안의) 처리, 통과
☐ spark	⑧ 촉발하다, 유발하다	☐ expose	⑧ 드러내다; 폭로하다
☐ industry	⑲ 산업 (industrial ⑱ 산업의)	☐ harsh	⑱ 가혹한, 냉혹한
☐ rapidly	⑲ 빠르게 (= quickly) (rapid ⑱ 빠른)	☐ revolution	⑲ 혁명
☐ steady	⑱ 안정적인	☐ employ	⑧ 고용하다
☐ steel mill	제철소	☐ laborer	⑲ 노동자 (labor ⑲ 노동)
☐ regard	⑧ ~을 …으로 여기다[평가하다]	☐ reveal	⑧ 드러내다, 밝히다
☐ economic	⑱ 경제의 (economy ⑲ 경제)	☐ committee	⑲ 위원회
☐ likely	⑱ 가능성 있는, 그럴듯한	☐ investigative	⑱ 조사[수사]의 (investigate ⑧ 조사하다)
☐ flare	⑲ (순간적으로) 확 타오르는 불길, 불꽃	☐ pretend	⑧ ~인 척하다, ~라고 가장하다
☐ oil-soaked	⑱ 기름에 흠뻑 젖은	☐ insurance	⑲ 보험; 보험업
☐ beneath	⑳ 아래에	☐ inspector	⑲ 조사관, 감독관
☐ article	⑲ (신문·잡지의) 글, 기사	☐ helpless	⑱ 무력한
☐ feature	⑧ 특별히 포함하다, 특징으로 삼다	☐ weave	⑧ 짜다[엮다], 짜서[엮어서] 만들다
☐ flame	⑲ 불길, 불꽃	☐ equipment	⑲ 장비, 용품
☐ occur	⑧ 발생하다 (occurrence ⑲ 발생)	☐ tragic	⑱ 비극적인, 비극의 (tragedy ⑲ 비극)
☐ impact	⑲ 영향	☐ exhibition	⑲ 전시회, 전시 (exhibit ⑧ 전시하다)
☐ attitude	⑲ 태도	☐ ban	⑧ 금하다, 금지하다
☐ environmental	⑱ 환경의 (environment ⑲ 환경)	☐ congress	⑲ 의회, 국회
☐ protect	⑧ 보호하다 (protection ⑲ 보호)	☐ illegal	⑱ 불법적인 (↔ legal 합법적인)

Phrases

☐ grab hold of	~을 (움켜)잡다	☐ set fire to	~을 태우다, ~에 불지르다
☐ in an instant	순식간에, 즉시	☐ take a picture of	~의 사진을 찍다
☐ a number of	다수의, 많은	☐ become aware of	~을 알게 되다
☐ provide A to B	A를 B에게 제공하다	☐ have an impact on	~에 영향을 주다
☐ regard A as B	A를 B로 간주하다	☐ go on strike	파업하다
☐ catch fire	불이 붙다	☐ gain access to	~에 접근하다

put out (불을) 끄다	It took about ten hours to **put out** the massive fire last night. 어젯밤 대형 화재를 진화하는 데 대략 열 시간이 걸렸다.
take advantage of ~을 이용하다	The company was criticized for **taking advantage of** its employees. 그 회사는 직원들을 이용하는 것에 대한 비판을 받았다.
can't help but+동사원형 ~하지 않을 수 없다	**I can't help but** wonder why my friend hasn't texted me back in weeks. 나는 내 친구가 몇 주 동안 왜 나에게 다시 문자를 하지 않았는지 궁금해 하지 않을 수 없다.

Collocations

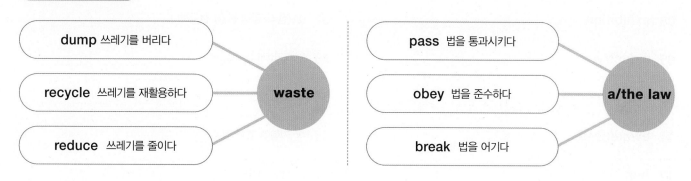

dump 쓰레기를 버리다
recycle 쓰레기를 재활용하다
reduce 쓰레기를 줄이다
waste

pass 법을 통과시키다
obey 법을 준수하다
break 법을 어기다
a/the law

English-English Dictionary

☐ **capture** 정확히 포착하다, 담아내다   to represent or record accurately in words or pictures

☐ **convey** (생각·감정 등을) 전달하다   to communicate or express (a thought, feeling, etc.)

☐ **flare** 확 타오르는 불길, 불꽃   a short flash of a light or flame

☐ **article** (신문·잡지의) 기사   a piece of writing about a particular subject that is included in a newspaper, magazine, etc.

☐ **awareness** 의식, 관심   the state of having knowledge about a situation or fact

☐ **passage** 통로; (법안의) 처리, 통과   the process of passing a law

☐ **expose** 드러내다; 폭로하다   reveal something that was hidden or covered

☐ **harsh** 가혹한, 냉혹한   unpleasantly rough or severe

☐ **committee** 위원회   a group of people who work for a specific purpose

☐ **helpless** 무력한   unable to protect or take care of oneself

☐ **equipment** 장비, 용품   tools or supplies needed for a specific purpose

☐ **exhibition** 전시회, 전시   a display of art, artifacts, or other items of interest

☐ **illegal** 불법적인   prohibited by law

✤ 다음 영어는 우리말로, 우리말은 영어로 쓰시오.

01	beneath	(전) _____	25	(동) 드러내다, 밝히다 _____
02	inspector	(명) _____	26	(형) 가혹한, 냉혹한 _____
03	capture	(동) _____	27	(동) 촉발시키다, 유발하다 _____
04	tragic	(형) _____	28	(명) 감정 _____
05	pretend	(동) _____	29	(동) 짜다[엮다], 짜서[엮어서] 만들다 _____
06	feature	(동) _____	30	(형) 무력한 _____
07	environmental	(형) _____	31	(형) 복잡한 _____
08	exhibition	(명) _____	32	(동) (생각·감정 등을) 전달하다 _____
09	industry	(명) _____	33	(동) 드러내다; 폭로하다 _____
10	article	(명) _____	34	(형) 불법적인 _____
11	awareness	(명) _____	35	(형) 기름에 흠뻑 젖은 _____
12	ban	(동) _____	36	(명) 장비, 용품 _____
13	revolution	(명) _____	37	(명) 통로; (법안의) 처리, 통과 _____
14	flare	(명) _____	38	(명) 수준, 기준 _____
15	investigative	(형) _____	39	(명) 위원회 _____
16	congress	(명) _____	40	(명) 노동자 _____
17	rapidly	(부) _____	41	(동) 설립[설정]하다; 수립하다 _____
18	occur	(동) _____	42	(형) 경제의 _____
19	photograph	(명) _____	43	(동) 간주하다 _____
20	likely	(형) _____	44	(동) 고용하다 _____
21	grab hold of	_____	45	파업하다 _____
22	put out	_____	46	~의 사진을 찍다 _____
23	take advantage of	_____	47	~에 영향을 주다 _____
24	can't help but+동사원형	_____	48	~에 접근하다 _____

A 다음 보기 에서 알맞은 말을 골라 빈칸에 쓰시오.

> 보기   grab hold of   put out   can't help but   go on strike   take advantage of

01   Please make sure to _____ the fire before you leave the campground.

02   We should not _____ others' weaknesses for our own benefit.

03   Aiden broke his promise to her, so he _____ feel sorry for her now.

04   The railroad union declared that they would _____ .

05   As quickly as a camera captures a scene, an image can _____ our emotions.

B 다음 빈칸에 들어갈 말을 보기 에서 골라 알맞은 형태로 바꿔 쓰시오.

> 보기   obey   dump   recycle   pass

01   Steel mills and factories started _____ large amounts of waste into the river.
제철소와 공장은 대량의 폐기물을 강에 버리기 시작했다.

02   Many states _____ stronger laws to ban the employment of children.
많은 주가 아동 고용을 금지하기 위해 더 강력한 법안들을 통과시켰다.

C 다음 밑줄 친 단어의 영어 뜻풀이로 알맞은 것을 골라 기호를 쓰시오.

> ⓐ the process of passing a law
> ⓑ tools or supplies needed for a specific purpose
> ⓒ a piece of writing included with others in a newspaper, magazine, or other publication

01   This was thanks to an <u>article</u> published in *Time* magazine that year. (   )

02   These included picking vegetables, weaving baskets, and even handling dangerous <u>equipment</u>.   (   )

03   National water quality standards were established with the <u>passage</u> of the Clean Water Act.
(   )

교과서 핵심 대화문

Function 1 정의하기

B I've started my own video channel.
= I have

G What's it about?

B It's focused on teaching how to play the guitar to beginners.
focus on: ~에 초점을 맞추다   의문사+to부정사(~하는 방법)

You know I really love music!
(that)

G That's great! My sister wants to learn how to play an instrument.
의문사+to부정사
want+to부정사: ~하기를 원하다

I'll definitely recommend your channel to her.
recommend A to B: B에게 A를 추천하다

B Thanks! I hope it helps her learn.
(that) help+목적어+(to-)v

G It's so nice that you are willing to make helpful videos.
가주어   진주어   be willing to: 기꺼이 ~하다

B Many people are doing it these days.

This means we can learn new things more easily than ever before.
(that)   비교급+than: ~보다 더 …한

G You're right.

《 B: 나 자신의 비디오 채널을 시작했어.

G: 어떤 내용이야?

B: 초보자들에게 기타 연주하는 법을 가르치는 데 초점을 맞추고 있어. 내가 음악을 정말 좋아하는 거 알잖아!

G: 그거 정말 좋다! 우리 언니가 악기 연주하는 법을 배우고 싶어 하거든. 언니한테 네 채널을 꼭 추천해줄게.

B: 고마워! 네 언니가 배우는 데 도움이 되길 바라.

G: 네가 도움이 되는 비디오를 만들려고 하다니 정말 좋다.

B: 요즘은 많은 사람들이 그렇게 하고 있어. 이것은 우리가 그 어느 때보다 쉽게 새로운 것들을 배울 수 있다는 걸 의미해.

G: 네 말이 맞아.

Study Point ✂

This means ~는 '이것은 ~를 의미한다'라는 뜻으로 앞서 언급된 내용의 의미나 결과를 설명하거나 정의할 때 사용하는 표현이다.

More Expressions ✂

정의하는 표현들

This shows that ~(이것은 ~을 나타낸다), This implies that ~(이것은 ~을 시사한다), This indicates that ~(이것은 ~을 나타낸다), This suggests that ~(이것은 ~을 암시한다) 등이 비슷한 의미의 표현이다. 여기서 that은 모두 생략할 수 있다.

This shows (that) people are more engaged in political issues than before.

이것은 사람들이 이전보다 정치적 이슈에 더 관심을 가지고 있음을 나타낸다.

This suggests (that) we need to take immediate action to reduce our carbon emissions.

이것은 우리가 탄소 배출을 줄이기 위해 즉각적인 조치를 취해야 한다는 것을 암시한다.

Check-up ✂

다음 대화에서 밑줄 친 부분의 의도로 적절한 것은?

> A I can't imagine how people used to live without streaming platforms.
>
> B Also, they are becoming more and more convenient to use.
>
>   This means we can watch TV shows and movies anytime and anywhere.

① 충고하기   ② 희망 표현하기   ③ 정의하기

④ 관심 표현하기   ⑤ 능력 유무 표현하기

Function 2 선호 표현하기

Ethan Social media <u>has changed</u> <u>the way</u> we consume news. Today, younger
현재완료   = how
generations are <u>much more likely</u> to get their news <u>from social media</u>
비교급 수식 부사+비교급   A
<u>than</u> from traditional sources <u>like</u> TV and newspapers.
B   ~ 같은(전치사)
Which do you prefer?
선호하는 것을 묻는 표현

Sophia I <u>prefer</u> social media. <u>It has completely transformed</u> <u>the way</u> we get
= I like social media better.   현재완료   = how
information. <u>It</u> has become <u>so much quicker</u> and easier <u>to access and</u>
가주어   비교급 수식 부사+비교급   진주어
<u>share news.</u>

Liam Absolutely. However, there is a negative side to this. People <u>don't</u>
항상 ~하는 것은 아니야
<u>always</u> check whether information is accurate. <u>As a result,</u> false or
그 결과
misleading information can also spread very quickly online.

Ava That's so true. <u>That's why</u> I prefer more traditional sources of news.
'그래서 ~이다' 또는 '그것이 ~한 이유이다' (앞서 언급된 내용의 결과나 이유를 설명할 때 사용)
<u>We should never</u> share news on social media <u>without checking</u> it first.
~해서는 안 된다   전치사+동명사

《 Ethan: 소셜 미디어는 우리가 뉴스를 소비하는 방식을 변화시켰어. 오늘날 젊은 세대들은 TV나 신문 같은 전통적인 매체보다 소셜 미디어에서 뉴스를 접할 가능성이 훨씬 더 높아. 너희는 어떤 것을 선호해?

Sophia: 나는 소셜 미디어를 선호해. 소셜 미디어는 우리가 정보를 얻는 방식을 완전히 바꿔놓았어. 뉴스에 접근하고 공유하는 것이 훨씬 더 빠르고 쉬워졌어.

Liam: 사람들이 항상 정보의 정확성을 확인하지는 않아. 그 결과, 거짓이나 오해의 소지가 있는 정보도 온라인에서 매우 빠르게 퍼질 수 있어.

Ava: 정말 맞아. 그래서 나는 더 전통적인 뉴스 출처를 선호해. 우리는 먼저 확인하지 않고 소셜 미디어에서 뉴스를 공유해서는 안 돼.

Study Point ♉

Which do you prefer?는 '어떤 것을 더 선호하나요?'라는 의미로 두 가지 이상의 선택지 중에서 상대방의 취향이나 선호를 묻는 질문이다.

More Expressions ♉

선호를 묻는 표현들

What's your preference?(무엇을 선호하니?), Which option do you favor?(어떤 선택을 선호하니?), Which one do you like better?(어느 것을 더 좋아하니?) 등이 선호를 묻는 다른 표현들이다.

A: **Which one do you like better?** 너는 어느 것을 더 좋아하니?

B: I like ordering from electronic kiosks better. 나는 전자 키오스크에서 주문하는 것을 더 좋아해.

Check-up ♉

다음 밑줄 친 문장과 같은 의미가 되도록 할 때 빈칸에 알맞은 단어를 쓰시오.

A <u>Which one do you like better?</u> (= Which one do you _____?)

B I like online shopping better than offline shopping.

교과서 기타 대화문

TOPIC 1 **C. Listen and Interact**

M Look at this picture. I **①** prepared dinner for my family last weekend.

W Wow, that looks great! Did you make everything?

M No. Actually, I used a meal kit. Meal kits make cooking meals easier, and they save a lot of time.

W Now I understand **②** why they are so popular **③** these days.

M **④** Why don't you try cooking with one? There is **⑤** a wide variety of options **⑥** to choose from.

W Well, they are definitely convenient. But I **⑦** worry about the excessive use of plastic packaging.

M Yes, that is a problem. **⑧** It would be great if there were more eco-friendly packaging options for them.

① prepare A for B: B를 위해 A를 준비하다 **②** 간접의문문(의문사+주어+동사) **③** these days: 요즘 **④** Why don't you ~?: ~하는 게 어때?
⑤ a wide variety of: 다양한 종류의 **⑥** 앞의 명사 options 를 수식하는 형용사적 용법의 to부정사 **⑦** worry about: ~에 대해 걱정하다
⑧ 가정법 과거 구문

Q1 Meal kits are an environmentally friendly option for cooking. (T / F)

TOPIC 4 **B. While You View**

W The Hubble Space Telescope **①** has been orbiting just above Earth's atmosphere **②** for more than thirty years. Ever since it was launched by NASA in 1990, Hubble **③** has transformed the way we view outer space. For example, it helped scientists to accurately estimate the age and size of the universe. In 1995, Hubble took a photograph of an area of deep space **④** that appeared to be empty. However, the picture revealed **⑤** something amazing. There were actually more than 1,500 **⑥** galaxies located in the area. This kind of information has **⑦** helped scientists learn **⑧** how many galaxies there are. Hubble has also taught us about the rate **⑨** at which the universe is expanding. Scientists thought it was slowing down, but it is actually getting faster.
In 2021, NASA launched a much more advanced telescope **⑩** called the James Webb Space Telescope. Scientists hope this new telescope, **⑪** which was inspired by Hubble's achievements, will reveal even more secrets of the universe.

① 현재완료 진행형 **②** 30년이 넘는 동안 **③** 앞에 since가 있는 현재완료 계속 용법 **④** 주격 관계대명사절 **⑤** -thing으로 끝나는 대명사+형용사
⑥ 앞의 명사 galaxies를 수식하는 과거분사구 **⑦** help+목적어+동사원형: 목적어가 ~하는 것을 돕다 **⑧** 간접의문문 **⑨** 전치사+관계대명사
⑩ 앞의 명사 telescope를 수식하는 과거분사구 **⑪** 관계대명사 삽입절

Q2 The Hubble Space Telescope has helped scientists accurately estimate the age and size of the universe. (T / F)

Wrap Up **A. Listen and Write**

M Hey, cool watch!

W Thanks. I got **①** it last week.

M **②** I'm thinking of buying a new watch, too. **③** Are you satisfied with your purchase?

W Yeah! This one **④** keeps track of my heart rate, so it is very useful when I exercise.

M Wow! That's amazing!

W It has other cool functions, too. For example, I can use it **⑤** to pay for things. **⑥** This means that I don't need to carry my wallet with me anymore.

M That's great! We can do so **⑦** much more than telling time with watches nowadays.

① it = cool watch **②** I'm thinking of ~: ~을 생각하고 있다 **③** be satisfied with: ~에 만족하다 **④** keep track of: ~을 기록하다 **⑤** 부사적 용법의 to부정사(목적) **⑥** This means (that) ~: 이것은 ~을 의미한다 / not ~ anymore: 더 이상 ~ 아닌 **⑦** 비교급 수식 부사+비교급+than

Q3 The woman's new watch can only be used to tell time and monitor her heart rate. (T / F)

교과서 핵심 대화문 익히기

01 대화의 흐름상, 주어진 문장이 들어가기에 가장 적절한 곳은?

> This means we can learn new things more easily than ever before.

> **B** I've started my own video channel. (①)
> **G** What's it about?
> **B** It's focused on teaching how to play the guitar to beginners. You know I really love music!
> **G** That's great! My sister wants to learn how to play an instrument. I'll definitely recommend your channel to her. (②)
> **B** Thanks! I hope it helps her learn. (③)
> **G** It's so nice that you are willing to make helpful videos. (④)
> **B** Many people are doing it these days. (⑤)
> **G** You're right.

02 자연스러운 대화가 되도록 순서대로 바르게 배열하시오.

> (A) **Liam** Absolutely. However, there is a negative side to this. People don't always check whether information is accurate. As a result, false or misleading information can also spread very quickly online.
> (B) **Ethan** Social media has changed the way we consume news. Today, younger generations are much more likely to get their news from social media than from traditional sources like TV and newspapers. Which do you prefer?
> (C) **Ava** That's so true. That's why I prefer more traditional sources of news. We should never share news on social media without checking it first.
> (D) **Sophia** I prefer social media. It has completely transformed the way we get information. It has become so much quicker and easier to access and share news.

(   ) – (   ) – (   ) – (   )

03 다음 대화의 빈칸에 들어갈 말로 가장 적절한 것은?

> **M** Hey, cool watch!
> **W** Thanks. I got it last week.
> **M** I'm thinking of buying a new watch, too. Are you satisfied with your purchase?
> **W** Yeah! This one keeps track of my heart rate, so it is very useful when I exercise.
> **M** Wow! That's amazing!
> **W** It has other cool functions, too. For example, I can use it to pay for things. This means that _____.
> **M** That's great! We can do so much more than telling time with watches nowadays.

① I can check the time more accurately
② I can make phone calls without my smartphone
③ I don't need to carry my wallet with me anymore
④ it's easier to track my daily exercise routine
⑤ the watch can automatically update its software

교과서 핵심 문법

POINT 1 명사를 뒤에서 수식하는 현재분사

예제   That man **wearing the blue shirt** is my English teacher.

명사 ↑⎿⎽⎽⎽⎽⎯⎯⎯⎯⎯⎿ 현재분사구

파란 셔츠를 입고 있는 저 남자분은 나의 영어 선생님이다.

교과서   The article featured a shocking photograph of flames and smoke **rising from the river**.

명사 ↑⎿⎽⎽⎯⎯⎿ 현재분사구

그 기사는 강에서 피어오르는 불길과 연기의 충격적인 사진을 특종으로 다뤘다.

▶ 현재분사(v-ing)는 명사를 수식하는 역할을 하며, 능동(~하게 하는) 또는 진행(~하고 있는)의 의미를 갖는다.

Study Point ♋

1 명사를 수식하는 현재분사

현재분사가 단독으로 명사를 수식할 경우에는 명사 앞에, 목적어나 수식어구 등이 와서 길어질 경우에는 명사 뒤에 위치한다.

Do you know that **dancing** boy?   당신은 춤추고 있는 저 소년을 아나요?

The boy **dancing on the stage** looks happy.   무대에서 춤추고 있는 소년이 행복해 보인다.

The students **studying in the library** are preparing for exams. 도서관에서 공부하고 있는 학생들은 시험을 준비하고 있다.

2 명사를 수식하는 과거분사

과거분사(v-ed 또는 불규칙 과거분사)도 명사를 수식하는 역할을 하며, 수동(~된, ~당한) 또는 완료(~된, ~해진)의 의미를 갖는다.

The novel **written by the professor** became a bestseller.   그 교수에 의해 쓰여진 그 소설은 베스트셀러가 되었다.

The movie **produced by the new director** gained widespread popularity.

새로운 감독에 의해 제작된 영화가 광범위한 인기를 얻었다.

3 현재분사 vs. 동명사

현재분사는 수식하는 명사의 동작이나 상태를 나타내고, 동명사는 명사의 목적이나 용도를 나타낸다.

a **sleeping** boy 잠자고 있는 아기 (= a baby who is sleeping) [현재분사]

a **sleeping** bag 잠자는 용도의 가방 (= a bag for sleeping) [동명사]

Q 다음 네모 안에서 어법상 올바른 것을 고르시오.

1 We watched the leaves | falling / fallen | from the trees.

2 The children | playing / played | in the park look very happy.

3 The car | parking / parked | in front of the house belongs to my neighbor.

Check-up ♂

01 다음 괄호 안의 동사를 알맞은 형태로 고쳐 쓰시오.

(1) The dog _____ next door keeps me awake at night. (bark)

(2) The woman _____ the red dress is a famous actress. (wear)

(3) The document _____ by the president is very important. (sign)

02 다음 문장의 빈칸 (A), (B)에 들어갈 말로 가장 적절한 것은?

> • I saw a man _____(A)_____ a sandcastle on the beach.
> • The house _____(B)_____ last year is already for sale.

	(A)		(B)			(A)		(B)
①	build	⋯	built		②	built	⋯	building
③	built	⋯	to build		④	building	⋯	built
⑤	building	⋯	building					

03 다음 문장에서 밑줄 친 부분을 바르게 고쳐 쓰시오.

(1) The car <u>damaging</u> in the accident needs to be repaired.

(2) I saw a group of students <u>painted</u> a poster for the school festival.

(3) She carefully picked up the pieces of the <u>breaking</u> vase.

04 다음 괄호 안의 단어들을 바르게 배열하여 문장을 완성하시오. 교과서 91쪽

> **The Cake Castle**
>
> • Come visit (1) _____!
>   (cakes / the most delicious / selling / the shop / in town)
>
> • (2) _____ has started.
>   (featuring / of cupcakes / our cupcake sale / flavors / various)
>   But don't forget to try our special birthday cakes, too!
>
> • The Cake Castle is open every day from 8:00 a.m. to 8:00 p.m. Why don't you stop by today?

(POINT 2) 관계대명사의 계속적 용법

예제   He kept shaking his legs, **which** was annoying.
                _{계속적 용법의 관계대명사(= and it)}
    그는 계속해서 다리를 흔들었고, 그것은 짜증스러웠다.

교과서   But this was not a photograph of the 1969 fire, **which** was put out so quickly that nobody took a
                                     _{계속적 용법의 관계대명사 (= and it)}
    picture of it.
    그러나 이것은 1969년 화재의 사진이 아니었는데, 그것은 너무 빨리 진압되어 아무도 사진을 찍지 못했다.

▶ 관계대명사 앞에 콤마(,)를 붙인 뒤, 선행사에 대한 추가적인 정보를 나타내는 것을 관계대명사의 계속적 용법이라고 한다. 「접속사 (and, but, for)+대명사」의 의미를 나타내며, which는 앞 절 전체를 대신할 수도 있다. 관계대명사 that은 계속적 용법으로 사용할 수 없으며, 계속적 용법으로 쓰인 관계대명사는 생략할 수 없다.

Study Point 🏅

1 계속적 용법의 관계대명사

I said nothing, **which**(= and it) made my parents feel disappointed. (선행사는 앞 문장 전체)
나는 아무 말도 하지 않았는데, 그것이 부모님들을 실망하게 했다.

My sister decorated the Christmas tree, **which**(= and it) looks great. (선행사는 the Christmas tree)
내 여동생이 크리스마스 트리를 장식했고, 그것은 멋져 보인다.

I talked to Sam, **who**(= and he) will move to Canada next month. (선행사는 Sam)
나는 Sam과 얘기했는데, 그는 다음 달에 캐나다로 이사를 갈 것이다.

2 한정적 용법의 관계대명사

Some countries have laws **which[that]** are very unusual. 일부 국가들은 매우 특이한 법률을 가지고 있다.

Sharks have special skin **which[that]** helps them swim fast.

상어는 그들이 빠르게 수영할 수 있게 해주는 특별한 피부를 가지고 있다.

Having someone **who** listens to you at school can really help.

학교에서 당신의 이야기를 들어주는 누군가가 있는 것은 정말 도움이 될 수 있다.

3 한정적 용법 vs. 계속적 용법

I have an aunt **who** is a doctor. 나는 의사인 이모가 한 분 있다. (여러 명의 이모가 있을 수 있음)

I have an aunt, **who** is a doctor. 나는 이모가 한 분 있는데, 그녀는 의사이다. (이모가 한 분뿐임)

Q 다음 네모 안에서 어법상 올바른 것을 고르시오.

1 I saw Mike, | who / which | was the captain of our soccer team.

2 Her garden has beautiful trees, | which / that | attract many birds and butterflies.

3 The 1988 Summer Olympics was held in Seoul, | what / which | is the capital of Korea.

Check-up

01 다음 빈칸에 알맞은 것을 보기 에서 골라 쓰시오.

> 보기   that   who   which   what

(1) This is my grandmother, _____ turned 90 last month.

(2) The city was hit by a storm, _____ caused great damage.

(3) She forgot to bring her umbrella, _____ made her get wet in the rain.

02 다음 문장의 밑줄 친 부분을 바르게 고쳐 쓰시오.

(1) He was reading a book, <u>who</u> was quite interesting.

(2) She got a new bicycle for her birthday present, <u>that</u> has a red frame.

(3) I enjoy spending time at my grandparents' house, <u>who</u> makes me laugh.

03 다음 글의 밑줄 친 부분 중, 어법상 틀린 것을 2개 찾아 번호를 쓰고 바르게 고쳐 쓰시오. (교과서 91쪽)

> **Palace Night Tour**
>
> Welcome to *Changdeokgung*, ①<u>who</u> was the favorite palace of many kings of the Joseon Dynasty. While ②<u>walking</u> along the ponds and through the trees, you can ③<u>enjoy</u> the peaceful atmosphere under the moon. You will also be able to watch a show ④<u>performed</u> by traditional Korean dancers, ⑤<u>which</u> will be dressed up in beautiful *hanbok*.

(1) _____ → _____

(2) _____ → _____

04 다음 중 밑줄 친 부분이 어법상 틀린 문장끼리 짝지어진 것은?

> ⓐ I lost the watch, <u>which</u> I had borrowed from my sister.
> ⓑ This is a gift from my cousin, <u>which</u> lives in Canada.
> ⓒ She has a friend, <u>that</u> does volunteer work at a hospital.
> ⓓ One good fruit is an orange, <u>which</u> has a lot of vitamin C.
> ⓔ Susan is wearing a sweater, <u>who</u> her mother made for her.

① ⓐ, ⓑ   ② ⓐ, ⓒ, ⓔ   ③ ⓑ, ⓒ, ⓔ   ④ ⓒ, ⓓ   ⑤ ⓒ, ⓓ, ⓔ

교과서 본문 분석

Pictures Worth a Thousand Words
천 단어의 가치가 있는 사진들

01 As quickly as a camera captures a scene, an image can grab hold of our emotions.
as+부사[형용사]의 원급+as: …만큼 ~하게[한]   ~을 (움켜)잡다

카메라가 장면을 포착하는 것만큼 빠르게, 이미지는 우리의 감정을 사로잡을 수 있다.

02 Through speech or written text, it can be difficult [to convey a complex message quickly].
가주어   진주어

연설이나 글로 쓰인 텍스트를 통해 복잡한 메시지를 빠르게 전달하는 것은 어려울 수 있다.

03 Yet photographs can change people's hearts and minds in an instant.
접속사(그렇지만, 그런데도)   순식간에, 즉시

그렇지만 사진은 사람들의 가슴과 마음을 순식간에 바꿀 수 있다.

04 And when the magic of photography sparks an emotional reaction in a great number of people,
a number of: 다수의, 많은
it can change history.

그리고 사진 촬영의 마법이 많은 사람들에게 감정적인 반응을 유발할 때, 그것은 역사를 바꿀 수 있다.

The Burning River That Started a Movement
운동을 시작하게 한 불타는 강

05 In the 1880s, industry began to grow rapidly along the Cuyahoga River in the city of Cleveland.
명사적 용법(began의 목적어) = growing

1880년대에, 산업이 클리블랜드 시의 쿠야호가 강을 따라 빠르게 성장하기 시작했다.

06 This industrial growth provided steady jobs to people [in the area].
전치사구
provide A to B: A를 B에게 제공하다 = provide B with A

이러한 산업 성장은 그 지역 사람들에게 안정적인 일자리를 제공했다.

07 Meanwhile, steel mills and factories started dumping large amounts of waste [into the river].
한편   동명사(started의 목적어) = to dump   전치사구

한편, 제철소와 공장은 대량의 폐기물을 강에 버리기 시작했다.

08 Although the river became polluted, most people simply regarded this as a sign of the area's
접속사(비록 ~이긴 하지만)   regard A as B: A를 B로 여기다[간주하다]
economic success.

비록 강이 오염되긴 했지만, 대부분의 사람들은 이를 단순히 그 지역의 경제적 성공의 신호로 여겼다.

09 In June 1969, the polluted river caught fire.
과거분사 ⎿___↑   catch fire: 불이 붙다

1969년 6월, 그 오염된 강에 불이 붙었다.

10 The likely cause was a burning flare [falling from a train], [which set fire to oil-soaked waste
↑_____⎦ 현재분사구   계속적 용법의 관계대명사   set fire to: ~을 태우다, ~에 불지르다
beneath a bridge].

가능성 있는 원인은 열차에서 떨어지던 타오르는 불꽃이었고, 그것은 다리 밑의 기름에 흠뻑 젖은 폐기물에 불을 붙였다.

11 At that time, few people in Cleveland cared.
(부정적) 거의 없는, 극히 소수의

당시 클리블랜드에는 관심을 가지는 사람이 거의 없었다.

12 This was because fires had been recorded [on the Cuyahoga] more than ten times before, and
과거완료 수동태: had been p.p.   전치사구
some of them had been much worse.
= fires   비교급 수식 부사(훨씬)

이것은 이전에 쿠아호가에서 열 번 넘는 화재가 기록되었었고, 그것들 중 일부는 훨씬 더 심했었기 때문이다.

13 However, it wasn't long before the 1969 fire became famous.
it is not long before ~: 머지않아 ~, 이윽고 ~

하지만 머지않아 1969년의 화재가 유명해졌다.

14 This was thanks to an article [published in *Time* magazine that year].
~ 덕분에   ↑____⎦ 과거분사구

이것은 그해 타임지에 실린 기사 덕분이었다.

15 The article featured a shocking photograph of flames and smoke [rising from the river].
↑_____⎦ 현재분사구

그 기사는 강에서 피어오르는 불길과 연기의 충격적인 사진을 특종으로 다뤘다.

16 But this was not a photograph of the 1969 fire, [which was put out so quickly that nobody took a
동사구의 수동태   so+부사[형용사]++that++주어+동사: 너무 ~해서 …하다
picture of it].
= the 1969 fire

그러나 이것은 1969년 화재의 사진이 아니었는데, 그것은 너무 빨리 진압되어 아무도 사진을 찍지 못했다.

17 In fact, it was a picture of a much worse fire [that had occurred on the river several years earlier].
↑_____⎦ 주격 관계대명사절

사실, 그것은 몇 년 전에 그 강에서 발생했던 훨씬 더 심한 화재의 사진이었다.

18 Still, the image had a great impact on people.

have an impact on: ~에 영향을 주다

그럼에도 불구하고 그 이미지는 사람들에게 큰 영향을 주었다.

19 Around that time, the attitudes of Americans [toward environmental problems] were starting
   to change.

S / 전치사구 / V

명사적 용법(were starting의 목적어) = changing

그 무렵, 환경 문제에 대한 미국인들의 태도가 바뀌기 시작하고 있었다.

20 become aware of: ~을 알게 되다

More and more people were becoming aware of the need [to protect the environment], and

S1 / V1 / 형용사적 용법

the shocking image [of the burning river] sparked public anger [about water pollution].

S2 / 전치사구 / V2 / O2 / 전치사구

점점 더 많은 사람들이 환경을 보호할 필요성을 인지하게 되는 중이었고, 불타는 강의 충격적인 이미지는 수질 오염에 대한 대중의 분노를 촉발시켰다.

21 As a result, the Cuyahoga River fire of 1969 became a symbol of pollution.

S / V / SC

그 결과, 1969년 쿠야호가 강 화재는 오염의 상징이 되었다.

22 계속적 용법의 주격 관계대명사절

A national environmental awareness event was held on April 22, 1970, [which later became

S / V(수동태) / become known as: ~로 알려지다

known as the first Earth Day].

전국적인 환경 의식 행사가 1970년 4월 22일에 열렸는데, 이날은 이후 제1회 지구의 날로 알려지게 되었다.

23 And in 1972, national water quality standards were established with the passage of the Clean
   Water Act.

S / V(수동태)

그리고 1972년, 청정수법의 통과와 함께 국가 수질 기준이 수립되었다.

Exposing the Harsh Reality of Child Labor
아동 노동의 가혹한 현실을 폭로하기

24 In the 19th century, the Industrial Revolution led to a dramatic increase in factory production in
   the United States.

lead to: ~로 이어지다, ~을 초래하다

19세기에, 산업혁명은 미국의 공장 생산량의 극적인 증가로 이어졌다.

25 The demand for workers increased, and many new positions were filled by children.

노동자에 대한 수요가 증가했고, 많은 새로운 일자리들이 아동들로 채워졌다.

26 「퍼센트+of+명사」일 때는 뒤에 오는 명사에 수 일치
By 1900, about twenty percent of all children [in the United States] were employed, and some of those [working in factories] were only four years old.

1900년쯤에는, 미국의 전체 아동의 약 20퍼센트가 고용되었고, 공장에서 일하는 아동 중 일부는 겨우 4살이었다.

27 The work was difficult and dangerous, [leaving many child laborers with health problems].

일은 힘들고 위험해서 많은 아동 노동자들에게 건강 문제를 남겼다.

28 Factory owners turned to child labor for several reasons.
turn to: ~에 의지[의존]하다

공장주들은 여러 가지 이유로 아동 노동에 의존했다.

29 For example, children could be paid less than adult workers.
조동사가 있는 수동태   ~보다 적게

예를 들어, 아이들은 성인 노동자보다 임금을 적게 받을 수 있었다.

30 They were also less likely to go on strike.
= Children   be less likely to-v: ~할 가능성이 더 적다

그들은 또한 파업을 할 가능성도 더 적었다.

31 Lewis Hine, a teacher and photographer, wanted to reveal [how cruel this system was].

교사이자 사진작가인 루이스 하인은 이 제도가 얼마나 잔인한지 밝히고 싶었다.

32 = working
So he quit his teaching job and started to work for the National Child Labor Committee as an investigative photographer.

그래서 그는 교사직을 그만두고 전국아동노동위원회에서 탐사 사진작가로 일하기 시작했다.

33 He gained access to factories by pretending to have different jobs [like insurance agent or fire inspector].
gain access to: ~에 접근하다   by v-ing: ~함으로써   전치사구

그는 보험 설계사나 화재 조사관 같은 다른 직업들을 가진 것처럼 가장함으로써 공장에 접근했다.

34 Once inside, he would photograph the children [working there].
(he was) · 현재분사구

일단 안에 들어가면, 그는 그곳에서 일하고 있는 아이들의 사진을 찍었다.

35 He would also ask their names and ages and record information [about their living and working
S V1 (would) V2 전치사구
conditions].

그는 또한 그들의 이름과 나이를 묻고 그들의 생활과 노동 환경에 대한 정보를 기록했다.

36 From 1908 to 1912, he secretly gathered information and took photographs [to expose factory
from A to B: A에서 B까지 S V1 V2 부사적 용법(목적) 선행사
owners {who were taking advantage of helpless children}].
take advantage of: ~을 이용하다
주격 관계대명사절

1908년부터 1912년까지, 그는 무력한 아이들을 이용하고 있던 공장주들을 폭로하기 위해 몰래 정보를 수집하고 사진을 찍었다.

37 Hine's photographs captured young children [doing all sorts of jobs].
· 현재분사구

하인의 사진들은 온갖 종류의 일을 하는 어린아이들을 포착했다.

38 These included picking vegetables, weaving baskets, and even handling dangerous equipment.
= all sorts of jobs 동명사구(목적어) 병렬 연결

이것들은 채소 따기, 바구니 짜기, 그리고 심지어 위험한 장비를 다루는 일까지 포함했다.

39 What is more, the children's faces showed the tragic impact of hard labor.
더욱이, 게다가

게다가, 그 아이들의 얼굴은 고된 노동의 비극적인 영향을 보여주었다.

40 When people saw the children's joyless expressions, they could not help but feel heartbroken.
can't (help) but+동사원형: ~하지 않을 수 없다(= can't help v-ing)

사람들이 그 아이들의 기쁨이 없는 표정을 보았을 때, 그들은 비통함을 느끼지 않을 수 없었다.

41 The pictures were later shown in exhibitions, lectures, magazine articles, and so on.
수동태 기타 등등

그 사진들은 이후 전시회, 강연, 잡지 기사 등에 공개되었다.

42 As a result, the public realized just [how serious the situation was].
간접의문문(realized의 목적어): 「의문사+주어+동사」의 어순

그 결과, 대중은 상황이 얼마나 심각한지 깨달았다.

43 Soon, many states passed stronger laws [to ban the employment of children].
부사적 용법(목적)

곧, 많은 주가 아동 고용을 금지하기 위해 더 강력한 법안들을 통과시켰다.

44 In 1938, the United States Congress passed an act [that made it illegal for children under sixteen
가목적어
VI O OC(형용사) 의미상 주어(for+목적격)

{to work in factories during school hours}].
진주어

1938년에, 미국 의회는 16세 미만 아동이 수업 시간 동안 공장에서 일하는 것을 불법으로 하는 법안을 통과시켰다.

45 These examples show [that photographs can bring meaningful change to society].
명사절(show의 목적어)   bring A to B: A를 B로 가져오다[데려오다]

이러한 사례들은 사진이 의미 있는 변화를 사회에 가져올 수 있음을 보여준다.

46 They prove [that, sometimes, a picture truly is worth a thousand words].
명사절(prove의 목적어)

그것들은 때로는 한 장의 사진이 진정 천 단어의 가치가 있다는 것을 증명한다.

♣ 다음 빈칸에 알맞은 말을 쓰시오.

01   As quickly as a camera captures a scene, an image can _____ our emotions.
카메라가 장면을 포착하는 것만큼 빠르게, 이미지는 우리의 감정을 사로잡을 수 있다.

02   Through speech or written text, it can be difficult to _____ quickly.
연설이나 글로 쓰인 텍스트를 통해 복잡한 메시지를 빠르게 전달하는 것은 어려울 수 있다.

03   Yet photographs can change people's hearts and minds _____.
그렇지만 사진은 사람들의 가슴과 마음을 순식간에 바꿀 수 있다.

04   And when the magic of photography sparks _____ in a great number of people, it can change history.
그리고 사진 촬영의 마법이 많은 사람들에게 감정적인 반응을 유발할 때, 그것은 역사를 바꿀 수 있다.

05   In the 1880s, industry began to _____ along the Cuyahoga River in the city of Cleveland. 1880년대에, 산업이 클리블랜드 시의 쿠야호가 강을 따라 빠르게 성장하기 시작했다.

06   This industrial growth _____ to people in the area.
이러한 산업 성장은 그 지역 사람들에게 안정적인 일자리를 제공했다.

07   Meanwhile, steel mills and factories started _____ into the river.
한편, 제철소와 공장은 대량의 폐기물을 강에 버리기 시작했다.

08   In June 1969, the polluted river _____. 1969년 6월, 그 오염된 강에 불이 붙었다.

09   The likely cause was a burning flare falling from a train, _____ oil-soaked waste beneath a bridge.
가능성 있는 원인은 열차에서 떨어지던 타오르는 불꽃이었고, 그것은 다리 밑의 기름에 흠뻑 젖은 폐기물에 불을 붙였다.

10   _____ fires had been recorded on the Cuyahoga more than ten times before, and some of them had been _____.
이것은 이전에 쿠야호가에서 열 번 넘는 화재가 기록되었고, 그것들 중 일부는 훨씬 더 심했었기 때문이다.

11   However, _____ the 1969 fire became famous.
하지만 머지않아 1969년의 화재가 유명해졌다.

12   This was _____ published in *Time* magazine that year.
이것은 그해 타임지에 실린 기사 덕분이었다.

13   The article _____ of flames and smoke rising from the river.
그 기사는 강에서 피어오르는 불길과 연기의 충격적인 사진을 특종으로 다뤘다.

14   But this was not a photograph of the 1969 fire, which was _____ that nobody took a picture of it. 그러나 이것은 1969년 화재의 사진이 아니었는데, 그것은 너무 빨리 진압되어 아무도 사진을 찍지 못했다.

15   In fact, it was a picture of a much worse fire that _____ on the river several years earlier. 사실, 그것은 몇 년 전에 그 강에서 발생했던 훨씬 더 심한 화재의 사진이었다.

16   Still, the image _____ people. 그럼에도 불구하고 그 이미지는 사람들에게 큰 영향을 주었다.

17   Around that time, the attitudes of Americans _____ were starting to change.
그 무렵, 환경 문제에 대한 미국인들의 태도가 바뀌기 시작하고 있었다.

18   More and more people were _____ the need to protect the environment, and the
shocking image of the burning river sparked public anger about water pollution.
점점 더 많은 사람들이 환경을 보호할 필요성을 인지하게 되는 중이었고, 불타는 강의 충격적인 이미지는 수질 오염에 대한 대중의
분노를 촉발시켰다.

19   As a result, the Cuyahoga River fire of 1969 became _____.
그 결과, 1969년 쿠야호가 강 화재는 오염의 상징이 되었다.

20   And in 1972, national water quality standards were _____ of the Clean Water Act.
그리고 1972년, 청정수법의 통과와 함께 국가 수질 기준이 수립되었다.

21   In the 19th century, the Industrial Revolution _____ in factory production
in the United States.
19세기에, 산업혁명은 미국의 공장 생산량의 극적인 증가로 이어졌다.

22   By 1900, about twenty percent of all children in the United States _____, and some
of those working in factories were only four years old.
1900년쯤에는, 미국의 전체 아동의 약 20퍼센트가 고용되었고, 공장에서 일하는 아동 중 일부는 겨우 4살이었다.

23   The work was difficult and dangerous, _____ with health problems.
일은 힘들고 위험해서 많은 아동 노동자들에게 건강 문제를 남겼다.

24   Factory owners turned to child labor _____.
공장주들은 여러 가지 이유로 아동 노동에 의존했다.

25   For example, children could be _____ adult workers.
예를 들어, 아이들은 성인 노동자보다 임금을 적게 받을 수 있었다.

26   They were also less likely to _____.
그들은 또한 파업을 할 가능성도 더 적었다.

27   Lewis Hine, a teacher and photographer, wanted to reveal _____.
교사이자 사진작가인 루이스 하인은 이 제도가 얼마나 잔인한지 밝히고 싶었다.

28   So he quit his teaching job and started to work for the National Child Labor Committee
_____.
그래서 그는 교사직을 그만두고 전국아동노동위원회에서 탐사 사진작가로 일하기 시작했다.

29   He _____ factories by pretending to have different jobs like insurance agent or fire
inspector. 그는 보험 설계사나 화재 조사관 같은 다른 직업들을 가진 것처럼 가장함으로써 공장에 접근했다.

30   Once inside, he _____ the children working there.

일단 안에 들어가면, 그는 그곳에서 일하고 있는 아이들의 사진을 찍었다.

31   He would also ask their names and ages and record information about _____.

그는 또한 그들의 이름과 나이를 묻고 그들의 생활과 노동 환경에 대한 정보를 기록했다.

32   From 1908 to 1912, he secretly gathered information and took photographs to expose factory owners who were _____ helpless children.

1908년부터 1912년까지, 그는 무력한 아이들을 이용하고 있던 공장주들을 폭로하기 위해 몰래 정보를 수집하고 사진을 찍었다.

33   Hine's photographs _____ doing all sorts of jobs.

하인의 사진들은 온갖 종류의 일을 하는 어린아이들을 포착했다.

34   These included picking vegetables, weaving baskets, and even _____.

이것들은 채소 따기, 바구니 짜기, 그리고 심지어 위험한 장비를 다루는 일까지 포함했다.

35   _____, the children's faces showed the tragic impact of hard labor.

게다가, 그 아이들의 얼굴은 고된 노동의 비극적인 영향을 보여주었다.

36   When people saw the children's joyless expressions, they _____ heartbroken.

사람들이 그 아이들의 기쁨이 없는 표정을 보았을 때, 그들은 비통함을 느끼지 않을 수 없었다.

37   The pictures were later _____, lectures, magazine articles, and so on.

그 사진들은 이후 전시회, 강연, 잡지 기사 등에 공개되었다.

38   Soon, many states _____ to ban the employment of children.

곧, 많은 주가 아동 고용을 금지하기 위해 더 강력한 법안들을 통과시켰다.

39   In 1938, the United States Congress passed an act that _____ for children under sixteen to work in factories during school hours.

1938년에, 미국 의회는 16세 미만 아동이 수업 시간 동안 공장에서 일하는 것을 불법으로 하는 법안을 통과시켰다.

40   These examples show that photographs can _____ to society.

이러한 사례들은 사진이 의미 있는 변화를 사회에 가져올 수 있음을 보여준다.

41   They prove that, sometimes, a picture truly is _____.

그것들은 때로는 한 장의 사진이 진정 천 단어의 가치가 있다는 것을 증명한다.

교과서 **본문 익히기** ② 옳은 어법·어휘 고르기

♣ 다음 네모 안에서 옳은 것을 고르시오.

01 As quick / quickly as a camera captures a scene, an image can grab hold of our emotions.

02 Through speech or written text, it can be difficult convey / to convey a complex message quickly.

03 Yet photographs can change peoples' / people's hearts and minds in an instant.

04 And when the magic of photography sparks an emotional reaction in a great amount / number of people, it can change history.

05 In the 1880s, industry began to grow slowly / rapidly along the Cuyahoga River in the city of Cleveland.

06 This industrial growth provided steady jobs to / with people in the area.

07 Meanwhile, steel mills and factories started dump / dumping large amounts of waste into the river.

08 Although the river became polluted, most people simply regarded this as / like a sign of the area's economic success.

09 In June 1969, the polluting / polluted river caught fire.

10 The likely cause was a burning flare falling from a train, who / which set fire to oil-soaked waste beneath a bridge.

11 At that time, few / little people in Cleveland cared.

12 This was because fires had been recorded on the Cuyahoga more than ten times before, and some / any of them had been much worse.

13 However, it wasn't long after / before the 1969 fire became famous.

14 This was thanks to an article publishing / published in *Time* magazine that year.

15 The article featured a shocking photograph of flames and smoke rising / falling from the river.

16 But this was not a photograph of the 1969 fire, which was put out so / such quickly that nobody took a picture of it.

17 In fact, it was a picture of a many / much worse fire that had occurred on the river several years earlier.

18 Still, the image had a small / great impact on people.

19 Around that time, the minds / attitudes of Americans toward environmental problems were starting to change.

20 More and more people were becoming awareness / aware of the need to protect the environment, and the shocking image of the burning river sparked public anger about water pollution.

21 As a result, the Cuyahoga River fire of 1969 became a symbol of pollution / pollute .

22 A national environmental awareness event was held on April 22, 1970, which / that later became known as the first Earth Day.

23 And in 1972, national water quality standards established / were established with the passage of the Clean Water Act.

24 In the 19th century, the Industrial Revolution leads / led to a dramatic increase in factory production in the United States.

25 The demand for workers increased / decreased , and many new positions were filled by children.

26 By 1900, about twenty percent of all children in the United States were employed, and some of these / those working in factories were only four years old.

27 The work was difficult and dangerous, leaving / left many child laborers with health problems.

28 Factory owners turned to child labor for / of several reasons.

29 For example, children could be paid more / less than adult workers.

30 They were also less like / likely to go on strike.

31   Lewis Hine, a teacher and photographer, wanted revealing / to reveal how cruel this system was.

32   So he quit his teaching job and started work / to work for the National Child Labor Committee as an investigative photographer.

33   He gained excess / access to factories by pretending to have different jobs like insurance agent or fire inspector.

34   Once inside, he would photograph the children working / worked there.

35   He would also ask their names and ages and record / recorded information about their living and working conditions.

36   From 1908 to 1912, he secretly gathered information and took photographs to expose factory owners who / which were taking advantage of helpless children.

37   Hine's photographs captured young children doing all sort / sorts of jobs.

38   These included picking vegetables, weaving baskets, and even handle / handling dangerous equipment.

39   That / What is more, the children's faces showed the tragic impact of hard labor.

40   When people saw the children's joyless expressions, they could not help but feel / to feel heartbroken.

41   The pictures were later showing / shown in exhibitions, lectures, magazine articles, and so on.

42   As a result, the public realized just how serious / seriously the situation was.

43   Soon, many states passed stronger laws to ban the employ / employment of children.

44   In 1938, the United States Congress passed an act that made it illegal for children under sixteen to work in factories for / during school hours.

45   These examples show that photographs can bring / bringing meaningful change to society.

46   They prove that, sometimes, a picture truly is worth / worthy a thousand words.

교과서 본문 익히기 ③ 틀린 부분 고치기

♣ 다음 밑줄 친 부분을 바르게 고쳐 쓰시오.

01   As <u>quick</u> as a camera captures a scene, an image can grab hold of our emotions.

02   And when the magic of photography sparks an emotional reaction in a great <u>amount</u> of people, it can change history.

03   In the 1880s, industry began to grow <u>rapid</u> along the Cuyahoga River in the city of Cleveland.

04   This industrial growth provided steady jobs <u>with</u> people in the area.

05   Although the river became <u>polluting</u>, most people simply regarded this as a sign of the area's economic success.

06   In June 1969, the polluted river <u>catches</u> fire.

07   The likely cause was a burning flare falling from a train, <u>who</u> set fire to oil-soaked waste beneath a bridge.

08   At that time, <u>little</u> people in Cleveland cared.

09   This was because fires had been recorded on the Cuyahoga more than ten times before, and some of them had been <u>more</u> worse.

10   This was thanks to an article <u>publishing</u> in *Time* magazine that year.

11   The article featured a <u>shocked</u> photograph of flames and smoke rising from the river.

12   In fact, it was a picture of a much <u>bad</u> fire that had occurred on the river several years earlier.

13   Still, the image had a great impact <u>to</u> people.

14   More and more people were becoming aware of the need to protect the environment, and the shocking image of the <u>burnt</u> river sparked public anger about water pollution.

15   A national environmental awareness event <u>held</u> on April 22, 1970, which later became known as the first Earth Day.

16   And in 1972, national water quality standards <u>were establishing</u> with the passage of the Clean Water Act.

17   <u>On</u> the 19th century, the Industrial Revolution led to a dramatic increase in factory production in the United States.

18   The demand for workers increased, and many new positions were filled <u>with</u> children.

19 The work was difficult and dangerous, <u>left</u> many child laborers with health problems.

20 Factory owners turned to child labor <u>of</u> several reasons.

21 For example, children could <u>pay</u> less than adult workers.

22 They were also less likely to go <u>to</u> strike.

23 Lewis Hine, a teacher and photographer, wanted <u>revealing</u> how cruel this system was.

24 So he quit his teaching job and started to work for the National Child Labor Committee <u>like</u> an investigative photographer.

25 He gained access to factories by <u>pretend</u> to have different jobs like insurance agent or fire inspector.

26 Once inside, he would <u>photography</u> the children working there.

27 He would also ask their names and ages and <u>records</u> information about their living and working conditions.

28 From 1908 to 1912, he secretly gathered information and took photographs to expose factory owners <u>which</u> were taking advantage of helpless children.

29 Hine's photographs captured young children <u>done</u> all sorts of jobs.

30 These included picking vegetables, weaving baskets, and even <u>handled</u> dangerous equipment.

31 What is <u>most</u>, the children's faces showed the tragic impact of hard labor.

32 When people saw the children's joyless expressions, they could not help but <u>to feel</u> heartbroken.

33 The pictures were later <u>showing</u> in exhibitions, lectures, magazine articles, and so on.

34 Soon, many states passed stronger laws <u>ban</u> the employment of children.

35 In 1938, the United States Congress passed an act that made it <u>illegally</u> for children under sixteen to work in factories during school hours.

36 These examples show <u>what</u> photographs can bring meaningful change to society.

37 They prove that, sometimes, a picture <u>true</u> is worth a thousand words.

교과서 본문 외 지문 분석

TOPIC 5 A. Preview

Are Online Classes Helpful?

❶ In my opinion, online classes are helpful ❷ for several reasons. First, they use online learning tools ❸ that students find interesting. These tools, ❹ such as screen sharing and ❺ live chats, keep students' attention and ❻ help them learn more effectively. ❼ In addition, online classes save time and energy. ❽ As the classes can be accessed anywhere, students ❾ do not have to ❿ spend much time and energy going to and from school. ⓫ This means they can study more efficiently. For these reasons, ⓬ I think online classes are helpful for students.

❶ in my opinion: 제 생각에 ❷ for several reasons: 여러 가지 이유로 ❸ 목적격 관계대명사절 ❹ such as: ~같은 ❺ live: 실시간의 (형용사)
❻ help+목적어+(to)동사원형: 목적어가 ~하는 것을 돕다 ❼ In addition: 게다가, 또한 ❽ As: 이유를 나타내는 접속사 (~ 때문에)
❾ do not have to: ~할 필요가 없다 ❿ spend ~ v-ing: ~을 …하는 데 쓰다 ⓫ This means (that) ~: 이것은 ~을 의미한다
⓬ I think (that) ~: 나는 ~라고 생각한다

Q1 The author thinks that online classes allow students to study more efficiently. (T / F)

Wrap Up B. Read and Discuss

Everybody ❶ sees change as a challenge. The difference is ❷ that ❸ some people ❹ regard it as something blocking our progress, ❺ while others see it as an opportunity. ❻ What's important about change is ❼ how we prepare for it and react to it.

Although change is unavoidable, does living in a fast-paced, digital world ❽ force us to change? I don't think most changes ❾ have anything to do with true innovation. ❿ At times, ⓫ it's wiser to hold onto what we already have.

Change is the only thing ⓬ that brings progress. If we ⓭ are not willing to change our minds and ⓮ let go of old ideas and beliefs, we cannot change anything.

❶ see A as B: A를 B로 보다 ❷ 보어 역할을 하는 명사절을 이끄는 접속사 ❸ some ~, others …: 일부 사람들은 ~하고, 다른 사람들은 …하다
❹ regard A as B: A를 B로 간주하다 ❺ while: 반면에 ❻ 주어 역할을 하는 명사절: 변화에 대해 중요한 것 ❼ 보어 역할을 하는 간접의문문
❽ force A to B: A에게 B 하도록 강요하다 ❾ have something to do with: ~와 관련이 있다 / 부정문이어서 anything이 쓰임 ❿ At times: 때로는
⓫ 「가주어 it, 진주어 to부정사」 구문 ⓬ 선행사에 the only가 있는 경우 관계대명사는 that을 쓴다. ⓭ be willing to: ~하려고 하다
⓮ let go of: ~을 놓다, ~을 포기하다

Q2 We can change things without altering our mindset or letting go of old ideas. (T / F)

❤ 다음 빈칸에 알맞은 말을 쓰시오.

01 In my opinion, online classes are helpful _____.
제 생각에 온라인 수업은 여러 가지 이유들로 도움이 됩니다.

02 First, they use _____ that students find interesting.
먼저, 그것들은 학생들이 흥미롭게 여길 온라인 학습 도구들을 활용합니다.

03 These tools, _____ and live chats, keep students' attention and help them learn more effectively.
화면 공유 및 실시간 채팅과 같은 이러한 도구들은 학생들의 관심을 유지시키고 그들이 더 효과적으로 배울 수 있도록 돕습니다.

04 _____, online classes save time and energy.
게다가, 온라인 수업은 시간과 에너지를 절약합니다.

05 As the classes _____, students do not have to spend much time and energy going to and from school.
수업이 어디에서나 접속될 수 있기 때문에 학생들은 등하교에 많은 시간과 에너지를 쓸 필요가 없습니다.

06 This means they can _____. 이는 그들이 더 효율적으로 학습할 수 있다는 것을 의미합니다.

07 For these reasons, I think online classes _____ students.
이러한 이유들로, 저는 온라인 수업이 학생들에게 도움이 된다고 생각합니다.

08 Everybody sees change _____. 모든 사람은 변화를 도전으로 본다.

09 The difference is that some people regard it as something blocking our progress, while others _____.
차이는 어떤 사람들은 그것을 우리의 진전을 방해하는 것이라고 여기는 반면, 다른 사람들은 그것을 기회로 본다는 것이다.

10 What's important about change is _____ and react to it.
변화에 관해 중요한 것은 우리가 어떻게 그것을 준비하고 그것에 대응하는지다.

11 Although change _____, does living in a fast-paced, digital world force us to change?
비록 변화는 피할 수 없다 할지라도, 빨리 진행되는, 디지털 세상에서 살아가는 것은 우리에게 변화를 강요하는 것일까?

12 I don't think most changes _____ true innovation.
나는 대부분의 변화들은 실제 혁신과 어떤 연관이 있다고 생각하지 않는다.

13 At times, it's wiser to hold onto _____.
때로는, 이미 우리가 가지고 있는 것을 고수하는 것이 더 현명하다.

14 Change is the only thing _____. 변화는 진전을 가져오는 유일한 것이다.

15 If we _____ change our minds and _____ old ideas and beliefs, we cannot change anything.
우리가 기꺼이 마음을 바꾸고 오래된 관념과 믿음을 버리지 않는다면, 우리는 아무것도 바꿀 수 없다.

01 (A), (B), (C)의 각 네모 안에서 문맥에 맞는 낱말로 가장 적절한 것은?

As quickly as a camera captures a scene, an image can grab hold of our (A) thoughts / emotions . Through speech or (B) spoken / written text, it can be difficult to convey a complex message quickly. Yet photographs can change people's hearts and minds in an instant. And when the magic of photography sparks an emotional reaction in a great (C) number / amount of people, it can change history.

	(A)	(B)	(C)
①	thoughts	spoken	number
②	thoughts	written	amount
③	emotions	spoken	number
④	emotions	written	number
⑤	emotions	written	amount

02 (A), (B), (C)의 각 네모 안에서 문맥에 맞는 낱말로 가장 적절한 것은?

In the 1880s, industry began to grow rapidly along the Cuyahoga River in the city of Cleveland. This (A) industrial / cultural growth provided steady jobs to people in the area. Meanwhile, steel mills and factories started dumping large (B) numbers / amounts of waste into the river. Although the river became polluted, most people simply regarded this as a sign of the area's economic (C) success / failure .

	(A)	(B)	(C)
①	industrial	numbers	failure
②	industrial	numbers	success
③	industrial	amounts	success
④	cultural	amounts	failure
⑤	cultural	numbers	success

03 다음 글의 밑줄 친 부분 중, 문맥상 낱말의 쓰임이 적절하지 않은 것은?

In June 1969, the polluted river caught fire. The likely cause was a ① burning flare falling from a train, which set fire to oil-soaked waste beneath a bridge. At that time, few people in Cleveland cared. This was because fires had been recorded on the Cuyahoga more than ten times before, and some of them had been much ② better.

However, it wasn't long before the 1969 fire became ③ famous. This was thanks to an article published in *Time* magazine that year. The article featured a ④ shocking photograph of flames and smoke rising from the river. But this was not a photograph of the 1969 fire, which was put out so quickly that nobody took a picture of it. In fact, it was a picture of a much worse fire that had occurred on the river several years earlier. Still, the image had a great ⑤ impact on people.

①   ②   ③   ④   ⑤

04 다음 글의 밑줄 친 부분 중, 문맥상 낱말의 쓰임이 적절하지 않은 것은?

Around that time, the ① attitudes of Americans toward environmental problems were starting to change. More and more people were becoming aware of the need ② to protect the environment, and the shocking image of the burning river sparked public anger about water pollution. As a result, the Cuyahoga River fire of 1969 became a symbol of ③ progress. A national environmental ④ awareness event was held on April 22, 1970, which later became known as the first Earth Day. And in 1972, national water quality standards were established with the ⑤ passage of the Clean Water Act.

①   ②   ③   ④   ⑤

05 (A), (B), (C)의 각 네모 안에서 문맥에 맞는 낱말로 가장 적절한 것은?

In the 19th century, the Industrial Revolution led to a dramatic (A) increase / decrease in factory production in the United States. The demand for workers increased, and many new positions were filled by children. By 1900, about twenty percent of all children in the United States were employed, and some of those working in factories were only four years old. The work was (B) easy / difficult and dangerous, leaving many child laborers with health problems.

Factory owners turned to child labor for several reasons. For example, children could be paid (C) less / more than adult workers. They were also less likely to go on strike.

	(A)	(B)	(C)
①	increase	easy	less
②	increase	difficult	less
③	increase	difficult	more
④	decrease	easy	more
⑤	decrease	difficult	less

06 (A), (B), (C)의 각 네모 안에서 문맥에 맞는 낱말로 가장 적절한 것은?

The pictures were later shown in exhibitions, lectures, magazine articles, and so on. As a result, the public realized just how (A) serious / trivial the situation was. Soon, many states passed stronger laws to ban the (B) employment / unemployment of children. In 1938, the United States Congress passed an act that made it (C) legal / illegal for children under sixteen to work in factories during school hours.

These examples show that photographs can bring meaningful change to society. They prove that, sometimes, a picture truly is worth a thousand words.

	(A)	(B)	(C)
①	serious	employment	legal
②	serious	employment	illegal
③	serious	unemployment	illegal
④	trivial	employment	illegal
⑤	trivial	unemployment	legal

07 다음 글의 밑줄 친 부분 중, 문맥상 낱말의 쓰임이 적절하지 않은 것은?

Lewis Hine, a teacher and photographer, wanted to reveal how cruel this system was. So he quit his teaching job and started to work for the National Child Labor Committee as an investigative photographer. He gained ①excess to factories by pretending to have different jobs like insurance agent or fire inspector.

Once inside, he would photograph the children working there. He would also ask their names and ages and record information about their living and working conditions. From 1908 to 1912, he secretly gathered information and took photographs to expose factory owners who were taking ②advantage of helpless children.

Hine's photographs ③captured young children doing all sorts of jobs. These included picking vegetables, ④weaving baskets, and even handling dangerous equipment. What is more, the children's faces showed the tragic impact of hard labor. When people saw the children's joyless expressions, they could not help but feel ⑤heartbroken.

①   ②   ③   ④   ⑤

01 (A), (B), (C)의 각 네모 안에서 어법에 맞는 표현으로 가장 적절한 것은?

As (A) quick / quickly as a camera captures a scene, an image can grab hold of our emotions. Through speech or written text, it can be difficult (B) convey / to convey a complex message quickly. (C) Yet / So photographs can change people's hearts and minds in an instant. And when the magic of photography sparks an emotional reaction in a great number of people, it can change history.

	(A)		(B)		(C)
①	quick	···	convey	···	Yet
②	quick	···	to convey	···	So
③	quickly	···	to convey	···	So
④	quickly	···	to convey	···	Yet
⑤	quickly	···	convey	···	Yet

02 (A), (B), (C)의 각 네모 안에서 어법에 맞는 표현으로 가장 적절한 것은?

In the 1880s, industry began (A) grow / to grow rapidly along the Cuyahoga River in the city of Cleveland. This industrial growth provided steady jobs (B) to / with people in the area. Meanwhile, steel mills and factories started dumping large amounts of waste into the river. Although the river became polluted, most people simply regarded this (C) as / like a sign of the area's economic success.

	(A)		(B)		(C)
①	grow	···	to	···	as
②	grow	···	with	···	like
③	to grow	···	to	···	like
④	to grow	···	with	···	as
⑤	to grow	···	to	···	as

03 다음 글의 밑줄 친 부분 중, 어법상 틀린 것은?

In June 1969, the ①polluted river caught fire. The likely cause was a burning flare falling from a train, which set fire to oil-soaked waste beneath a bridge. At that time, few people in Cleveland cared. This was because fires had been recorded on the Cuyahoga more than ten times before, and some of them had been ②much worse.

However, it wasn't long before the 1969 fire became famous. This was thanks to an article published in *Time* magazine that year. The article featured a shocking photograph of flames and smoke ③rising from the river. But this was not a photograph of the 1969 fire, ④that was put out so quickly that nobody took a picture of it. In fact, it was a picture of a much worse fire that ⑤had occurred on the river several years earlier. Still, the image had a great impact on people.

①   ②   ③   ④   ⑤

04 다음 글의 밑줄 친 부분 중, 어법상 틀린 것은?

Around that time, the attitudes of Americans toward environmental problems were starting ①to change. ②More and more people were becoming aware of the need to protect the environment, and the ③shocking image of the burning river sparked public anger about water pollution. As a result, the Cuyahoga River fire of 1969 became a symbol of pollution. A national environmental awareness event ④held on April 22, 1970, which later became known as the first Earth Day. And in 1972, national water quality standards ⑤were established with the passage of the Clean Water Act.

①   ②   ③   ④   ⑤

05 (A), (B), (C)의 각 네모 안에서 어법에 맞는 표현으로 가장 적절한 것은?

In the 19th century, the Industrial Revolution led to a dramatic increase in factory production in the United States. The demand for workers increased, and many new positions were filled by children. By 1900, about twenty percent of all children in the United States were employed, and some of those (A) working / worked in factories were only four years old. The work was difficult and dangerous, (B) leaving / left many child laborers with health problems.

Factory owners turned to child labor for several reasons. For example, children could (C) pay / be paid less than adult workers. They were also less likely to go on strike.

	(A)	(B)	(C)
①	working	⋯ leaving	⋯ pay
②	working	⋯ leaving	⋯ be paid
③	working	⋯ left	⋯ pay
④	worked	⋯ left	⋯ be paid
⑤	worked	⋯ leaving	⋯ pay

06 다음 글의 밑줄 친 부분 중, 어법상 틀린 것은?

The pictures were later ①showing in exhibitions, lectures, magazine articles, and so on. As a result, the public realized just how serious the situation was. Soon, many states passed ②stronger laws to ban the employment of children. In 1938, the United States Congress passed an act ③that made it illegal for children under sixteen to work in factories during school hours.

These examples show ④that photographs can bring meaningful change to society. They prove that, sometimes, a picture ⑤truly is worth a thousand words.

①   ②   ③   ④   ⑤

07 다음 글의 밑줄 친 부분 중, 어법상 틀린 것은?

Lewis Hine, a teacher and photographer, wanted to reveal ①how cruel this system was. So he quit his teaching job and started to work for the National Child Labor Committee as an investigative photographer. He gained access to factories ②by pretending to have different jobs like insurance agent or fire inspector.

Once inside, he would photograph the children working there. He would also ask their names and ages and record information about their living and working conditions. From 1908 to 1912, he secretly gathered information and took photographs to expose factory owners ③who were taking advantage of helpless children.

Hine's photographs captured young children doing all sorts of jobs. These included picking vegetables, weaving baskets, and even ④handled dangerous equipment. What is more, the children's faces showed the tragic impact of hard labor. When people saw the children's joyless expressions, they ⑤could not help but feel heartbroken.

①   ②   ③   ④   ⑤

01 다음 대화의 흐름으로 보아, 주어진 문장이 들어가기에 가장 적절한 곳은?

> This means that I don't need to carry my wallet with me anymore.

M Hey, cool watch!

W Thanks. I got it last week. (①)

M I'm thinking of buying a new watch, too. Are you satisfied with your purchase? (②)

W Yeah! This one keeps track of my heart rate, so it is very useful when I exercise. (③)

M Wow! That's amazing! (④)

W It has other cool functions, too. For example, I can use it to pay for things. (⑤)

M That's great! We can do so much more than telling time with watches nowadays.

①   ②   ③   ④   ⑤

02 다음 대화의 주제로 가장 적절한 것은?

B I've started my own video channel.

G What's it about?

B It's focused on teaching how to play the guitar to beginners. You know I really love music!

G That's great! My sister wants to learn how to play an instrument. I'll definitely recommend your channel to her.

B Thanks! I hope it helps her learn.

G It's so nice that you are willing to make helpful videos.

B Many people are doing it these days. This means we can learn new things more easily than ever before.

G You're right.

① The importance of music education
② Starting a video channel for teaching guitar
③ The challenges of learning a musical instrument
④ The benefits of online learning platforms
⑤ The future of music education technology

03 다음 중, 밑줄 친 부분의 의미가 바르지 <u>않은</u> 것은?

> ①<u>As quickly as</u> a camera captures a scene, an image can ②<u>grab hold of</u> our emotions. Through speech or written text, it can be difficult ③<u>to convey a complex message</u> quickly. Yet photographs can change people's hearts and minds ④<u>in an instant</u>. And when the magic of photography sparks an emotional reaction in ⑤<u>a great number of people</u>, it can change history.

① ~만큼 빠르게
② ~을 움켜잡다
③ 복잡한 메시지를 전달하는 것
④ 잠시 동안
⑤ 많은 수의 사람들

04 다음 글의 빈칸 (A), (B)에 들어갈 말로 가장 적절한 것은?

> In the 1880s, industry began to grow rapidly along the Cuyahoga River in the city of Cleveland. This industrial growth provided steady jobs to people in the area. ____(A)____, steel mills and factories started dumping large amounts of waste into the river. ____(B)____ the river became polluted, most people simply regarded this as a sign of the area's economic success.

	(A)		(B)
①	Meanwhile	···	Although
②	Moreover	···	As a result
③	However	···	Meanwhile
④	In addition	···	Even though
⑤	Furthermore	···	Meanwhile

[05~06] 다음 글을 읽고, 물음에 답하시오.

In June 1969, the polluted river caught fire. The likely cause was a burning flare falling from a train, which set fire to oil-soaked waste beneath a bridge. At that time, ①few people in Cleveland cared. This was because fires had been recorded on the Cuyahoga more than ten times before, and some of them had been much worse.

However, it wasn't long before the 1969 fire became ②famous. This was thanks to an article published in *Time* magazine that year. The article featured a ③shocking photograph of flames and smoke rising from the river. But this was not a photograph of the 1969 fire, which was put out so ④quickly that nobody took a picture of it. In fact, it was a picture of a much worse fire that had occurred on the river several years ⑤later. Still, the image had a great impact on people.

05 다음 글의 밑줄 친 부분 중, 문맥상 낱말의 쓰임이 적절하지 않은 것은?

①   ②   ③   ④   ⑤

06 윗글의 밑줄 친 rising과 쓰임이 같은 것을 모두 고르면?

ⓐ One of my responsibilities is taking care of children.

ⓑ Scientists studying climate change warn of increasing global temperatures.

ⓒ She is reading a fascinating book in the library right now.

ⓓ The chef cooking in the kitchen is known for his delicious pasta dishes.

ⓔ Feeling hungry, I opened the fridge and found something to eat.

① ⓐ, ⓑ   ② ⓐ, ⓒ   ③ ⓑ, ⓒ

④ ⓑ, ⓓ   ⑤ ⓒ, ⓓ, ⓔ

[07~08] 다음 글을 읽고, 물음에 답하시오.

Around that time, the attitudes of Americans toward environmental problems were starting to change. More and more people were becoming aware of the need (A) protect / to protect the environment, and the shocking image of the burning river sparked public anger about water pollution. As a result, the Cuyahoga River fire of 1969 became a symbol of pollution. A national environmental awareness event was held on April 22, 1970, (B) that / which later became known as the first Earth Day. And in 1972, national water quality standards (C) established / were established with the passage of the Clean Water Act.

07 (A), (B), (C)의 각 네모 안에서 어법에 맞는 표현으로 가장 적절한 것은?

	(A)	(B)	(C)
①	protect	that	established
②	protect	which	were established
③	to protect	that	established
④	to protect	which	were established
⑤	to protect	that	were established

08 윗글의 내용과 일치하지 않는 것은?

① 1969년 쿠야호가 강 화재 이후 미국인들의 환경 문제에 대한 태도가 변화하기 시작했다.

② 불타는 강의 충격적인 이미지는 수질 오염에 대한 대중의 분노를 불러일으켰다.

③ 1969년 쿠야호가 강 화재는 환경 오염의 상징이 되었다.

④ 1970년 4월 22일에 열린 국가적 환경 인식 행사는 후에 첫 번째 지구의 날로 알려졌다.

⑤ 1972년 청정수법(Clean Water Act) 제정으로 국가 대기 질 기준이 수립되었다.

[09~10] 다음 글을 읽고, 물음에 답하시오.

In the 19th century, the Industrial Revolution led to a dramatic increase in factory production in the United States. The demand for workers ⓐ increasing, and many new positions were filled by children. By 1900, about twenty percent of all children in the United States ⓑ were employed, and some of those ⓒ worked in factories were only four years old. The work was difficult and dangerous, _____.

Factory owners turned to child labor for several reasons. For example, children could be paid ⓓ less than adult workers. They were also less likely ⓔ to go on strike.

09 윗글의 밑줄 친 부분 중, 어법상 틀린 것을 모두 고른 것은?

① ⓐ, ⓒ   ② ⓐ, ⓓ   ③ ⓑ, ⓓ
④ ⓒ, ⓓ   ⑤ ⓓ, ⓔ

10 윗글의 빈칸에 들어갈 말로 가장 적절한 것은?

① causing high mortality rates among adults
② resulting in poor educational outcomes
③ leaving many child laborers with health problems
④ leading to increased productivity in factories
⑤ creating a skilled workforce for the future

[11~12] 다음 글을 읽고, 물음에 답하시오.

The pictures were later shown in exhibitions, lectures, magazine articles, and so on. As a result, the public realized just how serious the situation was. Soon, many states passed stronger laws to ban the employment of children. In 1938, the United States Congress passed an act that made it illegal for children under sixteen to work in factories during school hours.

These examples show that photographs can bring meaningful change to society. They prove that, sometimes, a picture truly is worth a thousand words.

11 윗글의 밑줄 친 to ban과 쓰임이 같은 것은?

① The government decided to ban smoking in all public places.
② They tried to ban the man from entering the building.
③ The school decided to ban students from using cell phones during class.
④ The effort to ban junk food advertisements during children's TV shows is ongoing.
⑤ The committee voted to ban the use of single-use plastics in the city.

12 주어진 영어 뜻풀이에 해당하는 단어를 윗글에서 찾아 쓰시오.

(1) _____: a display of art, artifacts, or other items of interest
(2) _____: prohibited by law

Lewis Hine, a teacher and photographer, wanted ⓐto reveal how cruel this system was. So he quit his teaching job and started to work for the National Child Labor Committee ___(A)___ an investigative photographer. (①) He gained access to factories by ⓑpretending to have different jobs ___(B)___ insurance agent or fire inspector.

Once inside, he would photograph the children ©working there. (②) He would also ask their names and ages and record information about their living and working conditions. (③) From 1908 to 1912, he secretly gathered information and took photographs ⓓto expose factory owners who were taking advantage ___(C)___ helpless children. (④)

Hine's photographs captured young children doing all sorts of jobs. These included ⓔpicking vegetables, weaving baskets, and even handling dangerous equipment. (⑤) When people saw the children's joyless expressions, they could not help but feel heartbroken.

13 윗글의 빈칸 (A), (B), (C)에 들어갈 전치사로 알맞은 것을 다음 보기 에서 찾아 쓰시오.

보기 in   as   on   like   for   of

(A) _____   (B) _____   (C) _____

14 윗글의 흐름으로 보아, 주어진 문장이 들어가기에 가장 적절한 곳은?

What is more, the children's faces showed the tragic impact of hard labor.

①   ②   ③   ④   ⑤

15 윗글의 밑줄 친 ⓐ~ⓔ에 대해 잘못 설명한 것은?

① ⓐ: to reveal은 동사 wanted의 목적어 역할을 하는 to부정사이다.

② ⓑ: pretending은 전치사 by의 목적어 역할을 하는 동명사이다.

③ ©: working은 앞에 있는 명사 the children을 후치 수식하는 현재분사이다.

④ ⓓ: to expose는 '~하기 위해서'라는 의미의 목적을 나타내는 to부정사이다.

⑤ ⓔ: picking은 '~하면서'라는 의미의 분사이다.

01 (A), (B), (C)의 각 네모 안에서 어법에 맞는 표현으로 가장 적절한 것은?

As quickly as a camera captures a scene, an image can grab hold of our emotions. Through speech or (A) writing / written text, it can be difficult to convey a complex message quickly. Yet photographs can change people's hearts and minds (B) in / for an instant. And when the magic of photography sparks an emotional reaction in a great (C) number / amount of people, it can change history.

	(A)		(B)		(C)
①	writing	…	in	…	number
②	writing	…	for	…	amount
③	written	…	in	…	number
④	written	…	for	…	amount
⑤	written	…	in	…	amount

02 다음 글의 밑줄 친 부분 중, 쓰임이 어색한 것은?

①In the 1880s, industry began to grow rapidly along the Cuyahoga River in the city ②of Cleveland. This industrial growth provided steady jobs ③with people in the area. Meanwhile, steel mills and factories started dumping large amounts of waste ④into the river. Although the river became polluted, most people simply regarded this ⑤as a sign of the area's economic success.

① ② ③ ④ ⑤

[03~04] 다음 글을 읽고, 물음에 답하시오.

In June 1969, the polluted river caught fire. The likely cause was a burning flare falling from a train, which ①set fire to oil-soaked waste beneath a bridge. At that time, few people in Cleveland cared. This was because fires had been recorded on the Cuyahoga more than ten times before, and some of them had been much worse.

However, it wasn't long before the 1969 fire became famous. This was ②thanks to an article published in *Time* magazine that year. The article featured a shocking photograph of flames and smoke rising from the river. But this was not a photograph of the 1969 fire, which was ③put out so quickly that nobody ④took a picture of it. In fact, it was a picture of a much worse fire that had occurred on the river several years earlier. Still, the image ⑤had a great impact on people.

03 윗글의 밑줄 친 부분 중, 의미가 바르지 않은 것은?

① set fire to: ~에 불지르다
② thanks to: ~에 감사하다
③ put out: (불을) 끄다
④ take a picture of: ~을 사진 찍다
⑤ have a great impact on: ~에 큰 영향을 주다

04 윗글의 내용과 일치하지 않는 것은?

① 1969년 화재의 원인은 기차에서 떨어진 불꽃이었다.
② 클리블랜드 사람들은 처음에 화재에 대해 크게 신경 쓰지 않았다.
③ 타임지에 실린 사진은 1969년 화재를 찍은 것이었다.
④ 1969년 화재는 빠르게 진압되어 사진이 찍히지 않았다.
⑤ 잡지에 실린 사진은 사람들에게 큰 영향을 미쳤다.

[05~06] 다음 글을 읽고, 물음에 답하시오.

Around that time, the ①attitudes of Americans toward environmental problems were starting to change. More and more people were becoming aware of the need to ②protect the environment, and the shocking image of the burning river sparked public anger about ③air pollution. As a result, the Cuyahoga River fire of 1969 became a symbol of ④pollution. A national environmental awareness event held on April 22, 1970, which later became known as the first Earth Day. And in 1972, national water quality standards were established with the ⑤passage of the Clean Water Act.

05 윗글의 밑줄 친 부분 중, 문맥상 낱말의 쓰임이 적절하지 <u>않은</u> 것은?

①   ②   ③   ④   ⑤

06 윗글의 밑줄 친 문장에서 <u>틀린</u> 것을 찾아 바르게 고쳐 쓰시오.

     틀린 것   고친 것

  _____ → _____

[07~09] 다음 글을 읽고, 물음에 답하시오.

In the 19th century, the Industrial Revolution led to _____ in the United States. The demand for workers increased, and many new positions were filled by children. By 1900, about twenty percent of all children in the United States were employed, and 공장에서 일하는 아동 중 일부는 겨우 4살이었다. The work was difficult and dangerous, leaving many child laborers with health problems.

Factory owners turned to child labor for several reasons. For example, children could be paid less than adult workers. They were also less likely to go on strike.

07 윗글의 빈칸에 들어갈 말로 가장 적절한 것은?

① a decline in agricultural employment
② an increase in labor unions
③ improved working conditions
④ a dramatic increase in factory production
⑤ a rise in adult unemployment

08 윗글을 통해 답을 찾을 수 있는 질문이 <u>아닌</u> 것은?

① 19세기 미국에서 아동 노동이 증가한 이유는 무엇인가?
② 1900년경 미국에서 일하는 아동의 비율은 얼마나 되었는가?
③ 아동 노동자들이 주로 일했던 산업 분야는 무엇이었는가?
④ 공장주들이 아동 노동을 선호한 이유는 무엇인가?
⑤ 아동 노동이 노동자들의 건강에 미친 영향은 무엇인가?

09 윗글의 밑줄 친 우리말과 같은 뜻이 되도록 보기의 단어를 바르게 배열하여 문장을 완성하시오.

> 보기 of / working / in / some / only / factories / those / were / four / years / old

> By 1900, about twenty percent of all children in the United States were employed, and _____
> _____.

[10~11] 다음 글을 읽고, 물음에 답하시오.

> Lewis Hine, a teacher and photographer, wanted to reveal how cruel this system was. So he (A) quit / continued his teaching job and started to work for the National Child Labor Committee as an investigative photographer. He gained access to factories by pretending to have different jobs like insurance agent or fire inspector.
>
> Once inside, he would photograph the children working there. He would also ask their names and ages and record information about their living and working conditions. From 1908 to 1912, he secretly gathered information and took photographs to expose factory owners who were taking advantage of (B) helpful / helpless children.
>
> Hine's photographs captured young children doing all sorts of jobs. These (C) excluded / included picking vegetables, weaving baskets, and even handling dangerous equipment. What is more, the children's faces showed the tragic impact of hard labor. When people saw the children's joyless expressions, they could not help but feel heartbroken.

10 윗글의 제목으로 가장 적절한 것은?

① The Rise of Child Labor in the 19th Century
② Lewis Hine: The Photographer Who Exposed Child Labor
③ The Impact of Industrial Revolution on American Society
④ The National Child Labor Committee's Fight Against Exploitation
⑤ Photography as a Tool for Social Change

11 (A), (B), (C)의 각 네모 안에서 문맥상 맞는 표현으로 가장 적절한 것은?

	(A)	(B)	(C)
①	quit	… helpless	… included
②	quit	… helpful	… included
③	quit	… helpless	… excluded
④	continued	… helpless	… excluded
⑤	continued	… helpful	… included

12 다음 대화의 주제로 가장 적절한 것은?

> **Ethan** Social media has changed the way we consume news. Today, younger generations are much more likely to get their news from social media than from traditional sources like TV and newspapers. Which do you prefer?
>
> **Sophia** I prefer social media. It has completely transformed the way we get information. It has become so much quicker and easier to access and share news.
>
> **Liam** Absolutely. However, there is a negative side to this. People don't always check whether information is accurate. As a result, false or misleading information can also spread very quickly online.
>
> **Ava** That's so true. That's why I prefer more traditional sources of news. We should never share news on social media without checking it first.

① 전통적인 뉴스 매체의 쇠퇴
② 젊은 세대의 정치 참여 방식
③ 온라인 저널리즘의 미래
④ 디지털 리터러시 교육의 필요성
⑤ 소셜 미디어를 통한 뉴스 소비의 장단점

14 윗글의 밑줄 친 부분 중, 전치사의 쓰임이 바르지 <u>않은</u> 것은?

①   ②   ③   ④   ⑤

[13~14] 다음 글을 읽고, 물음에 답하시오.

The pictures were later shown ①<u>in</u> exhibitions, lectures, magazine articles, and so ②<u>on</u>. As a result, the public realized just how serious was the situation. Soon, many states passed stronger laws to ban the employment of children. ③<u>In</u> 1938, the United States Congress passed an act that made it illegal ④<u>of</u> children under sixteen to work in factories ⑤<u>during</u> school hours.

13 윗글의 밑줄 친 문장에서 **틀린** 부분을 찾아 바르게 고쳐 문장을 다시 쓰시오.

As a result, the public realized just _____

_____ .

15 다음 대화의 ①~⑤ 중, 흐름상 불필요한 문장은?

B I've started my own video channel.
G What's it about?
B It's focused on teaching how to play the guitar to beginners. ①You know I really love music!
G That's great! My sister wants to learn how to play an instrument. ②I'll definitely recommend your channel to her.
B Thanks! ③I hope it helps her learn.
G It's so nice that you are willing to make helpful videos. ④I've been thinking about starting a cooking channel myself.
B ⑤Many people are doing it these days. This means we can learn new things more easily than ever before.
G You're right.

(1) _____ : to represent or record accurately in words or pictures

(2) _____ : to communicate or express a thought, feeling, etc.

01 다음 대화의 빈칸에 들어갈 말로 가장 적절한 것은?

> Ethan Social media has changed the way we consume news. Today, younger generations are much more likely to get their news from social media than from traditional sources like TV and newspapers. _____
>
> Sophia I prefer social media. It has completely transformed the way we get information. It has become so much quicker and easier to access and share news.
>
> Liam Absolutely. However, there is a negative side to this. People don't always check whether information is accurate. As a result, false or misleading information can also spread very quickly online.
>
> Ava That's so true. That's why I prefer more traditional sources of news. We should never share news on social media without checking it first.

① How do you consume news?
② Which do you prefer?
③ Do you think social media is reliable?
④ What are the benefits of social media news?
⑤ How often do you check the news?

02 다음 글에서 영어 뜻풀이에 알맞은 단어를 찾아 쓰시오.

> As quickly as a camera captures a scene, an image can grab hold of our emotions. Through speech or written text, it can be difficult to convey a complex message quickly. Yet photographs can change people's hearts and minds in an instant. And when the magic of photography sparks an emotional reaction in a great number of people, it can change history.

[03~04] 다음 글을 읽고, 물음에 답하시오.

> **The Burning River That Started a Movement**
>   ① In the 1880s, industry began to grow rapidly along the Cuyahoga River in the city of Cleveland. ② This industrial growth provided steady jobs to people in the area. ③ Meanwhile, steel mills and factories started dumping large amounts of waste into the river. ④ The region is also known for its rich cultural history and vibrant arts scene. ⑤ Although the river became polluted, most people simply regarded this as a sign of the area's economic success.

03 윗글의 전체 흐름으로 보아, 어색한 문장은?

①   ②   ③   ④   ⑤

04 윗글의 밑줄 친 That과 쓰임이 다른 것은?

① Mr. Smith is the teacher that everyone respects.
② The movie that we watched last night was boring.
③ I think that we should leave early tomorrow.
④ This is the restaurant that serves the best pizza in town.
⑤ The book that I borrowed from the library is very interesting.

05 다음 대화의 밑줄 친 우리말과 같은 뜻이 되도록 다음 보기 안의 단어를 알맞게 배열하여 영작하시오.

> **M** Hey, cool watch!
>
> **W** Thanks. I got it last week.
>
> **M** I'm thinking of buying a new watch, too. Are you satisfied with your purchase?
>
> **W** Yeah! This one keeps track of my heart rate, so it is very useful when I exercise.
>
> **M** Wow! That's amazing!
>
> **W** It has other cool functions, too. For example, I can use it to pay for things. 이것은 내가 더 이상 지갑을 가지고 다닐 필요가 없다는 것을 의미한다.
>
> **M:** That's great! We can do so much more than telling time with watches nowadays.

> 보기 means / that / I / this / need / my wallet / to carry / with me / don't / anymore

[06~07] 다음 글을 읽고, 물음에 답하시오.

> Around that time, the attitudes of Americans toward ____(A)____ problems were starting to change. More and more people were becoming aware of the need to protect the environment, and the shocking image of the burning river sparked public anger about water pollution. As a result, the Cuyahoga River fire of 1969 became a symbol of pollution. A national ____(B)____ awareness event was held on April 22, 1970, ____(C)____ later became known as the first Earth Day. And in 1972, national water quality standards were established with the passage of the Clean Water Act.

06 윗글의 빈칸 (A), (B)에 공통으로 들어갈 말로 알맞은 것은?

① ecological
② natural
③ sustainable
④ green
⑤ environmental

07 윗글의 빈칸 (C)에 들어갈 말로 알맞은 것은?

① who
② which
③ whose
④ that
⑤ what

[08~09] 다음 글을 읽고, 물음에 답하시오.

> In June 1969, the polluted river caught fire. The likely cause was a burning flare falling from a train, which set fire to oil-soaked waste beneath a bridge. At that time, few people in Cleveland cared. This was ____(A)____ fires had been recorded on the Cuyahoga more than ten times before, and some of them had been much worse.
>
> ____(B)____, it wasn't long before the 1969 fire became famous. This was thanks to an article published in *Time* magazine that year. 그 기사는 강에서 피어오르는 불길과 연기의 충격적인 사진을 특종으로 다뤘다. But this was not a photograph of the 1969 fire, which was put out so quickly that nobody took a picture of it. ____(C)____, it was a picture of a much worse fire that had occurred on the river several years earlier. Still, the image had a great impact on people.

08 윗글의 빈칸 (A), (B), (C)에 들어갈 말로 가장 적절한 것은?

	(A)	(B)	(C)
①	since	⋯ Yet	⋯ Actually
②	as	⋯ Still	⋯ Indeed
③	because	⋯ However	⋯ In fact
④	for	⋯ Though	⋯ Truly
⑤	due to	⋯ Nevertheless	⋯ Certainly

09 윗글의 우리말과 같은 뜻이 되도록 **보기**에서 동사를 골라 알맞은 형태로 바꿔 빈칸에 쓰시오.

> **보기** rise   capture   feature   convey

> The article _____ a shocking photograph of flames and smoke _____ from the river.

[10~11] 다음 글을 읽고, 물음에 답하시오.

In the 19th century, the Industrial Revolution led to a dramatic increase in factory production in the United States. The demand for workers increased, and many new positions were ⓐfill by children. By 1900, about twenty percent of all children in the United States were employed, and some of those working in factories were only four years old. The work was difficult and dangerous, ⓑleave many child laborers with health problems.

Factory owners turned to child labor for several reasons. For example, children could be paid less than adult workers. They were also less likely to _____.

10 윗글의 밑줄 친 ⓐ와 ⓑ를 어법에 맞게 고쳐 쓴 것으로 가장 적절한 것은?

① filled ⋯ left
② filled ⋯ leaving
③ filling ⋯ left
④ filling ⋯ leaving
⑤ to fill ⋯ leaving

11 윗글의 빈칸에 들어갈 말로 가장 적절한 것은?

① be physically strong
② work long hours
③ operate complex machinery
④ go on strike
⑤ adapt to new technologies

[12~13] 다음 글을 읽고, 물음에 답하시오.

Lewis Hine, a teacher and photographer, wanted to reveal how cruel this system was. So he quit his teaching job and started to work for the National Child Labor Committee as an investigative photographer. He gained access to factories by (A) pretending / pretended to have different jobs like insurance agent or fire inspector.

Once inside, he would photograph the children working there. He would also ask their names and ages and record information about their living and working conditions. From 1908 to 1912, he secretly gathered information and took photographs to expose factory owners (B) who / which were taking advantage of helpless children.

Hine's photographs captured young children doing all sorts of jobs. These included picking vegetables, weaving baskets, and even handling dangerous equipment. What is more, the children's faces showed the tragic impact of hard labor. When people saw the children's joyless expressions, they could not help but (C) feel / to feel heartbroken.

12 (A), (B), (C)의 각 네모 안에서 어법에 맞는 표현으로 가장 적절한 것은?

	(A)	(B)	(C)
①	pretending	⋯ who	⋯ feel
②	pretending	⋯ which	⋯ to feel
③	pretending	⋯ who	⋯ to feel
④	pretended	⋯ which	⋯ to feel
⑤	pretended	⋯ who	⋯ feel

13 Lewis Hine에 관한 내용으로 일치하지 <u>않는</u> 것은?

① 교사직을 그만두고 전국아동노동위원회에서 일했다.
② 보험 설계사나 소방 감독관으로 위장하여 공장에 들어갔다.
③ 1908년부터 1912년까지 아동 노동 실태를 비밀리에 조사했다.
④ 그의 사진은 다양한 종류의 아동 노동을 포착했다.
⑤ 그는 아동 노동자들의 이름과 나이를 공개적으로 물어보았다.

[14~15] 다음 글을 읽고, 물음에 답하시오.

The pictures were later shown in exhibitions, lectures, magazine articles, and so on. As a result, the public realized just how serious the situation was. Soon, many states passed (A) stronger / weaker laws to ban the employment of children. In 1938, the United States Congress passed an act <u>that</u> made it (B) legal / illegal for children under sixteen to work in factories during school hours.

These examples show that photographs can bring meaningful change to society. They prove that, sometimes, a picture (C) true / truly is worth a thousand words.

14 윗글의 밑줄 친 that과 쓰임이 같은 것의 개수는?

ⓐ The book <u>that</u> I am reading is interesting.
ⓑ I believe <u>that</u> honesty is the best policy.
ⓒ The museum <u>that</u> we visited yesterday was excellent.
ⓓ He said <u>that</u> he would come to the party.
ⓔ The red car <u>that</u> is parked over there is mine.

① 0개   ② 1개   ③ 2개   ④ 3개   ⑤ 4개

15 (A), (B), (C)의 각 네모 안에서 문맥에 맞는 낱말로 가장 적절한 것은?

	(A)	(B)	(C)
①	stronger	⋯ legal	⋯ true
②	stronger	⋯ illegal	⋯ truly
③	stronger	⋯ illegal	⋯ true
④	weaker	⋯ legal	⋯ truly
⑤	weaker	⋯ illegal	⋯ true

[01~02] 다음 글을 읽고, 물음에 답하시오.

> Just as a camera instantly captures a moment in time, a single image can immediately seize our emotions. It is challenging to convey a complex message through speech or writing quickly. However, photographs have the unique ability to ＿＿＿＿＿＿＿＿＿＿. When the magic of photography triggers a widespread emotional response among a large group of individuals, it has the potential to change history.

01 윗글의 빈칸에 들어갈 말로 가장 적절한 것은?

① document historical events accurately
② improve the quality of visual arts
③ swiftly alter our perspectives and feelings
④ replace traditional forms of communication
⑤ create lasting memories for individuals

02 윗글의 요지로 가장 적절한 것은?

① 사진은 복잡한 메시지를 전달하는 데 한계가 있다.
② 사진은 순간을 포착하는 능력이 뛰어나다.
③ 역사적 사건을 기록하는 데 있어 사진의 역할이 중요하다.
④ 사진은 사람들의 감정과 관점을 빠르게 변화시킬 수 있다.
⑤ 사진 기술의 발전으로 인해 대중의 반응이 더욱 즉각적으로 나타난다.

[03~05] 다음 글을 읽고, 물음에 답하시오.

> During the 1880s, the Cuyahoga River in Cleveland saw significant industrial (A) develop / development along its banks. (①) This growth brought steady ⓐ employment opportunities to residents. (②) However, it also led to steel mills and factories ⓑ dumping large (B) amounts / numbers of waste into the river. (③)
>
> In June 1969, the polluted river caught fire. The probable ⓒ result was a burning flare dropped from a passing train, which set fire to oil-soaked waste under a bridge. (④) At that time, few people in Cleveland cared. (⑤) This ⓓ lack of concern stemmed from the fact that the Cuyahoga had experienced more than ten previous fires, some of (C) which / that had been much ⓔ worse.

03 윗글의 흐름으로 보아, 주어진 문장이 들어가기에 가장 알맞은 곳은?

> Despite the polluted river, most people simply regarded this as a sign of the area's economic success.

①　　　②　　　③　　　④　　　⑤

04 윗글의 밑줄 친 ⓐ~ⓔ 중, 문맥상 낱말의 쓰임이 적절하지 <u>않은</u> 것은?

① ⓐ　　② ⓑ　　③ ⓒ　　④ ⓓ　　⑤ ⓔ

05 (A), (B), (C)의 각 네모 안에서 어법에 맞는 낱말로 가장 적절한 것은?

	(A)	(B)	(C)
①	develop	numbers	that
②	develop	amounts	which
③	development	numbers	which
④	development	amounts	that
⑤	development	amounts	which

[06~08] 다음 글을 읽고, 물음에 답하시오.

The fire on the Cuyahoga River in 1969 quickly became famous, primarily due to an article published in *Time* magazine that same year. The article included a striking photograph of flames and smoke rising from the river. ___(A)___, this image was not from the 1969 fire, ①which was extinguished so swiftly that no one managed to photograph it. Instead, it showed a ②much more severe fire that had taken place several years earlier. ___(B)___, the image left a significant impression on the public.

Around that time, the attitudes of Americans toward environmental issues began to change. Increasingly, people recognized the importance of ③protecting the environment, and the shocking image of the burning river sparked public anger about water pollution. ___(C)___, the 1969 Cuyahoga River fire became a symbol of environmental pollution. On April 22, 1970, a national event ④to raise environmental awareness took place, which later became known as the first Earth Day. In 1972, national water quality standards ⑤established with the passage of the Clean Water Act.

06 윗글의 제목으로 가장 적절한 것은?

① The History of Earth Day Celebrations
② Time Magazine's Influence on American Politics
③ The Development of National Water Quality Standards
④ Cleveland's Industrial Revolution and Its Consequences
⑤ The Cuyahoga River Fire: A Spark for Environmental Change

07 윗글의 밑줄 친 부분 중, 어법상 **틀린** 것은?

①   ②   ③   ④   ⑤

08 (A), (B), (C)의 각 빈칸에 들어갈 말로 가장 적절한 것은?

	(A)	(B)	(C)
①	However	Nonetheless	As a result
②	However	Therefore	As a result
③	Moreover	Nonetheless	Consequently
④	However	Additionally	Therefore
⑤	Moreover	Therefore	Consequently

[09~11] 다음 글을 읽고, 물음에 답하시오.

The Industrial Revolution in the 19th century sparked a significant (A) rise / fall in factory production across the United States. ① The Civil War turned Cleveland into a manufacturing city almost overnight. This surge in manufacturing created a high demand for workers, leading to the widespread (B) employment / unemployment of children. ② By 1900, approximately twenty percent of American children were part of the workforce, with some as young as four years old laboring in factories. ③ The working conditions were harsh and dangerous, often resulting in _____ for these young laborers.

④ Factory owners had multiple motivations for employing children. One key reason was (C) financial / industrial; children could be paid lower wages compared to adult workers. ⑤ Additionally, child workers were considered less likely to engage in labor strikes.

09 윗글의 ①~⑤ 중, 전체 흐름상 어색한 문장은?

①   ②   ③   ④   ⑤

10 (A), (B), (C)의 각 네모 안에서 어법에 맞는 표현으로 가장 적절한 것은?

	(A)	(B)	(C)
①	rise	employment	industrial
②	rise	employment	financial
③	rise	unemployment	financial
④	fall	employment	industrial
⑤	fall	unemployment	industrial

11 윗글의 빈칸에 들어갈 말로 가장 적절한 것은?

① higher wages for families
② increased job opportunities
③ improved living standards
④ severe health issues
⑤ greater educational access

[12~14] 다음 글을 읽고, 물음에 답하시오.

Lewis Hine, a teacher and photographer, was determined to (A) hide / expose the cruelty of child labor. He resigned from his teaching job to become an investigative photographer for the National Child Labor Committee. To gain access to factories, he pretended to have different jobs like insurance agent or fire inspector.

Once inside, Hine documented the working children through photographs. He also collected personal information, (B) including / excluding names and ages, and recorded details about their living and working conditions. Between 1908 and 1912, Hine secretly gathered evidence and took photographs to reveal how factory owners were taking advantage of helpless children.

Hine's photographs depicted young children doing all sorts of jobs. These included agricultural work like picking vegetables and industrial tasks such as weaving baskets and handling dangerous equipment. The photographs also revealed the children's faces, showing the tragic impact of hard labor. When people saw the children's (C) joyful / joyless expressions, they could not help but feel heartbroken.

12 윗글의 주제로 가장 적절한 것은?

① The impact of child labor on American society
② The role of photography in social reform
③ The history of child labor laws in the United States
④ The personal life of Lewis Hine
⑤ The economic benefits of child labor

13 (A), (B), (C)의 각 네모 안에서 문맥에 맞는 낱말로 가장 적절한 것은?

	(A)	(B)	(C)
①	hide	⋯ including	⋯ joyless
②	hide	⋯ excluding	⋯ joyful
③	expose	⋯ including	⋯ joyless
④	expose	⋯ including	⋯ joyful
⑤	expose	⋯ excluding	⋯ joyless

14 윗글을 요약문으로 만들 때 빈칸에 들어갈 말로 가장 적절한 것은?

Lewis Hine's work was crucial in raising awareness about child labor practices in the early 20th century. His photographs not only documented the harsh conditions but also _____ the public's consciousness regarding children's rights.

① ignored   ② awakened   ③ confused
④ diminished   ⑤ entertained

15 다음 글의 빈칸에 들어갈 말로 가장 적절한 것은?

Hine's photographs gained widespread exposure through various channels, including exhibitions, lectures, and magazine articles. As a result, many states passed stronger laws _____. In 1938, the United States Congress passed an act to make it illegal for children under sixteen to work in factories during school hours.

① to promote child labor awareness
② to improve working conditions in factories
③ to increase funding for educational programs
④ to prohibit the employment of children
⑤ to regulate industrial production methods

내신 1등급

서술형

01 다음 글의 밑줄 친 우리말과 같은 뜻이 되도록 빈칸에 알맞은 말을 조건에 맞게 쓰시오.

> As quickly as a camera captures a scene, an image can grab hold of our emotions. 연설이나 쓰인 텍스트를 통해 복잡한 메시지를 빠르게 전달하는 것은 어려울 수 있다. Yet photographs can change people's hearts and minds in an instant. And when the magic of photography sparks an emotional reaction in a great number of people, it can change history.

조건
- 「가주어 it, 진주어 to부정사」 구문으로 쓸 것
- can, convey, complex를 반드시 사용할 것

→ Through speech or written text, _____
_____ quickly.

02 괄호 안에 주어진 동사를 알맞은 형태로 바꿔 빈칸 (A), (B)에 쓰시오.

> The ____(A)____ (burn) River That Started a Movement
> In the 1880s, industry began to grow rapidly along the Cuyahoga River in the city of Cleveland. This industrial growth provided steady jobs to people in the area. Meanwhile, steel mills and factories started dumping large amounts of waste into the river. Although the river became ____(B)____ (pollute), most people simply regarded this as a sign of the area's economic success.

(A) _____   (B) _____

[03~04] 다음 글을 읽고, 물음에 답하시오.

> In June 1969, the polluted river caught fire. The likely cause was a ①burning flare falling from a train, which set fire to oil-soaked waste beneath a bridge. At that time, few people in Cleveland cared. This was because fires ②had been recorded on the Cuyahoga more than ten times before, and some of them had been much worse.
>
> However, it wasn't long before the 1969 fire became famous. This was thanks to an article ③published in *Time* magazine that year. The article featured a shocking photograph of flames and smoke ④rising from the river. But this was not a photograph of the 1969 fire, which was put out so quickly that nobody took a picture of it. In fact, it was a picture of a much worse fire that ⑤has occurred on the river several years earlier. Still, the image had a great impact on people.

03 윗글의 밑줄 친 부분 중, 어법상 틀린 것을 찾아 번호를 쓰고 바르게 고쳐 쓰시오.

_____ → _____

04 윗글의 내용을 바탕으로 다음 질문에 대한 대답을 5단어로 완성하시오.

> Q Why was there no photograph taken of the 1969 fire?
> A Because the fire _____ that nobody had time to take a picture of it.

[05~06] 다음 글을 읽고, 물음에 답하시오.

Around that time, the attitudes of Americans toward environmental problems were starting to change. More and more people were becoming aware of the need to protect the environment, and the shocking image of the burning river sparked public anger about water pollution. As a result, the Cuyahoga River fire of 1969 became a symbol of pollution. A national environmental awareness event was held on April 22, 1970, <u>which</u> later became known as the first Earth Day. And in 1972, national water quality standards established with the passage of the Clean Water Act.

05 윗글의 밑줄 친 which가 가리키는 것을 영어로 쓰시오.

_____

06 윗글의 밑줄 친 문장에서 틀린 부분을 바르게 고쳐 문장을 다시 쓰시오.

_____

[07~08] 다음 글을 읽고, 물음에 답하시오.

In the 19th century, the Industrial Revolution led to a dramatic increase in factory production in the United States. The demand for workers increased, and many new positions were filled by children. By 1900, about twenty percent of all children in the United States were employed, and some of those working in factories were only four years old. <u>일은 힘들고 위험해서 많은 아동 노동자들에게 건강 문제를 남겼다.</u>

Factory owners turned to child labor for several reasons. For example, children could be paid less than adult workers. They were also less likely to go on strike.

07 다음 영어 뜻풀이에 해당하는 단어를 윗글에서 찾아 쓰시오.

> _____ : unpleasantly rough or severe

08 윗글의 밑줄 친 우리말과 같은 뜻이 되도록 보기의 단어를 알맞게 배열하시오.

> 보기 many / health problems / with / leaving / child laborers

The work was difficult and dangerous, _____
_____ .

[09~10] 다음 글을 읽고, 물음에 답하시오.

교사이자 사진작가인 Lewis Hine은 이 제도가 얼마나 잔인한지 밝히고 싶었다. So he quit his teaching job and started to work for the National Child Labor Committee as an investigative photographer. ①He gained access to factories by pretending to have different jobs like insurance agent or fire inspector.

Once inside, he would photograph the children working there. ②He would also ask their names and ages and record information about their living and working conditions. ③From 1908 to 1912, he secretly gathered information and took photographs to expose factory owners who were taking advantage of helpless children.

④Hine's photographs captured young children doing all sorts of jobs. ⑤These included picking vegetables, weaving baskets, and even handling dangerous equipment. What is more, the children's faces showed the tragic impact of hard labor. When people saw the children's joyless expressions, they could not help but feel heartbroken.

09 윗글의 밑줄 친 우리말과 같은 뜻이 되도록 보기의 단어를 알맞게 배열하시오. (필요시 어형을 변형시킬 것)

> 보기 reveal / want / how / cruel / be / this system

Lewis Hine, a teacher and photographer, _____
_____.

10 다음 문장이 옳으면 T, 틀리면 F에 표시하고, 밑줄 친 ①~⑤ 중 판단의 근거가 되는 문장의 번호를 쓰시오.

(1) Lewis Hine openly entered factories as a photographer for the National Child Labor Committee. (T / F)
근거 문장: _____

(2) Hine's photographs depicted children engaged in a variety of jobs, including agricultural work and manufacturing. (T / F)

근거 문장: _____

[11~12] 다음 글을 읽고, 물음에 답하시오.

①The pictures were later shown in exhibitions, lectures, magazine articles, and so on. ②As a result, the public realized just how serious was the situation. Soon, many states passed stronger laws to ban the _____ of children. ③In 1938, the United States Congress passed an act that made it illegal for children under sixteen working in factories during school hours.

④These examples show that photographs can bring meaningful change to society. ⑤They prove that, sometimes, a picture truly is worth a thousand words.

11 윗글의 ①~⑤ 중, 틀린 문장을 두 개 찾아 번호를 쓰고 틀린 부분을 바르게 고쳐 문장을 다시 쓰시오.

틀린 문장	고친 문장

12 윗글의 빈칸에 주어진 단어를 알맞은 형태로 바꿔 쓰시오.

employ → _____

[01~02] 다음 글을 읽고, 물음에 답하시오.

Dear Tree,

Whenever I walk past you, your beautiful leaves bring a smile to my face. Whenever I stop in front of you and take a deep breath of fresh air, I appreciate the oxygen that you produce. 너와 네 모든 친구들이 없다면, 우리 인간들은 충분한 산소를 얻을 수 없을 거야. By the way, I noticed that a family of birds has made a nest in your branches. It's so kind of you to provide them with a home. I hope that more people realize how important you and all the other trees are to the environment. Have a nice day!

01 윗글에 나타난 필자의 심경으로 가장 적절한 것은?

① excited   ② anxious   ③ grateful
④ relieved   ⑤ disappointed

02 윗글의 밑줄 친 우리말과 같은 뜻이 되도록 괄호 안에서 알맞은 말을 골라 동그라미 하시오.

(With / Without) you and all your friends, we humans wouldn't (be / have been) able to get enough oxygen.

03 다음 중 어법상 어색한 문장의 개수로 알맞은 것은?

ⓐ Come visit the shop sold the most delicious cakes in town!
ⓑ Without fun and inspiring stories, life would be rather unexciting.
ⓒ We believe that we have everything you need for an enjoyable stay.
ⓓ The roads were covered with ice, who made walking a struggle.

① 0개   ② 1개   ③ 2개   ④ 3개   ⑤ 4개

[04~05] 다음 글을 읽고, 물음에 답하시오.

The story behind these emails begins with Melbourne's Urban Forest Strategy plan, a ① response to Australia's millennium drought. This drought lasted from the late 1990s to 2010. By the time it ended, 40 percent of the city's 77,000 trees were in a state of declining health. Furthermore, the overall number of trees was ②increasing.

As a result, the amount of shade provided by trees within the city, also known as canopy cover, decreased. The loss of canopy cover is a major threat to ③urban environments because it raises temperatures. Higher temperatures in cities can be dangerous for residents, as they increase the ④risk of heat exhaustion. They also lead to a rise in the use of air-conditioning. This speeds up climate change by increasing energy ⑤consumption and greenhouse gas emissions.

04 윗글의 제목으로 가장 적절한 것은?

① The Effects of Droughts on Urban Trees
② Climate Change and Urban Heat Islands
③ The Importance of Canopy Cover in Cities
④ The Purpose Behind Melbourne's Tree Email System
⑤ Air Conditioning and Greenhouse Gas Emissions

05 윗글의 밑줄 친 부분 중, 문맥상 낱말의 쓰임이 적절하지 않은 것은?

①   ②   ③   ④   ⑤

[06~07] 다음 글을 읽고, 물음에 답하시오.

Something had to be done to deal with the loss of Melbourne's trees. In 2012, the city government announced its Urban Forest Strategy plan. (①) It set the ambitious goal of (A) | planting / planted | more than 3,000 trees every year for the next twenty years. (②)

This interactive map shows the location of every single tree in the city's parks and along its roads. (③) It uses colors and symbols (B) | indicating / to indicate | each tree's age and genus. Also, users can click on a tree to find out its species and even send it an email. (④) At first, the "mail this tree" function had a specific purpose. (⑤) It was designed to allow people to easily inform council workers about trees (C) | that / what | were damaged or in poor health.

06 윗글의 흐름으로 보아, 주어진 문장이 들어가기에 가장 적절한 곳은?

The plan also involved the creation of an online map called the Urban Forest Visual.

①   ②   ③   ④   ⑤

07 (A), (B), (C)의 각 네모 안에서 어법상 옳은 것끼리 짝지어진 것은?

	(A)	(B)	(C)
①	planting	... to indicate	... that
②	planting	... to indicate	... what
③	planting	... indicating	... that
④	planted	... indicating	... that
⑤	planted	... to indicate	... what

[08~10] 다음 글을 읽고, 물음에 답하시오.

After the map was posted online, ①something unexpected happened. The trees started receiving thousands of emails, but many of them were not reports about damage or poor health. Instead, they were love letters, poems, greetings, and messages ②expressed appreciation for the trees. One person wrote, "I love the way the light shines on your leaves and how your branches hang so low. It is almost like you are trying to hug me." The tree mail phenomenon quickly spread, and people all over the world started sending messages.

A message that ③was sent all the way from Russia said, "When I read about this wonderful project, I was inspired to write to you, even though I live thousands of miles away. Although we are separated by a great distance, we share the same planet and the same environment. Perhaps one day we will meet. Until then, I hope you can ④stay healthy and strong."

The global popularity of the tree mail phenomenon reminds us that we are all connected to nature, and we are all involved in building a more sustainable world. Without collective action from people across the globe, we ⑤would have little hope of saving our planet for future generations.

08 윗글의 밑줄 친 부분 중, 어법상 **틀린** 것은?

①   ②   ③   ④   ⑤

09 윗글의 밑줄 친 sustainable의 영어 뜻풀이로 가장 적절한 것은?

① having characteristics of a town or city
② to create, make, or manufacture something
③ having a strong desire to achieve success or a specific goal
④ able to be maintained over time without harming the environment or depleting resources
⑤ involving communication or action between two or more things or people

10 윗글의 내용과 일치하지 <u>않는</u> 것은?

① The tree mail phenomenon started after a map was posted online.
② People sent various forms of writing to express their feelings in their emails.
③ A message from Russia mentioned a desire to meet one of the trees one day.
④ The global popularity of tree mail shows our connection to nature.
⑤ The tree mail phenomenon only attracted the interest of the locals.

[11~12] 다음 글을 읽고, 물음에 답하시오.

(A) Meanwhile, the Urban Forest Strategy's tree planting project has remained on track, and canopy cover is predicted to increase from 23 percent in 2012 to 40 percent by the year 2040. Melbourne's urban forest strategy will help keep the city cool. It will also allow residents to interact with nature and engage in outdoor activities every day.

(B) Locally, the tree mail phenomenon has inspired many Melbourne residents to offer their own ideas about building an environmentally friendly urban environment. Some have even volunteered to measure trees and monitor animals for nature programs in the city.

(C) As a result, residents will be happier and healthier as they move toward a greener future.

11 자연스러운 글이 되도록 순서대로 바르게 배열한 것은?

① (A) – (C) – (B)
② (B) – (A) – (C)
③ (B) – (C) – (A)
④ (C) – (A) – (B)
⑤ (C) – (B) – (A)

12 윗글의 요지로 가장 적절한 것은?

① 멜버른의 도시숲 전략은 기후 변화에 대응하기 위해 나무를 보호하고 늘리기 위한 계획이다.
② 나무 메일 현상은 멜버른 주민들이 나무에 대한 사랑을 표현하는 새로운 방법이다.
③ 멜버른의 도시숲 전략은 도시의 열섬 효과를 줄이고 주민들의 삶의 질을 향상시키는 데 기여한다.
④ 주민들은 도시숲 전략에 참여하여 나무를 심고 자연을 보호하는 데 도움을 준다.
⑤ 멜버른의 도시숲 전략은 생물 다양성을 증가시키고 지속 가능한 환경을 조성하기 위한 것이다.

13 다음 **보기** 에서 알맞은 단어를 골라 형태를 바꿔 빈칸에 쓰시오.

보기 usual   nerve   danger   expected

(1) Driving without a seatbelt is _____ and can lead to serious injuries.
(2) She felt _____ before her presentation, but she managed to speak confidently.
(3) It was _____ for him to stay up late studying, since he usually goes to bed early.
(4) The _____ rainstorm surprised everyone during the outdoor event.

14 다음 대화의 흐름으로 보아, 주어진 문장이 들어가기에 가장 적절한 곳은?

> This means we can learn new things more easily than ever before.

B I've started my own video channel. (①)

G What's it about?

B It's focused on teaching how to play the guitar to beginners. You know I really love music! (②)

G That's great! My sister wants to learn how to play an instrument. I'll definitely recommend your channel to her.

B Thanks! I hope it helps her learn. (③)

G It's so nice that you are willing to make helpful videos. (④)

B Many people are doing it these days. (⑤)

G You're right.

①   ②   ③   ④   ⑤

15 다음 담화의 목적으로 가장 적절한 것은?

W Would you like to contribute to research and make a difference in the world? Join Eco Trackers to participate in environmental citizen science projects! Scientists need data, but it's hard for them to collect the information they need alone. Our website allows people from around the world to collect data while they work together on research projects. Do you enjoy hiking? Help scientists study air quality by taking photographs from the tops of mountains. How about gardening? Try growing crops in your community garden and check your area's soil quality. You can even help scientists while looking at the stars! Just record light pollution by reporting how visible stars are. Come and join Eco Trackers today! I'm sure that we can make the world a better place.

① 과학 연구 장비를 위한 자금을 모으기 위해

② 등산가를 위한 새로운 하이킹 앱을 광고하기 위해

③ 커뮤니티 정원을 위한 원예 장비를 판매하기 위해

④ 천문학 애호가를 위한 별 관찰 이벤트를 홍보하기 위해

⑤ 환경 시민 과학 프로젝트를 위한 자원봉사자를 모집하기 위해

[16~17] 다음 글을 읽고, 물음에 답하시오.

> ① In the 1880s, industry began to grow rapidly along the Cuyahoga River in the city of Cleveland. ② This industrial growth provided steady jobs to people in the area. ③ Meanwhile, steel mills and factories started dumping large amounts of waste into the river. ④ People were optimistic that the increase in jobs meant an increase in wages. ⑤ Although the river became polluted, most people simply regarded this as a sign of the area's economic success.
>
> In June 1969, the (A) pollute river caught fire. The likely cause was a (B) burn flare falling from a train, which set fire to oil-soaked waste beneath a bridge. At that time, few people in Cleveland cared. This was because fires had been recorded on the Cuyahoga more than ten times before, and some of them had been much worse.

16 윗글의 전체 흐름상, 어색한 문장은?

①   ②   ③   ④   ⑤

17 윗글의 밑줄 친 동사 (A), (B)를 어법에 맞는 형태로 고쳐 쓰시오.

(A) pollute → _____

(B) burn → _____

However, it wasn't long before the 1969 fire became famous. This was thanks to an article published in *Time* magazine that year. The article featured a shocking photograph of flames and smoke <u>rising</u> from the river. But this was not a photograph of the 1969 fire, which was put out so quickly that nobody took a picture of it. In fact, it was a picture of a much worse fire that had occurred on the river several years earlier. Still, the image had a great ① <u>impact</u> on people.

Around that time, the ② <u>attitudes</u> of Americans toward environmental problems were starting to change. More and more people were becoming aware of the need to protect the ③ <u>environment</u>, and the shocking image of the burning river sparked public anger about water pollution. As a result, the Cuyahoga River fire of 1969 became a symbol of ④ <u>pollution</u>. A national environmental awareness event was held on April 22, 1970, which later became known as the first Earth Day. And in 1972, national ⑤ <u>air</u> quality standards were established with the passage of the Clean Water Act.

18 윗글의 밑줄 친 부분 중, 문맥상 낱말의 쓰임이 적절하지 <u>않은</u> 것은?

①   ②   ③   ④   ⑤

19 윗글의 밑줄 친 rising과 쓰임이 같은 것을 모두 고른 것은?

ⓐ The students are <u>studying</u> for their upcoming exams.

ⓑ The dog <u>barking</u> in the yard kept the neighbors awake all night.

ⓒ The children <u>laughing</u> in the park are having a great time

ⓓ <u>Feeling</u> thirsty, I opened the fridge and found something to drink.

ⓔ The chef <u>cooking</u> in the kitchen is preparing a delicious meal for the guests.

① ⓐ, ⓒ, ⓓ   ② ⓑ, ⓒ, ⓓ
③ ⓑ, ⓒ, ⓔ   ④ ⓑ, ⓓ, ⓔ
⑤ ⓒ, ⓓ, ⓔ

20 윗글의 내용과 일치하지 <u>않는</u> 것은?

① The image in *Time* magazine was of a 1969 fire.
② Americans' attitudes toward environmental problems were changing.
③ The image of the burning river made people feel strongly about water pollution.
④ The 1969 fire became a symbol of pollution.
⑤ The first Earth Day was held on April 22, 1970.

In the 19th century, the Industrial Revolution led to _____ in the United States. The demand for workers increased, and (A) <u>many new positions filled by children</u>. By 1900, about twenty percent of all children in the United States were employed, and (B) <u>some of those worked in factories were only four years old</u>. The work was difficult and dangerous, (C) <u>left many child laborers with health problems</u>.

Factory owners turned to child labor for several reasons. For example, (D) <u>children could be paid little than adult workers</u>. They were also less likely to go on strike.

21 윗글의 빈칸에 들어갈 말로 가장 적절한 것은?

① the emergence of labor unions
② a decline in agricultural employment
③ improved working conditions for adults
④ stricter regulations on child labor
⑤ a dramatic increase in factory production

최종 점검 **기말고사**

22 윗글의 밑줄 친 (A)~(D)에서 어법상 틀린 부분을 찾아 바르게 고쳐 쓰시오.

(A) _____ → _____
(B) _____ → _____
(C) _____ → _____
(D) _____ → _____

23 윗글의 밑줄 친 우리말과 같은 뜻이 되도록 조건에 맞게 영어로 쓰시오.

조건
• reveal, be, cruel, want, this system을 사용하여 8단어로 문장을 완성할 것
• 시제와 어법에 맞게 어형을 변화시킬 것

→ Lewis Hine, a teacher and photographer, _____
_____.

[23~25] 다음 글을 읽고, 물음에 답하시오.

교사이자 사진작가인 Lewis Hine은 이 제도가 얼마나 잔인한지 밝히고 싶었다. So he quit his teaching job and started to work for the National Child Labor Committee as an investigative photographer. He gained access to factories by pretending to have different jobs like insurance agent or fire inspector.

Once inside, he would photograph the children working there. He would also ask their names and ages and record information about their living and working conditions. From 1908 to 1912, he secretly gathered information and took photographs to expose factory owners who were taking advantage of ⓐhelpless children.

Hine's photographs ⓑcaptured young children doing all sorts of jobs. These included picking vegetables, weaving baskets, and even handling dangerous ⓒequipment. What is more, the children's faces showed the tragic impact of hard labor. When people saw the children's joyless expressions, they could not help but feel heartbroken.

The pictures were later shown in ⓓexhibitions, lectures, magazine articles, and so on. As a result, the public realized just how serious the situation was. Soon, many states passed stronger laws to ban the employment of children. In 1938, the United States Congress passed an act that made it ⓔillegal for children under sixteen to work in factories during school hours.

24 윗글의 밑줄 친 부분의 영어 뜻풀이로 알맞지 않은 것은?

① ⓐ: unable to protect or take care of oneself
② ⓑ: to communicate or express a thought, feeling, etc.
③ ⓒ: tools or supplies needed for a specific purpose
④ ⓓ: a display of art, artifacts, or other items of interest
⑤ ⓔ: prohibited by law

25 보기에서 알맞은 말을 골라 윗글의 요약문을 완성하시오.

보기 left   leading   documenting   revealed

Lewis Hine, a teacher and photographer, _____ his job to work for the National Child Labor Committee, _____ child labor in factories. His powerful photographs _____ the harsh conditions children faced, _____ to public awareness and, eventually, stronger child labor laws in the United States.

Two Thanksgiving Day Gentlemen

by O. Henry

교과서 본문 분석

Two Thanksgiving Day Gentlemen
추수감사절의 두 신사

01 There is one day [when all Americans gather {to eat a big dinner}].
관계부사절 / 부사적 용법(목적)
모든 미국인이 푸짐한 정찬을 먹기 위해 모이는 하루가 있다.

02 We don't actually remember much about the people [who had the first Thanksgiving].
주격 관계대명사절
우리는 사실 첫 번째 추수감사절을 지낸 사람들에 관해 많이 기억하지는 못한다.

03 But we know [they ate a large bird {called a turkey}], so it is served for Thanksgiving dinner.
(that) / 명사절(know의 목적어) / 과거분사구 / = a turkey / 수동태
그러나 우리는 그들이 칠면조라고 불리는 커다란 새를 먹었다는 것을 알고, 그리하여 그것이 추수감사절 정찬에 차려진다.

04 That is a tradition, and Thanksgiving Day is the one day of the year [that is purely American].
주격 관계대명사절
그것은 전통이며, 추수감사절은 전적으로 미국적인 일 년 중 하루이다.

05 Here is a story [to prove {that there are old traditions even in this new country}].
형용사적 용법 / 명사절(to prove의 목적어)
심지어 이 새로운 나라에도 오래된 전통들이 있다는 것을 증명해 줄 한 이야기가 여기 있다.

06 Stuffy Pete sat down on a seat in a New York City park.
Stuffy Pete는 뉴욕시 공원에 있는 자리에 앉았다.

07 Every Thanksgiving Day for nine years, he had sat there at one in the afternoon.
과거완료(대과거)
9년간 추수감사절마다, 그는 오후 1시에 그곳에 앉았다.

08 Every time he was there, something wonderful had happened to him.
-thing으로 끝나는 부정대명사는 형용사가 뒤에서 수식함 / 과거완료(대과거)
그가 그곳에 있을 때마다, 멋진 일이 그에게 일어났었다.

09 This filled his heart with joy, and it filled another part of him, too.
fill A with B: A를 B로 채우다
이는 그의 마음을 기쁨으로 채워 주었고, 그것은 그의 다른 부분도 채워 주었다.

10 On most ordinary days, Stuffy was hungry.
대부분의 평범한 날에, Stuffy는 배가 고팠다.

11 But on this day, he was not hungry at all.
전혀 ~하지 않은
하지만 이날, 그는 전혀 배고프지 않았다.

12 He had had a dinner [that was so big that he could barely move].
과거완료(대과거) / so+형용사+that+주어+동사: 너무 ~해서 …하다 / 주격 관계대명사절
그는 너무 푸짐해서 그가 거의 움직일 수 없는 정찬을 먹었었다.

13 His body seemed ready to break out of his clothes.
~에서 탈피하다, 벗어나다
그의 몸은 그의 옷을 벗어날 준비가 되어 있는 것 같았다.

14 It is a strange thing.
그것은 이상한 일이다.

15 There are rich people [who wish to help the poor], but many of them seem to think [that the poor

= poor people   = rich people   명사절(think의 목적어)
주격 관계대명사절   the+형용사: 복수 보통명사(~한 사람들)   seem to-v: ~인 것 같다

are hungry only on Thanksgiving Day].

가난한 사람들을 돕기를 바라는 부유한 사람들이 있지만, 그들 중 많은 이들은 가난한 사람들이 오직 추수감사절에만 배가 고프다고 생각하는 것 같다.

16 The dinner had been completely unexpected.

과거완료(대과거)

그 정찬은 완전히 예기치 않은 것이었다.

17 Near the park, there was a large house [where two elderly ladies lived].

관계부사절

공원 근처에, 두 노부인이 사는 커다란 집이 있었다.

18 Every Thanksgiving Day, they sent a servant to the front door of their house [to bring in the first

= two elderly ladies   부사적 용법(목적)

hungry-looking person {who was walking by} and offer the person a meal].

(to)
주격 관계대명사절   병렬 연결   간접목적어   직접목적어

매 추수감사절에, 그들은 지나가던 첫 번째로 배고파 보이는 사람을 들이고 그 사람에게 식사를 제공하기 위해 하인을 그들 집의 현관으로 보냈다.

19 This was their tradition.

= two elderly ladies'

이것이 그들의 전통이었다.

20 And on this day, Stuffy Pete was passing by on his way to the park when the ladies' servant came

on one's way to: ~으로 가는 길[도중]에   접속사(~할 때)

to the door.

그리고 이날, 그 부인들의 하인이 문간으로 왔을 때 Stuffy Pete는 공원으로 가는 길에 옆을 지나고 있었다.

21 She brought Stuffy into the house and fed him [until he could eat no more].

S   V1   V2   시간의 부사절

그녀는 Stuffy를 집 안으로 데려왔고 그가 더는 먹을 수 없을 때까지 그에게 먹을 것을 주었다.

22 Tradition was followed.

수동태

전통이 이어졌다.

23 From his seat in the park, a very full Stuffy Pete spotted something [that made his breath stop].

주격 관계대명사절
make+목적어+동사원형: ~가 … 하게 만들다

공원 안의 그의 자리에서, 매우 배부른 Stuffy Pete가 그의 숨을 멈추게 만드는 무언가를 발견했다.

24 The Old Gentleman was coming toward him.

come toward: ~을 향해 다가오다

그 노신사가 그를 향해 오고 있었다.

25 Every Thanksgiving Day for nine years, the Old Gentleman had come [to find Stuffy on his seat].

전치사(~동안)   과거완료(대과거) 부사적 용법(목적)

9년간 매 추수감사절에, 노신사는 자리에 앉은 Stuffy를 찾으러 왔었다.

26 After that, he led Stuffy to a restaurant and watched him eat a big dinner.

S   V1   V2

그 후에, 그는 Stuffy를 이끌고 한 식당에 가서 그가 푸짐한 정찬을 먹는 것을 지켜보았다.

27 This was the very thing [that the Old Gentleman was trying to make into a tradition].

바로 그(명사 강조)
목적격 관계대명사절   try to-v: ~ 하려고 노력하다

이것이 노신사가 전통으로 만들려고 애쓰던 바로 그 일이었다.

28 Buying dinner for Stuffy once a year was a small act, but the Old Gentleman believed [that he was
S(동명사구)   V   명사절(believed의 목적어)

helping to build a great American tradition].
help+(to-)v: ∼하는 것을 돕다
1년에 한 번 Stuffy에게 정찬을 사주는 것은 작은 행동이었지만, 노신사는 그가 위대한 미국 전통을 만드는 것을 돕고 있다고 생각했다.

29 In order to build a tradition, the same thing must be done again and again for a long time, and he
in order to-v: ∼하기 위하여   조동사가 있는 수동태   몇 번이고, 되풀이해서

had been doing very well.
과거완료진행
전통을 만들기 위해서는, 같은 일이 오랫동안 반복해서 행해져야 하고, 그는 매우 잘해 왔었다.

30 Nine years is a long time in America, as it is a young country compared to old countries like
S(단수 취급)   V   접속사(∼ 때문에)   전치사(∼와 같은)

England.

9년은 미국에서 긴 시간인데, 이는 그것이 영국과 같은 오래된 나라들과 비교하여 신생 국가이기 때문이다.

31 The Old Gentleman was thin and tall, and he was dressed all in black.
S1   V1   S2   V2(수동태)
노신사는 마르고 키가 컸으며, 온통 검은색으로 입고 있었다.

32 His hair was whiter and thinner than it had been the previous year.
비교급++than: …보다 더 ∼한   과거완료(대과거)
그의 머리카락은 이전 해에 그랬던 것보다 더 희고 가늘었다.

                                                    과거완료(대과거)
33 His legs did not seem as strong as they had seemed the year before.
as+형용사(부사)의 원급+as: …만큼 ∼한[하게]
그의 다리는 이전 해에 보였던 것만큼 튼튼해 보이지 않았다.

                                                                    (that)
34 As this kind Old Gentleman came toward him, Stuffy wished [he could fly away].
접속사(∼할 때)   명사절(wished의 목적어)
이 친절한 노신사가 그를 향해 올 때, Stuffy는 그가 날아가 버릴 수 있으면 좋겠다고 생각했다.

35 But he could not move from his seat.
         = Stuffy
하지만 그는 그의 자리에서 움직일 수 없었다.

                                    명사절(see의 목적어)
36 "I am glad to see [that the troubles of another year have not hurt you]," said the Old Gentleman.
             부사적 용법(감정의 원인)   현재완료
"나는 또 다른 해의 문제들이 당신을 다치게 하지 않은 것을 보게 되어 기쁘군요."라고 노신사가 말했다.

                                            직접목적어   as+형용사(부사)의 원급+as: ∼만큼 …한[하게]
37 "If you come with me, I will give you a dinner [that will surely make your body feel as thankful as
접속사(∼한다면)   간접목적어   ↑_____ 주격 관계대명사절   make+목적어+동사원형: ∼가 …하게 하다

your mind]."

"만약 당신이 나와 함께 간다면, 나는 분명 당신의 몸을 당신의 마음만큼이나 감사하게 느끼게 해줄 정찬을 제공하겠소."

38 That was [what the Old Gentleman had said every Thanksgiving Day for nine years].
                  관계대명사절(주격보어)   과거완료(대과거)
그것은 노신사가 9년간 매 추수감사절에 말해 왔던 것이었다.

39 The words themselves were almost a tradition.
                  재귀대명사 <강조 용법>
그 말들 자체가 거의 전통이었다.

40 For the past nine years, they had always been music to Stuffy's ears.

= the words

과거완료 · music to a person's ears: 아주 반가운 소식

지난 9년 동안, 그것들은 항상 Stuffy에게 반가운 소리였다.

41 But now as he looked up at the Old Gentleman's face, Stuffy had tears of suffering in his eyes.

접속사(~할 때)

그러나 이제 그가 노신사의 얼굴을 올려다볼 때, Stuffy는 그의 눈에 고통의 눈물을 머금고 있었다.

42 Stuffy had always wondered [why the Old Gentleman seemed sad as he spoke].

간접의문문(had wondered의 목적어): 「의문사+주어+동사」의 어순

과거완료 · 접속사(~할 때)

Stuffy는 노신사가 말할 때 왜 슬퍼 보이는지 항상 궁금해 했었다.

43 He was unaware that the Old Gentleman was wishing [that he had a son].

be unaware that: ~임을 알지 못하다 · 명사절(was wishing의 목적어)

그는 노신사가 아들이 있기를 바랐던 것을 알지 못했다.

44 A son could come there once the Old Gentleman himself was gone.

접속사(일단 ~하면) · 재귀대명사 <강조 용법>

아들은 일단 노신사 자신이 죽고 나면 그곳에 올 수 있을 것이다.

45 He would stand proud and strong before Stuffy, and say, "I have come in remembrance of my father."

(would)

병렬 연결 · 현재완료(결과)

그는 Stuffy 앞에 자랑스럽고 굳세게 서서 "저는 저의 아버지를 추모하러 왔습니다."라고 말할 것이다.

46 Then it would really be a tradition.

그러면 그것은 정말로 전통이 될 것이다.

47 But the Old Gentleman had no family.

하지만 노신사는 가족이 없었다.

48 He lived alone in a room in one of the old houses near the park.

one of+복수 명사: ~ 중 하나

그는 공원 근처의 오래된 집들 중 하나의 방에서 혼자 살았다.

49 [Feeling helpless and very sorry for himself], Stuffy Pete looked up at him for a minute.

분사구문(부대상황) · = the Old Gentleman

그 자신에 대해 무력함과 매우 유감스러움을 느끼며, Stuffy Pete는 그를 잠시 동안 올려다보았다.

50 The Old Gentleman's eyes were bright with the pleasure of giving.

동명사(전치사 of의 목적어)

노신사의 눈은 주는 것에 대한 기쁨으로 빛났다.

51 After a while, with great effort, Stuffy spoke. "Thank you. I'm very hungry."

잠시 후, 대단히 애를 써서, Stuffy가 "감사합니다. 배가 정말 고프네요."라고 말했다.

52 Stuffy was very full, but he understood [that he was part of a tradition].

명사절(understood의 목적어)

Stuffy는 매우 배불렀지만, 그는 자신이 전통의 일부라는 것을 이해했다.

53 The Old Gentleman led Stuffy to the restaurant and to the same table as before.

lead A to B: A를 B로 이끌다

노신사는 이전과 같이 Stuffy를 그 식당, 그리고 동일한 테이블로 이끌었다.

54 The Old Gentleman sat at the table and watched the waiters bring large amounts of food.

S · V1 · V2 · watch(지각동사)+목적어+동사원형: ~가 …하는 것을 보다

노신사는 테이블에 앉았고 종업원들이 많은 양의 음식을 가져오는 것을 지켜보았다.

55 Stuffy struggled with his full stomach as he ate and ate.
접속사(~할 때)
Stuffy는 그가 먹고 또 먹는 동안 그의 부른 배와 씨름했다.

56 However, he couldn't stop eating, as he saw the look of happiness on the Old Gentleman's face.
접속사(~ 때문에)
stop v-ing: ~하는 것을 멈추다 (cf. stop to-v: ~하려고 멈추다)
하지만, 그는 먹는 것을 멈출 수 없었는데, 그가 노신사의 얼굴에서 행복한 표정을 보았기 때문이다.

57 So he continued until he finished the whole meal.
접속사(~할 때까지)
그래서 그는 그가 모든 식사를 마칠 때까지 계속했다.

58 When the struggle was finished, Stuffy said, "Thank you for my Thanksgiving dinner."
접속사(~할 때)   수동태
분투가 끝났을 때, Stuffy는 "저의 추수감사절 정찬에 감사드립니다."라고 말했다.

59 Then he stood up heavily [to leave].
부사적 용법(목적)
그러고 나서 그는 떠나기 위해 힘겹게 일어섰다.

60 The Old Gentleman carefully counted out one dollar and thirty cents and left fifteen cents more
S   V1   V2
for the waiter.

노신사는 1달러 30센트를 조심스럽게 하나씩 셌고 종업원을 위해 15센트를 더 놓아두었다.

61 The two men said goodbye at the door, and the Old Gentleman went south, while Stuffy went north.
접속사(~인 반면에)
두 남자는 문간에서 작별 인사를 했고, 노신사는 남쪽으로 간 반면, Stuffy는 북쪽으로 갔다.

62 [After turning the first corner], Stuffy stood for a moment, then collapsed.
접속사를 생략하지 않은 분사구문(때)   S   V1   V2
첫 번째 모퉁이를 돈 후에, Stuffy는 잠깐 서 있었고, 그러고는 쓰러졌다.

63 Before long, he was picked up and taken to a hospital.
동사구의 수동태   (was)
오래지[머지] 않아, 이윽고   병렬 연결
오래지 않아, 그는 들어 올려져 병원으로 이송되었다.

64 An hour later, the Old Gentleman was brought to the same hospital.
수동태
한 시간 뒤, 노신사가 같은 병원으로 이송되었다.

65 After a while, one of the doctors met another doctor, and they discussed the Old Gentleman's case.
one of+복수 명사: ~ 중 하나
잠시 후, 의사들 중 한 명이 또 다른 의사를 만났고, 그들은 노신사의 사례에 관해 논의했다.

66 "Did you hear [what's wrong with that nice old gentleman over there]?
지시형용사(저, 그)
간접의문문(hear의 목적어):「의문사(주어)+동사」의 어순
"당신은 저기 있는 저 친절한 노신사에게 무슨 일이 있는지 들었나요?

67 He almost died from hunger.
die from: ~으로 죽다
그는 거의 굶주림으로 죽을 뻔했어요.

68 He seems like a very proud man.
seem like: ~ 처럼 보이다
그는 매우 자부심이 있는 남자처럼 보여요.

69 He told me [he hadn't eaten for three days]."
(that) 명사절 (told의 직접목적어)
간접목적어   과거완료(대과거)
그는 내게 그가 3일 동안 먹지 않았었다고 했어요."

교과서 **본문 익히기** ❶ 빈칸 완성하기

♣ 다음 빈칸에 알맞은 말을 쓰시오.

01 There is one day when all Americans _____ a big dinner.

모든 미국인이 푸짐한 정찬을 먹기 위해 모이는 하루가 있다.

02 But we know they ate a large bird _____, so it _____
for Thanksgiving dinner.

그러나 우리는 그들이 칠면조라고 불리는 커다란 새를 먹었다는 것을 알고, 그리하여 그것이 추수감사절 정찬에 차려진다.

03 Here is a story to prove that _____ even in this new country.

심지어 이 새로운 나라에도 오래된 전통들이 있다는 것을 증명해 줄 한 이야기가 여기 있다.

04 Every time he was there, something wonderful _____ to him.

그가 그곳에 있을 때마다, 멋진 일이 그에게 일어났었다.

05 This _____, and it filled another part of him, too.

이는 그의 마음을 기쁨으로 채워 주었고, 그것은 그의 다른 부분도 채워 주었다.

06 But on this day, he was _____.

하지만 이날, 그는 전혀 배고프지 않았다.

07 He had had a dinner that was so big that he _____.

그는 너무 푸짐해서 그가 거의 움직일 수 없는 정찬을 먹었었다.

08 His body seemed ready to _____.

그의 몸은 그의 옷을 벗어날 준비가 되어 있는 것 같았다.

09 There are rich people _____, but many of them seem to think that the poor
are hungry only on Thanksgiving Day.

가난한 사람들을 돕기를 바라는 부유한 사람들이 있지만, 그들 중 많은 이들은 가난한 사람들이 오직 추수감사절에만 배가 고프다고
생각하는 것 같다.

10 Near the park, there was a large house _____.

공원 근처에, 두 노부인이 사는 커다란 집이 있었다.

11 Every Thanksgiving Day, they sent a servant to the front door of their house _____
_____ who was walking by and offer the person a meal.

매 추수감사절에, 그들은 지나가던 첫 번째로 배고파 보이는 사람을 들이고 그 사람에게 식사를 제공하기 위해 하인을 그들 집의
현관으로 보냈다.

12 And on this day, Stuffy Pete _____ on his way to the park when the ladies'
servant came to the door.

그리고 이날, 그 부인들의 하인이 문간으로 왔을 때 Stuffy Pete는 공원으로 가는 길에 옆을 지나고 있었다.

13 She brought Stuffy into the house and _____ he could eat no more.

그녀는 Stuffy를 집 안으로 데려왔고 그가 더는 먹을 수 없을 때까지 그에게 먹을 것을 주었다.

14 From his seat in the park, a very full Stuffy Pete spotted something that _____.

공원 안의 그의 자리에서, 매우 배부른 Stuffy Pete가 그의 숨을 멈추게 만드는 무언가를 발견했다.

15 After that, he led Stuffy to a restaurant and _____ a big dinner.

그 후에, 그는 Stuffy를 이끌고 한 식당에 가서 그가 푸짐한 정찬을 먹는 것을 지켜보았다.

16 This was the very thing that the Old Gentleman was _____ a tradition.

이것이 노신사가 전통으로 만들려고 애쓰던 바로 그 일이었다.

17 Buying dinner for Stuffy once a year was a small act, but the Old Gentleman believed that he was helping to _____.

1년에 한 번 Stuffy에게 정찬을 사주는 것은 작은 행동이었지만, 노신사는 그가 위대한 미국 전통을 만드는 것을 돕고 있다고 생각했다.

18 _____ a tradition, the same thing must be done again and again for a long time, and he had been doing very well.

전통을 만들기 위해서는, 같은 일이 오랫동안 반복해서 행해져야 하고, 그는 매우 잘해 왔었다.

19 Nine years is a long time in America, as it is a young country _____ old countries like England.

9년은 미국에서 긴 시간인데, 이는 그것이 영국과 같은 오래된 나라들과 비교하여 신생 국가이기 때문이다.

20 His hair was _____ it had been the previous year.

그의 머리카락은 이전 해에 그랬던 것보다 더 희고 가늘었다.

21 His legs did not _____ they had seemed the year before.

그의 다리는 이전 해에 보였던 것만큼 튼튼해 보이지 않았다.

22 As this kind Old Gentleman came toward him, Stuffy wished he _____.

이 친절한 노신사가 그를 향해 올 때, Stuffy는 그가 날아가 버릴 수 있으면 좋겠다고 생각했다.

23 "I am glad to see that _____ have not hurt you," said the Old Gentleman.

"나는 또 다른 해의 문제들이 당신을 다치게 하지 않은 것을 보게 되어 기쁘군요."라고 노신사가 말했다.

24 "If you come with me, I will give you a dinner that will surely make your body feel _____."

"만약 당신이 나와 함께 간다면, 나는 분명 당신의 몸을 당신의 마음만큼이나 감사하게 느끼게 해줄 정찬을 제공하겠소."

25 But now as he looked up at the Old Gentleman's face, Stuffy had _____ in his eyes.

그러나 이제 그가 노신사의 얼굴을 올려다볼 때, Stuffy는 그의 눈에 고통의 눈물을 머금고 있었다.

26 Stuffy _____ the Old Gentleman seemed sad as he spoke.

Stuffy는 노신사가 말할 때 왜 슬퍼 보이는지 항상 궁금해 했다.

27   He _____ the Old Gentleman was wishing that he had a son.

그는 노신사가 아들이 있기를 바랐던 것을 알지 못했다.

28   He would stand proud and strong before Stuffy, and say, "I have come _____

my father."

그는 Stuffy 앞에 자랑스럽고 굳세게 서서 "저는 저의 아버지를 추모하러 왔습니다."라고 말할 것이다.

29   He lived alone in a room in _____ near the park.

그는 공원 근처의 오래된 집들 중 하나의 방에서 혼자 살았다.

30   _____ and very sorry for himself, Stuffy Pete looked up at him for a minute.

그 자신에 대해 무력함과 매우 유감스러움을 느끼며, Stuffy Pete는 그를 잠시 동안 올려다보았다.

31   The Old Gentleman's eyes were bright _____.

노신사의 눈은 주는 것에 대한 기쁨으로 빛났다.

32   The Old Gentleman sat at the table and watched the waiters _____.

노신사는 테이블에 앉았고 종업원들이 많은 양의 음식을 가져오는 것을 지켜보았다.

33   Stuffy _____ as he ate and ate.

Stuffy는 그가 먹고 또 먹는 동안 그의 부른 배와 씨름했다.

34   However, he _____, as he saw the look of happiness on the Old

Gentleman's face.

하지만, 그는 먹는 것을 멈출 수 없었는데, 그가 노신사의 얼굴에서 행복한 표정을 보았기 때문이다.

35   After turning the first corner, Stuffy _____, then collapsed.

첫 번째 모퉁이를 돈 후에, Stuffy는 잠깐 서 있었고, 그러고는 쓰러졌다.

36   Before long, he was picked up and _____.

오래지 않아, 그는 들려서 병원으로 이송되었다.

37   An hour later, the Old Gentleman _____ the same hospital.

한 시간 뒤, 노신사가 같은 병원으로 이송되었다.

38   Did you hear _____ that nice old gentleman over there?

당신은 저기 있는 저 친절한 노신사에게 무슨 일이 있는지 들었나요?

39   He almost _____.

그는 거의 굶주림으로 죽을 뻔했어요.

40   He told me he _____ three days.

그는 내게 그가 3일 동안 먹지 않았었다고 했어요.

♣ 다음 네모 안에서 옳은 것을 고르시오.

01 There is one day when / where all Americans gather to eat a big dinner.

02 But we know they ate a large bird calling / called a turkey, so it is served for Thanksgiving dinner.

03 Every Thanksgiving Day for / during nine years, he had sat there at one in the afternoon.

04 Every time he was there, wonderful something / something wonderful had happened to him.

05 This filled his heart of / with joy, and it filled another part of him, too.

06 On most / mostly ordinary days, Stuffy was hungry.

07 He have had / had had a dinner that was so big that he could barely move.

08 His body seemed ready breaking / to break out of his clothes.

09 There are rich people who wish to help the poor, but many of them seem to think that the poor is / are hungry only on Thanksgiving Day.

10 The dinner had / had been completely unexpected.

11 Near the park, there was a large house which / where two elderly ladies lived.

12 Every Thanksgiving Day, they sent a servant to the front door of their house to bring in the first hungry-looking person who / which was walking by and offer the person a meal.

13 And on this day, Stuffy Pete was passing by on his way to the park when / where the ladies' servant came to the door.

14 She brought Stuffy into the house and fed him until / by he could eat no more.

15 From his seat in the park, a very full Stuffy Pete spotted something that made his breath to stop / stop.

16 After that, he led Stuffy to a restaurant and watched him eat / to eat a big dinner.

17 This was the very thing which / that the Old Gentleman was trying to make into a tradition.

18 Buy / Buying dinner for Stuffy once a year was a small act, but the Old Gentleman believed that he was helping to build a great American tradition.

19 Nine years is / are a long time in America, as it is a young country compared to old countries like England.

20 The Old Gentleman was thin and tall, and he dressed / was dressed all in black.

21 His hair was whiter and thinner than / as it had been the previous year.

22 His legs did not seem as strong / stronger as they had seemed the year before.

23 As this kind Old Gentleman came toward him, Stuffy wishes / wished he could fly away.

24 "If you come with me, I will give you a dinner that will surely make your body feel / to feel as thankful as your mind."

25 That was which / what the Old Gentleman had said every Thanksgiving Day for nine years.

26 The words itself / themselves were almost a tradition.

27 For / During the past nine years, they had always been music to Stuffy's ears.

28 But now as he looked up at the Old Gentleman's face, Stuffy had tears of suffer / suffering in his eyes.

29 Stuffy had always wondered why / how the Old Gentleman seemed sad as he spoke.

30 A son could come there once the Old Gentleman itself / himself was gone.

31 He would stand proud and strong before Stuffy, and say, "I have come / came in remembrance of my father."

32 He lived alone in a room in one of the old house / houses near the park.

33 Feeling / Felt helpless and very sorry for himself, Stuffy Pete looked up at him for a minute.

34 The Old Gentleman's eyes were bright with the pleasure of give / giving.

35 The Old Gentleman sat at the table and watched the waiters bring / to bring large amounts of food.

36 However, he couldn't stop eating / to eat, as he saw the look of happiness on the Old Gentleman's face.

37 Before long, he was picked up and took / taken to a hospital.

38 After a while, one of the doctors met another / the other doctor, and they discussed the Old Gentleman's case.

39 He almost died of / from hunger.

40 He told me he hasn't / hadn't eaten for three days.

♣ 다음 밑줄 친 부분을 바르게 고쳐 쓰시오.

01   There is one day <u>where</u> all Americans gather to eat a big dinner.

02   But we know they ate a large bird <u>calling</u> a turkey, so it is served for Thanksgiving dinner.

03   Every Thanksgiving Day <u>during</u> nine years, he had sat there at one in the afternoon.

04   Every time he was there, <u>wonderful something</u> had happened to him.

05   This filled his heart <u>of</u> joy, and it filled another part of him, too.

06   On <u>mostly</u> ordinary days, Stuffy was hungry.

07   He <u>have had</u> a dinner that was so big that he could barely move.

08   His body seemed ready <u>broke</u> out of his clothes.

09   There are rich people who wish to help the poor, but many of them seem to think that the poor <u>is</u> hungry only on Thanksgiving Day.

10   The dinner <u>had</u> completely unexpected.

11   Near the park, there was a large house <u>which</u> two elderly ladies lived.

12   Every Thanksgiving Day, they sent a servant to the front door of their house to bring in the first hungry-looking person <u>which</u> was walking by and offer the person a meal.

13   And on this day, Stuffy Pete was passing by on his way to the park <u>where</u> the ladies' servant came to the door.

14   She brought Stuffy into the house and fed him <u>by</u> he could eat no more.

15   From his seat in the park, a very full Stuffy Pete spotted something that made his breath <u>to stop</u>.

16   After that, he led Stuffy to a restaurant and watched him <u>to eat</u> a big dinner.

17   This was the very thing <u>which</u> the Old Gentleman was trying to make into a tradition.

18   <u>Buy</u> dinner for Stuffy once a year was a small act, but the Old Gentleman believed that he was helping to build a great American tradition.

19   In order to build a tradition, the same thing must <u>do</u> again and again for a long time, and he had been doing very well.

20   Nine years <u>are</u> a long time in America, as it is a young country compared to old countries like England.

21   The Old Gentleman was thin and tall, and he <u>dressed</u> all in black.

22   His hair was whiter and thinner <u>as</u> it had been the previous year.

23   His legs did not seem as <u>stronger</u> as they had seemed the year before.

24   As this kind Old Gentleman came toward him, Stuffy <u>wishes</u> he could fly away.

25   "If you come with me, I will give you a dinner that will surely make your body <u>to feel</u> as thankful as your mind."

26   That was <u>which</u> the Old Gentleman had said every Thanksgiving Day for nine years.

27   The words <u>itself</u> were almost a tradition.

28   <u>During</u> the past nine years, they had always been music to Stuffy's ears.

29   But now as he looked up at the Old Gentleman's face, Stuffy had tears of <u>suffer</u> in his eyes.

30   Stuffy had always wondered <u>how</u> the Old Gentleman seemed sad as he spoke.

31   He was unaware <u>if</u> the Old Gentleman was wishing that he had a son.

32   A son could come there once the Old Gentleman <u>itself</u> was gone.

33   He would stand proud and strong before Stuffy, and say, "I have <u>came</u> in remembrance of my father."

34   He lived alone in a room in one of the old <u>house</u> near the park.

35   <u>Felt</u> helpless and very sorry for himself, Stuffy Pete looked up at him for a minute.

36   The Old Gentleman's eyes were bright with the pleasure of <u>give</u>.

37   The Old Gentleman sat at the table and watched the waiters <u>to bring</u> large amounts of food.

38   However, he couldn't stop <u>to eat</u>, as he saw the look of happiness on the Old Gentleman's face.

39   The Old Gentleman carefully counted out one dollar and thirty cents and <u>leaves</u> fifteen cents more for the waiter.

40   After <u>turned</u> the first corner, Stuffy stood for a moment, then collapsed.

41   Before long, he was picked up and <u>took</u> to a hospital.

42   After a while, one of the doctors met <u>the other</u> doctor, and they discussed the Old Gentleman's case.

43   He almost died <u>of</u> hunger.

44   He told me he hasn't eaten for three days.

[01~02] 다음 글을 읽고, 물음에 답하시오.

There is one day when all Americans gather ①to eat a big dinner. We don't actually remember much about the people ②who had the first Thanksgiving. But we know they ate a large bird ③calling a turkey, so it is served for Thanksgiving dinner. That is a tradition, and Thanksgiving Day is the one day of the year ④that is purely American. Here is a story ⑤to prove that there are old traditions even in this new country.

01 윗글의 밑줄 친 부분 중, 어법상 어색한 것은?

①   ②   ③   ④   ⑤

02 윗글 바로 뒤에 이어질 내용으로 가장 적절한 것은?

① a story about Thanksgiving celebrations that have been passed down for generations

② an explanation of how to cook a turkey for Thanksgiving

③ a comparison of Thanksgiving traditions in different countries

④ a discussion about the economic impact of Thanksgiving on the retail industry

⑤ an analysis of the nutritional value of a typical Thanksgiving meal

[03~05] 다음 글을 읽고, 물음에 답하시오.

Stuffy Pete sat down on a seat in a New York City park. Every Thanksgiving Day for nine years, he had sat there at one in the afternoon. 그가 그곳에 있을 때마다, 멋진 일이 그에게 일어났다. This filled his heart with joy, and it filled another part of him, too.

On most ①ordinary days, Stuffy was hungry. But on this day, he was not hungry at all. He had had a dinner that was so big that he could ②barely move. His body seemed ready to break out of his clothes. It is a strange thing. There are rich people who wish to help the poor, but many of them seem to think that the poor are ③hungry only on Thanksgiving Day.

The dinner had been completely ④expected. Near the park, there was a large house where two elderly ladies lived. Every Thanksgiving Day, they sent a servant to the front door of their house to bring in the first hungry-looking person who was walking by and offer the person a ⑤meal. This was their tradition. And on this day, Stuffy Pete was passing by on his way to the park when the ladies' servant came to the door. She brought Stuffy into the house and fed him until he could eat no more. T_____ was followed.

03 윗글의 밑줄 친 부분 중, 문맥상 낱말의 쓰임이 적절하지 않은 것은?

①   ②   ③   ④   ⑤

04 윗글의 밑줄 친 우리말과 같은 뜻이 되도록 보기 의 단어를 바르게 배열하여 문장을 완성하시오.

> 보기   wonderful / something / happened / to / had / him

Every time he was there, _____
_____.

05 다음 영어 뜻풀이를 참고하여 윗글의 빈칸에 들어갈 적절한 단어를 주어진 철자로 시작하여 쓰시오.

> T_____ : a thought, belief, or practice that has been passed down through generations

06 (A), (B), (C)의 각 네모 안에서 어법에 맞는 표현으로 가장 적절한 것은?

From his seat in the park, a very full Stuffy Pete spotted something that made his breath stop. The Old Gentleman was coming toward him.

Every Thanksgiving Day for nine years, the Old Gentleman had come to find Stuffy on his seat. After that, he led Stuffy to a restaurant and watched him (A) to eat / eat a big dinner. This was the very thing that the Old Gentleman was trying to make into a tradition. Buying dinner for Stuffy once a year was a small act, but the Old Gentleman believed that he was helping to build a great American tradition. In order to build a tradition, the same thing must be done again and again for a long time, and he had been doing very well. Nine years (B) is / are a long time in America, as it is a young country compared to old countries like England.

The Old Gentleman was thin and tall, and he was dressed all in black. His hair was whiter and thinner (C) that / than it had been the previous year. His legs did not seem as strong as they had seemed the year before. As this kind Old Gentleman came toward him, Stuffy wished he could fly away. But he could not move from his seat.

	(A)		(B)		(C)
①	to eat	⋯	is	⋯	than
②	to eat	⋯	are	⋯	that
③	eat	⋯	is	⋯	than
④	eat	⋯	is	⋯	that
⑤	eat	⋯	are	⋯	than

[07~08] 다음 글을 읽고, 물음에 답하시오.

"I am glad to see that the troubles of another year have not hurt you," said the Old Gentleman. "If you come with me, I will give you a dinner that will surely make your body feel as thankful as your mind."

That was what the Old Gentleman had said every Thanksgiving Day for nine years. The words themselves were almost a tradition. For the past nine years, _____. But now as he looked up at the Old Gentleman's face, Stuffy had tears of suffering in his eyes.

Stuffy had always wondered why the Old Gentleman seemed sad as he spoke. He was unaware that the Old Gentleman was wishing that he had a son. A son could come there once the Old Gentleman himself was gone. He would stand proud and strong before Stuffy, and say, "I have come in _____ (remember) of my father." Then it would really be a tradition. But the Old Gentleman had no family. He lived alone in a room in one of the old houses near the park.

07 윗글의 빈칸에 들어갈 말로 가장 적절한 것은?

① Stuffy Pete had avoided meeting the Old Gentleman
② they had always been music to Stuffy's ears
③ the Old Gentleman had forgotten to come to the park
④ Stuffy Pete had brought food for the Old Gentleman
⑤ they had celebrated Thanksgiving at Stuffy Pete's home

08 윗글의 괄호 안에 주어진 단어를 알맞은 형태로 바꿔 빈칸에 쓰시오.

_____

[09~10] 다음 글을 읽고, 물음에 답하시오.

As he felt helpless and very sorry for himself, Stuffy Pete looked up at him for a minute. The Old Gentleman's eyes were bright with the pleasure of giving. After a while, with great effort, Stuffy spoke. "Thank you. I'm very hungry."

Stuffy was very full, but he understood that he was part of a tradition. The Old Gentleman led Stuffy to the restaurant and to the same table as before. The Old Gentleman sat at the table and watched the waiters bring large amounts of food. Stuffy struggled with his full stomach as he ate and ate. However, he couldn't stop eating, as he saw the look of happiness on the Old Gentleman's face. So he continued until he finished the whole meal.

When the struggle was finished, Stuffy said, "Thank you for my Thanksgiving dinner." Then he stood up heavily to leave. The Old Gentleman carefully counted out one dollar and thirty cents and left fifteen cents more for the waiter.

09 윗글의 밑줄 친 문장을 분사구문으로 바꿔 쓰시오.

→ _____ ,

Stuffy Pete looked up at him for a minute.

10 윗글의 내용과 일치하지 <u>않는</u> 것은?

① The Old Gentleman was happy to offer Stuffy Pete a meal.
② Stuffy Pete and the Old Gentleman sat at the same table as previous years.
③ Stuffy Pete ate the entire meal despite already being full.
④ The Old Gentleman paid for the meal and left a tip for the waiter.
⑤ Stuffy Pete enjoyed the meal and was grateful for the delicious food.

[11~12] 다음 글을 읽고, 물음에 답하시오.

The two men said goodbye at the door, and the Old Gentleman went south, _____(A)_____ Stuffy went north. After turning the first corner, Stuffy stood for a moment, then collapsed. _____(B)_____ long, he was picked up and taken to a hospital. An hour later, 노신사가 같은 병원으로 이송되었다.

After a while, one of the doctors met another doctor, and they discussed the Old Gentleman's case. "Did you hear what's wrong with that nice old gentleman over there? He almost died from hunger. He seems like a very proud man. He told me he hadn't eaten for three days."

11 윗글의 빈칸 (A), (B)에 들어갈 말로 가장 적절한 것은?

	(A)		(B)
①	while	…	After
②	while	…	Before
③	as	…	While
④	because	…	After
⑤	because	…	Before

12 윗글의 밑줄 친 우리말과 같은 뜻이 되도록 조건 에 맞게 쓰시오.

조건
• the Old Gentleman을 주어로 한 수동태 문장으로 쓸 것
• bring, hospital을 사용하고 필요시 어형을 변형시킬 것

An hour later, _____

_____ .

NE 능률

어휘서의 표준, 대한민국 NO.1 어휘 학습서

시리즈 구성

어원편 Lite	고교기본
어원편	고교필수 2000
	수능완성 2200
	숙어
	고난도

1 **교육부 지정 주요 어휘 수록**
교육부 지정 중고등 교과 어휘 및
EBS 교재들에 사용된 주요 기출 어휘 수록

2 **풍부한 어휘 확장**
각 어휘의 파생어, 유/반의어 수록과
어휘의 실제적 쓰임을 잘 보여주는 예문 제시로 어휘력 확장

3 **체계적이고 완벽한 암기력 향상**
암기 효과를 극대화 시켜주는 클래스 카드 QR과
워크북 및 휴대가 편리한 mini 능률 VOCA제공

고등

BOOK LIST

도/서/목/록

어휘 · 문법 · 구문

능률VOCA

대한민국 어휘서의 표준

어원편 Lite | 어원편 | 고교기본 | 고교필수 2000 |
수능완성 2200 | 숙어 | 고난도

GRAMMAR ZONE

대한민국 영문법 교재의 표준

입문 | 기초 | 기본 1 | 기본 2 | 종합 (각 Workbook 별매)

 시리즈

필히 통하는

시험에 필히 통하는 고등 영문법과 서술형

필히 통하는 고등 영문법 기본편 | 실력편
필히 통하는 고등 서술형 기본편 | 실전편

문제로 마스터하는 고등영문법

고등학생을 위한 문법 연습의 길잡이

천문장

구문이 독해로 연결되는 해석 공식

입문 | 기본 | 완성

능률 기본 영어

최신 수능과 내신을 위한 고등 영어 입문서

내신
백신,

NE 능률

정답 및 해설

고등 기출문제집

Common
English 1

오선영

LESSON 01 | A Journey into Yourself

교과서 어휘 익히기 ·················· pp. 8-9

STEP 1

01 극장	25 discover
02 장담하다, 확언하다	26 absorbed
03 얕은	27 relationship
04 성격	28 positive
05 도전	29 discomfort
06 분위기	30 involve
07 집중이 안 되게 하다, (주의를) 딴 데로 돌리다	31 satisfying
08 얻다	32 confident
09 안락, 편안함	33 researcher
10 과제, 임무	34 forehead
11 반응	35 perspective
12 흥분, 신남	36 photographer
13 극복하다	37 lonely
14 기회	38 preference
15 경험	39 definitely
16 포착하다	40 realize
17 (기분이) 어색한	41 capable
18 강사, 교사	42 properly
19 시도하다, 한번 해보다	43 be curious about
20 자기 스스로	44 worry about
21 ~을 우연히 발견하다	45 draw attention to
22 간신히[용케] 해내다	46 sign up
23 ~에 영향을 미치다	47 step out of
24 ~의 초반에	48 capable of

STEP 2

A 01 excitement 02 comfortable
   03 suitable 04 acceptable
   05 agreement
B 01 joined 02 make
C 01 ⓑ 02 ⓒ 03 ⓐ

교과서 핵심 대화문 ·················· pp. 10-11

Function 1 능력 유무 표현하기
Check-Up 🏅 ⑤
Function 2 관심 표현하기
Check-Up 🏅 ③

교과서 기타 대화문 ·················· p. 12

Q1 T	Q2 T	Q3 F

TOPIC 1 C. Listen and Interact

M: 자신의 강점을 찾는 것은 자기 발견의 중요한 부분입니다. 그리고 이것은 쉽습니다! 그냥 펜을 잡고 몇 가지 간단한 질문에 대한 답을 적어보세요. 우선, 자신을 어떻게 인식하는지 생각해보세요. 당신의 좋은 자질은 무엇이라고 생각하나요? 다른 사람들보다 잘하는 것은 무엇인가요? 다음으로, 다른 사람들이 당신을 어떻게 보는지 생각해보세요. 다른 사람들이 자주 칭찬하는 것은 무엇인가요? 가족과 친구들이 당신이 가지고 있다고 생각하는 강점은 무엇인가요? 일단 이러한 질문에 모두 답하면, 다시 돌아가서 자신의 답을 검토하세요. 그런 다음 눈에 띄는 단어에 동그라미를 치세요. 당신 자신에 대해 무엇을 발견했나요?

TOPIC 4 B. While You View

M: 모든 사람은 자신의 고유한 정체성을 가지고 있으며, 이는 다양한 요소로 구성되어 있습니다. 어떤 정체성 표지는 눈에 보이는 반면, 다른 표지는 보이지 않습니다. 이러한 표지는 당신이 세상을 어떻게 인식하는지에 영향을 미칩니다. 또한 세상이 당신을 어떻게 인식하는 지에도 영향을 줍니다.
이러한 표지를 식별하는 쉬운 방법은 정체성 초상화를 만드는 것입니다. 만드는 방법은 다음과 같습니다. 첫째, 얼굴, 목, 어깨의 그림을 그립니다. 그런 다음 얼굴의 중앙에 수직선을 그립니다. 선의 한 쪽에는 얼굴의 특징을 색칠합니다. 다른 쪽에는 보이지 않는 정체성 표지를 추가합니다. 그것들은 단어 또는 그림일 수 있습니다. 선택은 당신의 몫입니다!
정체성 초상화를 그리는 것은 단순히 재미있고 창의적인 활동이 아닙니다. 그것은 당신 자신과 다른 사람들에 대해 배우는 방법입니다. 그것은 또한 모든 사람의 정체성이 우리 자신의 것만큼 복잡하고 아름답다는 것을 상기시켜줍니다!

Wrap Up A. Listen and Write

G: Marco, 너의 발표가 다음 주에 있지, 그렇지?
B: 응, 그런데 나 긴장돼. 사람들 앞에서 말하는 게 잘 안 돼.
G: 이해해. 하지만 두려움을 극복하고 싶다면 안전지대에서 벗어나야 해.
B: 그 말도 맞네. 너는 어떤 걸 제안해?
G: 작은 것부터 시작해봐. 오늘 수업에서 질문을 해보는 건 어때?
B: 그건 그렇게 어렵지 않은 것 같아. 그것이 도움이 될 거라고 생각해?
G: 물론이지! 첫 단계를 밟고 나면 다음 단계는 더 쉬워질 거야.
B: 알겠어. 한번 해볼게.

교과서 핵심 대화문 익히기 ·················· p. 13

01 ⑤	02 ①

03 I'm interested in seeking new opportunities

2

POINT 1 동명사

> **Q** 1 Eating 2 walking 3 Traveling
> **Check-Up**
> **01** (1) Swimming (2) Playing (3) Traveling
> **02** ④
> **03** (1) is (2) watching (3) managing[to manage]
>   (4) Learning[To learn]
> **04** (1) looking (2) Painting (3) Making

01 (1)~(3) 모두 동사가 문장에서 주어 역할을 해야 하므로 동명사형이 알맞다. to부정사도 문장에서 주어 역할을 할 수 있는데 그런 경우 「가주어 It, 진주어 to부정사」 구문으로 자주 쓰인다.

02 (A) 주어로 사용되며, healthy food에 대한 행동을 나타내야 하므로 동명사 주어인 Eating(먹는 것)이 알맞다.
(B) to a better quality of life는 결과를 나타내는 부분으로 동사가 필요하며, 주어와 동사의 일치에 따라 contributes가 알맞다.

03 (1) 동명사구(Painting landscapes)가 주어이므로 단수 취급하여 단수동사 is가 와야 한다.
(2) enjoy는 동명사를 목적어로 취하는 동사이므로 watching이 알맞다.
(3) be동사 뒤에서 보어 역할을 해야 하므로 managing이나 to manage가 알맞다.
(4) 동사가 주어 역할을 하기 위해서는 동명사 Learning이나 to부정사 To learn이 알맞다. to부정사가 주어인 경우 주로 「가주어 It, 진주어 to부정사」 구문으로 쓴다.

04
> **봉사자들이 필요합니다**
> 재미있는 봉사 기회를 찾고 있나요? 그러면 우리 프로그램에 합류해서 우리가 지역사회에서 벽을 칠하는 것을 도와주세요! 오래된 공공의 벽을 칠하는 것은 지역사회를 더 밝게 만들고 당신에게 당신의 창의력을 표현할 기회를 줄 것입니다. 우리 도시 안에서의 다채로운 변화를 불러오는 것은 당신으로부터 시작됩니다!

(1) look for: ~을 찾다 / 앞에 be동사가 있고 현재 진행형 문장이 되어야 하므로 looking이 알맞다.
(2) paint walls: 벽에 페인트칠을 하다 / 주어 역할을 해야 하므로 동명사형 Painting이 알맞다.
(3) make a difference: 변화를 만들다 / 주어 역할을 해야 하므로 동명사형 Making이 알맞다.

POINT 2 사역동사

> **Q** 1 performing 2 believe 3 to understand
> **Check-Up**
> **01** (1) help (2) complete (3) stay
> **02** (1) The coach made the players practice hard for the big game.

(2) The birthday wishes that Susan received made her smile all day.
(3) My older brother made me apologize for using his tablet without asking.
03 (1) made me feel inspired
  (2) made me cry
  (3) make you want to recommend
04 ②

01 (1) had는 사역동사로서 동사원형 help를 목적격보어로 취한다.
(2) made는 사역동사로서 동사원형 complete를 목적격보어로 취한다.
(3) let은 사역동사로서 동사원형 stay를 목적격보어로 취한다.

02 「사역동사+목적어+동사원형」의 어순에 유의하면서 단어를 배열하여 문장을 완성한다.

03
> **영화 제목: 「원더」**
> 안면 차이가 있는 한 남자 아이에 관한 이 영화는 내가 영감을 느끼게 했다. 그 남자아이가 많은 어려움들을 극복하는 것을 보는 것은 감동적이었고, 그것은 나를 울게 했다. 또한, 그 영화의 주제들은—차이를 이해하는 것, 다른 사람들을 받아들이는 것, 그리고 우정을 쌓는 것과 같은—내게 생각해 볼만한 많은 것들을 주었다. 나는 「원더」를 보는 것이 당신이 그것을 당신의 친구들에게도 추천하고 싶게 할 거라고 확신한다!

「사역동사+목적어+동사원형」의 어순에 유의하면서 단어를 배열하여 문장을 완성한다.

04 모두 「사역동사+목적어+동사원형」 구조의 문장이다. ⓐ to submit → submit, ⓒ helping → help, ⓓ to play → play가 알맞다.

교과서 **본문 익히기 ❶** ·························· pp. 24-26

> **01** should not stay
> **02** by pushing ourselves
> **03** gave us an assignment
> **04** could involve hobbies
> **05** trying something new
> **06** share our experiences with
> **07** tend to watch movies
> **08** watch an action or science fiction movie
> **09** the kinds of movies
> **10** had never done before
> **11** give it a try
> **12** It was nice to choose
> **13** have to worry about
> **14** as a good opportunity
> **15** awkward and lonely
> **16** became completely absorbed in
> **17** nothing to distract
> **18** made me realize

19 make my own choices
20 been afraid of water
21 felt comfortable
22 decided to try to overcome
23 came across
24 it took place
25 signed up for
26 At the beginning of
27 managed to surf a few waves
28 a rush of excitement
29 Being in the water
30 did help me discover
31 draw attention to
32 that suited me
33 as difficult as
34 have such a positive effect on
35 through this assignment
36 while another joined
37 push ourselves to try
38 gained different perspectives
39 to keep learning and growing
40 what we're capable of

교과서 본문 익히기 ❷ pp. 27-29

01 To grow	02 first
03 to start, comfort	04 assignment
05 trying	06 with
07 theater	08 kinds
09 was, before	10 to give
11 It	12 preferences
13 something different, had been	14 by
15 absorbed	16 nothing
17 realize, doing	18 make
19 felt	20 to try, discomfort
21 surfing	22 fun, shallow
23 beginner	24 beginning
25 properly, a few	26 excitement
27 Being	28 While, discover
29 most	30 the same
31 confident	32 find
33 surprised	34 as
35 feel	36 stepping, such
37 myself	38 another
39 push	40 fun
41 ourselves	42 what

교과서 본문 익히기 ❸ pp. 30-31

01 To grow	02 pushing
03 ourselves	04 something new
05 watch	06 Going
07 to give	08 to choose
09 have to	10 had been
11 absorbed	12 satisfying
13 realize	14 to make
15 felt	16 surfing
17 that	18 how
19 excitement	20 bad
21 did	22 most
23 because	24 had
25 find	26 surprised
27 trying	28 feel
29 stepping	30 did
31 another	32 it is
33 fun	34 setting
35 growing	36 what

교과서 본문 외 지문 분석 pp. 32-33

Q1 F Q2 T

Check-Up

01 decided to develop	02 This is because
03 To keep my resolution	04 help me organize
05 to limit my screen time	06 By removing distractions
07 require hard work	08 Learning about yourself
09 make better decisions	10 let others tell
11 make us happy	12 based on
13 feel more confident	14 what others think of you
15 allows you to love	16 why don't you start

TOPIC 5 A. Preview

새 학기를 위한 다짐으로, 나는 더 나은 시간 관리 기술을 계발하기로 결심했다. 이는 바쁜 학기 동안 좋은 시간 관리 기술이 매우 중요할 것이기 때문이다. 내 다짐을 지키기 위해, 나는 플래너(일정 계획 수첩)를 사용할 것이다. 나의 과제들과 마감일들을 적어 두는 것은 내가 나의 일정을 정리하고 과업들을 능률적으로 완수하는 데 도움이 될 것이다. 또한, 나는 나의 스크린 타임(전자 기기 사용 시간)을 제한해 줄 앱을 사용할 것이다. 공부나 숙제를 하는 동안 집중을 방해하는 것들을 제거함으로써, 나는 내가 더 잘 집중하고 내 시간을 더 효과적으로 쓸 수 있다고 생각한다. 나는 내 다짐을 지키는 것이 힘든 일을 요할 것임을 알지만, 나는 내 목표를 달성하기 위해 최선을 다할 것이다.

당신 자신에 관해 배우는 것은 매우 중요하다. 무엇보다도, 그것은 당신이 더 나은 결정을 하는 것을 도와준다. 우리는 흔히 다른 사람들이 우리에게 우리가 해야 할 것을 말하게 한다. 그 결과, 우리는 우리를 행복하게 해주지 않을 목표들을 위해 노력한다. 하지만, 만약 당신이 당신 자신을 잘 알면, 당신은 당신의 진정한 요구에 기반하여 결정들을 할 수 있다. 당신 자신에 관해 배우는 것은 또한 당신이 더 자신감을 느끼게 한다. 일단 당신이 당신의 진정한 모습을 알면, 당신은 다른 이들이 당신에 대해 생각하는 것에 관해 신경을 덜 쓰게 될 것이다. 이는 당신이 있는 그대로의 당신 자신을 사랑하게 해줄 것이다. 그러니 오늘 당신의 자아 발견 여정을 시작하는 게 어떨까?

내신 1등급 어휘 공략
pp. 34-35

01 ③   02 ④
03 ④   04 ②
05 ③   06 ③
07 ③   08 ④

01 (A) 글의 시작 부분에서 언급된 내용으로, 학교의 첫날에 대한 이야기이므로 first가 적절하다.
(B) 학생들이 자신을 도전하게 하고 성장하도록 유도하는 의미가 있으므로 pushing이 적절하다.
(C) 과제가 완료된 후에 경험을 공유하라는 것이 맥락상 자연스러우므로 finished가 적절하다.

02 ④ 문맥상 물속에 있는 것이 생각했던 것만큼 나쁘지 않았다고 하는 것이 자연스러우므로 good이 아니라 bad가 적절하다.

03 ④ references는 보통 '추천'이나 '인용' 등을 의미하는데 문맥상 영화에 대한 다른 사람들의 '선택'이나 '취향'을 이야기하고 있으므로 preferences가 알맞다.

04 (A) 영화에 집중하는 것이 만족스러운 경험임을 나타내므로 satisfying이 적절하다.
(B) 아무것도 방해가 되지 않음을 강조하므로 nothing이 적절하다.
(C) choices와 함께 '선택을 하다'라고 할 때는 make를 사용한다.

05 (A) 물과 관련된 활동에서 편안함을 느낀 적이 없는 것이므로 comfortable이 적절하다.
(B) 두려움이나 불편함을 극복하고자 하는 상황이므로 discomfort가 적절하다.
(C) 얕은 실내 수영장에서 서핑을 한다는 사실이 좋았다는 것이므로 shallow가 적절하다.
▨ (A) 물과 관련된 활동에서 편안함을 느낀 적이 없는 것이므로 uncomfortable이라고 생각하고 ⑤를 답으로 고르지 않도록 주의한다. felt는 앞에 나온 have never enjoyed와 병렬 구조를 이루는 동사로 부정의 의미인 never가 있으므로 comfortable이 되어야 한다.

06 (A) 친구들의 반응이 대체로 긍정적이라는 것을 나타내기 위해서는 positive가 적절하다.
(B) 새로운 모습을 시도하는 것이 생각보다 어렵지 않았다는 의미를 전달하기 위해서는 difficult가 적절하다.

(C) 문맥상 '익숙하고 안전한 영역'을 나타내는 comfort zone이 오는 것이 자연스럽다.

07 ③ 두 번의 도전으로 자신감을 얻은 상태이므로 'disappointed(실망한)'가 아니라 'confident(자신감 있는)'가 적절하다.

08 (A) 문맥상 한 친구가 다른 나라의 새로운 음식을 시도했다는 의미가 적절하므로 different가 알맞다.
(B) 새로운 경험을 통해 얻은 것을 설명하는 부분으로 삶에 대한 다양한 perspectives를 얻었다는 의미가 문맥에 더 잘 맞는다.
(C) 마지막 부분에서 계속 배우고 성장하는 것에 대한 긍정적인 태도를 표현하고 있으므로 exciting이 더 적절하다.

내신 1등급 어법 공략
pp. 36-37

01 ②   02 ②
03 ⑤   04 ⑤
05 ③   06 ③
07 ③   08 ②

01 ② 앞에 있는 by pushing과 병렬 구조를 이루는 동사이므로 learning이 되어야 한다.

02 (A) '혼자'라는 의미가 와야 하므로 by myself가 적절하다.
(B) 영화에 집중하는 것이 만족스러운 것이므로 satisfying이 적절하다.
(C) 사역동사 make는 목적격보어로 동사원형을 취하므로 realize가 적절하다.

03 (A) 앞에 those가 있으므로 kinds가 적절하다.
(B) 「가주어 it, 진주어 to부정사」 구문이므로 to choose가 적절하다.
(C) 역사 드라마를 선택한 시점이 과거인데 그 전부터 호기심을 가져온 것이므로 과거완료 had been이 적절하다.

04 강조동사(did) 뒤에는 동사원형이 와야 하므로 did help가 되어야 한다.

05 (A) 물 활동을 즐기지 않았다는 의미가 자연스러우므로 never가 적절하다.
(B) decide는 to부정사를 목적어로 취하므로 to try가 적절하다.
(C) 앞에 있는 the fact의 동격절을 이끌므로 접속사 that이 적절하다.

06 (A) for와 during 모두 '~동안'이라는 의미이다. for는 숫자를 나타내는 말과 함께 쓰이고, during은 특정 기간을 나타내는 말과 함께 쓰인다.
(B) feeling 뒤에서 보어 역할을 하므로 형용사 confident가 적절하다.
(C) help는 목적격보어로 동사원형이나 to부정사를 쓸 수 있다.

07 (A) 친구들이 놀란 것이므로 surprised가 적절하다.
(B) that절에서 주어 역할을 하므로 동명사형 trying이 적절하다.
(C) make는 목적격보어로 동사원형을 취하므로 feel이 적절하다.

08 (A) 앞에 one of them이 있으므로 여러 개 중에 다른 하나라는 의미의 another가 적절하다.
(B) 전치사 about의 목적어 역할이므로 동명사 setting이 적절하다.
(C) of의 목적어를 포함하는 관계대명사 what이 적절하다.

01 ③	02 I'm good at creating
03 ②	04 ⑤
05 ③	06 ⑤
07 ①	08 ⑤
09 ②	

10 Being in the water wasn't as bad as

11 He listened to my concerns and helped me (to) find a shorter hairstyle that suited me

12 ④	13 ②
14 ②	

15 I'm not good at speaking in front of others.

01 ③ Austin의 마지막 말 It's quite fun. Plus, you can gain a better understanding of yourself.를 통해서 그는 색상 성격 검사(color personality test)를 '자신을 더 잘 이해하는 재미있는 방법'이라고 생각한다는 것을 알 수 있다.
  오답 ① Austin은 그것이 지루하고 재미없다고 생각한다.
  ② Austin은 그것이 그의 친구들에게만 유용하다고 생각한다.
  ④ Austin은 진정한 성격 특성을 반영하는 데 있어서 그것의 정확성을 의심한다.
  ⑤ Austin은 그것이 너무 복잡해서 쓸모가 없다고 생각한다.

02 자신이 잘하는 것을 말할 때는 I'm good at을 사용한다. 이어서 동사 create를 써야 하는데 전치사 at 뒤에 오므로 동명사형 creating이 알맞다.

03 ②는 목적어 역할을 하는 명사적 용법의 to부정사이고, To help와 나머지는 모두 목적을 나타내는 부사적 용법의 to부정사이다.
  ① 그녀는 새 노트북을 사기 위해 돈을 모았다.
  ② 우리는 금요일까지 프로젝트를 끝내야 한다.
  ③ 회원들은 다가오는 행사를 계획하기 위해 만났다.
  ④ Kevin은 기타 실력을 향상시키기 위해 매일 연습했다.
  ⑤ 그들은 에펠탑을 보기 위해 파리로 여행했다.

04 ⑤ 교사가 학생들에게 도전 과제를 주어 자신을 발전시키도록 하려는 의도를 나타내므로 'an assignment(과제)'가 적절하다.
  오답 ① 규칙 ② 제안 ③ 아이디어, 생각 ④ 지시, 설명

05 (B)는 친구나 가족과 함께 영화를 보는 일반적인 상황을 설명한다. -(C)는 혼자서 영화관에 간 경험을 설명한다. - (A)는 그 경험을 긍정적으로 받아들인 후 자신이 궁금해해왔던 영화를 선택한 이야기를 이어간다.

06 ⑤ '스스로'라는 의미가 와야 자연스럽다. '스스로'라는 의미는 on my own이다.

07 이 글은 혼자 영화를 보면서 혼자 하는 활동의 즐거움을 깨달았다는 내용이므로 ① '혼자만의 경험에서 오는 기쁨 발견하기'가 제목으로 가장 적절하다.
  오답 ② 친구들과 영화 보기의 장점
  ③ 최고의 영화관 좌석을 선택하는 방법
  ④ 영화관에서의 방해 요소 다루기
  ⑤ 단체로 영화 보기의 문제점

08 밑줄 친 itself는 강조 용법으로 사용되었다. ⑤의 ourselves도 같은 강조 용법으로, 주어(we)가 스스로 준비했다는 의미를 강조하는 쓰임이다. 강조 용법은 생략해도 의미 전달에 문제가 없다. 나머지는 모두 재귀 용법으로 사용되었으며 생략하여 쓸 수 없다.
  ① 그는 컴퓨터를 완전히 혼자서 고쳤다.
  ② 그녀는 수학 문제를 혼자서 풀었다.
  ③ 우리는 마감 시간을 맞추기 위해 더 열심히 노력했다.
  ④ 아이들은 놀이공원에서 하루 종일 즐겁게 놀았다.
  ⑤ 우리는 모든 식사를 직접 준비했다.

09 (A) 문맥상 불편함을 극복하려고 했지만 무엇을 해야 할지 몰랐다고 했으므로 'However(그러나)'가 적절하다.
  (B) 결과적으로 초보자 과정에 등록했다는 의미로 'so(그래서)'가 적절하다.

10 제시된 단어와 「as+원급+as」 구문을 사용하되 be동사가 주어 역할을 해야 하므로 Being을 쓰는 것에 주의한다.

11 help는 목적격보어로 동사원형이나 to부정사가 올 수 있으므로 finding을 find 또는 to find로 고쳐야 한다.

12 (A) 필자는 헤어스타일을 바꾸는 것에 대한 두려움을 극복했으므로 overcame이 적절하다.
  (B) 긍정적인 피드백을 받았다는 내용이므로 received가 적절하다.

13 여러 명의 사람들 중에서 '한 사람'은 one으로 나타내고, '또 다른 한 사람'은 another로 나타낸다.

14 ②는 명사절을 이끄는 접속사이고, 나머지는 모두 관계대명사이다.
  ① 그는 뉴욕에 사는 친구가 있다.
  ② 나는 그가 그 일에 가장 적합하다고 생각한다.
  ③ 나는 네가 나에게 소개한 그 남자를 안다.
  ④ 내가 어젯밤에 본 영화는 정말 재미있었다.
  ⑤ 내가 도서관에서 빌린 책은 오늘 반납일이다.

15 주어진 문장은 be not good at을 사용하여 잘하지 못하는 것을 표현해야 한다. 부정문이므로 I'm not good at을 먼저 쓰고, 전치사의 목적어 speaking을 쓴다. 이어서 in front of others로 문장을 완성한다.

01 ②	02 ⑤
03 ③	04 ④

05 It was nice to choose the movie and the seat on my own.

06 ④	07 ②
08 ②	09 ⑤
10 ③	11 ③
12 ③	13 perspective
14 ④	15 strengths

01 ②가 Marco가 제안을 따르고 두려움을 극복하기 위한 첫 걸음을 내딛을 의향이 있음을 보여주는 응답이다.
  ① 아니, 그것이 도움이 될 것 같지 않아.
  ② 좋아. 한번 시도해 볼게.

③ 나는 수업 중에 질문하는 것을 좋아하지 않아.
④ 아마도 그냥 발표를 건너뛰어야 할 것 같아.
⑤ 마지막 순간까지 기다렸다가 준비할게.
▨ ①은 거절, ③은 개인적 선호, ④와 ⑤는 회피나 미루기 등의 태도를 보여주는 응답으로 대화의 흐름상 적절하지 않다.

02 ①~④는 모두 자신감을 키우거나 공개 발표 능력을 향상시키기 위한 긍정적인 조언인 반면, ⑤ '대중 연설을 피해라.'는 부정적인 조언으로 문제를 회피하는 방법을 제시하고 있다.
▨ ① 수업 중에 질문하는 것부터 시작해라.
② 자신감을 키우기 위해 작은 단계부터 시작해라.
③ 거울 앞에서 말하는 연습을 해라.
④ 안전지대에서 벗어나라.

03 ③ '교실은 동기 부여 포스터로 밝게 꾸며져 있었다.'는 교실 꾸미기에 관한 내용으로, 본문의 핵심 주제인 자기 성장과 교사의 과제와는 직접적인 관련이 없다.

04 (A) '~하기 위해서'라는 뜻의 목적을 나타내기 위해서는 부사적 용법의 to부정사 To grow가 알맞다.
(B) 보어 역할을 해야 하므로 trying 또는 to try가 알맞다.

05 주어진 문장을 가주어 it과 진주어 to부정사를 사용하여 바꾸면 It was nice to choose the movie and the seat on my own. 이 된다.

06 ④의 as는 '~로서'라는 뜻의 전치사이고, 나머지 as는 모두 접속사이다. ①과 ⑤는 '~때문에'라는 뜻의 '이유'를 나타내는 접속사이고, ②와 ③은 '~할 때', '~하면서'라는 뜻의 시간을 나타내는 접속사이다.
① 그는 중요한 회의가 있어서 일찍 떠났다.
② 그녀는 연설을 하기 위해 무대에 올라가면서 긴장했다.
③ 해가 지면서 하늘은 아름다운 주황빛으로 변했다.
④ 그녀는 유명한 가수가 되기 전에 교사로 일했다.
⑤ 밖이 매우 추웠기 때문에, 그녀는 코트를 입었다.

07 (A) 동사 felt의 보어 역할이므로 형용사 awkward가 알맞다. lonely는 형태는 부사처럼 보이지만 형용사이다.
(B) 주어가 영화에 몰입되었음을 표현하므로 과거분사 absorbed가 알맞다.
(C) 사역동사 made의 목적격보어이므로 동사원형 realize가 알맞다.

08 문맥상 뒤에 있는 my own choices와 함께 '선택하다'라는 의미가 되어야 하므로 make가 적절하다.

09 ⑤ 여기서 signed up은 '등록했다'라는 뜻이다.

10 흥분감을 주었던 원인이 It에 해당한다. It은 강사의 도움을 받아 균형 잡는 법을 배우고 약간의 파도를 탄 것이므로 주어진 문장이 들어갈 위치로 알맞은 곳은 ③이다.

11 ③ 문맥상 jokes(농담)가 아니라 '걱정, 우려'라는 의미의 concerns가 알맞다.

12 (A) Since는 이유를 나타내는 접속사로 왜 스타일 변경을 시도할 수 있었는지 설명한다.
(B) In fact는 스타일 변경의 결과가 기대 이상으로 긍정적이었다는 점을 강조하여 경험의 효과를 구체화하고 있다.

13 '어떤 것을 보거나 이해하는 특정한 방식'이라는 뜻이므로 '관점'이라는 의미의 perspective가 알맞다.

14 (A) 여기서 that은 명사절을 이끄는 접속사로 found out의 목적어 역할을 한다.
(B) 여기서 while은 '반면에'라는 뜻으로 One과 another의 행동 사이의 대조를 나타낸다.
(C) 여기서 until은 행동이 발생하기 전까지의 상태를 설명한다.

15 자기 성찰(self-reflection)과 타인들의 의견(feedback from others)을 통해 자신의 강점(strengths)을 파악하는 방법을 설명하고 있으므로, 빈칸에는 strengths가 적절하다.

내신 1등급 실전 3회   pp. 46-49

01 ⑤   **02** ④
03 by pushing ourselves out of our comfort zones and learning more about ourselves
04 ②   **05** ④
06 ④   **07** ⑤
08 ③   **09** overcome
10 ⓒ → excitement   **11** ①
12 ①   **13** ④
14 ②
15 Through these experiences, we all realized how important it is to push ourselves to try new things.

01 ⑤ Janis Smith는 주로 사람들의 표정을 통해 감정을 포착하는 사진을 찍는다고 했다. 풍경과 자연 경치를 주로 촬영한다는 언급은 없다.
① 그녀는 사진작가, 여행 가이드, 그리고 연구원으로서 여러 직업을 가지고 있다.
② 그녀는 일을 위해 전 세계를 여행한다.
③ 그녀는 사진 작업에서 얼굴 표정을 통해 인간의 감정을 표현하는 것을 강조한다.
④ 그녀는 사람들에게 꿈을 추구하고 자신을 행복하게 만드는 일을 하라고 조언한다.
⑤ 그녀는 주로 풍경과 자연 경관을 포착하는 데 중점을 둔다.

02 ⓒ: challenge herself는 주어가 we인데 herself로 되어 있어 어법상 맞지 않으며 challenge ourselves가 알맞다.
ⓔ: 「share A with B」 구문으로 'B와 A를 공유하다'는 의미가 되어야 하므로 of가 아니라 with가 알맞다.

03 전치사 by 뒤에 동명사형을 써야 한다는 것과 접속사 and 뒤에 오는 동사도 병렬 구조에 따라 동명사형을 써야 한다는 것에 주의한다.

04 ② 필자가 혼자 극장에 가고 영화 선택을 혼자서 할 수 있었던 것에 대해 긍정적이고 만족스러운 감정을 가지고 있음을 알 수 있으므로 'content(만족한)'가 적절하다
▨ ① 불안해하는 ③ 놀란 ④ 좌절한 ⑤ 무관심한

05 worry about: ~에 대해 걱정하다 / be curious about: ~에 대해 궁금해하다

06 혼자 영화관에 있는 것에서 오는 처음의 어색함과 외로움을 경험한 후, 영화에 몰입하게 되는 변화를 강조하고 있기 때문에 ④ '어색하고 외로운'이 적절하다.

　　① 친숙하고 따뜻한 ② 흥미진진하고 스릴 넘치는 ③ 편안하고 즐거운 ⑤ 실망스럽고 좌절스러운

07 (A) nothing을 수식하는 형용사적 용법의 to부정사가 적절하다.
(B) enjoy의 목적어 역할을 하는 동명사가 적절하다.

08 필자는 '물에 대한 두려움을 극복하기 위해' 초보자 과정에 등록하기로 결정했다고 했으므로 ③이 질문에 대한 대답으로 적절하다.

　　① 사촌의 조언을 따르기 위해
② 친구들과 경쟁하기 위해
④ 바다에서 수영을 즐기기 위해
⑤ 소셜 미디어 존재감을 높이기 위해

09 '문제나 어려움을 성공적으로 처리하거나 극복하다'는 의미이므로 overcome이 적절하다.

10 전치사 뒤에는 명사 형태가 와야 하므로 excite의 명사형 excitement가 적절하다.

11 ① suitable for나 capable of가 맞는 표현으로 My sister is capable of fixing broken things.(내 여동생은 고장 난 물건들을 고칠 수 있는 능력이 있다.)가 되어야 한다.

　　② Alex는 비행기를 탈 때 창가 좌석에 앉는 것을 선호한다.
③ 나는 책에 너무 몰두해서 늦게까지 깨어 있었다.
④ 친절한 작은 행동이 누군가의 하루에 큰 차이를 만들 수 있다.
⑤ 박물관 규칙에 따르면, 사진 촬영은 허용되지 않는다.

12 (A) 헤어스타일을 변경하려는 이유와 고민을 설명한다. – (C) 헤어스타일 변화 후의 반응을 다루며, 필자가 느낀 변화에 대해 서술한다. – (B) 새로운 헤어스타일이 필자에게 긍정적인 영향을 미쳤음을 강조하며 마무리한다.

13 ⓐ '~이후로'라는 의미의 전치사로, 과거의 특정 시점부터 현재까지 계속되는 상황을 나타낸다.
ⓑ '~때문에'라는 의미의 이유를 나타내는 접속사이다.
ⓒ '~이후로'라는 의미의 전치사로, 현재완료형과 함께 사용되어 과거의 특정 시점 이후 현재까지의 상황을 나타낸다.
ⓓ '~때문에'라는 의미의 이유를 나타내는 접속사이다.

　　ⓐ 나는 2020년부터 이 도시에서 살고 있다.
ⓑ 비가 오고 있었기 때문에, 우리는 실내에 머물기로 결정했다.
ⓒ 그는 지난 여름 이후로 우리를 방문하지 않았다.
ⓓ 콘서트가 취소되었기 때문에, 나는 그 티켓에 대한 환불을 받았다.

14 (A) 전치사 about 뒤에는 동명사 형태인 setting이 적절하다.
(B) 「가주어 it, 진주어 to부정사」 구문으로 진주어 역할을 하는 to keep이 적절하다.

15 realized의 목적어 역할을 하는 명사절로 「how+형용사+주어+동사」의 어순이 되어야 한다.

01 ①	02 ③
03 ④	04 ⑤
05 ⑤	06 ③
07 ④	08 ②
09 ③	10 ②
11 ④	12 ④
13 ②	14 ⑤
15 ③	

[01-02] 해석

> "더 나은 모습의 우리가 되기 위해서는 우리는 같은 상태로 머물러서는 안 됩니다." 이것은 학기 첫날 우리 선생님이 하신 첫 말씀이었다. 선생님은 우리가 안전지대에서 벗어나 우리 자신에 대해 더 많이 알아가면서 학기를 시작하도록 격려하셨다. 이를 돕기 위해, 선생님은 우리에게 세 가지 다른 방식으로 자신에게 도전하는 과제를 내주셨다. 이러한 도전들은 취미, 운동, 공부, 심지어 인간관계와 관련된 것일 수 있었다. 중요한 점은 각각의 도전에서 새로운 것을 시도하는 것이었다. 우리가 도전들을 완수하면, 선생님은 우리에게 우리의 경험을 반 친구들과 공유하도록 요청하셨다.

01 교사가 학생들에게 새로운 경험을 통해 자신을 발견하고 성장하도록 격려하는 내용이므로 ① '자아 발견과 개인적 성장'이 주제로 가장 적절하다.

　　② 도전을 피하고 편안함을 유지하기
③ 학교 프로젝트에서 팀워크의 중요성
④ 오래된 습관을 효과적으로 유지하는 방법
⑤ 전통적인 교육 방법의 이점

02 ③ and 앞에 있는 by stepping과 병렬 구조를 이루므로 discovering이 알맞다.

　　① '목적'을 나타내는 부사적 용법의 to부정사
② encourage A to B: A에게 B 하도록 권장하다
④ 앞에 있는 명사 a task를 수식하는 형용사적 용법의 to부정사
⑤ ask A to B: A에게 B 하도록 요청하다

[03-04] 해석

> 최근에 나는 보통 스트리밍 서비스에서 영화를 본다. 하지만 극장에 가면 친구들이나 가족과 함께 그들이 좋아하는 액션이나 공상과학 영화를 주로 본다.
> 혼자서 극장에 가는 것은 내가 한 번도 시도해본 적이 없는 일이었다. 그래서 첫 번째 도전으로 그것을 해보기로 결심했다. 다른 사람의 취향을 고려하지 않고 영화를 고르고 자리를 선택할 수 있어서 좋았다. 나는 이것을 새로운 것을 볼 수 있는 좋은 기회로 생각했고, 관심이 있었던 역사 드라마를 선택했다.

03 주어진 문장은 혼자 영화관에 가기로 결정한 직후의 즉각적인 느낌을 표현하므로, ④의 위치가 가장 적절하다.

04 I typically watch action or science fiction films with my friends or family because those are their favorites.에서 필자는 주로 친구나 가족이 좋아하는 영화를 보았다는 것을 알 수 있으므로 ⑤가 일치하지 않는 내용이다.

[05-06] 해석

> 처음에는 극장에 혼자 앉아 있는 것이 조금 이상하고 외롭게 느껴졌다. 하지만 영화가 시작되자, 나는 완전히 이야기에 빠져들었다. 어떤 방해도 없이 오로지 영화에만 집중할 수 있어서 굉장히 만족스러웠다. 이 경험을 통해 나는 때때로 혼자 무언가를 하는 것을 즐긴다는 것을 깨달았다. 영화가 끝난 후, 나는 앞으로 더 자주 내 스스로 선택을 하고 혼자서 더 많은 활동을 즐기겠다고 다짐했다.

05 ⑤ '내 스스로 선택하다'는 make my own choices이므로 take가 아니라 make를 써야 한다.

06 ③ 필자는 처음에는 혼자 영화관에 앉아 있을 때 '어색한(awkward)' 감정을 느끼다가 영화가 시작된 후, 이야기에 몰입하게 되어 '만족스러운(satisfied)' 기분을 느꼈다.

[07-08] 해석

> 어렸을 때부터 나는 항상 물에 대한 두려움이 있어서 물에서 하는 스포츠 활동을 불편해했다. 두 번째 도전으로, 나는 이 두려움에 맞서기로 결심했다. 처음에는 어떻게 접근해야 할지 확신이 서지 않았다. 어느 날, 소셜 미디어에서 사촌이 실내 수영장에서 서핑하는 영상을 보았다. 재미있어 보였고, 바다가 아닌 얕은 수영장에서 이루어진다는 점이 마음에 들었다. 나는 사촌에게 연락했고, 그는 그것이 그리 어렵지 않다고 확신시켜 주었다. 그래서 나는 초보자 과정에 등록했다.

07 물에 대한 두려움을 극복하려는 필자의 노력을 서술하고 있으므로 제목으로 알맞은 것은 ④ '물에 대한 두려움 극복하기'이다.
　　① 수영의 기쁨 ② 바다에서의 새로운 모험 ③ 수영장에서의 가족 놀이 ⑤ 내가 좋아하는 여름 활동

08 (A) 앞 문장을 선행사로 하는 관계대명사는 which가 알맞다.
(B) decide는 to부정사를 목적어로 취하므로 to confront가 알맞다.
(C) 앞에 있는 명사 my cousin을 뒤에서 수식하는 현재분사 surfing이 알맞다.

[09-10] 해석

> 수업 초반에는 단순히 보드 위에 서는 것조차 힘들었다. 하지만 강사의 도움으로 제대로 균형을 잡는 법을 배웠고, 결국에는 몇 개의 파도를 서핑하는 데 성공했다! 그것은 정말 흥미진진한 경험이었다. 물속에 있는 것이 내가 생각했던 것보다 훨씬 덜 무서웠다. 비록 물 스포츠에 대한 내 생각을 완전히 바꾸지는 못했지만, 내 안의 모험심을 발견하는 데 도움을 주었다.

09 주어진 문장의 It은 ③의 앞에 나온 문장 I learned to balance properly and even managed to surf a few waves!를 나타내므로 주어진 문장이 들어갈 위치로 알맞은 곳은 ③이다.

10 (A) 문맥상 수업의 시작을 언급하고 있으며, 처음에 어려움을 겪었다고 하므로 beginning이 적절하다.
(B) 수업에서 도움을 준 사람을 지칭하므로 instructor가 적절하다.
(C) 물속에서의 경험이 생각했던 것보다 두려움이 덜하다는 점을 강조하고 있으므로 scary가 적절하다.

[11-12] 해석

> 내가 선택한 모든 도전들 중에서 세 번째 도전이 나를 가장 긴장되게 했다: 헤어스타일을 바꾸는 것이었다. 수년 동안 나는 이마 때문에 걱정하여 같은 헤어스타일을 유지해 왔다. 내 이마가 넓다고 늘 생각했고, 그것에 주목을 받고 싶지 않았다. 첫 두 번의 도전 후 자신감을 얻어, 나는 미용실을 방문하여 스타일리스트와 내 옵션에 대해 상의하기로 결정했다. 그는 내 걱정을 경청하고 나에게 어울리는 더 짧은 헤어스타일을 선택하는 데 도움을 주었다.

11 필자가 직면한 여러 가지 '도전'을 나타내기 때문에 ④가 가장 적절하다.

12 ④ 주어가 생략된 분사구문으로 Feeling confident가 알맞다.
　　① '~중에서'라는 의미의 전치사 among의 쓰임이 적절하다.
② 앞에 있는 had kept와 호응을 이루며 had been worried는 과거완료 형태로 적절하다.
③ want는 to부정사를 목적어로 취하므로 to draw가 적절하다.
⑤ help는 목적격보어로 동사원형이나 to부정사를 취하므로 choose가 적절하다.

[13-14] 해석

> 다음 날 학교에서 나의 반 친구들은 조금 놀랐지만, 전반적인 반응은 긍정적이었다. 새로운 모습을 시도하는 것이 내가 생각했던 것만큼 어렵지 않다는 것을 깨달았다. 사실, 그것은 나로 하여금 더 자신감 있게 느끼게 해주었다. 안전지대에서 벗어나는 것이 나 자신에 대한 느낌에 이렇게 긍정적인 영향을 줄 것이라고는 전혀 예상하지 못했다.

13 (A) 문맥상 친구들이 약간 놀라기는 했지만 전체적으로 긍정적이라는 것이 자연스러우므로 positive가 적절하다.
(B) 새로운 모습을 시도해 보면서 자신감이 생겼다는 내용과 잘 연결되므로 confident가 적절하다.
(C) comfort zone에서 벗어나는 것이 긍정적인 영향을 미쳤다고 하는 것이 자연스러우므로 comfort가 적절하다.

14 ⑤ 문맥상 trying out a new look은 새로운 시도를 의미하며, 일반적으로 이러한 경험은 긴장되거나 힘든 면이 있을 수 있으므로 challenging(어려운, 힘든)이 이러한 의미를 잘 전달한다.
　　① 기쁜, 즐거운 ② 만족스러운 ③ 편안한 ④ 우울한, 침울한

[15] 해석

> 이 과제를 통해 나는 나 자신에 대해 많은 것을 발견했고, 나의 반 친구들도 마찬가지였다. 그들 중 한 명은 다양한 나라의 음식을 먹어 보았고, 다른 한 명은 창의적 글쓰기 동아리에 가입했다. 이러한 경험들은 우리에게 새로운 것을 시도하기 위해 스스로를 밀어붙이는 것의 중요성을 가르쳐 주었다. 우리는 인생에 대한 새로운 관점을 얻었고, 정말 즐거운 시간도 보냈다! 나와 반 친구들은 심지어 우리 자신에게 더 많은 도전 과제를 설정하는 것에 대해 논의했다. 우리는 항상 우리 자신에 대해 더 많은 것을 발견할 수 있으며, 계속해서 배우고 성장하는 것은 흥미진진하다. 우리는 직접 시도해보기 전까지는 우리의 진정한 능력을 알 수 없다!

15 (B) 친구들이 과제를 통해 구체적으로 어떤 경험을 했는지 설명하는 부분으로 도입부에서 언급된 my classmates did as well의 구체적인 예시에 해당하므로 첫 번째로 나오는 것이 적절하다.
(A) 친구들과 함께 앞으로 더 많은 도전을 논의한 내용으로 새로운 도전을 계속해 나가는 것에 대한 생각을 담고 있으므로 (B)에서 제시된 경험에 이어 나오는 것이 적절하다.
(C) 도전의 중요성과 시도를 통해 스스로의 능력을 알 수 있다는 결론을 맺는 문장으로 앞의 내용들을 종합하는 역할로 적절하다.

내신 1등급 서술형

pp. 54-56

01 우리 자신의 더 나은 모습으로 성장하기 위해서, 우리는 지금 모습 그대로 머물러 있어서는 안 됩니다.

02 She wanted us to start the semester by pushing ourselves out of our comfort zones and learning more about ourselves.

03 The important part was trying something new for each one.

04 action or science fiction movies

05 (A) Going to the theater alone was something I had never done before.
(B) I didn't have to worry about anyone else's preferences.

06 was so satisfying just to focus on the movie itself

07 awkward and lonely → satisfying

08 (A) comfortable
(B) excitement

09 I came across a video clip of my cousin surfing at an indoor pool on social media

10 did help

11 ⓐ (c)onfident ⓑ (p)ositive

12 (A) The next day at school, my classmates were a bit surprised.
(B) I realized that trying a different look wasn't as difficult as I thought it would be.
(C) In fact, it made me feel more confident about myself.

13 while another joined a creative writing club

14 (1) assignment
(2) importance
(3) perspectives
(4) excited

01 부사적 용법의 to부정사는 '~하기 위해서'라고 해석한다.

02 want는 to부정사를 목적어로 취하므로 start가 아니라 to start가 되어야 한다. learn은 앞에 나오는 by pushing과 병렬 구조를 이루므로 learn이 아니라 동명사인 learning이 되어야 한다.

03 주어로 The important part를 쓰고 과거형 be동사 was를 쓰고 보어로 동명사형 trying을 쓰고 '새로운 어떤 것'에 해당하는 something new를 쓰고 마지막으로 for each one을 쓴다. new something으로 쓰지 않도록 주의한다.

04 Those는 앞에 나온 an action or science fiction movie를 가리킨다. Those가 복수이므로 action or science fiction movies가 알맞다.

05 (A) 동명사(구) 주어는 단수 취급을 하므로 were가 아니라 was가 알맞다.
(B) must의 과거형 부정형은 didn't have to이다.

06 It 뒤에 be동사 was와 보어 so satisfying을 쓰고, just to focus on the movie itself를 이어서 쓴다.

07 처음에는 어색하고 외로웠지만(awkward and lonely) 나중에는 만족감(satisfying)을 느꼈다.

08 (A) felt의 보어이므로 형용사 comfortable이 알맞다.
(B) 전치사 뒤이므로 excite의 명사형 excitement가 알맞다.

09 주어와 동사인 I came across를 쓰고 목적어 a video clip of my cousin을 쓰고 뒤에서 수식하는 현재분사구 surfing at an indoor pool과 부사구 on social media로 마무리한다.

10 과거형 동사이므로 강조동사 did를 쓰고 뒤에는 동사원형 help를 쓴다.

11 ⓐ '어떤 것에 대해 확신을 느끼거나 보여주는; 자신감 있는'은 'confident(자신감 있는)'에 대한 설명이다.
ⓑ '낙관적이거나 건설적인; 좋은 태도나 효과를 가진'은 'positive(긍정적인)'에 대한 설명이다.

12 (A) 주어가 사람이므로 과거분사 형용사 surprised가 알맞다.
(B) 이 문장은 「as+원급+as」 구문으로 than이 아니라 as가 알맞다.
(C) made는 사역동사로 동사원형 feel이 목적격보어로 알맞다.

13 '반면에'에 해당하는 while을 쓰고 주어인 another, 동사 joined를 쓰고 목적어 a creative writing club을 쓴다.

14 이 과제를 통해 우리는 새로운 것을 시도하는 것의 중요성을 깨달았다. 우리는 삶에 대한 새로운 관점들을 발견했고, 계속 배우고 성장하는 것이 기대된다.

교과서 어휘 익히기 ········· pp. 60-61

STEP 1

01 시력, 비전	25 friendship
02 (~을 할) 여유[형편]가 되다	26 therapy
03 부상을 입은, 다친; (마음이) 상한	27 depressed
04 영감을 주다	28 effort
05 창립자, 설립자	29 transportation
06 구할[이용할] 수 있는	30 reliable
07 의학의	31 recovery
08 심하게, 극심하게	32 incredibly
09 부족	33 region
10 접근 가능한	34 volunteer
11 확대[확장]하다; 확대[확장]시키다	35 struggle
12 게다가	36 emotional
13 의미 있는	37 face-to-face
14 상담가	38 ability
15 우울증	39 recovery
16 공감, 감정이입	40 patient
17 불안(감), 염려	41 psychiatrist
18 연세가 드신	42 population
19 치료	43 engage in
20 생각을 떠올리다	44 pass away
21 ~을 부끄러워하다	45 be encouraged to
22 ~와 같은	46 deal with
23 ~을 겪다	47 be connected to
24 ~로 고심하다	48 relate to

STEP 2

A 01 be ashamed of 02 come up with
  03 engage in 04 go through
  05 relate to
B 01 support 02 Seeking
C 01 ⓑ 02 ⓐ 03 ⓒ

교과서 핵심 대화문 ········· pp. 62-63

Function 1 충고하기
Check-Up ✓ ⑤
Function 2 희망, 기대 표현하기
Check-Up ✓ I hope

교과서 기타 대화문 ········· p. 64

Q1 T Q2 F Q3 T

TOPIC 1 C. Listen and Interact

B: 나 살이 좀 찐 것 같아. 이 셔츠가 꽉 끼는 느낌이야.
G: 아, 너는 왜 살이 찐 것 같아?
B: 나는 간식을 너무 자주 먹는 것 같아, 특히 밤에.
G: 그건 나쁜 습관이야. 네가 그것을 고칠 수 있는 방법을 찾아보자.
B: 좋아. 오, 이 웹사이트에서는 물을 더 많이 마시라고 제안하고 있어. 사람들이 종종 목마름을 배고픔으로 착각한다고 해.
G: 맞아. 그리고 여기에는 낮에 식사를 거르지 말라고 하네. 그렇게 하면 밤에 더 배고파져. 또한, 만약 간식이 필요하다면, 과일이나 견과류를 먹는 것이 좋대.
B: 좋은 팁들이네. 나도 한번 해봐야겠어.
G: 응, 너의 건강을 챙기는 것이 중요해.

TOPIC 4 B. While You View

M 시험을 보려던 마지막 순간을 생각해보세요. 만약 여러분이 불안했다면, 손이 땀에 젖었나요? 아마도 반 친구가 여러분을 웃게 만들어서 좀 더 편안해졌을 거예요. 이와 비슷하게, 여러분은 때때로 건강한 식사를 한 후에 기분이 좋아지는 것을 느낄 수도 있어요. 이러한 상황들은 마음과 몸의 연결을 반영해요.
이 개념에 따르면, 우리의 마음과 몸은 서로 영향을 미칠 수 있어요. 예를 들어, 지속적인 걱정은 위장 문제를 일으킬 수 있어요. 따라서 여러분은 정신적, 신체적 건강을 모두 돌봐야 해요. 기분이 우울할 때는 숨을 깊게 들이쉬고 내쉬는 데 집중하세요. 이것은 부정적인 생각이나 감정을 다루는 효과적인 전략이에요. 스트레스를 느낀다면, 밖에서 걷거나 조깅하세요. 집중력이 떨어질 때는 잠시 쉬거나 스트레칭을 하세요. 그렇게 하면 몸과 마음을 다시 연결할 수 있어요. 안팎으로 건강하게 지내기 위해서는 마음과 몸의 연결을 잘 챙기세요.

Wrap Up A. Listen and Post

G: 그게 뭐야, Jake?
B: 이건 내 식단 계획이야. 각 식사에 무엇을 먹을지 보여줘. 그것을 미리 생각하는 것이 건강한 식단을 유지하는 데 도움이 돼.
G: 좋은 생각이야! 나는 무엇을 먹을지 결정하지 못해서 종종 건강에 좋지 않은 패스트푸드를 먹게 돼.
B: 정말? 그럼 너도 식단 계획을 세워야 할 것 같아.
G: 각 식사를 어떻게 건강하게 만드는지 설명해줄 수 있어?
B: 물론이지. 나는 곡물, 단백질, 채소의 균형이 잘 맞도록 해. 그리고 다양한 음식을 먹으려고 노력해.
G: 알겠어. 나도 그렇게 해볼게!

교과서 핵심 대화문 익히기 ········· p. 65

01 ④

02 I hope these tips help you enjoy your favorite shows in a healthy way.

03 ⑤

교과서 핵심 문법 ········· pp. 66-69

POINT 1 to부정사의 형용사적 용법

Q 1 to play　　　2 to prepare　　　3 to skip

Check-Up ✍

01 (1) to improve (2) to watch (3) to be ashamed of

02 ③

03 (1) hopes to travel (2) a book to read (3) to avoid traffic

04 (1) share (2) to keep (3) check (4) to be

01 (1) 앞의 명사 a new coach를 수식하는 형용사적 용법의 to부정사가 알맞다.
(2) 앞의 명사 a great movie를 수식하는 형용사적 용법의 to부정사가 알맞다.
(3) nothing은 be ashamed of 즉, 전치사의 목적어이므로 of를 빠뜨리지 않도록 주의한다.

02 친구들과 재미있게 놀기 위해서는 함께 즐길 활동을 계획해야 한다. 나는 공원에 가거나 영화를 보는 것을 좋아한다.
(A) '~하기 위해서'라는 의미의 목적을 나타내는 부사적 용법의 to부정사가 알맞다.
(B) 앞의 명사 activities를 수식하는 형용사적 용법의 to부정사가 알맞다.
(C) love의 목적어 역할을 하는 명사적 용법의 to부정사가 알맞다.

03 (1) '여행하기를 희망하다'가 되어야 하므로 hopes to travel이 알맞다.
(2) '읽을 책'이므로 형용사적 용법의 to부정사를 사용한 a book to read가 알맞다.
(3) '교통 체증을 피하기 위해서'가 되어야 하므로 to avoid traffic이 알맞다.

04
　　　뉴욕행 123 항공편에 탑승하신 것을 환영합니다. 여러분의 안전을 위해서, 저희는 몇 가지 중요한 정보를 공유하고 싶습니다. 여러분의 안전 벨트가 채워졌는지 확인해 주세요. 이것이 비행 중에 여러분을 안전하게 지켜 주는 최고의 방법이기 때문입니다. 또한, 가장 가까운 비상구의 위치를 확인해 주세요. 저희는 여러분의 여행 경험의 일부가 될 기회를 얻게 되어 기쁩니다.

(1) would like to+동사원형: ~하고 싶다
(2) 앞의 명사 the best way를 수식하는 형용사적 용법의 to부정사가 알맞다.
(3) 명령문이므로 동사원형 check가 알맞다.
(4) 앞의 명사 the opportunity를 수식하는 형용사적 용법의 to부정사가 알맞다.

POINT 2 가주어 it

Q 1 to go　　　2 It　　　3 that　　　4 for you

Check-Up ✍

01 (1) that (2) to maintain (3) It

02 (1) It is fun to go camping with friends during the summer.
(2) It is a fact that regular exercise improves both physical and mental health.

03 (1) It was nice to have
(2) It was truly wonderful to see
(3) It was hard for us to thank

04 ③

01 (1) 「It ~ that ... 가주어·진주어」 구문이다.
(2), (3) 「It ~ to ... 가주어·진주어」 구문이다.

02 (1) 가주어 It과 is fun을 쓰고 뒤에 to부정사구를 쓴다.
(2) 가주어 It과 is a fact를 쓰고 뒤에 that절을 쓴다.

03
　　　친애하는 Nicky에게,
　　　저희는 당신이 자선 행사에서 저희와 함께해 주신 것에 감사를 전하고 싶습니다. 당신의 지지를 받게 되어 좋았습니다. 당신의 참석은 실질적인 변화를 가져왔으며, 모든 이가 이런 대단한 목적을 위해 모인 것을 보는 것은 정말로 멋졌습니다. 저희가 행사에서 당신에게 개인적으로 감사를 표하는 것은 어려웠지만, 저희는 당신의 친절과 지지에 감사드립니다.
　　　진심으로,
　　　희망 자선 단체 드림

「It is/was+형용사+(for+목적격)+to부정사 ~」 구문이다.

04 ⓑ 앞의 명사 a friend를 수식하는 형용사적 용법의 to부정사 to help가 알맞다.
ⓒ to부정사의 의미상의 주어는 to부정사 앞에 「for+목적격」 형태로 쓰므로 for students가 알맞다.
ⓓ 「가주어 It, 진주어 to부정사」 구문으로 to attend가 알맞다.

교과서 본문 익히기 ❶ ········· pp. 76-78

01 the founder of
02 inspired you to come up with
03 came from an experience
04 had become, depressed
05 was unable to afford
06 considered such a problem
07 to pay for transportation
08 eleven psychiatrists serving
09 bring, into the community
10 as a way to provide
11 people dealing with issues
12 respected elderly women
13 provide them with emotional support

14 are deeply connected to

15 the ability to engage in

16 to support mental health

17 who have been trained

18 are encouraged to join, made up of

19 can easily relate to

20 build a sense of community

21 incredibly successful

22 face-to-face counseling

23 available in more than

24 within walking distance

25 started expanding

26 reach even more people

27 how you got involved with

28 have been volunteering for

29 struggle with

30 heal their wounded hearts

31 about your experience

32 nothing to be ashamed of

33 make a difference

34 going through

35 begin her recovery journey

36 is back on track

37 make me so proud

38 such a rewarding experience

39 sharing your experiences with

40 It's truly inspiring to see

41 thanks to

39 Seeking   40 make

41 mine   42 recovery

43 make   44 positive

45 sharing   46 truly

교과서 본문 익히기 ❸ ························· pp. 82-83

01 called   02 to come

03 had   04 become

05 never   06 for

07 for   08 serving

09 to bring   10 works

11 created   12 to

13 provided   14 called

15 What   16 because

17 ability   18 which

19 made   20 one another

21 because   22 to

23 more   24 walking

25 expanding   26 even

27 amazing   28 who

29 yourself   30 volunteering

31 to do   32 wounded

33 Seeking   34 it can

35 begin   36 make

37 such   38 sharing

39 to see   40 to

교과서 본문 익히기 ❷ ··············· pp. 79-81

01 called   02 founder

03 to come   04 psychiatrist

05 depressed   06 afford

07 such   08 to pay

09 for   10 serving

11 to find   12 beginning, to

13 was created   14 dealing

15 elderly   16 provide

17 What   18 were chosen

19 to engage   20 which

21 with   22 have been trained

23 after   24 to join

25 another   26 similar

27 build   28 to

29 more than   30 happen

31 expanding   32 even

33 grandmothers   34 how you got

35 volunteering   36 something

37 heal   38 as

교과서 본문 외 지문 분석 ··············· pp. 84-85

Q1 F   Q2 F

Check-Up 🏅

01 give a presentation

02 felt confident

03 went blank

04 ruined my presentation

05 felt so disappointed

06 spent some time working

07 faded away

08 mess up

09 shouldn't worry, about

10 can do better

11 your posture can influence

12 plays a large role

13 decrease your stress

14 walking with, raised

15 Don't you feel

16 highly beneficial

17 easier for them to concentrate

TOPIC 5 A. Preview

나를 그렇게 느끼게 한 것

나는 오늘 영어 수업 중에 발표를 해야 했다. 나는 열심히 연습했으므로, 처음에는 자신감을 느꼈다. 하지만, 내가 학생들 앞에 서자, 머릿속이 하얘졌다. 나는 무엇을 말할지 잊어버리고 나의 발표를 망쳤다. 나는 스스로에게 매우 실망했다.

내가 내 감정에 대처한 방법

집에 온 후에, 나는 내 모형 비행기를 작업하는 데 약간의 시간을 보냈다. 내가 부품들을 조립하는 동안, 그날의 좌절감이 사라졌고, 나 자신에게 느낀 실망감을 잊을 수 있었다.

내가 그 경험으로부터 배운 것

누구나 망칠 수 있다. 또한, 나는 이미 일어난 일에 관해 너무 많이 걱정하지 말아야 한다. 나는 내가 다음번에 더 잘할 수 있다고 확신한다.

Wrap Up B. Read and Discuss

놀랍게도, 당신의 자세가 당신의 마음과 감정에 영향을 줄 수 있다. 사실, 마음과 신체 사이의 관계는 너무 강력해서 당신의 신체 자세가 당신이 생각하고, 느끼고, 행동하는 방식에 큰 역할을 한다. 예를 들어, 똑바로 앉고 서는 것은 당신의 자신감을 높이고 당신의 스트레스를 낮출 것이다. 당신의 가슴을 내밀고 당신의 턱을 든 채로 한번 걸어 보라. 이 자세에서 더 자신감을 느끼지 않는가? 또한, 연구는 좋은 자세가 학생들에게 매우 이로울 수 있다는 것을 보여 주었다. 만약 학생들이 좋은 자세를 지니고 있다면, 그들이 집중하고 좋은 기분으로 있기가 더 쉽다.

내신 1등급 어휘 공략
pp. 86-87

01 ③	02 ③
03 ④	04 ②
05 ②	06 ⑤
07 ④	08 recovery

01 (A) 환자가 병원에 가는 버스 요금을 감당할 수 없었다는 의미가 적절하므로 unable이 알맞다.
(B) 짐바브웨에 정신과 의사가 부족했다는 의미가 문맥에 맞으므로 lack이 알맞다.
(C) 문맥상 '문명(civilization)'보다는 '인구(population)'가 알맞다.

02 ③ respected(존경받는)와 grandmothers라는 호칭은 나이가 많고 경험이 풍부한 여성들을 가리키는 것이므로 young women과는 어울리지 않는다.

03 ④ 우정 벤치 프로그램은 주로 정신 건강 서비스 제공이 목적이므로 physical health보다는 mental health가 알맞다.

04 (A) 맥락상 할머니들과 세션을 완료하는 것은 '의사들(psychiatrists)'이 아니라 '환자들(patients)'이다.

(B) 프로그램의 다음 단계로 지역 사회 지원 그룹에 참여하도록 '권장된다(encouraged)'는 의미가 문맥상 알맞다.
(C) 지원 그룹 구성원들이 서로 쉽게 공감하고 지원할 수 있는 이유로 '비슷한(similar)' 어려움을 경험했다는 것이 논리적이다.

05 (A) 프로그램이 매우 성공적이었는지 묻는 사회자의 말에 동의하는 것이 문맥상 적절하므로 '맞는(correct)'이 알맞다.
(B) 우정 벤치가 20개 이상의 지역에서 '이용 가능하다(available)'는 것은 프로그램의 확장을 나타내므로 적절하다.
(C) 앱을 통한 상담을 제공한다는 것은 '온라인(online)' 서비스를 의미하므로 적절하다.

06 ⑤ 우정 벤치 프로그램은 정신 건강 문제를 다루는 프로그램이고 heal their healthy hearts라는 표현은 모순된다. 이미 건강한 것을 치유할 필요가 없기 때문에 wounded가 알맞다.

07 (A) 정신 건강 문제에 대한 도움을 구하는 것이 '부끄러운(ashamed)' 일이 아니라는 메시지가 자연스럽다.
(B) 어머니의 사망 후 겪는 시간은 '어려운(difficult)' 시기이다.
(C) Moyo 할머니가 사람들의 삶에 긍정적인 변화를 만드는 것을 돕는 경험을 보상적이라고 표현하고 있으므로 'positive(긍정적인)'가 알맞다.

08 '질병이나 부상 후 정상 상태로 돌아가는 것'은 '회복'이므로 recovery가 알맞다.

내신 1등급 어법 공략
pp. 88-89

01 ③	02 ④
03 ⑤	04 ⑤
05 ①	06 ②
07 ③	

08 It is[It's] truly inspiring to see the influence that the Friendship Bench program has had.

01 (A) 환자의 상태를 설명하는 것이므로 depressed가 알맞다.
(B) to부정사의 의미상의 주어는 「for+목적격」으로 나타낸다.
(C) '~할 방법을 찾다'라는 의미가 되어야 하므로 앞의 명사 a way를 수식하는 형용사적 용법의 to부정사가 알맞다.

02 ④ These women은 주어이고, volunteer가 동사이다. grandmothers는 이 여성들을 지칭하는 것으로 '불리는' 것이므로 과거분사 called가 알맞다.

03 ⑤ 선행사(grandmothers)가 사람이므로 who가 알맞다.

04 (A) 「be encouraged to+동사원형(~하도록 권장받다)」의 형태로, to부정사가 알맞다.
(B) 동사 relate와 support를 수식하므로 부사 easily가 알맞다.
(C) '이것은 ~때문이다'라는 의미의 This is because ~ 구문이다.

05 ① provide A with B = provide B to A: A에게 B를 제공하다 / 이 문장은 「provide B to A」 구문이므로 to가 알맞다.

06 (A) grandmothers가 선행사이므로 관계대명사는 who가 알맞다.

(B) Moyo 할머니가 약 8년 동안 계속해서 자원봉사를 해오고 있음을 의미하므로 과거부터 현재까지 계속되고 있는 행동을 나타내는 현재완료 진행형(have been v-ing)이 알맞다.
(C) 전치사 뒤에는 동명사가 오므로 supporting이 알맞다.

07 (A) 문장의 주어 역할을 하므로 동명사 Seeking이 알맞다.
(B) 간접의문문의 어순이므로 「의문사(how) + 주어(it) + 조동사(can) + 동사(make)」의 순서가 알맞다.
(C) 「such(+a(n))(+형용사) + 명사」 구문이 알맞다. so는 형용사나 부사를 수식할 때 사용되므로 여기에는 적절하지 않다.

08 가주어 It과 is truly inspiring을 쓰고 to부정사구를 문장의 뒤로 보낸다.

01 ⑤
02 what inspired you to come up with the program
03 ③   **04** (A) ⓐ, ⓓ (B) ⓑ, ⓒ
05 ③   **06** anxiety
07 ②   **08** ⑤
09 ②
10 we provided about 90,000 patients in Zimbabwe with face-to-face counseling
11 ①   **12** ②
13 ①
14 It is such a rewarding experience to help people make positive changes
15 experience(s)

01 점심 식사 후 도서관에 있을 때 자주 배탈이 난다고 말하는 Lisa에게 남자아이는 식사 직후에 앉아있는 것은 건강에 좋지 않을 수 있으니 식사 후에 산책을 해보는 게 좋을 것 같다고 조언하고 있다. 따라서 ⑤ '식사 후 산책하다'가 정답이다.
   ① 점심을 거르다 ② 더 가벼운 식사를 하다 ③ 도서관을 피하다 ④ 다른 동아리에 가입하다

02 Can you tell us로 질문을 시작하는 공손한 표현이다. what inspired you(무엇이 당신에게 영감을 주었는지)를 쓴다. 여기서 inspire는 과거형으로 써야 한다. to come up with(떠올리다, 생각해내다)를 쓰고 the program으로 마무리한다.

03 Furthermore(게다가)라는 단어는 앞서 언급된 문제에 추가적인 정보를 제공할 때 사용된다. 이는 ③의 앞 문장에서 언급된 일반적인 의료 접근성 문제에 정신과 의사 부족이라는 특정 문제를 추가하는 역할을 하므로 ③의 위치에 오는 것이 문맥상 자연스럽다.

04 전치사 as 뒤에는 주로 명사가 오고, 접속사 as 뒤에는 주어와 동사가 있는 절이 온다.
ⓐ 그녀는 고등학교에서 교사로 일한다.
ⓑ 해가 지자 기온이 떨어지기 시작했다.
ⓒ 그는 행복했던 순간을 떠올리며 미소 지었다.

ⓓ 그들은 피크닉을 위해 오래된 상자를 테이블로 사용했다.

05 Chibanda 박사의 답변이 프로그램의 운영 방식에 대해 설명하고 있으므로 ③ '우정 벤치 프로그램이 어떻게 운영되는지 설명해 주시겠어요?'가 빈칸에 들어갈 질문으로 알맞다.
   ① 당신이 정신과 의사가 되도록 영감을 준 것은 무엇인가요?
② 몇 명의 사람들이 우정 벤치 프로그램을 이용할 수 있나요?
④ 프로그램에서 할머니들은 무엇을 하나요?
⑤ 프로그램에서 '할머니들'을 어떻게 선발하고 훈련하나요?

06 '미래의 사건이나 상황에 대한 걱정이나 두려움의 감정'은 'anxiety(불안)'를 나타낸다.

07 ② 할머니들은 프로그램으로부터(from our program) 선택된 것이 아니라, 프로그램을 위해(for our program) 선택되었다.

08 ⑤ 우정 벤치 프로그램의 '할머니들'은 전문가들이 아니라, 지역 사회에서 선발되어 훈련받은 자원봉사자들이므로 일치하지 않는 내용이다.
① 할머니들은 지역 사회와의 연계성 때문에 선택되었다.
② 할머니들은 뛰어난 경청 능력과 공감 능력을 가지고 있다.
③ 프로그램은 14명의 자원봉사 할머니들로 시작되었다.
④ 지금은 수천 명의 할머니들이 치료를 제공하기 위해 훈련받는다.
⑤ 할머니들은 경험이 있는 유급 전문가들이다.

09 (A) '할머니들과의 세션이 끝났을 때'라는 의미로, 시간을 나타내는 접속사 When이 가장 적절하다.
(B) '이는 대부분이 같은 지역 사회 출신이며 비슷한 어려움을 겪었기 때문이다'라는 의미로, 이유를 나타내는 접속사 because가 가장 적절하다.

10 「provide B to A」와 「provide A with B」는 모두 'A에게 B를 제공하다'라는 의미이다.

11 ① 선행사가 one of the grandmothers로 사람이므로 관계대명사는 who 또는 that이 알맞다.

12 ①, ③, ④, ⑤: ~동안 / ②: ~을 위해
① 우리는 고속도로에서 3시간 동안 운전했다.
② 나는 가난한 아이를 위해 약간의 돈을 기부했다.
③ 그녀는 10년 동안 뉴욕에 살고 있다.
④ 그 음악 축제는 5일 동안 계속되었다.
⑤ 우리는 몇 달 동안 유럽을 여행했다.

13 ① 동사가 문장에서 주어 역할을 하기 위해서는 동명사(Seeking) 형태가 되어야 한다.

14 가주어 It을 사용하여 It is로 문장을 시작한다. to help people make positive changes가 진주어 역할을 한다. 보어 자리에 such a rewarding experience를 쓴다.

15 사회자의 첫 번째 질문에서 경험에 대해 말해 달라고 요청했고 Moyo 할머니는 그에 대한 답을 했다. 이어서 사회자가 마무리하는 말이므로 '경험(experiences)'을 공유해주셔서 감사하다는 말이 오는 것이 자연스럽다.

01 ⑤   **02** ④

03 ③   **04** (A) as (B) for (C) into

05 Could you explain to us how the Friendship Bench program works?

06 ③: paid → free

이유: 우정 벤치 프로그램의 대화 치료 세션은 '무료(free)'이기 때문이다.

07 ②   **08** that → which

09 ③   **10** ⑤

11 a great way to continue the support and build a sense of community

12 ④

13 Can you introduce yourself and tell us how you got involved with the Friendship Bench program?

14 ⑤   **15** ④

01 빈지 워칭의 개념 소개 → 위험성 언급 → 예방 방법 제시 순으로 구성되어 ⑤ '빈지 워칭의 위험성과 그것들을 피하는 방법'이 주제로 가장 적절하다.

① 스트리밍 플랫폼의 이점
② TV 시리즈의 인기
③ 신체 활동의 중요성
④ 최고의 스트리밍 서비스를 선택하는 방법

02 ④ 알람이 울리면 프로그램 중간이라도 시청을 멈추는 것이 중요하다고 말하고 있다.

03 이 글은 Chibanda 박사가 우정 벤치 프로그램을 시작하게 된 배경과 짐바브웨의 정신 건강 관리 상황에 대해 설명하고 있으므로 ③ '많은 짐바브웨 사람들이 전통 음악과 춤을 즐긴다.'는 전체 흐름과 어울리지 않는다.

04 (A) '정신과 의사로서'라는 의미로, Chibanda 박사의 직업적 역할을 나타내고 있으므로 '~로서'라는 의미의 전치사 as가 알맞다.
(B) '오랫동안'이라는 의미의, 시간의 지속을 나타내는 전치사 for가 알맞다.
(C) '정신의학을 지역사회로 가져오다'라는 의미의 「bring A into B」 구문이므로 '~안으로'라는 의미의 into가 알맞다.

05 공손한 표현인 Could you로 문장을 시작하고 동사원형 explain, 이어서 to us를 쓴다. 뒤에는 간접의문문의 어순인 「의문사＋주어＋동사」의 어순으로 써야 하므로 how the Friendship Bench program works를 쓰고 물음표를 붙여 마무리한다.

07 (A) 할머니들이 프로그램에 선택된 이유를 설명하고 있으므로 because가 적절하다.
(B) 할머니들의 자질에 대한 추가적인 설명을 제공하고 있으므로 추가적인 정보나 이유를 제시할 때 사용되는 Moreover가 적절하다.
(C) 초기의 적은 수의 할머니들과 현재의 많은 수를 대조하고 있으므로 대조를 나타내는 접속사 But이 적절하다.

08 관계대명사 that은 계속적 용법으로 쓸 수 없으며 앞 문장 전체를 선행사로 받는 관계대명사는 which이다.

09 (A) made up of는 '~로 구성된'이라는 의미로 앞의 명사 a community support group을 수식하는 과거분사구가 알맞다.
(B) 동사 relate와 support를 수식하므로 부사 easily가 알맞다.
(C) 과거의 경험이 현재까지 영향을 미치고 있음을 나타내므로 현재완료 have experienced가 적절하다.

10 ⑤ This is because most of them come from the same community and have experienced similar struggles.에서 그룹 구성원들은 비슷한 어려움을 경험했다는 것을 알 수 있다.

12 (C) 이 문장은 2022년의 구체적인 통계를 제공하므로 제일 앞에 오는 것이 적절하다.
(A) (C)에 이어 Now라는 단어로 시작하여 현재 상황을 설명하고, 미래의 비전을 제시한다.
(B) We've also started라는 표현은 이전에 언급된 내용에 추가적인 정보를 제공함을 나타낸다. 온라인 상담 앱의 도입은 프로그램의 최신 발전 사항을 보여주며, 논리적으로 마지막에 위치하는 것이 적절하다.

13 Can you introduce yourself and tell us 뒤에는 간접의문문(의문사＋주어＋동사)의 어순이 와야 한다. 이어서 how you got involved with the Friendship Bench program?을 쓴다.

14 ⑤ Moyo 할머니는 정신과 의사가 아니라 자원봉사자로서 우정 벤치 프로그램에 참여하고 있으며 전문적인 의학적 치료가 아닌, 경청과 지지를 통해 지역 사회 구성원들의 정신 건강을 돕고 있다.

15 ④ pass away는 '돌아가시다'라는 의미로 잘못된 해석이다.

01 ②   **02** ③

03 ④   **04** ③

05 ③   **06** ④

07 ②   **08** ⑤

09 ②   **10** ②

11 expanding

12 (1) encouraging → encouraged (2) making → made

13 ②, ④   **14** ③

15 (1) are → is (2) 동명사(구) 주어는 단수 취급하므로 is가 되어야 한다

01 Jake의 조언에 긍정적으로 반응하고 meal plan을 시도해보겠다는 의지를 보여주는 말 ② '좋아. 그걸 시도해 볼게'가 가장 자연스럽다.

① 그건 나에게 너무 복잡하게 들려.
③ 나는 내가 원하는 건 무엇이든 먹는 것을 선호해.
④ 대신 나를 위한 식단 계획을 세워 줄 수 있니?
⑤ 나는 균형 잡힌 식사가 중요하다고 생각하지 않아.

02 ③ 충고의 표현은 I think you should ~.이다.

① 동명사 주어는 단수 취급하므로 helps가 알맞다.
② end up v-ing: 결국 ~하게 되다
④ make＋목적어＋형용사: 목적어를 ~하게 만들다
⑤ try＋to부정사: ~하려고 애쓰다, 노력하다

03 (A) 환자가 심각한 우울증에 걸렸지만 도움을 받지 못했다는 대조적인 상황을 나타내므로 However가 알맞다.
(B) 짐바브웨의 일반적인 상황에 대한 추가 설명이므로 In fact가 알맞다.
(C) 정신과 의사 부족 문제를 추가로 언급하며 상황의 심각성을 더하고 있으므로 Furthermore가 알맞다.

04 환자의 어려움에 대한 깊은 이해와 공감으로 지역사회 기반 정신 건강 프로그램을 시작한 것이므로 ③ 'empathetic(공감하는)'이 가장 적절하다.
⬛ ① 비판적인 ② 무관심한 ④ 전문적인 ⑤ 객관적인

05 ③ 우정 벤치 프로그램은 '할머니'라고 불리는 지역사회 어르신들이 무료 대화 치료를 제공한다.

06 provide B to A = provide A with B (A에게 B를 제공하다)

07 (A) 앞 문장의 내용 전체를 선행사로 받아 부연 설명할 때 사용하는 관계대명사 which가 적절하다.
(B) 선행사가 grandmothers로 사람이므로 관계대명사 who가 적절하다.

08 '목적'을 나타내는 부사적 용법의 to부정사로 ⑤와 쓰임이 같다.
①, ③, ④는 목적어 역할을 하는 명사적 용법의 to부정사이고, ②는 명사 a book을 수식하는 형용사적 용법의 to부정사이다.
① Katie는 세계 여행을 하고 싶어 한다.
② 나는 휴가 동안 읽을 책이 필요하다.
③ 나의 형은 대학에서 공학을 공부할 계획이다.
④ 우리는 그 프로젝트에 참여하기로 동의했다.
⑤ Lucy는 성적을 향상시키기 위해 열심히 공부한다.

09 이 글은 전체에 걸쳐 '우리의 자세가 정신적, 감정적 상태에 어떻게 영향을 미치는지'를 말하고 있으므로 ②가 정답이다.

10 이 글은 자세가 마음과 감정에 미치는 영향에 대해 설명하고 있다. 문맥상 올바른 자세가 긍정적인 영향을 준다는 내용이므로, ② 'nervousness(긴장, 불안)'라는 단어는 적절하지 않고 'confidence(자신감)'가 알맞은 단어이다.

11 '크기, 부피, 또는 범위가 증가하다; 퍼지거나 더 커지다'는 'expand (확대[확장]하다)'의 의미이다. 빈칸에는 started의 목적어가 필요하므로 expanding이 알맞다.

12 (1) 환자들이 '격려되는' 것이므로, 과거분사 형태인 encouraged가 올바른 표현이다.
(2) 지원 그룹이 '만들어진' 것이므로, 과거분사 형태인 made가 올바른 표현이다.

13 Moyo 할머니의 가족 관계와 프로그램을 알게 된 시점은 언급되어 있지 않으므로 ②, ④가 정답이다.
① 나이는 76세이다.
③ 프로그램에 참여한 이유는 지역 사회에서 정신 건강 문제로 어려움을 겪고 있는 사람들을 돕고 싶어서이다.
⑤ 약 8년 동안 자원봉사를 해왔다.

14 (A) 선행사 one of the grandmothers가 단수이므로, 동사도 단수 형태 volunteers가 알맞다.
(B) 현재완료 진행형이므로 have been 뒤에 현재분사형

volunteering이 알맞다.
(C) 상처받은 마음을 의미하므로 '상처를 입은'이라는 뜻의 과거분사 wounded가 알맞다.

15 동명사(구) 주어는 단수 취급하므로 are가 아니라 is가 되어야 한다. 앞에 있는 명사 problems를 보고 are를 쓰지 않도록 주의한다.

내신 1등급 수능형 고난도

pp. 102-105

01 ①	02 ②
03 ②	04 ③
05 ②	06 ③
07 ④	08 ②
09 ⑤	10 ②
11 ④	12 ①
13 ③	14 ③
15 ④	

[01-02] 해석

진행자: 오늘 방송에서는 짐바브웨의 특별한 공원 벤치인 우정 벤치에 대해 알아보겠습니다. 두 분의 귀한 손님을 모셨습니다. 먼저 우정 벤치 프로그램의 창립자인 Dixon Chibanda 박사님을 환영합니다. 이 프로그램을 만들게 된 계기를 말씀해 주시겠습니까?

Chibanda 박사: 물론입니다. 이 아이디어는 제가 정신과 의사로 일하면서 겪은 경험에서 비롯되었습니다. 제 환자 중 한 명이 심각한 우울증에 빠졌지만 병원까지 가는 버스 요금을 감당할 수 없어 도움을 받지 못했습니다. 이런 문제를 전에는 생각해 본 적이 없어서 이 사실을 알게 되었을 때 충격을 받았습니다. 짐바브웨의 많은 사람들이 교통비를 내고 의료 서비스를 받는 데 어려움을 겪고 있습니다. 게다가 오랫동안 국내 정신과 의사가 부족했습니다. 2006년 우정 벤치 프로그램이 시작되었을 때, 1200만 명이 넘는 짐바브웨 인구를 위해 단 11명의 정신과 의사만 있었습니다. 저는 정신과 치료를 지역사회로 가져와야 한다는 것을 알았습니다.

01 ① 앞에 있는 special park benches in Zimbabwe를 수식하는 과거분사 'known(알려진)'이 적절하다.

02 많은 사람들이 교통비 부담으로 병원에 갈 수 없었고, 짐바브웨의 정신과 의사 부족 문제를 해결하기 위해, Chibanda 박사는 정신 건강 지원을 제공할 방법으로 프로그램을 시작했으므로 ②가 정답이다.

[03-04] 해석

진행자: 아, 그렇게 시작되었군요. 우정 벤치 프로그램이 어떻게 운영되는지 설명해 주시겠습니까?

Chibanda 박사: 물론입니다. 이 프로그램은 접근하기 쉬운 정신 건강 관리를 제공하기 위해 설계되었습니다. 우울증이나 불안과 같은 어려움을 겪고 있는 사람들에게 무료 대화 치료 세션을 제공합니다. 이 세션들은 지역사회에서 존경받는 연세 드신 여성분들, 일명 '할머니들'이 이끕니다. 이분들은 벤치에서 환자들과 함께 앉아 그들의 이야기를 듣고 정서적 지지를 제공하는 자원봉사를 합니다.

03 지역 사회의 노인 여성들을 활용하여 정신 건강 문제를 겪는 사람들에게 무료 상담을 제공하는 ② '짐바브웨에서 비용 효율적인 정신 건강 중재'가 주제로 적절하다.

　　① 아프리카 공동체에서 노년 여성들의 역할
③ 개발도상국에서 정신 건강 치료를 제공하는 데에 따른 어려움
④ 우울증에 대한 전문 치료의 중요성
⑤ 정신 질환 치료에서의 문화적 차이

04 우정 벤치 프로그램은 접근 가능한 정신 건강 관리를 제공하기 위해 설계되었다. 이 프로그램은 우울증이나 불안과 같은 문제에 직면한 사람들을 위해 ③ '무료 상담 치료 세션'을 제공한다고 하는 것이 가장 자연스럽다.

　　① 약물 치료와 임상 치료
② 재정 지원과 직업 훈련
④ 신체 운동과 영양 조언
⑤ 종교 상담과 영적 지도

[05-06] 해석

> 진행자: 정말 환상적인 아이디어네요! 이 놀라운 할머니들은 어떻게 프로그램에 참여하게 되셨나요?
>
> Chibanda 박사: 할머니들은 지역사회와 강한 유대관계를 가지고 있기 때문에 우리 프로그램에 선택되었습니다. 그들은 뛰어난 경청 능력, 공감 능력, 의미 있는 대화를 나눌 수 있는 능력 등 상담사의 필수적인 자질을 갖추고 있습니다. 많은 할머니들이 여가 시간에 정원 가꾸기를 즐기시는데, 이는 그들의 휴식에 도움이 됩니다. 또한 그들은 매우 신뢰할 수 있는 분들이어서 정신 건강을 지원하는 우리의 노력에 중요합니다. 처음에는 단 14명의 자원봉사 할머니들로 시작했지만, 지금은 짐바브웨 전역에서 수천 명의 할머니들이 우정 벤치 치료를 제공할 수 있도록 훈련받았습니다.

05 할머니들의 정원 가꾸기 취미는 우정 벤치 프로그램의 운영이나 효과와 직접적인 관련이 없다. 이는 프로그램의 목적이나 할머니들의 역할을 설명하는 데 불필요한 정보이므로 ②가 정답이다.

06 (A) get involved in은 '~에 관여하다', '~에 참여하다'라는 뜻이다.
(B) 앞 문장 전체를 선행사로 받는 관계대명사는 which이다.
(C) 문맥상 할머니들이 훈련을 받은 것이므로 현재완료 수동태 have been trained가 알맞다.

[07-08] 해석

> 진행자: 흥미롭네요! 환자들이 할머니들과의 세션을 마친 후에는 어떤 일이 일어나나요?
>
> Chibanda 박사: 할머니들과의 세션이 끝난 후, 환자들은 프로그램의 이전 참가자들로 구성된 지역사회 지원 그룹에 참여하도록 권장됩니다. 이 그룹의 구성원들은 보통 같은 지역사회 출신이고 비슷한 어려움을 겪었기 때문에 서로 쉽게 연결되고 지원할 수 있습니다.

07 (A) 환자들이 할머니들과의 세션을 마친 후에 무슨 일이 일어나는지 묻는 것이 자연스러우므로 finish가 알맞다.
(B) 세션이 끝난 후 환자들이 지원 그룹에 참여하는 내용이므로 patients가 알맞다.
(C) 지원 그룹의 구성원들이 비슷한 어려움을 경험했다는 점을 강조하므로 similar가 알맞다.

08 (A) 우정 벤치 프로그램에서 할머니들과의 세션이 끝난 후의 시점을 나타내므로 When이 알맞다.
(B) former participants를 수식하는 관계대명사 who가 알맞다.
(C) 지원 그룹이 참가자들의 연결과 상호 지원을 가능하게 한다는 의미이므로 분사 enabling이 알맞다.

[09-10] 해석

> 진행자: 지원을 지속하고 공동체 의식을 조성하는 훌륭한 방법 같습니다. 프로그램이 매우 성공적이었군요, 그렇죠?
>
> Chibanda 박사: 그렇습니다. 2022년에 우리는 짐바브웨에서 약 90,000명의 환자들에게 대면 상담을 제공했습니다. 현재 우정 벤치는 전국 20개 이상의 지역에 위치해 있습니다. 우리의 목표는 모든 사람이 걸어갈 수 있는 거리 내에 우정 벤치를 갖는 것이며, 우리는 그 목표를 향해 열심히 노력하고 있습니다. 또한 프로그램을 확장하기 시작했고 이제는 앱을 통한 온라인 상담도 제공하고 있어 더 많은 사람들에게 다가갈 수 있게 되었습니다.

09 ⑤ 「allow A to B(A가 B하도록 허락하다)」 구문으로 to reach가 알맞다.

10 ② 우정 벤치는 짐바브웨의 20개 이상의 지역에 위치해 있으므로 일치하지 않는다.

[11-12] 해석

> 진행자: 정말 놀라운 일이군요! 시간 내주셔서 감사합니다, Chibanda 박사님. 이제 프로그램에서 자원봉사를 하시는 할머니 한 분의 이야기를 들어보겠습니다. 자기소개와 함께 우정 벤치 프로그램에 어떻게 참여하게 되셨는지 말씀해 주시겠습니까?
>
> Moyo 할머니: 안녕하세요, 제 이름은 Judith Moyo입니다만, 모두들 저를 Moyo 할머니라고 부릅니다. 저는 76세이고, 우정 벤치 프로그램에서 약 8년 동안 자원봉사를 해왔습니다. 제가 이 프로그램에 참여하게 된 이유는 우리 지역사회의 많은 사람들이 정신 건강 문제에 직면해 있고, 저는 무언가 행동을 취하고 싶었기 때문입니다. 제가 지원을 제공함으로써 그들의 상처받은 마음을 치유하는 데 도움을 줄 수 있다고 느꼈습니다.

11 Moyo 할머니의 답변이 자기 소개를 하고 있으므로 ④ '자기소개를 하다'가 빈칸에 들어갈 말로 가장 적절하다.

　　① 당신의 이야기를 우리에게 들려주다
② 당신의 역할을 설명해주다
③ 당신의 경험을 설명해주다
⑤ 당신의 배경을 설명해주다

12 Moyo 할머니는 지역 사회의 정신 건강 문제를 해결하기 위해서 우정 벤치 프로그램에 자원봉사자로 참여하게 되었다고 말하고 있으므로 ①이 일치하는 내용이다.

　　② 우정 벤치 프로그램은 70세 이상의 자원봉사자만을 받아들인다.
③ Moyo 할머니는 8년 동안 전문 치료사로 일해 왔다.
④ 우정 벤치 프로그램은 자원봉사자들에게 높은 급여를 지급한다.
⑤ Moyo 할머니는 개인적 발전을 위해 새로운 기술을 배우고자 프로그램에 참여했다.

진행자: 정말 친절하시군요. 우정 벤치 프로그램에 참여하신 할머니로 서의 경험을 나눠주시겠습니까?

Moyo 할머니: 정말 놀라운 경험이었습니다. 정신 건강 문제로 도움을 구하는 것에는 부끄러움이 없습니다. 저는 이 프로그램이 사람들의 삶에 미치는 긍정적인 영향을 직접 목격했습니다. 제 환자 중 한 명인 19세 소녀는 어머니가 돌아가신 후 힘든 시기를 겪었습니다. 저는 그녀를 상담하고 회복의 여정을 시작하도록 도왔습니다. 지금은 그녀의 삶이 정상 궤도에 올랐고, 심지어 자신의 사업도 시작했습니다! 이런 이야기들은 제가 이 프로그램의 일원이라는 것에 자부심을 느끼게 합니다. 사람들이 삶에서 긍정적인 변화를 만들도록 돕는 것은 정말 보람 있는 경험입니다.

진행자: 오늘 경험을 나눠주셔서 감사합니다, Moyo 할머니. 우정 벤치 프로그램이 미친 영향을 보니 정말 감동적입니다. 그리고 이 모든 것은 할머니와 Chibanda 박사님 같은 분들의 노고 덕분입니다.

13 소녀의 어려움 → 상담 및 회복 시작 → 현재의 긍정적인 결과로 이어지는 시간적 흐름이다. 주어진 문장의 her는 앞에 나온 a nineteen-year-old girl을 가리킨다.

14 ③ was born은 문맥상 적절하지 않다. 19세 소녀가 어려움을 겪게 된 것은 어머니가 태어난(was born) 후가 아니라, 어머니가 돌아가신(passed away) 후일 것이다.

15 사회자가 It's truly inspiring to see the impact that the Friendship Bench program has had.라고 말한 것으로 보아, Moyo 할머니가 프로그램의 실제 영향을 보여주는 경험을 공유했음을 알 수 있다. 따라서 ④ 'experiences(경험들)'가 빈칸에 알맞다.
　① 감정들 ② 생각들 ③ 의견들 ⑤ 지식

내신 1등급 서술형

pp. 106-108

01 needed to find a way to bring
02 (1) depressed (2) population
03 it is difficult, to pay for transportation and receive medical treatment
04 help, transportation, lack
05 Could you explain to us how the Friendship Bench program works?
06 (A) happen (B) expanding/to expand (C) (to) reach
07 (1) ⓑ: were chosen → 할머니들이 선정된 것이기 때문에 수동태 were chosen으로 써야 한다.
(2) ⓔ: who → 선행사가 grandmothers로 사람이므로 관계대명사 who를 써야 한다.
08 therapy **09** who volunteers for
10 (1) Judith Moyo (2) 76세 (3) (약) 8년
(4) 지역사회의 많은 사람들이 정신 건강 문제로 어려움을 겪고 있어서 그들을 돕고 싶었기 때문에
11 Seeking, is, of **12** like

01 시제는 과거형 needed가 되어야 하고 need는 to부정사를 목적어로 취한다. 이어서 a way를 쓰고 명사를 수식하는 형용사적 용법의 to부정사를 쓴다.
Q: 우정 벤치 프로그램을 개발하는 데 있어 당신의 주요 목표는 무엇이었습니까?
A: 저는 정신의학을 지역 사회에 도입할 방법을 찾아야 했습니다.

02 (1) '매우 슬프거나 절망적인 감정을 느끼는'은 'depressed(우울한)'에 대한 설명이다.
(2) '특정 지역이나 영역에 살고 있는 전체 사람의 수'는 'population(인구)'에 대한 설명이다.

03 it is difficult로 문장을 시작한다. 의미상의 주어 '짐바브웨의 많은 사람들(for many people in Zimbabwe)' 뒤에 진주어인 to부정사 to pay for transportation and receive medical treatment를 이어서 쓴다.

04 Chibanda 박사는 짐바브웨에서 교통비와 정신과 의사의 부족으로 인해 심각한 우울증에 대한 도움을 받을 수 없었던 환자를 목격한 후 우정 벤치 프로그램을 시작했다.

05 Could you explain to us?와 How does the Friendship Bench program work?를 한 문장으로 만들 때 간접의문문의 어순 「의문사+주어+동사」에 따라 써야 한다.

06 (A) 사역동사 make는 목적격보어로 동사원형을 취하므로 happen이 알맞다.
(B) start는 목적어로 동명사와 to부정사를 모두 취할 수 있으므로 expanding과 to expand가 모두 올 수 있다.
(C) help는 준사역동사로 reach나 to reach가 모두 올 수 있다.

08 '의학적 또는 정신 건강 문제를 완화하거나 치유하는 것을 목표로 하는 치료'는 'therapy(치료)'에 해당하는 영어 뜻풀이다.

09 빈칸에 들어갈 말은 앞에 있는 the grandmothers를 수식하는 구조가 되어야 한다. 따라서 앞에 있는 명사를 수식하는 주격 관계대명사절이 알맞다. 동사는 단수 형태인 volunteers로 쓴다는 점에 주의한다.

10 (1) my name is Judith Moyo에서 이름을 알 수 있다.
(2) I'm 76 years old에서 나이를 알 수 있다.
(3) I have been volunteering for the Friendship Bench program for about eight years에서 봉사 기간을 알 수 있다.
(4) I joined the program because many people in my community struggle with mental health problems, and I wanted to do something about it. I knew that I could help heal their wounded hearts by supporting them.에서 가입 이유를 알 수 있다.

11 동사가 주어 역할을 해야 하므로 Seeking이 알맞다. 동명사(구) 주어는 단수 취급하므로 is가 알맞다. be ashamed of는 '~을 부끄러워하다'라는 뜻으로 전치사를 빠뜨리지 않도록 주의한다.

12 빈칸에 공통으로 들어갈 단어는 '~처럼, ~같은'이라는 의미의 전치사 like이다.

최종 점검 **중간고사** pp. 109~114

01 ②   **02** ⑤

03 ④

04 to start the semester by pushing ourselves out of our comfort zones and learning more about ourselves

05 ②   **06** ③

07 ②

08 (A) comfortable   (B) excitement

09 Being in the water wasn't as bad as

10 ③   **11** ③

12 ③   **13** ②

14 depression, transportation, shortage, mental

15 (1) ©: wanting → want / make는 목적격보어로 동사원형이 와야 한다.

  (2) ⓔ: thanking → to thank / 「가주어 it, 진주어 to부정사」 구문으로 to부정사 형태가 와야 한다.

16 ④

17 존경받는 지역사회의 할머니들을 활용하여 무료로 접근 가능한 정신건강 서비스를 제공하는 혁신적인 방법

18 ②   **19** ③

20 ①   **21** ①

22 ②

23 Can you introduce yourself and tell us how you got involved with the Friendship Bench program?

24 are → is

25 It is such a rewarding experience to help people make positive changes

---

01 '문제나 어려움을 성공적으로 처리하거나 극복하다'는 'overcome (극복하다)'의 정의이므로 ②가 정답이다.
① 그녀는 그것이 너무 어렵지 않다고 나를 안심시켰다.
② 나는 이 불편함을 극복하려고 노력하기로 결심했다.
③ 나를 방해할 것이 아무것도 없었다!
④ 우리는 삶에 대한 다양한 관점을 얻었다.
⑤ 그녀는 병원까지 가는 버스 요금을 감당할 수 없었다.

02 과도한 연속 시청(binge-watching)의 개념을 소개하고, 이러한 시청 습관의 부정적인 영향(수면 문제, 신체 활동 감소)을 언급한 후 건강에 미치는 영향을 예방하기 위한 구체적인 팁들을 제시하고 있으므로 이 담화의 주제로 알맞은 것은 ⑤이다.

03 ④ The important part was 다음에는 보어 역할을 하는 동명사 (v-ing) 형태가 와야 하므로 trying이 알맞다.
  ① '~하기 위해서'라는 목적을 나타내는 부사적 용법의 to부정사로 알맞다.
② 서수 first 앞에는 정관사 the가 필요하므로 알맞다.
③ we의 재귀대명사 ourselves가 알맞다.
⑤ '~할 때'라는 의미의 부사절 접속사 when이 알맞다.

04 전치사 by 뒤에 동명사형을 써야 한다는 것과 접속사 and 뒤에 오는 동사도 동명사형을 써야 한다는 것에 주의한다.

05 혼자 영화관에 있는 것에서 오는 처음의 어색함과 외로움을 경험한 후, 영화에 몰입하게 되는 변화를 강조하고 있기 때문에 ② '어색하고 외로운'이 적절하다.
  ① 흥미진진하고 스릴 넘치는 ③ 익숙하고 지루한 ④ 편안하고 휴식을 취하게 하는 ⑤ 실망스럽고 좌절감을 주는

06 (A) 문장의 주어 역할이므로 Going이 적절하다.
(B) 앞에 선행사(a historical drama)가 있으므로 관계대명사 that이 적절하다.
(C) 사역동사 made의 목적격보어 자리에는 동사원형이 와야 하므로 realize가 적절하다.

07 ⓑ came across는 '~을 우연히 발견했다'라는 의미이다.

08 (A) felt의 보어이므로 형용사 comfortable이 알맞다.
(B) 전치사 뒤이므로 excite의 명사형 excitement가 알맞다.

09 제시된 단어와 「as+원급+as」 구문을 이용하되 be동사가 주어 역할을 해야 하므로 Being을 쓰는 것에 주의한다. 시제는 과거형을 쓴다.

10 필자는 새로운 헤어스타일 도전을 통해 자신감을 얻고 긍정적인 반응을 경험하며 만족감을 느꼈다. 또한, 새로운 것을 시도하는 것의 중요성을 깨닫고 계속해서 배우고 성장하는 것에 대한 흥미를 표현하고 있으므로 ③ 'content(만족한)'가 적절하다.
  ① 화난 ② 좌절한 ④ 무관심한 ⑤ 실망한

11 ③ 필자가 자신의 '안전지대(comfort zone)'를 벗어나 새로운 것을 시도했다는 의미가 문맥상 자연스러우므로 ©는 discomfort가 아니라 comfort가 되어야 한다.
  ⓐ attention은 '주목'을 끌고 싶지 않다는 맥락에 적절하다.
ⓑ positive는 학급 친구들이 놀라기는 했지만 반응은 '긍정적'이었으므로 적절하다.
ⓓ assignment는 '과제'라는 의미로 적절하다.
ⓔ challenges는 더 많은 '도전'을 설정한다는 맥락에 적절하다.

12 ③ 급우들이 놀라기는 했지만 반응은 전반적으로 긍정적이었다고 했으므로 글의 내용과 일치하지 않는다.

13 (A) However는 환자가 우울증이 심했지만 도움을 받지 못했다는 상황을 나타내는 데 적합하다.
(B) In fact는 짐바브웨의 일반적인 상황에 대한 추가 설명을 도입하는 데 적절하다.
(C) Furthermore는 정신과 의사 부족이라는 또 다른 문제점을 추가로 언급하는 데 적합하다.

14 Chibanda 박사는 심각한 우울증을 앓고 있는 환자가 교통비를 감당할 수 없어 도움을 받지 못하는 것을 목격한 후 우정 벤치 프로그램을 시작했다. 그는 또한 짐바브웨의 정신과 의사 부족을 인식하고, 이로 인해 더 접근하기 쉬운 정신 건강 지원 시스템을 만들도록 동기부여를 받았다.

16 이 문장은 할머니들의 다른 자질들(뛰어난 경청 능력, 공감 능력, 의미 있는 대화를 나눌 수 있는 능력)을 언급한 문장 다음인 ④의 위치에 오는 것이 가장 적절하다.

18 세 빈칸 모두 '지역사회, 공동체'를 의미하는 community가 적절하다.

20

19 (B)는 2022년의 실적을 언급하며 프로그램의 성공을 보여준다. – (A)는 현재 프로그램의 확장 상황과 미래 비전을 설명한다. – (C)는 온라인 상담 앱을 통한 추가적인 확장을 언급하며 가장 최근의 발전 사항을 보여준다.

20 ① In 2022, we provided face-to-face counseling to about 90,000 patients in Zimbabwe.로 보아 일치하는 내용이다.

▬▬ ② 언급되지 않은 내용이다.

③ 20개 이상의 지역에서 이용 가능하다고 했으므로 틀린 내용이다.

④ 온라인 상담 앱이 더 많은 사람들에게 도달하는 데 도움이 되었다고 했으므로 틀린 내용이다.

⑤ 지원 그룹의 구성원들은 대부분 같은 지역 출신이며 비슷한 어려움을 겪었다고 했으므로 틀린 내용이다.

21 Marco가 상대방의 제안을 따르고 두려움을 극복하기 위한 첫 걸음을 내딛을 의향이 있음을 보여주는 응답 ① '좋아. 한번 해볼게.'가 빈칸에 알맞다.

▬▬ ② 나는 그걸 할 수 없을 것 같아.

③ 그것이 나에게 효과가 있을지 잘 모르겠어.

④ 나는 그냥 발표를 건너뛰고 싶어.

⑤ 그건 시간 낭비처럼 들려.

22 (A) 선행사가 one of the grandmothers이므로 who가 적절하다.

(B) 현재완료 진행형이므로 volunteering이 적절하다.

(C) want는 to부정사를 목적어로 취하는 동사이므로 to do가 적절하다.

23 간접의문문인 「의문사+주어+동사」의 어순이 되어야 한다.

24 동명사구(Seeking help for mental health problems) 주어는 단수 취급하므로 is가 알맞다.

25 가주어 It을 사용하여 It is로 문장을 시작한다. to help people make positive changes가 진주어 역할을 한다. such a rewarding experience가 보어 역할을 한다.

교과서 **어휘 익히기** ·················· pp. 118-119

STEP 1

01 나뭇가지	25 nest
02 도시의	26 produce
03 전략	27 environment
04 협박, 위협	28 drought
05 고마워하다	29 consumption
06 배출; 배출물, 배기가스	30 decline
07 포함하다	31 ambitious
08 상호적인; 대화형의	32 species
09 목적	33 indicate
10 현상	34 specific
11 예기치 않은, 예상 밖의	35 damage
12 기능	36 separate
13 인기	37 sustainable
14 게다가	38 collective
15 총액, 양	39 millennium
16 의회	40 oxygen
17 퍼지다	41 predict
18 지역적으로	42 measure
19 추적 관찰하다	43 meanwhile
20 A에게 B를 제공하다	44 greenhouse gas
21 그 결과	45 take a deep breath
22 ~에서 벗어나다	46 believe it or not
23 ~와 상호작용하다	47 lead to
24 ~할 희망이 거의 없다	48 set a goal

STEP 2

A 01 courageous   02 nervous
   03 humorous   04 unexpected
   05 unusual
B 01 threat   02 set
C 01 ©   02 ⓐ   03 ⓑ

교과서 **핵심 대화문** ·················· pp. 120-121

Function 1 동의나 이의 여부 묻기
Check-Up ✓ ②
Function 2 확실성 정도 표현하기
Check-Up ✓ ④

교과서 **기타 대화문** ·················· p. 122

Q1 F	Q2 T	Q3 T

TOPIC 1 **C. Listen and Interact**

W 자연의 모든 것은 연결되어 있으며, 우리는 자연의 일부이다. 따라서 우리의 행동은 우리 주변 환경에 직접적인 영향을 미칠 수 있다. 그렇다면 우리는 어떻게 지구를 보호하는 데 도움이 될 수 있을까? 재활용, 나무 심기, 전기 사용 줄이기와 같은 간단한 방법들이 많이 있다. 제품을 덜 구매하는 것도 환경을 돕는 매우 효과적인 방법이 될 수 있다. 이는 제품을 만드는 데 많은 물이 필요하기 때문이다. 뿐만 아니라, 제품 생산 과정에서 온실가스가 방출된다. 게다가 너무 많은 제품을 구매하면 많은 가정 쓰레기를 발생시킬 것이다. 따라서 다음 번 쇼핑을 할 때는 구매하기 전에 그 물건이 정말 필요한지 고려해보아라. 결국, 지구를 보호하는 것은 당신으로부터 시작된다!

TOPIC 4 **B. While You View**

M 1979년, Jadav Payeng이라는 젊은 인도 남성이 고향 근처의 모래 땅을 발견했다. 그곳은 한때 나무와 야생동물로 가득 차 있었다. 그러나 숲이 파괴되고 심각한 홍수가 발생하면서 땅이 황폐해지기 시작했다. Payeng은 뭔가 해야 한다는 것을 알았다.
그래서 그는 하루에 한 그루의 나무를 심기 시작했다. 처음에는 땅이 매우 천천히 변했다. 그러나 그는 노력을 계속했고, 곧 나무들이 스스로 번식하기 시작했다. 40년이 넘게 지난 지금, 한때 모래로 가득했던 그 땅은 울창한 숲이 되었다. 사실, 그 숲은 뉴욕의 센트럴 파크보다 거의 두 배나 큰 면적을 자랑한다. Payeng은 이제 '인도의 포레스트 맨'으로 알려져 있다. 사람들은 이 숲을 Jadav의 별명 중 하나인 '몰라이'라고 부른다.
몰라이 숲은 지금 다양한 식물과 동물 종의 서식지가 되었다. 포레스트 맨은 나무 심기를 계속할 계획이다.

Wrap Up **A. Listen and Post**

M: 요즘 날씨가 정말 이상해요. 그렇지 않나요?
W: 네, 맞아요. 베니스가 해수면 상승 때문에 홍수로 고생하고 있다는 소식을 들었어요.
M: 그것 참 안타깝네요. 그게 기후 변화 때문인가요?
W: 네, 맞아요. 지구상의 모든 것은 연결되어 있어요. 그래서 극지방의 얼음이 녹으면, 베니스처럼 해수면이 낮은 도시들이 홍수를 겪을 수 있어요.
M: 나는 해안 근처에 있는 다른 도시들도 홍수를 겪을까 걱정이에요.
W: 나도 그래요. 이것은 모두에게 영향을 미치는 전 세계적인 문제예요. 그래서 우리는 모두 함께 그것을 해결해야 해요.

교과서 **핵심 대화문 익히기** ·················· p. 123

01 ①	02 ④

03 I'm sure that we can make the world a better place.

교과서 핵심 문법 ························· pp. 124-127

POINT 1 Without 가정법

> **Q 1** fail   **2** have won   **3** Without   **4** were not
>
> **Check-Up** ✿
>
> **01** (1) If it were not for (2) If it were not for
>   (3) If it had not been for
> **02** (1) But for (2) If it were not for
> **03** (1) couldn't complete (2) would have made
> **04** (1) Without (2) would, be

01 주절의 동사 형태로 가정법 과거와 과거완료를 구분할 수 있다.
  (1), (2)는 가정법 과거이고, (3)은 가정법 과거완료이다.
  (1) 물이 없다면, 지구상의 모든 생명체는 죽을 것이다.
  (2) 현대 기술이 없다면, 삶이 훨씬 힘들 것이다.
  (3) GPS가 없었더라면, 우리는 여행 중 길을 잃었을 것이다.

02 「Without ~+가정법 과거」 문장은 현재 사실에 대한 가정으로 「If it were not for[But for] ~+가정법 과거」로 바꿔 쓸 수 있다.

03 (1) 현재 사실에 대한 가정이므로 「Without ~, 주어+조동사의 과거형+동사원형」 형태의 문장이 되어야 하므로 couldn't complete가 알맞다.
  (2) 과거 사실에 대한 가정이므로 「Without ~, 주어+조동사의 과거형+have+p.p.」 형태의 문장이 되어야 하므로 would have made가 알맞다.

04
> 제5회 추계 소설 박람회 / 10월 25~28일
>   재미있고 영감을 주는 이야기들이 없다면, 삶은 다소 따분할 것입니다. 우리가 TV와 영화를 통해 이야기들을 경험할 수 있는 것은 사실입니다. 하지만, 소설들이 우리의 마음과 영혼에 미치는 영향을 아무것도 대신할 수 없습니다. 소설이 없다면, 세상은 확실히 상상력이 덜 풍부한 곳이 될 것입니다. 그러니 이번 달에는, 소설 한 권을 집어 들 것을 기억하세요!

  (1) If it were not for는 Without이나 But for로 바꿔 쓸 수 있다.
  (2) 해석으로 보아 현재 사실에 대한 가정이므로 가정법 과거이다. 따라서 would와 be가 알맞다.

POINT 2 명사절을 이끄는 접속사 that

> **Q 1** 목적어   **2** 주어   **3** 목적어   **4** 목적어   **5** 보어
>
> **Check-Up** ✿
>
> **01** ④
> **02** (1) I believe that hard work leads to success.
>   (2) It is clear that climate change is affecting our planet.
> **03** ②   **04** that

01 〈보기〉에 쓰인 that은 명사절을 이끄는 접속사 that이다. ④는 목적격 관계대명사 that이고, 나머지는 모두 명사절을 이끄는 접속사 that이다.

02 (1) '나는 ~을 믿는다'는 I believe that ~으로 표현한다.
  (2) 주어가 긴 경우이므로 가주어 It을 쓰고 that절을 뒤로 보낸다.

03 ⓐ, ⓒ: 목적어 역할 ⓑ, ⓔ: 주어 역할 ⓓ: 보어 역할

04
> Royal Hotel에 오신 것을 환영하며, 저희를 선택해 주신 것에 감사드립니다! 저희는 무료 와이파이 접속, 비즈니스 센터, 실내 수영장 등을 제공합니다. 저희는 당신의 즐거운 투숙을 위해 당신이 필요로 하는 모든 것을 갖고 있다고 생각합니다. 저희 직원은 당신을 어느 때나 도울 준비가 되어 있으니 저희에게 저희가 무엇을 할 수 있는지 알려 주세요. 저희는 당신이 이곳에서 멋진 경험을 하시기를 바랍니다!
> 진심으로,
> Mark Richard
> 총지배인 드림

목적어 역할을 하는 명사절을 이끄는 접속사 that이 빈칸에 공통으로 알맞다.

교과서 본문 익히기 ❶ ························· pp. 134-136

01 take a deep breath
02 wouldn't be able to get
03 I noticed that
04 to the environment
05 Believe it or not
06 a response to
07 This drought lasted
08 a state of declining health
09 was decreasing
10 also known as
11 urban environments
12 Higher temperatures
13 lead to a rise
14 energy consumption
15 deal with the loss
16 the city government
17 set the ambitious goal
18 involved the creation of
19 interactive map shows
20 had a specific purpose
21 inform council workers
22 something unexpected
23 started receiving
24 expressing appreciation
25 how your branches hang
26 started sending messages
27 was inspired to write
28 by a great distance
29 stay healthy and strong
30 reminds us that
31 Without, would have
32 building an environmentally friendly
33 volunteered to measure
34 has remained on track
35 engage in outdoor activities
36 happier and healthier

01 Whenever	02 air
03 Without	04 that
05 of	06 that
07 receive	08 possible
09 sending	10 begins
11 lasted	12 declining
13 was	14 provided
15 because	16 Higher
17 rise	18 increasing
19 be done	20 its
21 more than	22 online
23 every	24 to indicate
25 its	26 specific
27 poor	28 something unexpected
29 many	30 expressing
31 low	32 quickly
33 inspired	34 Although
35 healthy	36 building
37 Without	38 environmentally
39 monitor	40 increase
41 keep	42 to interact
43 happier	

01 Whenever	02 that
03 wouldn't	04 with
05 or	06 begins
07 to	08 percent
09 was	10 known
11 loss	12 as
13 also	14 increasing
15 be done	16 its
17 more	18 called
19 location	20 to indicate
21 send	22 were damaged
23 something unexpected	24 many
25 expressing	26 to hug
27 quickly	28 are separated
29 that	30 Without
31 building	32 by
33 (to) keep	34 to interact
35 healthier	

Q1 T   **Q2** F
Check-Up ✿

01 most common items	02 make up
03 more than	04 as common, as
05 seven percent of ocean waste	
06 the least common	07 a wide variety of
08 plants are grown	09 pleasant to look at
10 many other benefits	11 by reducing
12 keep surrounding areas cool	13 contribute to
14 provide shelter and food	
15 remind us of our connection	16 we must protect nature

TOPIC 5 A. Preview

위 그래프는 세계의 해양을 오염시키는 여덟 가지의 가장 흔한 품목들을 보여 준다. 비닐봉지가 가장 흔한 폐기물 품목이며 해양 쓰레기의 약 14퍼센트를 차지한다. 플라스틱 병은 해양 쓰레기의 10퍼센트를 넘게 차지하며 두 번째로 가장 흔한 폐기물 품목이다. 포장지는 세계의 해양에서 거의 식품 용기만큼 흔하다. 낚시용품은 플라스틱 뚜껑과 유리병보다 약간 더 많은, 해양 쓰레기의 7퍼센트를 넘게 차지한다. 음료수 캔은 열거된 품목들 중에서 가장 덜 흔하다. 이 그래프로부터, 우리는 인간이 만든 매우 다양한 품목들이 우리의 해양을 오염시키고 있음을 알 수 있다.

Wrap Up B. Read and Present

그린월은 그 위에 식물들이 자라는 수직 구조물이다. 당신은 그것들이 그저 보기 좋다고 생각할지도 모른다. 하지만, 그것들은 많은 다른 이점들을 제공한다. 첫 번째로, 그린월은 에어컨의 필요성을 줄임으로써 에너지를 절약하는 데 도움을 준다. 식물들이 햇빛의 많은 양을 흡수하고 반사하기 때문에, 그것들은 주변 지역을 시원하게 유지하는 데 도움을 준다. 그린월은 또한 더 많은 산소를 만들어 냄으로써 더 건강한 생활 환경에 기여한다. 그것들은 심지어 작은 동물들에게 살 곳과 먹이를 제공한다! 마지막으로, 그린월은 우리에게 자연과 우리의 연관성을 일깨워 준다. 그린월의 이점들을 즐기고 우리가 자연을 보호해야 한다는 것을 기억하자.

---

01 ③	02 ⑤
03 ②	04 ⑤
05 ③	06 ④
07 ②	08 phenomenon

01 (A) take a deep breath는 '깊은 숨을 쉬다'라는 뜻이다. 나무 앞에서 신선한 공기를 깊게 들이마시는 상황이므로 deep이 적절하다.
(B) made a nest in your branches라는 표현에서 가지(branches)에 둥지를 만드는 것은 새(birds)이다.

(C) 나무가 새들에게 집을 제공하는 것을 긍정적으로 표현하고 있으므로 kind가 적절하다.

02 ⑤ 문맥상 나무의 전체 수가 증가하고 있었다는 것은 맞지 않다. 가뭄으로 인해 나무들의 건강이 악화되고 있었다는 내용과 일치하려면 decreasing이 적절하다.

03 (A) shade는 셀 수 있는 명사가 아니므로 amount가 적절하다.
(B) 임관 피복도의 손실은 온도를 높이므로 raises가 적절하다.
(C) 도시의 높은 온도가 주민들에게 위험할 수 있다는 맥락이므로 dangerous가 적절하다.

04 나무가 손상되었거나 건강이 좋지 않다는 것을 의회 직원들에게 '알리는' 기능을 설명하고 있으므로 ⑤는 'inform(알리다)'이 적절하다.

05 (A) 사람들이 나무에게 사랑의 편지를 보내는 것은 원래 의도와 다른 예상치 못한 결과이므로 unexpected가 알맞다.
(B) 원래 이메일 기능의 목적이 손상되거나 건강이 좋지 않은 나무에 대해 보고하는 것이었으므로 poor가 적절하다.
(C) 나무에게 메일을 보내는 현상이 빠르게 퍼져나갔다는 것이 문맥상 자연스러우므로 quickly가 알맞다.

06 문맥상 우리가 더 '지속 가능한(sustainable)' 세계를 만드는 데 관여하고 있다는 의미가 되어야 하므로 ④ 'unsustainable(지속 불가능한)'은 적절하지 않다.

07 (A) 문맥상 멜버른 시의 도시 환경에 대해 이야기하고 있으므로 urban이 알맞다.
(B) 도시숲 전략의 목표가 캐노피 커버를 23%에서 40%로 늘리는 것이므로 increase가 알맞다.
(C) 도시의 주민들이 자연과 상호작용하고 야외 활동에 참여할 수 있게 한다는 내용이므로 residents가 알맞다.

08 '특히 비범하거나 주목할 만한, 관찰 가능한 사건이나 사실'은 '현상(phenomenon)'이다.

03 ① 이 문맥에서는 shade를 꾸며주는 과거분사가 와야 하므로 provided가 알맞다.

04 (A) '무언가가 행해져야 했다'는 의미가 되어야 하므로 Something had to be done이 알맞다.
(B) '다음 20년 동안'이라는 의미는 for the next twenty years로 뒤에 숫자가 나오는 경우는 for를 사용한다. during은 주로 특정 기간 내내 계속되는 행위를 나타낼 때 사용된다.
(C) Urban Forest Visual이라고 '불리는' 온라인 지도라는 의미이므로 과거분사 called가 알맞다.

05 (A) '색상과 기호를 사용하여 나타내기 위해'라는 의미로 목적을 나타내는 부사적 용법의 to부정사 to indicate가 알맞다.
(B) 앞의 to find와 병렬 구조를 이루므로 send가 알맞다. to는 반복하여 쓰지 않는다.
(C) 선행사 trees를 수식하는 관계대명사 that이 알맞다.

06 (A) something은 형용사가 뒤에서 수식하므로 something unexpected가 알맞다.
(B) 감사를 '표현하는' 메시지들이라는 의미로 현재분사 expressing이 알맞다.
(C) 문맥상 '거의'라는 의미의 부사가 자연스러우므로 almost가 알맞다.

07 ⑤ 현재 사실에 대한 가정을 하는 「Without ~, 가정법 과거」 구문으로 would have had가 아니라 would have가 알맞다.

08 ④ help 다음에는 동사원형이나 to부정사가 와야 하므로 keep이나 to keep이 알맞다.

내신 1등급 어법 공략   pp. 146-147

01 ④	**02** ⑤
03 ①	**04** ③
05 ④	**06** ③
07 ⑤	**08** ④

01 (A) '내가 당신 앞에 멈출 때마다'라는 의미로, 반복적인 행동을 나타내므로 Whenever가 적절하다.
(B) '당신과 당신의 모든 친구들이 없다면, 우리 인간은 충분한 산소를 얻을 수 없을 것이다.'라는 의미이므로 Without이 적절하다.
(C) 주어가 a family of birds로 단수이므로 단수 동사 has가 적절하다.

02 (A) 주어가 The story로 3인칭 단수이므로, 단수형 동사 begins가 적절하다.
(B) '1990년대 후반'은 late 1990s가 관용적으로 사용된다. lately는 '최근에'라는 의미의 부사로 적절하지 않다.
(C) a state of 뒤에 와야 하므로 전치사 뒤에 쓸 수 있는 동명사형 declining이 적절하다.

내신 1등급 실전 1회   pp. 148-151

01 ④	**02** ③
03 ④	**04** ⓐ tree ⓑ (a family of) birds
05 ③	**06** ①
07 ②	**08** interactive
09 ②	**10** ③
11 ②	**12** ③
13 ④	**14** ①
15 ②	

01 (B) 질문에 대한 직접적인 응답으로 자연스럽게 이어진다.
(D) 상대방의 동의에 Right.로 답하고, 새로운 주제를 도입한다.
(A) 상대방이 언급한 흥미로운 사실에 대해 물어본다.
(C) 질문에 대한 답변으로, 곤충에 대한 흥미로운 사실을 설명한다.

02 ③ There are about one million insect species.에서 10만 종이 아니라 100만 종의 곤충이 있다는 것을 알 수 있다.

03 ④ 나무의 역할의 중요성을 강조하며 감사하는 마음으로 더 많은 사람들이 이를 깨닫기를 바라고 있으므로 필자의 전반적인 심경은 'grateful(감사하는)'이 가장 적절하다.
■■■ ① 안도한 ② 흥분된 ③ 불안해하는 ⑤ 실망한

04 ⓐ 이것이 나무에게 쓴 편지라는 점과 I appreciate the oxygen that you produce.를 통해 산소를 생산하는 것은 나무라는 것을 알 수 있으므로 you가 지칭하는 것은 tree이다.

ⓑ I noticed that a family of birds has made a nest in your branches.에서 새들의 가족이 언급되고 있으므로 뒤에 나오는 them은 바로 앞에 언급된 (a family of) birds를 가리킨다.

05 (A) 문맥상 나무를 지나칠 때마다의 상황을 설명하고 있으므로 Whenever가 적절하다.

(B) 나무와 다른 식물들이 없으면 인간이 충분한 산소를 얻지 못한다는 의미를 전달하므로 Without이 적절하다.

(C) 앞에 사람의 성격을 나타내는 형용사가 있으므로 to부정사의 의미상 주어는 「of+목적격」으로 나타낸다.

06 ① 주어가 The story로 단수이므로 동사는 begins가 되어야 한다.

07 (A) 앞 문장의 내용에 추가적인 정보를 제공하므로 'Furthermore (게다가)'가 알맞다.

(B) 앞의 상황으로 인한 결과를 나타내므로 'As a result(그 결과)'가 알맞다.

08 '두 개 이상의 사물이나 사람들 사이의 의사소통이나 행동을 포함하는'이므로 'interactive(상호적인)'의 영어 뜻풀이다.

09 (A) set the goal은 '목표를 설정하다'라는 뜻이다.

(B) 지도가 색상과 기호를 사용하여 나무의 나이와 속을 나타낸다고 (indicate) 하는 것이 문맥상 적절하다.

(C) 손상되거나 '건강이 좋지 않은(poor health)' 나무에 대해 알리는 것이 문맥상 적절하다.

10 이 글은 온라인 지도 게시 후 나무들이 예상치 못하게 이메일을 받기 시작했다는 내용과 그 이메일의 내용에 대해 설명하고 있다. ③ '시 정부는 공원 유지 관리와 나무 심기를 위한 예산을 늘리기로 결정했다.'는 전체 흐름상 어색하다.

11 Everything on Earth is connected.는 기후 변화로 인한 극지방 얼음의 융해가 해수면 상승을 초래하고, 그로 인해 베니스와 같은 저지대 도시가 침수될 수 있다는 설명을 연결하는 데 적합하기 때문에 ②가 정답이다.

12 (A) 멀리 떨어져 있다는 사실과 같은 행성과 환경을 공유한다는 내용 사이의 대조를 나타내므로 although가 알맞다.

(B) '그때까지'라는 의미로 until이 적절하다.

(C) reminds us that ~의 구조로, 명사절을 이끄는 접속사 that이 알맞다.

13 ④ Perhaps one day we will meet라고 말했지만, 이는 직접적인 만남의 계획이 아닌 가능성을 언급한 것이므로 일치하지 않는다.

14 나무 메일 현상이 시민들의 참여를 유도하고, 도시숲 전략이 환경 개선과 삶의 질 향상에 기여한다는 글의 핵심 내용을 포함하고 있는 ①이 요지이다.

15 ⓑ 앞에 있는 to measure와 병렬 구조를 이루므로 monitor가 알맞다. to는 한번 더 쓰지 않아도 된다.

ⓔ as는 '~함에 따라', '~하는 동안'의 의미로 시간의 동시성을 나타내는 부사절을 이끄는 접속사이다.

내신 1등급 실전 2회 pp. 152-155

01 ④
02 Without, wouldn't be able to get enough oxygen
03 ②   **04** ②
05 were → was   **06** ③
07 (A) ⓑ (B) ⓐ (C) ⓒ.   **08** ②
09 ⑤   **10** ⑤
11 ③   **12** ③
13 ④   **14** ③
15 (A) building (B) predicted (C) to interact

01 ④ 이 글은 나무가 새들에게 집을 제공하는 행위를 긍정적으로 평가하고 있으므로 문맥상 'kind(친절한)'가 적절하다.

03 ②는 the girl을 수식하는 주격 관계대명사 that이고, 나머지는 모두 목적어 역할을 하는 명사절을 이끄는 접속사 that이다.
① 관계자들은 콘서트가 취소되었다고 발표했다.
② 그녀는 작년에 노래 경연대회에서 우승한 소녀이다.
③ 나는 내일 우리의 캠핑 여행을 위해 날씨가 좋기를 바란다.
④ 많은 사람들이 모든 사람이 평등한 기회를 가질 자격이 있다고 믿는다.
⑤ 나는 기후 변화가 심각한 문제라고 생각한다.

04 ② 나무가 제공하는 것은 '빛(light)'이 아니라 '그늘(shade)'이다. 'canopy cover(임관 피복도)'는 '나무들이 만드는 그늘'을 의미하므로, 여기서는 shade가 올바른 표현이다.

05 the overall number of trees는 단수 주어이므로, 단수 동사 was를 사용해야 한다. trees가 아니라 number가 주어라는 것에 주의한다.

06 나무로 인한 그늘(캐노피 커버)의 양이 감소했고, 이로 인해 온도가 상승했다고 언급하고 있으므로 ③은 일치하지 않는 내용이다.

07 (A) 남자가 날씨가 이상하다는 의견을 제시하고 여자의 동의를 구하는 상황으로 Don't you agree?가 적절하다. 대답에 Yes, I do.도 정답의 단서가 된다.

(B) 여자가 베니스의 홍수 상황을 언급한 후, 남자가 이에 대한 유감을 표현하는 흐름이 자연스러우므로 That's too bad.가 적절하다.

(C) 남자가 다른 해안 도시들의 홍수 가능성에 대해 걱정을 표현하자 여자도 같은 걱정을 하는 흐름이 자연스러우므로 상대방의 말에 동의하는 표현 So am I.가 적절하다.

08 주어진 문장은 도시숲 전략 계획의 일부로 만들어진 온라인 지도에 대해 언급하고 있다. 이 문장은 계획의 목표를 설명한 문장 다음, 그리고 지도에 대한 구체적인 설명 전에 위치하는 것이 가장 자연스러우므로 ②가 정답이다.

09 mail this tree 기능은 처음에 '손상되거나 건강이 좋지 않은 나무에 대해 시의회 직원들에게 쉽게 알리기 위해' 설계되었다. 따라서 건강한 나무를 찾기 위해 만들어졌다는 ⑤는 일치하지 않는 내용이다.

10 빈칸 이후의 내용을 보면, 나무들이 받은 것들이 '연애편지, 시, 인사말, 그리고 나무들에 대한 고마움을 표현하는 메시지들'이라고 설명하고 있으므로 나무들이 ⑤ '수천 개의 이메일들을 받기 시작했다'가 빈칸에 가장 적절하다.

▨▨▨ ① 더 빨리 자라기 시작했다 ② 베어졌다 ③ 다른 지역으로 옮겨졌다 ④ 질병에 더 저항력이 생겼다

11 (A) 나무에게 이메일을 보내는 현상이 예상치 못한 일이었음을 나타내므로 unexpected가 적절하다.
(B) 사람들이 나무에 대한 감사를 표현하는 메시지를 보냈다는 내용이므로 expressing이 적절하다.
(C) 나무의 가지가 거의 사람을 껴안으려는 것 같다는 비유적 표현을 나타내므로 almost가 적절하다.

12 ①, ②, ④, ⑤는 모두 수동태의 쓰임이 적절하다. ③의 share는 '공유하다'라는 의미를 가진 동사이므로 수동태가 아닌 share가 알맞다.

13 sustainable은 '지속 가능한'이라는 뜻으로 ④ '환경을 해치거나 자원을 고갈시키지 않고 시간이 지나도 유지될 수 있는'이 알맞은 영어 뜻풀이다.
① 도시나 마을의 특성을 가진 → urban(도시의)
② 성공이나 특정 목표를 달성하려는 강한 욕구를 가진 → ambitious(야심 있는)
③ 두 개 이상의 사물이나 사람 사이의 의사소통이나 행동을 포함하는 → interactive(상호적인)
⑤ 무언가를 창조하거나, 만들거나, 제조하다 → produce(생산하다)

14 도시숲 전략의 직접적이고 종합적인 결과로 주민들의 행복과 건강 증진을 예측하는 것이 가장 적절하므로 ③ '주민들이 더 행복하고 건강해질 것이다'가 정답이다.
① 도시가 인기 있는 관광지가 될 것이다
② 나무들이 더 빨리 그리고 더 강하게 자랄 것이다
④ 대기 오염이 극적으로 감소할 것이다
⑤ 그 지역의 부동산 가치가 크게 상승할 것이다

15 (A) 전치사 about 뒤에는 동명사 형태 building이 알맞다.
(B) '예상되다'는 의미로 수동태가 와야 하므로 is predicted가 알맞다.
(C) 「allow A to B」 구문으로 allow는 목적격보어로 to부정사가 와야 하므로 to interact가 알맞다.

내신 **1등급** 실전 3회	pp. 156-159
01 ①	02 ⑤: worse → better
03 ①	04 ③
05 ①	06 ③
07 ②	08 ③
09 ④	10 ①: posting → posted
11 ②	12 (A) popularity (B) collective
13 ④	14 If it were not for
15 ④	

01 첫 문장에서 Would you like to contribute to research and make a difference in the world?라고 묻고, 이어서 Join Eco Trackers to participate in environmental citizen science projects!라고 말하며 환경 시민 과학 프로젝트 참여를 직접적으로 권유하고 있으므로 위 담화의 목적은 ① '환경 시민 과학 프로젝트를 위한 자원봉사자를 모집하기 위해'이다.

▨▨▨ ② 등산객을 위한 새로운 하이킹 앱을 광고하기 위해
③ 공동체 정원을 위한 원예 장비를 판매하기 위해
④ 천문학 애호가들을 위한 별 관측 행사를 홍보하기 위해
⑤ 과학 연구 장비를 위한 기금을 모으기 위해

02 전체 메시지의 긍정적인 어조와 환경 개선을 위한 노력이라는 주제와 어울리기 위해서는 ⑤의 worse를 better로 바꿔야 한다.

03 '무언가의 가치를 인식하거나 감사하다'는 ① 'appreciate(고마워하다)'에 대한 영어 뜻풀이다.

04 ③ (A)와 (B) 모두 반복적인 행동이나 상황을 나타내고 있다. 글쓴이가 나무를 지나갈 때마다, 또는 나무 앞에 멈출 때마다 일어나는 일을 설명하고 있으므로 '~할 때마다'라는 의미의 Whenever가 적절하다.

05 이 글은 멜버른의 나무들이 이메일 주소를 가지고 있고 사람들이 그 나무들에게 메시지를 보내는 독특한 현상에 대해 소개하고 있다. 따라서 ① '멜버른의 독특한 나무 이메일 시스템'이 제목으로 적절하다.
▨▨▨ ② 도시 나무들에 대한 가뭄의 영향
③ 기후 변화와 도시 열섬 현상
④ 도시에서의 캐노피 커버의 중요성
⑤ 에어컨과 온실가스 배출

06 (B)는 멜버른의 도시숲 전략 계획의 배경을 설명하며, 가뭄으로 인한 나무들의 건강 악화와 수의 감소를 언급하고 있다.
(C)는 (B)의 결과로 나타난 그늘(캐노피 커버)의 감소와 그로 인한 도시 온도 상승 문제를 설명하고 있다.
(A)는 (C)에서 언급된 높은 온도로 인한 에어컨 사용 증가와 그에 따른 기후 변화 가속화를 설명하고 있다.

07 ② '그 계획은 또한 도시숲 시각 자료라고 불리는 온라인 지도 제작을 포함했다'이므로 앞에 있는 명사 the creation of an online map을 수식하는 과거분사 'called (불리는)'가 올바른 표현이다.

08 빈칸이 있는 문장은 'mail this tree' 기능의 목적을 설명하고 있다. 이 기능은 의회에서 일하는 사람들에게 나무의 상태에 대해 알리기 위한 것이다. poor health(건강 상태가 좋지 않음)와 함께 언급되는 단어이므로, 나무의 부정적인 상태를 나타내는 ③ 'damaged(손상된)'가 가장 적절하다.

09 (A) 지도가 온라인에 게시된 후에(After) 예상치 못한 일이 일어났다는 시간적 순서를 나타낸다.
(B) 이메일들이 손상이나 건강 악화에 대한 보고가 아니라, 그 대신에(Instead) 연애편지나 시 등이었다는 것을 나타내는 전환어로 Instead가 적절하다.
(C) It is almost like you are trying to hug me.는 나무의 모습을 사람의 행동에 비유하는 표현으로 like가 적절하다.

10 the map은 게시되는 것이므로 수동태 was posted가 되어야 한다.

11 윗글의 밑줄 친 that은 A message를 수식하는 관계대명사이다. ①, ③, ④, ⑤의 that도 모두 관계대명사인 반면, ②의 that은 관계대명사가 아니라 believe의 목적어 역할을 하는 명사절을 이끄는 접속사이다.

정답 및 해설 **27**

12 (A) 나무 이메일 현상의 전 세계적 '인기'라는 의미가 자연스러우므로 'popular(인기 있는)'의 명사형 popularity가 알맞다.

(B) 문맥상 '집단적 행동'이 자연스러우므로 'collect(모으다)'의 형용사형 collective가 알맞다.

13 ④ 빈칸 뒤의 내용이 각각 We believe와 We hope의 목적어 역할을 하는 명사절이므로 명사절을 이끄는 접속사 that이 적절하다.

14 「Without ~, 가정법 과거」에서 Without은 If it were not for로 바꿔 쓸 수 있다.

15 (C) 나무 이메일 현상이 멜버른 주민들에게 미친 영향을 설명하며 글을 시작하는데 이는 전체 상황의 배경과 시작점을 제공한다.

(A) Meanwhile(한편)로 시작하며, 도시숲 전략의 진행 상황과 구체적인 목표를 설명한다.

(B) As a result(결과적으로)로 시작하며, 앞서 언급된 주민들의 참여(C)와 도시숲 전략(A)의 결과를 제시한다. 이는 전체 내용의 결론 역할을 한다.

내신 1등급 수능형 고난도

pp. 160-163

01 ①	02 ④
03 ③	04 ④
05 ④	06 ⑤
07 ④	08 ⑤
09 ③	10 ⑤
11 ④	12 ③
13 ③	14 ④
15 ④	

[01-02] 해석

> 나무에게,
>
> 내가 너의 곁을 지날 때마다 너의 아름다운 이파리가 나를 미소 짓게 만들어. 너의 앞에 멈춰 서서 신선한 공기를 깊이 들이쉬면, 나는 네가 만들어내는 산소에 감사하게 돼. 너와 다른 나무들이 없었다면, 우리 인간은 숨 쉴 충분한 산소를 얻지 못했을 거야. 또한, 내가 보니 너의 가지에 새 가족이 둥지를 틀고 있더구나. 그들에게 집을 제공해 준 것은 정말 너그러운 일이야. 더 많은 사람들이 너와 다른 모든 나무들이 우리 환경에 얼마나 중요한 존재인지 이해하길 바라. 멋진 하루가 되길 바라!

01 이 글은 나무에게 보내는 편지 형식으로, 나무의 아름다움과 중요성에 대한 감사의 마음을 표현하고 있다. 따라서 ①이 가장 적절하다.

02 (A) 형용사 뒤에 와야 하므로 명사형 breath가 알맞다.

(B) I noticed 뒤의 명사절을 이끌어야 하므로 명사절을 이끄는 접속사 that이 알맞다.

(C) 앞에 사람의 성격을 나타내는 형용사 generous가 있으므로 의미상 주어는 「of+목적격」 형태가 적절하다.

[03-04] 해석

> 놀랍게도 호주 멜버른의 나무들은 이메일을 받는다. 여러분은 나무들이 어떻게 이메일 주소를 가질 수 있는지, 그리고 왜 사람들이 나무들에게 메시지를 보내는지 궁금해 할 수 있다.
>
> 이 독특한 소통 체계의 기원은 멜버른의 도시숲 전략 계획으로 거슬러 올라간다. 이 계획은 1990년대 후반부터 2010년까지 호주를 괴롭힌 심각한 밀레니엄 가뭄에 대응하여 개발되었다. 가뭄이 마침내 끝났을 때, 멜버른의 77,000그루의 나무 중 40%가 건강 악화로 고통 받고 있다는 사실이 밝혀졌다. 게다가 도시의 전체 나무 수가 감소하고 있었다.

03 주어진 문장은 멜버른의 도시숲 전략 계획이 개발된 배경을 설명하고 있다. 이 문장은 도시숲 전략에 대한 언급 직후에 오는 것이 가장 자연스럽다. 주어 It은 앞에 나온 '멜버른의 도시숲 전략 계획(Melbourne's Urban Forest Strategy plan)'을 가리킨다.

04 나무에 이메일 주소를 부여한 원래 목적은 시민들이 위험한 가지나 나무 건강 악화의 징후와 같은 문제를 쉽게 보고할 수 있도록 하기 위한 것이었다. 시민들의 개인적인 메시지를 받는 것은 의도하지 않은 결과였으므로 ④는 글의 내용과 일치하지 않는다.

[05-06] 해석

> 결과적으로, 나무의 캐노피 커버, 즉 도시 지역에서 나무가 제공하는 그늘이 줄어들었다. 이러한 캐노피 커버의 감소는 도시 환경에 상당한 위험을 초래하며, 이는 온도 상승으로 이어진다. 도시 지역에서의 높은 온도는 주민들에게 위험할 수 있으며, 열 관련 질병의 가능성을 높인다. 또한, 이러한 따뜻한 조건은 에어컨 사용을 증가시킨다. 냉방 기술에 대한 의존도가 높아지면 에너지 사용이 증가하고 온실가스가 대기 중으로 방출되어 기후 변화가 가속화된다.

05 도시 지역의 나무 캐노피 커버 감소가 가져오는 여러 가지 부정적인 결과에 대해 설명하고 있다. 온도 상승, 건강 위험 증가, 에어컨 사용 증가로 인한 기후 변화 가속화 등이 언급되고 있다. 따라서 이 글의 주제로 가장 적절한 것은 ④ '도시의 나무 캐노피 커버 감소의 부정적 결과'이다.

〔오답〕 ① 도시 지역에서 나무 캐노피 커버의 중요성 ② 나무 캐노피 커버와 관련된 건강 위험 ③ 에어컨 사용과 기후 변화 간의 관계 ⑤ 도시의 나무 캐노피 커버를 증가시키는 방법

06 ⑤ release는 '방출'이라는 의미이고, consumption은 '소비, 소모'라는 의미이므로 바꿔 쓸 수 없다.

[07-08] 해석

> 멜버른의 나무 감소 문제를 해결하기 위한 조치가 필요했다. 2012년, 시 정부는 도시 숲 전략(Urban Forest Strategy)을 도입하여 향후 20년 동안 매년 3,000그루 이상의 나무를 심는 것을 목표로 했다. 이 계획에는 도시숲 시각 자료라고 불리는 대화형 온라인 지도 개발도 포함되었다.
>
> 이 지도는 멜버른의 공원과 거리의 모든 나무에 대한 종합적인 정보를 제공한다. 각 나무의 나이와 속성을 나타내기 위해 색상과 기호 시스템을 사용한다. 또한 사용자는 개별 나무를 클릭하여 그 종에 대한 정보를 알아보고, 심지어 전자 메시지를 보낼 수 있다. 처음에 '이 나무에게 메일 보내기' 기능은 시민들이 손상되거나 건강이 좋지 않은 나무를 시 당국에 쉽게 보고할 수 있도록 하기 위한 실용적인 도구로 의도되었다.

07 글의 주요 내용인 멜버른의 도시숲 전략과 그 혁신적인 접근 방식(나무 심기 계획, 상호 작용 지도, 나무에 이메일 보내기 등)을 포괄하는 제목으로 ④ '멜버른의 혁신적인 도시숲 계획'이 적절하다.

⬛ ① 멜버른의 공원과 정원의 역사
② 호주 도시들에 대한 기후 변화의 영향
③ 도시 계획에서의 대중 참여
⑤ 현대 조경 건축에서의 기술

08 ⑤ trees를 수식하는 분사가 적절하다. damaged or unhealthy trees는 '손상되었거나 건강하지 않은 나무들'이라는 의미이다.

⬛ ① introduced에 이어지는 분사구문으로 적절하게 사용되었다.
② an interactive online map을 수식하는 과거분사로 올바르게 사용되었다.
③ employs의 목적을 나타내는 부사적 용법의 to부정사로 올바르게 사용되었다.
④ 전치사 by 다음에 동명사 형태로 올바르게 사용되었다.

[09-10] 해석

지도가 온라인에 게시된 후, 예상치 못한 일이 발생했다. 나무들이 수많은 이메일을 받기 시작했지만, 놀랍게도 그 중 많은 이메일이 손상이나 건강 문제에 대한 보고가 아니었다. 대신, 사람들은 나무들에게 연애편지, 시, 인사말, 감사의 메시지를 보냈다. 이 도시는 또한 많은 방문객을 끌어모으는 연례 음식 축제를 개최한다. 한 개인은 이렇게 썼다: '나는 네 잎에 빛이 비치는 모습과 네 가지가 이렇게 낮게 드리워져 있는 것을 정말 좋아해. 마치 네가 나를 안으려고 손을 내미는 것처럼 느껴져.' 이러한 나무와의 소통 트렌드는 빠르게 인기를 얻었고, 전 세계 사람들이 나무들에게 메시지를 보내기 시작했다.

09 이 글은 온라인 지도에 게시된 나무들에 대한 예상치 못한 반응과 사람들이 나무에게 보내는 메시지에 대한 내용이다. 그러나 ③ '이 도시는 또한 많은 방문객을 끄는 연례 음식 축제를 개최한다'는 나무와의 소통이라는 주제와 전혀 관련이 없는 내용으로 전체 흐름과 무관하다.

10 (A) 문맥상 나무들이 이메일을 받기 시작한 것은 예상치 못한 일이었으므로 unexpected가 자연스럽다.
(B) 뿌리(roots)보다 나무의 가지(branches)가 낮게 드리워져 있다는 표현이 자연스럽다.
(C) 전 세계 사람들이 나무에게 메시지를 보내기 시작했다는 내용으로 보아, 이 트렌드가 '인기(popularity)'를 얻었다고 할 수 있다.

[11-12] 해석

러시아의 한 사람이 멜버른의 나무에게 이렇게 썼다: '이 멋진 프로젝트에 대해 알게 된 것이 나를 감동시켜 메시지를 보내게 되었어. 비록 나는 수천 마일 떨어져 살고 있지만, 우리는 같은 지구에 살고 있으며 공통의 환경을 공유하고 있어. 언젠가 만날 수 있기를 바라. 그때까지 네가 건강하고 강하게 지낼 수 있기를 바라.'
나무 이메일 프로젝트의 광범위한 인기는 자연과의 보편적인 연결 및 더 지속 가능한 세상을 만드는 데 있어 우리의 공동 책임을 일깨워 준다. 미래 세대를 위해 지구를 보존하는 것은 전 세계적인 협력 노력에 크게 의존하며, 이러한 단합된 행동 없이는 성공할 가능성이 희박할 것이다.

11 이 글은 나무에게 보내는 메시지를 통해 자연과의 연결성과 환경에 대한 공동 책임을 강조하고 있다. 따라서 빈칸에는 ④ '더 지속 가능한 세상을 만드는 것'이 가장 적절하다.

⬛ ① 국제 관광 촉진 ② 첨단 기술 개발 ③ 경제 성장 증대 ⑤ 도시 개발 확대

12 (A) Until then은 '그때까지'라는 의미로, 미래의 어떤 시점까지를 나타내는 표현이다.
(B) serve as는 '~로서의 역할을 하다'라는 뜻이다.
(C) rely on은 '~에 의존하다'라는 뜻이다.

[13-15] 해석

지역적으로 나무 이메일 현상은 많은 멜버른 주민들에게 환경 친화적인 도시 환경을 구축하기 위한 아이디어를 제공했다. 일부 열정적인 주민들은 도시 자연 프로그램을 위한 나무 측정 및 야생 동물 모니터링에 도움을 주겠다고 제안하기도 했다. 한편, 도시의 도시숲 전략의 나무 심기 프로젝트는 계획대로 진행되고 있다. 시는 2012년 23%에서 2040년까지 40%로 캐노피 커버가 확장될 것으로 예상하고 있다. 이 도시숲 계획은 멜버른의 온도를 낮추고, 주민들이 자연과 연결되고 야외 활동에 참여할 수 있는 기회를 매일 제공하기 위해 설계되었다. 결과적으로, 도시가 더 푸르러짐에 따라 주민들은 더 행복하고 건강해질 것이다.

13 이 글은 멜버른의 도시숲 전략(Urban Forest Strategy)이 어떻게 시민 참여를 이끌어내고, 도시 환경을 개선하며, 주민들의 삶의 질을 향상시키는지에 대해 전반적으로 다루고 있으므로 ③ '멜버른의 도시숲 전략의 긍정적인 영향'이 주제로 가장 적절하다.

⬛ ① 멜버른의 나무 이메일 프로젝트의 예상치 못한 성공
② 기후 변화 대응에 있어 도시숲의 중요성
④ 도시 환경 프로그램에서의 시민 참여 역할
⑤ 녹지 공간 증가에 따른 건강상의 이점

14 it will provide daily opportunities for residents to connect with nature and participate in outdoor activities라고 언급하고 있다. 따라서 도시숲 전략(Urban Forest Strategy)이 주민들에게 제공하는 것은 '일상적인 자연과의 연결'이다.

⬛ ① 재정적 인센티브 ② 일자리 기회 ③ 교육 프로그램 ⑤ 도시 농업 공간

15 This urban forest plan is designed to maintain lower temperatures in Melbourne.으로 보아 도시숲 계획은 멜버른의 기온을 낮추기 위해 설계되었다는 것을 알 수 있으므로 ④가 일치하지 않는 내용이다.

내신 1등급 서술형

pp. 164-166

01 (A) tree (B) environment
02 ②: Without you and all your friends, we humans wouldn't be able to get enough oxygen.
03 is a major threat to urban environments because it raises temperatures
04 ⓐ: response ⓑ: consumption
05 set, goal, more than, for
06 ⓐ: This interactive map ⓑ: the "mail this tree" function
07 (1) something unexpected happened
(2) how your branches hang so low

01 이 편지는 <u>나무</u>가 산소를 제공하고 새들에게 쉼터를 제공하는 것에 대
해 감사를 표현하면서, 나무가 <u>환경</u>에 미치는 중요성을 강조하고 있
다.

02 ② 문맥상 '나무들이 없으면 인간이 충분한 산소를 얻을 수 없을 것이
다'가 되어야 하므로 With가 아니라 Without이 알맞다.

03 '주요한 위협'은 a major threat로, '도시 환경에'는 to urban
environments로, '기온을 상승시키기 때문에'는 because it raises
temperatures로 연결한다.

04 ⓐ respond는 동사형이므로, 여기서는 명사형인 response로 바꿔
야 한다. a response to는 '~에 대한 대응'이라는 의미이다.
ⓑ consume은 동사형이므로, 여기서는 명사형인 consumption
으로 바꿔야 한다. energy consumption은 '에너지 소비'라는 의
미이다.

05 '야심찬 목표를 설정하다'는 set the ambitious goal이다. '~이상'은
more than이다. '~동안'은 전치사 for를 쓴다.

06 ⓐ It은 바로 앞 문장에서 언급된 This interactive map을 가리킨다.
ⓑ It은 바로 앞 문장에서 언급된 the "mail this tree" function을
가리킨다.

07 (1) '예상치 못한 무언가'를 의미하는 something unexpected를 쓰
고 동사 happened를 이어서 쓴다.
(2) how로 시작한 후 주어 your branches와 동사 hang을 쓰고
동사를 수식하는 부사구 so low를 쓴다.

08 (1) 나쁜 공기 질은 특히 어린 아이들에게 <u>위험하다</u>.
(2) 대부분의 날에는 자전거를 타고 등교하기 때문에 Sally가 걸어서
등교하는 것은 <u>드문</u> 일이다.
(3) 친구들이 그를 격려하러 왔음에도 불구하고, 그는 여전히 시험에
대해 <u>긴장하고</u> 있었다.
(4) 팀의 <u>예상치 못한</u> 우승은 모든 팬들을 충격에 빠뜨렸다.

09 ① 메시지는 보내지는 것이므로 수동태인 was sent가 어법상 올바르
다.
④ 「remind A B」 구문으로 'A에게 B를 상기시키다'는 뜻이므로 명
사절을 이끄는 접속사 that이 어법상 올바르다.

10 주어진 문장은 「Without ~, 가정법 과거」 문장으로 이때 Without은
But for 또는 If it were not for로 바꿔 쓸 수 있다.

교과서 어휘 익히기 ·········· pp. 170-171

STEP 1

01 아래에	25 reveal
02 조사관, 감독관	26 harsh
03 정확히 포착하다, 담아내다	27 spark
04 비극적인, 비극의	28 emotion
05 ~인 척하다, ~라고 가장하다	29 weave
06 특별히 포함하다, 특징으로 삼다	30 helpless
07 환경의	31 complex
08 전시회, 전시	32 convey
09 산업	33 expose
10 (신문·잡지의) 글, 기사	34 illegal
11 의식[관심]	35 oil-soaked
12 금하다, 금지하다	36 equipment
13 혁명	37 passage
14 (순간적으로) 확 타오르는 불길, 불꽃	38 standard
15 조사[수사]의	39 committee
16 의회[국회]	40 laborer
17 빠르게	41 establish
18 발생하다	42 economic
19 사진	43 regard
20 가능성이 있는, 그럴듯한	44 employ
21 ~을 (움켜)잡다	45 go on strike
22 (불을) 끄다	46 take a picture of
23 ~을 이용하다	47 have an impact on
24 ~하지 않을 수 없다	48 gain access to

STEP 2

A 01 put out 02 take advantage of
03 can't help but 04 go on strike
05 grab hold of
B 01 dumping 02 passed
C 01 ⓒ 02 ⓑ 03 ⓐ

교과서 핵심 대화문 ·········· pp. 172-173

Function 1 정의하기
Check-Up ✕ ③
Function 2 선호 표현하기
Check-Up ✕ prefer

교과서 기타 대화문 ·········· p. 174

Q1 F Q2 T Q3 F

TOPIC 1 C. Listen and Interact
M: 이 사진을 봐. 나는 지난 주말에 가족을 위해 저녁을 준비했어.
W: 와, 정말 멋지다! 모든 걸 네가 만들었어?
M: 아니. 사실, 나는 밀키트를 사용했어. 밀키트는 요리를 더 쉽게 해주고 많은 시간을 절약해줘.
W: 이제 나는 요즘 왜 그렇게 그것들이 인기가 있는지 이해했어.
M: 너도 하나로 요리해보는 건 어때? 선택할 수 있는 다양한 옵션이 있어.
W: 음, 확실히 편리하긴 해. 하지만 플라스틱 포장의 과도한 사용이 걱정돼.
M: 맞아, 그건 문제야. 더 많은 친환경 포장 옵션이 있으면 좋겠어.

TOPIC 4 B. While You View
W 허블 우주망원경은 30년 이상 동안 지구 대기 위에서 궤도를 돌고 있습니다. 1990년 NASA에 의해 발사된 이후, 허블은 우리가 우주를 바라보는 방식을 변화시켰습니다. 예를 들어, 허블은 과학자들이 우주의 나이와 크기를 정확하게 추정하는 데 도움을 주었습니다. 1995년, 허블은 비어 있는 것처럼 보이는 심우주 지역의 사진을 찍었습니다. 그러나 이 사진은 놀라운 것을 드러냈습니다. 실제로 그 지역에는 1,500개 이상의 은하가 존재했습니다. 이러한 정보는 과학자들이 은하의 수를 배우는 데 도움을 주었습니다. 허블은 또한 우주가 팽창하는 속도에 대해서도 우리에게 알려주었습니다. 과학자들은 그것이 느려지고 있다고 생각했지만, 실제로는 더 빨라지고 있습니다. 2021년, NASA는 제임스 웹 우주 망원경이라는 훨씬 더 발전된 망원경을 발사했습니다. 과학자들은 허블의 업적에서 영감을 받은 이 새로운 망원경이 우주의 더 많은 비밀을 밝혀줄 것이라고 기대하고 있습니다.

Wrap Up A. Listen and Write
M: 야, 멋진 시계네!
W: 고마워. 지난주에 샀어.
M: 나도 새 시계를 사려고 생각 중이야. 너는 구매에 만족해?
W: 응! 이 시계는 내 심박수를 측정해줘서 운동할 때 매우 유용해.
M: 와! 정말 대단하다!
W: 다른 멋진 기능도 있어. 예를 들어, 이 시계를 사용해서 물건을 결제할 수 있어. 이것은 내가 더 이상 지갑을 들고 다닐 필요가 없다는 것을 의미하지.
M: 그거 좋네! 요즘 시계는 시간을 알려주는 것 외에도 할 수 있는 게 정말 많아.

교과서 핵심 대화문 익히기 ·········· p. 175

01 ⑤
02 (B) – (D) – (A) – (C)
03 ③

교과서 핵심 문법 ·········· pp. 176-179

POINT 1 명사를 뒤에서 수식하는 현재분사

Q 1 falling　　2 playing　　3 parked

Check-Up 🏅

01 (1) barking (2) wearing (3) signed
02 ④
03 (1) damaged (2) painting (3) broken
04 (1) the shop selling the most delicious cakes in town
　　(2) Our cupcake sale featuring various flavors of cupcakes

01 (1) 개가 현재 짖고 있는 동작을 나타내므로 현재분사 barking이 적절하다.
(2) 여성이 현재 빨간 드레스를 입고 있는 상태를 나타내므로 현재분사 wearing이 적절하다.
(3) 문서에 서명하는 행위가 이미 완료되었고, 문서가 서명을 '받은' 상태이므로 과거분사 signed가 적절하다.

02 (A) 나는 해변에서 모래성을 짓고 있는 한 남자를 보았다.
사람이 모래성을 만드는 진행 중인 동작이기 때문에 building이 적절하다.
(B) 작년에 지어진 그 집이 이미 판매 중이다.
집이 작년에 지어졌다는 것은 이미 완료된 동작이기 때문에 built가 적절하다.

03 (1) 차가 사고로 인해 이미 손상된 상태이므로 완료된 동작이나 상태를 나타내는 과거분사 damaged가 적절하다.
(2) 학생들이 포스터를 그리는 진행 중인 동작을 나타내는 현재분사 painting이 적절하다.
(3) 꽃병이 깨진 상태로 완료된 동작을 나타내는 과거분사 broken이 적절하다.

04

> **The Cake Castle**
> • 마을에서 가장 맛있는 케이크를 판매하고 있는 가게에 방문해 보세요!
> • 다양한 맛의 컵케이크를 특징으로 삼는 저희의 컵케이크 세일이 시작되었습니다. 하지만 저희의 특별한 생일 케이크를 맛보는 것도 잊지 마세요!
> • Cake Castle은 매일 오전 8시부터 오후 8시까지 열려 있습니다. 오늘 가는 길에 들러 보는 건 어떠세요?

(1) the shop을 수식하는 현재분사구 selling the most delicious cakes를 쓰고 장소를 나타내는 부사구 in town을 쓴다.
(2) Our cupcake sale을 수식하는 현재분사구 featuring various flavors of cupcakes를 쓴다.

POINT 2 관계대명사의 계속적 용법

Q 1 who　　2 which　　3 which

Check-Up 🏅

01 (1) who (2) which (3) which
02 (1) which (2) which (3) which
03 (1) ① → which (2) ⑤ → who
04 ③

01 (1) 선행사가 my grandmother이므로 관계대명사 who가 알맞다.
(2) 선행사가 a stomach이므로 관계대명사 which가 알맞다.
(3) 선행사가 앞 문장 전체이므로 관계대명사 which가 알맞다.

02 (1) 선행사가 사물이므로 관계대명사 which가 알맞다.
(2) 선행사가 사물이므로 관계대명사 which가 알맞다. 관계대명사 that은 계속적 용법으로 쓸 수 없다.
(3) 선행사가 앞 문장 전체이므로 관계대명사 which가 알맞다.

03

> **궁궐 야간 투어**
> 창덕궁에 오신 것을 환영하며, 이곳은 조선 왕조의 많은 왕들이 매우 좋아하는 궁궐이었습니다. 연못을 따라서, 그리고 나무 사이로 걷는 동안, 여러분은 달 아래 평화로운 분위기를 즐길 수 있습니다. 여러분은 또한 전통 한국 무용수들에 의해 공연되는 쇼도 볼 수 있는데, 이들은 아름다운 한복을 차려입을 것입니다.

(1) ① 선행사가 Changdeokgung으로 사물이므로 관계대명사 which가 알맞다.
(2) ⑤ 선행사가 dancers로 사람이므로 관계대명사 who가 알맞다.

04 ⓑ 선행사가 my cousin으로 사람이므로 관계대명사 who가 알맞다.
ⓒ 선행사가 a friend로 사람이므로 관계대명사 who가 알맞다. 관계대명사 that은 계속적 용법으로 쓸 수 없다.
ⓔ 선행사가 a sweater로 사물이므로 관계대명사 which가 알맞다.

교과서 본문 익히기 ❶ ·········· pp. 186-188

01 grab hold of
02 convey a complex message
03 in an instant
04 an emotional reaction
05 grow rapidly
06 provided steady jobs
07 dumping large amounts of waste
08 caught fire
09 which set fire to
10 This was because, much worse
11 it wasn't long before
12 thanks to an article
13 featured a shocking photograph
14 put out so quickly
15 had occurred
16 had a great impact on

17 toward environmental problems

18 becoming aware of

19 a symbol of pollution

20 established with the passage

21 led to a dramatic increase

22 were employed

23 leaving many child laborers

24 for several reasons

25 paid less than

26 go on strike

27 how cruel this system was

28 as an investigative photographer

29 gained access to

30 would photograph

31 their living and working conditions

32 taking advantage of

33 captured young children

34 handling dangerous equipment

35 What is more

36 could not help but feel

37 shown in exhibitions

38 passed stronger laws

39 made it illegal

40 bring meaningful change

41 worth a thousand words

41 shown

42 serious

43 employment

44 during

45 bring

46 worth

교과서 본문 익히기 ❸ ·················· pp. 192-193

01 quickly	02 number
03 rapidly	04 to
05 polluted	06 caught
07 which	08 few
09 much	10 published
11 shocking	12 worse
13 on	14 burning
15 was held	16 were established
17 In	18 by
19 leaving	20 for
21 be paid	22 on
23 to reveal	24 as
25 pretending	26 photograph
27 record	28 who
29 doing	30 handling
31 more	32 feel
33 shown	34 to ban
35 illegal	36 that
37 truly	

교과서 본문 익히기 ❷ ·················· pp. 189-191

01 quickly	02 to convey
03 people's	04 number
05 rapidly	06 to
07 dumping	08 as
09 polluted	10 which
11 few	12 some
13 before	14 published
15 rising	16 so
17 much	18 great
19 attitudes	20 aware
21 pollution	22 which
23 were established	24 led
25 increased	26 those
27 leaving	28 for
29 less	30 likely
31 to reveal	32 to work
33 access	34 working
35 record	36 who
37 sorts	38 handling
39 What	40 feel

교과서 본문 외 지문 분석 ·················· pp. 194-195

Q1 T   Q2 F

Check-Up ✓

01 for several reasons

02 online learning tools

03 such as screen sharing

04 In addition

05 can be accessed anywhere

06 study more efficiently

07 are helpful for

08 as a challenge

09 see it as an opportunity

10 how we prepare for it

11 is unavoidable

12 have anything to do with

13 what we already have

14 that brings progress

15 are not willing to, let go of

온라인 수업은 도움이 될까요?

제 생각에 온라인 수업은 여러 가지 이유들로 도움이 됩니다. 먼저, 그것들은 학생들이 흥미롭게 여길 온라인 학습 도구들을 활용합니다. 화면 공유 및 실시간 채팅과 같은 이러한 도구들은 학생들의 관심을 유지시키고 그들이 더 효과적으로 배울 수 있도록 돕습니다. 게다가, 온라인 수업은 시간과 에너지를 절약합니다. 수업이 어디에서나 접속될 수 있기 때문에 학생들은 등하교에 많은 시간과 에너지를 쓸 필요가 없습니다. 이는 그들이 더 효율적으로 학습할 수 있다는 것을 의미합니다. 이러한 이유들로, 저는 온라인 수업이 학생들에게 도움이 된다고 생각합니다.

Wrap Up B. Read and Discuss

모든 사람은 변화를 도전으로 본다. 차이는 어떤 사람들은 그것을 우리의 진전을 방해하는 것이라고 여기는 반면, 다른 사람들은 그것을 기회로 본다는 것이다. 변화에 관해 중요한 것은 우리가 어떻게 그것을 준비하고 그것에 대응하는지다.

비록 변화는 피할 수 없다 할지라도, 빨리 진행되는 디지털 세상에서 살아가는 것은 우리에게 변화를 강요하는 것일까? 나는 대부분의 변화들은 실제 혁신과 어떤 연관이 있다고 생각하지 않는다. 때로는, 이미 우리가 가지고 있는 것을 고수하는 것이 더 현명하다.

변화는 진전을 가져오는 유일한 것이다. 우리가 기꺼이 마음을 바꾸고 오래된 관념과 믿음을 버리지 않는다면, 우리는 아무것도 바꿀 수 없다.

내신 1등급 어휘 공략
pp. 196-197

01 ④	02 ③
03 ②	04 ③
05 ②	06 ②
07 ①	

01 (A) 이미지는 우리의 논리적 사고보다는 감정에 더 직접적이고 즉각적으로 영향을 미치는 경향이 있기 때문에 emotions가 더 자연스럽다. 또한 뒤에 나오는 emotional reaction과도 자연스럽게 연결된다.
(B) speech는 이미 구어를 의미하므로, 대조를 위해 written이 적절하다.
(C) 뒤에 people이 있으므로 수를 나타내는 number가 적절하다.

02 (A) 문맥상 '산업적 성장'이 더 적절하다. 앞에 있는 industry와도 자연스럽게 연결된다.
(B) 폐기물은 셀 수 없는 명사이므로, large amounts of waste가 적절하다.
(C) 강이 오염되었음에도 불구하고 대부분의 사람들이 이를 경제적 '성공(success)'의 징후로 여겼다는 내용이 문맥상 적절하다.

03 ② 이전의 화재들 중 일부가 '더 좋았다'는 것은 문맥상 어울리지 않으며, 실제로는 더 심각했다(worse)는 의미가 되어야 한다.

04 ③ 쿠야호가 강의 화재가 '진보의 상징'이 되었다는 것은 이 사건의 본질과 그 후의 환경 운동의 맥락에 맞지 않는다. '오염의 상징(symbol of pollution)'이 되었다는 의미가 되어야 자연스럽다.

05 (A) 산업혁명으로 인해 공장 생산이 급격히 증가했다는 것이 맥락상 자연스러우므로 increase가 알맞다.
(B) 아동 노동자들의 작업이 쉬웠다면 건강 문제를 겪지 않았을 것이다. 따라서 '어렵고(difficult)' 위험한 작업이었다는 것이 맥락상 적절하다.
(C) 공장 소유주들이 아동 노동을 선호한 이유는 성인보다 적은 임금을 줄 수 있었기 때문이므로 less가 적절하다.

06 (A) 아동 노동의 상황이 '심각하다'는 것을 대중이 깨달았다는 맥락이 적절하므로 serious가 알맞다.
(B) 아동의 '고용'을 금지하는 법안이 통과되었다는 내용이 맥락에 맞으므로 employment가 알맞다.
(C) 16세 미만 아동의 공장 노동을 '불법화'하는 법안이 통과되었다는 내용이 맥락에 맞으므로 illegal이 적절하다.

07 ① Hine이 공장에 들어가기 위해 다른 직업으로 가장했다는 내용이므로 '접근, 입장'을 의미하는 access가 올바른 단어이다. gain access to는 '~에 접근하다'라는 뜻이다. excess는 '과잉, 초과'를 의미하므로 문맥상 적절하지 않다.

내신 1등급 어법 공략
pp. 198-199

01 ④	02 ⑤
03 ④	04 ④
05 ②	06 ①
07 ④	

01 (A) 「as++형용사[부사]의 원급+as」 구문에서 동사 captures를 수식하는 부사가 필요하므로 quickly가 알맞다.
(B) 앞에 가주어 it이 있고 뒤에 진주어 to부정사가 나와야 하므로 to convey가 알맞다.
(C) 이 문장은 앞 문장과 대조를 이루고 있으므로 대조를 나타내는 접속사 Yet이 적절하다. So는 결과나 결론을 나타내므로 적절하지 않다.

02 (A) begin은 to부정사나 동명사를 목적어로 취하는 동사이므로 to grow가 올바른 형태이다.
(B) provide something to someone의 구조가 올바르므로 to가 적절하다.
(C) 「regard A as B」 구문으로 'A를 B로 여기다'라는 의미의 관용 표현이다. 따라서 as가 올바르다.

03 ④ that은 계속적 용법으로 쓸 수 없는 관계대명사로 which를 써야 한다.

04 ④ A national environmental awareness event가 개최된 것이므로 수동태(was held)가 적절하다.

05 (A) '공장에서 일하고 있는 사람들'이라는 의미로 앞에 있는 those를 수식하는 현재분사 working이 적절하다.

(B) 주절의 내용에 대한 결과나 부수적인 상황을 나타내는 분사구문으로 현재분사 leaving이 적절하다.

(C) 아이들이 '지불받을 수 있었다'는 의미이므로 조동사가 있는 수동태could be paid가 올바른 표현이다.

06 ① 사진들이 전시회, 강연, 잡지 기사 등에 공개된 것으로 수동태가 되어야 하므로 과거분사 shown이 알맞다.

07 ④ 이 문장은 병렬 구조를 묻는 문제로 picking, weaving과 같은 동명사 형태로 handling이 되어야 한다.

01 ⑤	**02** ②
03 ④	**04** ①
05 ⑤	**06** ④
07 ④	**08** ⑤
09 ①	**10** ③
11 ④	**12** (1) exhibition (2) illegal
13 (A) as (B) like (C) of	**14** ⑤
15 ⑤	

01 주어진 문장은 결제 기능에 대한 부연 설명으로, 지갑을 가지고 다닐 필요가 없다는 것을 의미한다. 따라서 결제 기능을 언급한 직후인 ⑤의 위치가 가장 적절하다.

02 이 대화는 전반적으로 기타를 가르치는 비디오 채널을 시작하는 것에 초점을 맞추고 있으므로 ② '기타를 가르치는 비디오 채널 시작하기'가 주제로 적절하다.
　　① 음악 교육의 중요성 ③ 악기 배우기의 어려움 ④ 온라인 학습 플랫폼의 이점 ⑤ 음악 교육 기술의 미래

03 ④ in an instant는 '순식간에'라는 의미이다.

04 (A) meanwhile: '한편'이라는 의미로, 산업 성장의 긍정적 측면(일자리 제공)과 부정적 측면(폐기물 투기)이 동시에 일어났음을 나타낸다.
(B) although: '비록 ~일지라도'라는 의미로, 강이 오염되었음에도 불구하고 사람들이 이를 긍정적으로 인식했다는 모순된 상황을 표현한다.

05 ⑤ 타임지에 실린 사진은 1969년 화재의 것이 아니라 몇 년 전에(several years earlier)에 발생한 더 심각한 화재의 사진이었다. 따라서 later(나중에)가 아닌 earlier(이전에)가 올바른 표현이다.

06 밑줄 친 rising은 현재분사로 flames and smoke를 수식하고 있다.
ⓐ taking은 보어 역할을 하는 동명사이다.
ⓑ studying은 scientists를 수식하는 현재분사이다.
ⓒ reading은 앞에 있는 be동사와 함께 현재진행형으로 쓰인 현재분사이다.
ⓓ cooking은 the chef를 수식하는 현재분사이다.
ⓔ Feeling은 분사구문에 쓰인 현재분사이다.

07 (A) 앞의 명사 the need를 수식하는 형용사적 용법의 to protect가 적절하다.
(B) 앞 문장 전체를 선행사로 하는 계속적 용법의 관계대명사 which가 필요하다. that은 계속적 용법으로 쓸 수 없다.
(C) national water quality standards가 '설립되었다'는 의미이므로 수동태 were established가 올바른 표현이다.

08 ⑤ 1972년 청정수법(Clean Water Act) 제정으로 국가 수질 기준이 수립되었다고 언급하고 있다. 대기질이 아닌 수질 기준에 대한 내용이다.

09 ⓐ 접속사 and 뒤에 문장이 왔고 앞에도 문장이 와야 한다. 따라서 과거 시제 동사인 increased가 알맞다.
ⓒ 이 문장의 동사는 뒤에 나오는 were이고 앞에 있는 some of those를 수식하므로 현재분사 working이 적절하다.

10 19세기 산업혁명 시기 아동 노동의 실태를 설명하고 있다. 빈칸은 어렵고 위험한 아동 노동의 결과를 나타내야 하므로 많은 아동 노동자들에게 건강 문제를 남겼다는 내용의 ③이 빈칸에 적절하다.
　　① 성인들 사이에 높은 사망률을 초래했다
② 열악한 교육 결과를 초래했다
④ 공장의 생산성 증가로 이어졌다
⑤ 미래를 위한 숙련된 노동력을 창출했다

11 본문의 to ban은 형용사적 용법의 to부정사이다. ④는 형용사적 용법의 to부정사이고 나머지는 모두 동사의 목적어 역할을 하는 명사적 용법의 to부정사이다.
① 정부는 모든 공공장소에서 흡연을 금지하기로 결정했다.
② 그들은 그 남자가 건물에 들어오는 것을 금지하려고 했다.
③ 학교는 수업 중 학생들의 휴대전화 사용을 금지하기로 결정했다.
④ 어린이 TV 프로그램 중 정크푸드 광고를 금지하려는 노력이 계속되고 있다.
⑤ 위원회는 도시 내 일회용 플라스틱 사용을 금지하는 것에 투표했다.

12 (1) '예술 작품, 유물 또는 기타 흥미로운 항목들의 전시'는 'exhibition(전시회, 전시)'의 영어 뜻풀이다.
(2) '법에 의해 금지된'이라는 의미는 'illegal(불법적인)'의 영어 뜻풀이다.

13 (A) '~로서'라는 의미의 as가 알맞다.
(B) '~와 같은'이라는 의미의 like가 알맞다.
(C) '~을 이용하다'라는 의미의 take advantage of이므로 of가 알맞다.

14 What is more는 추가적인 정보를 제공할 때 사용되는 표현으로 주어진 문장은 Hine의 사진이 포착한 아동 노동의 실상을 더 자세히 설명하는 내용이므로 ⑤의 위치가 적절하다.

15 ⓔ picking vegetables는 '채소 따기'라는 의미의 명사구로 여기서 picking은 동명사이다.

01 ③	02 ③
03 ②	04 ③
05 ③	06 held → was held
07 ④	08 ③
09 some of those working in factories were only four years old	
10 ②	11 ①
12 ⑤	
13 how serious the situation was	
14 ④	15 ④

01 (A) '쓰여진 글'을 의미해야 하므로 written text가 적절하다. 여기서 written은 과거분사로 text를 수식하는 형용사 역할을 한다. writing text는 '글을 쓰는 행위'를 의미하므로 문맥상 적절하지 않다.
(B) in an instant는 '순식간에'라는 의미이고 for an instant는 '잠시 동안'이라는 의미이다. 문맥상 적절한 것은 in an instant이다.
(C) a great number of people은 '많은 수의 사람들'이라는 의미이다. people은 셀 수 있는 명사이므로 number가 적절하다. amount는 주로 셀 수 없는 명사와 함께 사용된다.

02 ③ 'B에게 A를 제공하다'라는 의미는 provided A to B이다. (= provide B with A)

03 ② thanks to는 '~덕분에'라는 뜻이다. '~에 감사하다'라는 해석은 문맥상으로도 적절하지 않다.

04 ③ 타임지에 실린 사진은 1969년 화재의 것이 아니라 몇 년 전에 (several years earlier) 발생한 더 심각한 화재의 사진이었다.

05 ③ 쿠야호가 강의 화재는 수질 오염에 대한 공분을 불러일으킨 것이므로 air가 아니라 water가 알맞다.

06 A national environmental awareness event는 개최된 것이므로 수동태가 되어야 한다. 따라서 held가 아니라 was held가 알맞다.

07 The demand for workers increased, ~라는 문장이 바로 뒤에 나오는데, 이는 '공장 생산의 증가'의 직접적인 결과이므로 ④가 정답이다.
▨ ① 농업 고용의 감소 ② 노동조합의 증가 ③ 개선된 근로 조건 ⑤ 성인 실업률의 상승

08 윗글에서는 아동 노동자들이 주로 일했던 특정 산업 분야에 대한 정보는 제공하지 않고 있으므로 ③이 정답이다.
▨ 질문에 대한 답은 다음과 같다. ① 산업혁명으로 인한 공장 생산의 증가에 따른 노동력 수요 증가 ② 약 20% ④ 낮은 임금, 파업 가능성 낮음 ⑤ 건강 문제 발생

09 전체 중 일부를 나타내는 some of those가 주어이고 주어를 뒤에서 수식하는 현재분사구 working in factories를 쓰고 were only four years old를 쓴다.

10 이 글은 아동 노동의 실태를 사진으로 폭로한 Lewis Hine의 활동에 초점을 맞추고 있으므로 ② 'Lewis Hine: 아동 노동을 폭로한 사진작가'가 정답이다.

▨ ① 19세기 아동 노동의 증가
③ 산업혁명이 미국 사회에 미친 영향
④ 전국아동노동위원회의 착취와의 싸움
⑤ 사회 변화를 위한 도구로서의 사진

11 (A) and 뒤에 started to work가 나오는 것으로 보아 앞에는 일을 '그만두었다(quit)'는 말이 오는 것이 적절하다.
(B) 아동 노동의 피해자인 어린이들은 '무력한(helpless)' 상태였다.
(C) 뒤에 나오는 picking vegetables, weaving baskets, and even handling dangerous equipment에서 다양한 종류의 아동 노동을 열거하고 있으므로 '포함했다(included)'가 적절하다.

12 네 사람은 소셜 미디어가 뉴스 소비 방식에 미친 영향에 대해 논의하고 있다. Sophia는 소셜 미디어의 빠르고 쉬운 정보 접근성을 강조하며 선호한다고 말한다. Liam은 정보의 정확성 문제와 허위정보 확산의 위험성을 지적한다. Ava는 이를 인정하면서 전통적인 뉴스 출처를 선호한다고 말하고 있다.

13 간접의문문을 포함하고 있는 문장이다. 간접의문문의 어순은 「의문사+주어+동사」이다. 이 규칙에 따라 how serious the situation was가 올바른 어순이다.

14 ④ to부정사의 의미상의 주어는 「for+목적격」이다. 「of+목적격」은 앞에 사람의 성격을 나타내는 형용사가 나오는 경우에 쓴다.

15 ④ G가 I've been thinking about starting a cooking channel myself.라고 말함으로써 대화의 초점이 B의 기타 채널에서 G의 요리 채널로 갑자기 바뀌게 되므로 흐름상 적절하지 않다.

01 ②	02 (1) capture (2) convey
03 ④	04 ③
05 This means that I don't need to carry my wallet with me anymore.	
06 ⑤	07 ②
08 ③	09 featured, rising
10 ②	11 ④
12 ①	13 ⑤
14 ④	15 ②

01 Ethan이 소셜 미디어가 뉴스 소비 방식을 변화시켰다는 일반적인 설명으로 토론을 시작한다. 그 후 Sophia와 Liam이 각각 소셜 미디어를 통한 뉴스 소비의 장단점을 언급한다. 빈칸은 Ethan의 설명 직후에 위치하며, Sophia가 소셜 미디어를 선호한다고 말하는 문장 앞에 있다. 이 맥락에서 가장 자연스러운 질문은 토론에 참여한 사람들의 선호도를 묻는 것이므로 ② 'Which do you prefer?(어느 것을 더 선호하니?)'가 적절하다.
▨ ① 당신은 뉴스를 어떻게 소비하나요?
③ 당신은 소셜 미디어가 신뢰할 수 있다고 생각하나요?
④ 소셜 미디어 뉴스의 장점은 무엇인가요?
⑤ 당신은 얼마나 자주 뉴스를 확인하나요?

02 (1) '정확하게 단어나 그림으로 표현하거나 기록하다'라는 의미이므로 'capture(정확히 포착하다)'의 정의이다.

(2) '생각이나 감정 등을 전달하거나 표현하다'라는 의미이므로 'convey (전달하다)'의 정의이다.

03 ④ '이 지역은 풍부한 문화 역사와 활기찬 예술 현장으로도 알려져 있다.'는 산업 오염에 관한 본문의 주제와 맞지 않으므로 흐름상 적절하지 않다.

04 밑줄 친 That과 ①, ②, ④, ⑤의 that은 모두 관계대명사로 사용되었다. ③의 that은 명사절을 이끄는 접속사로 사용되었다.

06 (A) environmental problems: 1969년 쿠야호가 강 화재 사건은 미국인들의 환경 문제에 대한 인식을 변화시켰다.

(B) environmental awareness event: 1970년 4월 22일에 열린 행사는 첫 번째 지구의 날로, 환경 문제에 대한 대중의 인식을 높이는 중요한 계기가 되었다.

■■■ ① 생태학의, 생태적인 ② 자연의, 자연적인 ③ 지속 가능한 ④ 친환경적인, 녹색의

07 앞 문장의 내용 전체를 받아 부가적인 설명을 덧붙일 때 사용하는 관계대명사는 which이다. 계속적 용법이므로 that은 쓸 수 없다.

08 (A) 이유를 나타내는데 적합한 접속사는 because로 클리블랜드 사람들이 신경 쓰지 않았던 이유를 설명하고 있다.

(B) 앞선 내용과 대조되는 내용을 소개할 때 사용되는 접속사는 However로 사람들이 처음에는 관심이 없었지만, 곧 화재가 유명해졌다는 대조적인 상황을 연결하고 있다.

(C) 추가적인 정보나 더 정확한 설명을 제공할 때 사용되는 접속사는 In fact이다. 타임지에 실린 사진이 실제로는 1969년 화재의 것이 아니라는 사실을 강조하고 있다.

09 첫 번째 빈칸에는 '~을 특종으로 다루다'라는 의미의 동사가 들어가야 하므로 featured가 알맞다. 두 번째 빈칸에는 flames and smoke(불꽃과 연기)를 수식하여, 강에서 올라오는 모습을 묘사하고 있으므로 rising이 알맞다.

10 ⓐ 수동태 문장이므로 과거분사형 filled가 적절하다.

ⓑ 앞 문장과 연결되는 분사구문으로 leaving이 적절하다.

11 빈칸은 아동 노동자들이 성인 노동자들에 비해 덜 할 것 같은 행동을 설명해야 하므로 '파업을 덜할 것 같다'가 들어가는 것이 알맞다.

■■■ ① 신체적으로 강하다 ② 긴 시간을 일하다 ③ 복잡한 기계를 조작하다 ⑤ 새로운 기술에 적응하다

12 (A) 전치사 by 뒤에는 동명사 형태가 와야 한다.

(B) 선행사 factory owners가 사람이므로 주격 관계대명사 who가 알맞다.

(C) '~하지 않을 수 없다'라는 뜻의 「cannot help but+동사원형」 구문이다.

13 ⑤ Lewis Hine은 아이들의 이름과 나이를 물어보고 생활 및 근로 조건에 대한 정보를 기록했지만, 이를 '공개적으로' 했다는 언급은 없다. 오히려 비밀리에 정보를 수집했다고 명시되어 있다.

14 본문의 밑줄 친 that은 관계대명사이다. ⓐ, ⓒ, ⓔ는 관계대명사이고 ⓑ, ⓓ는 명사절을 이끄는 접속사이다.

ⓐ 내가 읽고 있는 그 책은 흥미롭다.

ⓑ 나는 정직이 최선의 방책이라고 믿는다.

ⓒ 우리가 어제 방문한 박물관은 훌륭했다.

ⓓ 그는 파티에 올 거라고 말했다.

ⓔ 저기 주차된 빨간 차는 내 것이다.

15 (A) 아동 노동을 금지하기 위해 더 강력한 법률이 필요했을 것이므로 stronger가 알맞다.

(B) 맥락상 16세 미만 아동의 공장 노동을 불법화하는 법안이 통과되었다는 것이므로 illegal이 알맞다.

(C) a picture is worth a thousand words는 관용구로, 여기서는 부사 truly가 적절하다.

내신 1등급 수능형 고난도   pp. 212-215

01 ③	02 ④
03 ③	04 ③
05 ⑤	06 ⑤
07 ⑤	08 ①
09 ①	10 ②
11 ④	12 ②
13 ③	14 ②
15 ④	

[01-02] 해석

> 카메라가 순간을 즉시 포착하듯이, 하나의 이미지가 우리의 감정을 즉각적으로 사로잡을 수 있다. 말이나 글로 복잡한 메시지를 빠르게 전달하는 것은 어려울 수 있다. 하지만 사진은 <u>사람들의 관점과 감정을 신속하게 바꿀 수 있는</u> 독특한 능력을 가지고 있다. 사진의 마법이 많은 사람들 사이에서 광범위한 감정적 반응을 일으킬 때, 그것은 역사를 바꿀 수 있는 잠재력을 갖게 된다.

01 ③ '사람들의 관점과 감정을 신속하게 변화시키다'가 글의 주제와 잘 어울린다.

■■■ ① 역사적 사건을 정확하게 기록하다

② 시각 예술의 질을 향상시키다

④ 전통적인 의사소통 방식을 대체하다

⑤ 개인에게 지속적인 기억을 만들어 주다

02 이 글은 사진이 즉각적으로 사람들의 감정을 사로잡고, 복잡한 메시지를 빠르게 전달할 수 있으며, 사람들의 관점과 감정을 신속하게 변화시킬 수 있는 독특한 능력을 가지고 있다고 설명하고 있다. 따라서 글의 요지로 가장 적절한 것은 ④이다.

[03-05] 해석

> 1880년대 동안 클리블랜드의 쿠야호가 강 주변에서 상당한 산업 발전이 이루어졌다. 이러한 성장은 지역 주민들에게 안정적인 고용 기회를 제공했다. 하지만 동시에 제철소와 공장들이 강에 대량의 폐기물을 버리는 결과를 낳았다. 오염된 강에도 불구하고, 대부분의 사람들은 이를 단순히 지역 경제 성공의 징표로 여겼다.
>
> 1969년 6월, 오염된 강에 불이 붙었다. 가장 유력한 원인은 지나가는 기차에서 떨어진 불타는 조명탄이 다리 밑의 기름에 젖은 폐기물에 불을 붙인 것이었다. 당시 클리블랜드의 거의 아무도 이를 신경 쓰지 않았다. 이러한 무관심은 쿠야호가 이전에 10번 이상 불이 났고, 그 중 일부는 훨씬 더 심각했다는 사실에서 비롯되었다.

03 주어진 문장은 강이 오염되었음에도 불구하고 사람들이 이를 경제적 성공의 징후로 여겼다는 내용이다. 이 문장은 강의 오염에 대한 언급 직후, 1969년 화재 사건 이전에 위치하는 것이 가장 적절하므로 ③이 정답이다.

04 ③ 화재의 원인을 설명하고 있으므로 ⓒ 'result(결과)'가 아니라 'cause(원인)'가 적절하다.

05 (A) 형용사 industrial의 수식을 받으므로 명사형 development가 적절하다.
(B) 셀 수 없는 명사인 waste와 함께 사용되므로 amounts가 적절하다. numbers는 셀 수 있는 명사와 함께 사용된다.
(C) 계속적 용법의 관계대명사 which가 자연스럽다. that은 계속적 용법으로 쓸 수 없다.

[06-08] 해석

1969년 쿠야호가 강에서 발생한 화재는 같은 해 타임지에 실린 기사로 인해 빠르게 유명해졌다. 이 기사에는 강에서 불길과 연기가 치솟는 충격적인 사진이 포함되어 있었다. 하지만 이 이미지는 1969년 화재의 것이 아니었다. 1969년 화재는 너무 빨리 진압되어 아무도 사진을 찍지 못했다. 대신, 이 사진은 몇 년 전에 발생했던 훨씬 더 심각한 화재를 보여주고 있었다. 그럼에도 불구하고 이 이미지는 대중에게 큰 인상을 남겼다.
그 무렵, 미국인들의 환경 문제에 대한 태도가 변하기 시작했다. 사람들은 점점 더 환경 보호의 중요성을 인식하게 되었고, 불타는 강의 충격적인 이미지는 수질 오염에 대한 대중의 분노를 불러일으켰다. 그 결과, 1969년 쿠야호가 강 화재는 환경오염의 상징이 되었다. 1970년 4월 22일, 환경 인식을 높이기 위한 전국적인 행사가 열렸고, 이는 후에 첫 번째 지구의 날로 알려지게 되었다. 그리고 1972년, 청정수법(Clean Water Act) 제정으로 국가 수질 기준이 수립되었다.

06 쿠야호가 강 화재 사건이 환경 변화의 불씨 역할을 했다는 점에서 ⑤ '쿠야호가 강 화재: 환경 변화의 불씨'가 글의 제목으로 적절하다.
▨ ① 지구의 날 기념 행사의 역사
② 타임지가 미국 정치에 미치는 영향
③ 국가 수질 기준의 발전
④ 클리블랜드의 산업혁명과 그 결과

07 ⑤ 주어가 national water quality standards이므로 수동태 'were established(설립되었다)'가 올바른 표현이다.

08 (A) 타임지에 실린 사진이 실제 1969년의 화재 사진이 아니라는 점을 대조적으로 보여주고 있으므로 앞선 내용과 대조되는 내용을 소개할 때 사용되는 'However(그러나)'가 적절하다.
(B) 1969년의 화재 사진이 아님에도 불구하고 대중에게 큰 인상을 남겼다는 점을 강조하고 있으므로 'Nonetheless(그럼에도 불구하고)'가 적절하다.
(C) 앞선 내용의 결과로 어떤 일이 발생했음을 나타낼 때 사용되는 'As a result(결과적으로)'가 적절하다.

[09-11] 해석

19세기 산업혁명은 미국 전역에서 공장 생산의 급격한 증가를 촉발했다. 남북전쟁은 클리블랜드를 하룻밤 사이에 제조업 도시로 변모시켰다. 이러한 제조업의 급증으로 노동자에 대한 수요가 크게 늘어났고, 이는 아동 노동의 광범위한 고용으로 이어졌다. 1900년경에는 미국 아동의 약 20%가 노동력의 일부였으며, 일부는 4세의 어린 나이에도 공장에서 일했다. 근로 조건은 열악하고 위험했으며, 종종 이 어린 노동자들에게 심각한 건강 문제를 초래했다.
공장주들이 아동을 고용한 데에는 여러 가지 이유가 있었다. 한 가지 주요 이유는 재정적인 것이었다; 아동 노동자들에게는 성인 노동자들보다 낮은 임금을 지급할 수 있었다. 또한, 아동 노동자들은 노동 파업에 참여할 가능성이 낮다고 여겨졌다.

09 윗글은 19세기 산업혁명 이후 미국 전역에서 아동 노동이 증가한 상황과 그 원인, 그리고 아동 노동의 실태에 대해 설명하고 있다. 그러나 ① '남북전쟁으로 클리블랜드가 하룻밤 사이에 제조업 도시로 변모했다'는 특정 도시의 변화에 대해 언급하고 있으므로 전체적인 미국의 아동 노동 문제를 다루는 글의 흐름과 무관하다.

10 (A) 산업혁명으로 인해 공장 생산이 증가했기 때문에 rise가 적절하다.
(B) 아동 노동의 증가를 설명하고 있기 때문에 employment가 적절하다.
(C) 공장주들이 아동을 고용한 주요 이유가 경제적이었음을 나타내므로 financial이 적절하다.

11 문맥상 어린이 노동자들이 열악한 근무 환경에서 일하면서 심각한 건강 문제를 겪는다는 내용이 적합하므로 ④ '심각한 건강 문제'가 빈칸에 적절하다.
▨ ① 가족을 위한 더 높은 임금 ② 증가된 일자리 기회 ③ 향상된 생활수준 ⑤ 더 나은 교육 접근성

[12-14] 해석

Lewis Hine은 교사이자 사진작가로, 아동 노동의 잔혹성을 폭로하기로 결심했다. 그는 교직을 사임하고 전국아동노동위원회(National Child Labor Committee)의 조사 사진작가가 되었다. 공장에 접근하기 위해 그는 보험 설계사나 소방 감독관 같은 다른 직업을 가진 것처럼 가장했다.
일단 공장 안에 들어가면, Hine은 사진을 통해 아동들의 노동을 기록했다. 그는 또한 이름과 나이를 포함한 개인 정보를 수집하고 그들의 생활 및 근로 조건에 대한 세부 사항을 기록했다. 1908년부터 1912년 사이에 Hine은 비밀리에 증거를 수집하고 사진을 찍어 공장주들이 어떻게 무력한 아동들을 이용하고 있는지를 폭로했다.
Hine의 사진들은 어린 아이들이 다양한 일을 하는 모습을 담았다. 여기에는 채소를 따는 농업 노동부터 바구니를 짜거나 위험한 장비를 다루는 산업 작업까지 포함되었다. 이 사진들은 또한 힘든 노동이 아이들에게 미친 비극적인 영향을 보여주는 그들의 얼굴을 드러냈다. 사람들은 아이들의 기쁨 없는 표정을 보고 가슴 아파하지 않을 수 없었다.

12 이 글은 Lewis Hine이 아동 노동의 잔혹함을 드러내기 위해 사진을 사용한 방법과 그로 인해 사회가 변화하는 과정을 설명하고 있다. 따라서 주제로 가장 적절한 것은 ② '사회 개혁에서 사진의 역할'이다.

오답 ① 아동 노동이 미국 사회에 미친 영향
③ 미국 아동 노동 법의 역사
④ 루이스 하인(Lewis Hine)의 개인 생활
⑤ 아동 노동의 경제적 이점

13 (A) Hine의 목적이 아동 노동의 잔혹성을 드러내는 것이므로 expose가 적절하다.
(B) Hine이 개인 정보를 수집했다는 맥락에서 including이 적절하다.
(C) 아이들의 표정이 고된 노동의 영향을 보여주므로 joyless가 적절하다.

14 ② Hine의 사진은 아동 노동의 열악한 조건을 기록했을 뿐만 아니라 대중의 아동 권리에 대한 의식을 '깨웠다'는 의미로, awakened가 문맥상 가장 적절하다.

[15] 해석

Hine의 사진들은 전시회, 강연, 잡지 기사 등 다양한 경로를 통해 널리 알려지게 되었다. 그 결과, 많은 주에서 아동 고용을 금지하는 더 강력한 법률을 통과시켰다. 1938년, 미국 의회는 16세 미만의 아동이 학교 수업 시간 동안 공장에서 일하는 것을 불법으로 만드는 법안을 통과시켰다.

빈칸 다음 문장에서 1938년에 16세 미만 아동의 공장 노동을 불법화하는 법안이 통과되었다고 언급하고 있다. 따라서 빈칸에는 이러한 법적 변화의 내용을 가장 직접적으로 표현하는 ④ '아동 고용을 금지하기 위해'가 가장 적절하다.
오답 ① 아동 노동 인식을 촉진하다
② 공장에서의 근무 조건을 개선하다
③ 교육 프로그램에 대한 자금을 늘리다
⑤ 산업 생산 방법을 규제하다

내신 1등급 서술형

pp. 216-218

01 it can be difficult to convey a complex message
02 (A) Burning (B) polluted
03 ⑤ → had occurred
04 was put out so quickly
05 a national environmental awareness event
06 And in 1972, national water quality standards were established with the passage of the Clean Water Act.
07 harsh
08 leaving many child laborers with health problems
09 wanted to reveal how cruel this system was
10 (1) F / ① (2) T / ④
11 ②: As a result, the public realized just how serious the situation was. ③: In 1938, the United States Congress passed an act that made it illegal for children under sixteen to work in factories during school hours.
12 employment

01 「가주어 it, 진주어 to부정사」 구문을 사용하고 can, convey, complex를 사용하여 문장을 쓰면 it can be difficult to convey a complex message가 된다.

02 (A) '불타는 강'이라는 의미로 명사 river를 수식하는 현재분사 burning이 알맞다.
(B) became이라는 동사 뒤에서 보어 역할을 한다. 「became+과거분사」는 '~하게 되었다'라는 의미를 나타내므로 polluted가 알맞다.

03 ⑤ has occurred는 현재완료 시제로, 과거의 특정 시점을 기준으로 그 이전에 일어난 사건을 나타내는 문맥에 맞지 않다. 이 문장에서는 1969년 화재보다 몇 년 전에 일어난 사건을 설명하고 있으므로, 과거완료 시제인 had occurred가 올바른 표현이다.

04 which was put out so quickly that nobody took a picture of it을 바탕으로, 1969년 화재의 사진이 없는 이유는 화재가 너무 빨리 진압되었기 때문임을 알 수 있다. 이를 5단어로 간결하게 표현하면 was put out so quickly가 된다.
Q. 왜 1969년 화재의 사진이 찍히지 않았나요?
A. 불이 너무 빨리 꺼져서 아무도 그것의 사진을 찍을 시간이 없었기 때문이다.

05 which는 바로 앞 문장의 A national environmental awareness event를 가리킨다.

06 이 문장은 수동태 구문이다. national water quality standards가 주어이고, 이것이 '설립되었다'는 의미를 나타내야 한다. 따라서 were established라는 수동태 형태가 필요하다. 주어가 복수이고 과거의 일을 말하고 있으므로 were가 필요하다.

07 '불쾌하게 거칠거나 심한'이라는 의미는 'harsh(가혹한, 냉혹한)'의 정의이다.

08 분사구문은 동사의 현재분사형으로 시작하므로, leaving이 맨 앞에 온다. leaving 다음에는 목적어가 오는데, 여기서는 many child laborers가 된다. with는 전치사로, health problems와 함께 사용되어 상태나 결과를 나타낸다.

09 '~하고 싶었다'는 의미의 과거형 동사 wanted가 알맞다. want는 to부정사를 목적어로 취하므로 to reveal이 적절하다. reveal의 목적어로는 간접의문문의 어순이 되어야 하므로 how cruel this system was가 알맞다.

10 (1) ①에서 Hine이 공장에 들어가기 위해 보험 설계사나 소방 감독관과 같은 다른 직업을 가진 것처럼 가장했다고 했으므로 그가 공개적으로(openly) 사진작가로서 공장에 들어갔다는 진술은 틀린 내용이다.
(2) ④에서 Hine의 사진이 다양한 종류의 일을 하는 어린 아이들을 포착했다고 했으므로 특히 채소 따기(농업 노동)와 바구니 짜기, 위험한 장비 다루기(제조업) 등을 언급하고 있어, 농업과 제조업을 포함한 다양한 직종에서 일하는 아이들의 모습을 찍었다는 것을 확인할 수 있다.

11 ② realized의 목적어 역할을 하는 간접의문문이므로 「의문사+주어+동사」의 어순으로 써야 한다. 따라서 올바른 어순은 how serious the situation was이다.
③ 가목적어 it과 진목적어 to부정사 구문이므로 working이 아니라 to work가 알맞다.

12 여기서는 명사형이 필요하므로 employment가 알맞다.

01 ③	**02** Without, be
03 ③	**04** ④
05 ②	**06** ②
07 ①	**08** ②
09 ④	**10** ⑤
11 ②	**12** ③
13 (1) dangerous (2) nervous (3) unusual	
(4) unexpected	
14 ⑤	**15** ⑤
16 ④	**17** (A) polluted (B) burning
18 ⑤	**19** ③
20 ①	**21** ⑤
22 (A) filled → were filled (B) worked → working	
(C) left → leaving (D) little → less	
23 wanted to reveal how cruel this system was	
24 ②	
25 left, documenting, revealed, leading	

01 ③ 필자는 나무의 아름다움과 나무로 인해 얻는 산소에 대해 감사하는 마음을 표현하고 있다. 또한 나무가 새에게 집을 제공하는 것에 대한 고마움도 나타내고 있다. 따라서 이 글에 나타난 필자의 전반적인 심경은 'grateful(감사하는)'이다.

02 현재 사실의 반대를 가정하는 「Without ~, 주어+과거형 조동사+동사원형」 구문으로 wouldn't 뒤에는 be가 적절하다.

03 ⓐ the shop을 수식하는 현재분사 selling이 알맞다.
ⓓ 선행사가 ice이므로 관계대명사는 which가 알맞다.

04 이 글은 멜버른의 나무들이 이메일 주소를 가지고 있고 사람들이 그 나무들에게 메시지를 보내는 독특한 현상에 대해 소개하고 있다. 따라서 ④ '멜버른의 나무 이메일 시스템 뒤의 목적'이 제목으로 적절하다.
▨ ① 도시 나무들에 미치는 가뭄의 영향
② 기후 변화와 도시 열섬 현상
③ 도시에서 캐노피 커버(임관 피복도)의 중요성
⑤ 에어컨 사용과 온실가스 배출

05 ② 문맥상 나무의 수가 줄어들고 있다는 내용이므로 decreasing이 알맞다.

06 주어진 문장은 도시숲 전략 계획의 일부로 만들어진 온라인 지도에 대해 언급하고 있다. 이 문장은 계획의 목표를 설명한 문장 다음, 그리고 지도에 대한 구체적인 설명 전에 위치하는 것이 가장 자연스러우므로 ②가 정답이다.

07 (A) 전치사 뒤이므로 동명사 형태인 planting이 적절하다.
(B) 목적을 나타내는 부사적 용법의 to부정사가 적절하다.
(C) 선행사 trees를 수식하는 관계대명사 that이 적절하다.

08 ② 앞에 있는 love letters, poems, greetings, and messages를 수식하는 현재분사 expressing이 알맞다.

① something unexpected: -thing으로 끝나는 대명사는 형용사가 뒤에서 수식한다.
③ A message를 수식하는 관계대명사절에 쓰인 동사로 수동태가 적절하다.
④ stay 뒤에 보어로 형용사 healthy and strong이 적절하다.
⑤ 「Without+가정법 과거」 구문으로 would have가 적절하다.

09 ④ 환경을 해치거나 자원을 고갈시키지 않고 시간이 지나도 유지될 수 있는'이 'sustainable(지속 가능한)'의 영어 뜻풀이로 알맞다.
▨ ① 도시나 마을의 특성을 가진: urban(도시의)
② 무언가를 창조하거나, 만들거나, 제조하다: produce(생산하다, 만들어 내다)
③ 성공이나 특정 목표를 달성하려는 강한 욕구를 가진: ambitious(야심 있는)
⑤ 두 개 이상의 사물이나 사람 사이의 의사소통이나 행동을 포함하는: interactive(상호적인)

10 ⑤ 나무 메일 현상은 오직 지역적인 관심만을 끌었다. / 나무 메일 현상이 전 세계적으로 인기를 끌었다고 언급하고 있으므로 일치하지 않는 내용이다.
▨ ① 나무 메일 현상은 온라인에 지도가 게시된 후 시작되었다.
② 사람들은 나무에 대한 감정을 표현하기 위해 다양한 형태의 메시지를 보냈다.
③ 러시아에서 온 메시지는 언젠가 나무를 만나고 싶다는 바람을 언급했다.
④ 나무 메일의 세계적 인기는 우리가 자연과 연결되어 있음을 보여준다.

11 (B) 나무 메일 현상이 멜버른 주민들에게 미친 영향을 설명하며 글을 시작하는데 이는 전체 상황의 배경과 시작점을 제공한다.
(A) Meanwhile(한편)로 시작하며, 도시숲 전략의 진행 상황과 구체적인 목표를 설명한다. 이는 (C)에서 언급된 주민들의 참여와 병행하여 진행되는 공식적인 프로젝트를 소개한다.
(C) As a result(결과적으로)로 시작하며, 앞서 언급된 주민들의 참여(B)와 도시숲 전략(A)의 결과를 제시한다. 이는 전체 내용의 결론 역할을 한다.

12 ③ 도시숲 전략이 열섬 효과를 줄이고 주민들의 삶의 질을 향상시키는 데 기여한다는 내용은 글의 핵심 주제를 잘 반영한다.
▨ ① 멜버른의 도시 숲 전략이 기후 변화에 대응하는 내용을 포함하고 있지만, 요지로서 다소 구체적이지 않다.
② 나무 메일 현상에 대한 설명이지만, 전체 요지를 나타내지는 않는다.
④ 주민들의 참여가 언급되지만, 이 역시 전체 요지를 나타내기에는 부족하다.
⑤ 생물 다양성을 증가시키는 목표가 있지만, 이 또한 전체적인 요지를 포괄하지는 않는다.

13 (1) 보어 자리이므로 형용사 dangerous가 알맞다.
(2) felt 뒤에서 보어 역할을 하는 형용사 nervous가 적절하다.
(3) usual에서 파생된 형용사로, 보통과 다른 상태를 나타내는 unusual이 알맞다.
(4) expected의 부정형으로 예상치 못한 상태를 나타내는 unexpected가 알맞다.
(1) 안전벨트를 매지 않고 운전하는 것은 위험하며 심각한 부상을 초래할 수 있다.

(2) 그녀는 발표 전에 긴장했지만, 자신감 있게 말하는 데 성공했다.

(3) 그는 보통 일찍 잠자리에 들기 때문에 그가 늦게까지 공부하느라 깨어 있는 것은 이례적인 일이었다.

(4) 예상치 못한 폭우가 야외 행사 중에 모든 사람을 놀라게 했다.

14 B의 마지막 말 Many people are doing it these days.는 교육 비디오 제작이 보편화되었다는 것을 의미한다. 주어진 문장은 이러한 현상(많은 사람들이 교육 비디오를 만드는 것)의 결과로 우리가 새로운 것을 더 쉽게 배울 수 있게 되었다는 결론을 제시한다. 따라서 이 문장은 B의 마지막 말 뒤에 오는 것이 가장 자연스럽다. G의 You're right.는 B의 말과 주어진 문장 모두에 대한 동의로 볼 수 있다.

15 담화의 시작 부분에서 Would you like to contribute to research and make a difference in the world?라고 묻고, Eco Trackers가 사람들이 연구 프로젝트에 참여할 수 있게 해준다고 설명한다. 하이킹, 정원 가꾸기, 별 관찰 등 다양한 활동을 통해 과학 연구에 기여할 수 있는 방법들을 소개하며 마지막에 Come and join Eco Trackers today!라고 직접적으로 참여를 권유하고 있으므로 이 담화의 주된 목적은 ⑤이다.

16 글의 주제가 산업 발전과 환경 오염에 관한 내용인데 ④ '사람들은 일자리 증가가 임금 상승을 의미할 것이라고 낙관적이었다.'는 글의 전체 흐름과 어울리지 않는다.

17 (A) pollute는 뒤의 명사 river를 수식하는 과거분사 형태인 polluted로 써야 한다.

(B) burn은 뒤의 명사 flare를 수식하는 현재분사 형태인 burning으로 써야 한다.

18 ⑤ 쿠야호가 강의 화재는 수질 오염에 대한 공분을 불러일으킨 것이므로 air가 아니라 water가 알맞다.

19 밑줄 친 rising은 명사를 수식하는 현재분사로 ⓑ, ⓒ, ⓔ가 쓰임이 같다.

ⓑ barking은 명사 The dog을 수식하는 현재분사이다.

ⓒ laughing은 명사 The children을 수식하는 현재분사이다.

ⓔ cooking은 명사 The chef를 수식하는 현재분사이다.

████ ⓐ 현재 진행형에 쓰인 현재분사이다.

ⓓ Feeling은 분사구문에 쓰인 현재분사이다.

20 ① 타임지에 실린 사진은 1969년 화재의 사진이 아니었다. 실제로는 몇 년 전에 발생한 더 심각한 화재 사진이었다. 1969년 화재는 너무 빨리 진압되어 사진을 찍을 시간이 없었다고 한다.

████ ② 환경 문제에 대한 미국인들의 태도가 변하고 있었다.

③ 불타는 강의 이미지는 사람들이 수질 오염에 대해 강한 감정을 느끼게 만들었다.

④ 1969년 화재가 오염의 상징이 되었다.

⑤ 첫 번째 지구의 날이 1970년 4월 22일에 열렸다.

21 ⑤ 산업혁명이 공장 생산의 급격한 증가로 이어졌다고 하는 것이 자연스럽다.

████ ① '노동조합의 출현'은 본문에서 언급되지 않았으며, 오히려 아동 노동의 증가와는 반대되는 개념이다.

② '농업 고용의 감소'는 직접적으로 언급되지 않았으며, 공장 노동의 증가를 설명하지 못한다.

③ '성인의 근로 조건 개선'은 본문의 내용과 맞지 않는다. 오히려 열악한 노동 조건을 암시하고 있다.

④ '아동 노동에 대한 더 엄격한 규제'는 본문의 내용과 정반대이다.

22 (A) 수동태가 되어야 하므로 were filled가 알맞다.

(B) some of those를 수식하는 현재분사 working이 알맞다.

(C) 앞의 was와 병렬 구조를 이루는 분사구문에 쓰인 현재분사 leaving이 알맞다.

(D) 뒤에 than이 있으므로 little의 비교급 less가 알맞다.

23 '~하고 싶었다'는 의미의 과거형 동사 wanted를 쓴다. want는 to부정사를 목적어로 취하므로 to reveal을 쓴다. reveal의 목적어로는 간접의문문의 어순이 되어야 하므로 how cruel this system was를 이어서 쓴다.

24 ⓑ '생각이나 감정 등을 전달하거나 표현하다'는 'convey(생각이나 감정 등을 전달하다)'의 정의이다.

████ ⓐ 자신을 보호하거나 돌볼 수 없는

ⓒ 특정 목적을 위한 도구 또는 용품

ⓓ 예술, 유물, 또는 기타 관심 있는 항목들의 전시

ⓔ 법에 의해 금지된

25 교사이자 사진작가인 Lewis Hine은 아동 노동을 기록하기 위해 교사직을 그만두고 전국아동노동위원회에서 일하기 시작했다. 그의 강렬한 사진들은 아이들이 처한 가혹한 환경을 보여주었고, 이를 통해 대중의 인식을 높였으며 결국 미국에서 더 강력한 아동 노동법이 제정되는 계기가 되었다.

SPECIAL LESSON
Two Thanksgiving Day Gentlemen

01 gather to eat
02 called a turkey, is served
03 there are old traditions
04 had happened
05 filled his heart with joy
06 not hungry at all
07 could barely move
08 break out of his clothes
09 who wish to help the poor
10 where two elderly ladies lived
11 to bring in the first hungry-looking person
12 was passing by
13 fed him until
14 made his breath stop
15 watched him eat
16 trying to make into
17 build a great American tradition
18 In order to build
19 compared to
20 whiter and thinner than
21 seem as strong as
22 could fly away
23 the troubles of another year
24 as thankful as your mind
25 tears of suffering
26 had always wondered why
27 was unaware that
28 in remembrance of
29 one of the old houses
30 Feeling helpless
31 with the pleasure of giving
32 bring large amounts of food
33 struggled with his full stomach
34 couldn't stop eating
35 stood for a moment
36 taken to a hospital
37 was brought to
38 what's wrong with
39 died from hunger
40 hadn't eaten for

01 when
02 called
03 for
04 something wonderful
05 with
06 most
07 had had
08 to break
09 are
10 had been
11 where
12 who
13 when
14 until
15 stop
16 eat
17 that
18 Buying
19 is
20 was dressed
21 than
22 strong
23 wished
24 feel
25 what
26 themselves
27 For
28 suffering
29 why
30 himself
31 come
32 houses
33 Feeling
34 giving
35 bring
36 eating
37 taken
38 another
39 from
40 hadn't

01 when
02 called
03 for
04 something wonderful
05 with
06 most
07 had had
08 to break
09 are
10 had been
11 where
12 who
13 when
14 until
15 stop
16 eat
17 that
18 Buying
19 be done
20 is
21 was dressed
22 than
23 strong
24 wished
25 feel
26 what
27 themselves
28 For
29 suffering
30 why
31 that
32 himself
33 come
34 houses
35 Feeling
36 giving
37 bring
38 eating
39 left
40 turning
41 taken
42 another
43 from
44 hadn't

01 ③
02 ①
03 ④
04 something wonderful had happened to him
05 (T)radition
06 ③
07 ②
08 remembrance
09 Feeling helpless and very sorry for himself
10 ⑤
11 ②
12 the Old Gentleman was brought to the same hospital

---

01 ③ 칠면조라고 '불리는' 큰 새라는 의미이므로 a large bird를 수식하는 과거분사 called가 알맞다.

02 마지막 문장에서 '여기 이 새로운 나라에도 오래된 전통이 있다는 것을 증명하는 이야기가 있다'고 언급하고 있으므로 ① '대대로 전해 내려온 추수감사절 축하에 대한 이야기'가 뒤에 이어질 내용으로 적절하다.
　　② 추수감사절 칠면조 요리 방법에 대한 설명
　　③ 다양한 국가에서의 추수감사절 전통 비교
　　④ 추수감사절이 소매 산업에 미치는 경제적 영향에 대한 논의
　　⑤ 전형적인 추수감사절 식사의 영양가 분석

03 ④ Stuffy Pete가 예상치 못하게 저녁을 먹게 된 상황을 설명하고 있으므로 'unexpected(예상치 못한)'가 적절하다.

05 '여러 세대를 거쳐 전해 내려온 생각, 신념 또는 관습'은 '전통(tradition)'의 영어 뜻풀이다.

06 (A) watch는 지각동사로 목적격보어로 동사원형이 와야 하므로 eat이 알맞다.
(B) Nine years는 하나의 기간을 나타내는 말로 단수 취급하므로 is가 알맞다.
(C) 앞에 whiter and thinner라는 비교급이 있으므로 than이 알맞다.

07 빈칸 앞부분에 나온 Old Gentleman의 말이 Stuff Pete에게는 반가운 소리였다는 내용이 자연스러우므로 ② '그것들은 항상 Stuffy의 귀에 음악과 같았다'가 빈칸에 들어갈 말로 가장 적절하다.
　　① Stuffy Pete는 노신사를 만나는 것을 피했다
③ 노신사가 공원에 오는 것을 잊었다
④ Stuffy Pete가 노신사를 위해 음식을 가져왔다
⑤ 그들은 Stuffy Pete의 집에서 추수감사절을 축하했다

08 전치사 뒤이므로 빈칸에는 명사형이 적절하다. remember의 명사형은 remembrance이다.

09 접속사 As를 지우고, 주어 he도 주절의 주어 Stuffy Pete와 같으므로 지우고, felt를 현재분사 Feeling으로 바꾼다.

10 Stuffy Pete가 음식을 즐기고 맛있어 했다는 내용은 없다. 오히려 배가 불러 고통스러워하면서도 Old Gentleman을 위해 먹었다고 설명하고 있으므로 ⑤ 'Stuffy Pete는 식사를 즐겼고 맛있는 음식에 대해 감사했다.'가 일치하지 않는 내용이다.
　　① 노신사는 Stuffy Pete에게 식사를 제공하게 되어 기뻤다.
② Stuffy Pete와 노신사는 이전 해들과 마찬가지로 같은 테이블에 앉았다.
③ Stuffy Pete는 이미 배가 불렀음에도 불구하고 전체 식사를 먹었다.
④ 노신사는 식사 비용을 지불하고 웨이터에게 팁을 남겼다.

11 (A) while은 두 행동이 동시에 일어남을 나타내는 접속사로, Old Gentleman이 남쪽으로 가는 동안 Stuffy가 북쪽으로 갔다는 의미를 적절하게 전달한다.
(B) 모퉁이를 돌아 잠시 서 있다가 쓰러졌고 오래지 않아(before long) 병원으로 이송된 것이므로 Before가 알맞다.

12 the Old Gentleman을 주어로 하고 bring의 과거분사형 brought를 사용하여 was brought와 to the same hospital로 완성한다.

· MEMO ·

독해

READING EXPERT
중고등 대상 7단계 원서 독해 교재
Level 1 | Level 2 | Level 3 | Level 4 | Level 5 |
Advanced 1 | Advanced 2

기강 잡고
기본을 강하게 잡아주는 고등영어
독해 잡는 필수 문법 | 기초 잡는 유형 독해

빠른 독해를 위한 바른 선택
기초세우기 | 구문독해 | 유형독해 | 수능실전

The 상승
독해 기본기에서 수능 실전 대비까지
직독직해편 | 문법독해편 | 구문편 |
수능유형편 | 어법·어휘+유형편

수능

맞수
맞춤형 수능영어 단기특강 시리즈
구문독해 기본편 | 실전편
수능유형 기본편 | 실전편
수능문법어법 기본편 | 실전편
수능듣기 기본편 | 실전편
빈칸추론

PICK
핵심만 콕 찍어주는 수능유형 필독서
독해 기본 | 독해 실력 | 듣기

특급
수능 1등급 만드는 특급 시리즈
독해 유형별 모의고사 | 듣기 실전 모의고사 24회 |
어법 | 빈칸추론 | 수능·EBS 기출 VOCA

얇빠 얇고 빠른 미니 모의고사 10+2회
수능 핵심유형들만 모아 얇게! 회당 10문항으로 빠르게!
입문 | 기본 | 실전

수능만만
만만한 수능영어 모의고사
기본 영어듣기 20회 | 기본 영어듣기 35회+5회 |
기본 영어독해 10+1회 | 기본 문법·어법·어휘 150제 |
영어듣기 20회 | 영어듣기 35회 |
영어독해 20회 | 어법·어휘 228제

지은이

오 선 영	現 서울대학교 영어교육과 교수	최 동 석	現 인천국제고등학교 교사	이 주 연	現 경일고등학교 교사
양 하 늬	現 덕수고등학교 교사	최 성 묵	現 경북대학교 영어교육과 교수	서 공 주	現 대구외국어고등학교 교감
신 유 승	現 ㈜NE능률 교과서개발연구소	한 정 은	前 ㈜NE능률 교과서개발연구소		

고등 **기출문제집**

내신백신
Common
English 1 오선영

펴 낸 날	2025년 3월 1일 (초판 1쇄)
펴 낸 이	주민홍
펴 낸 곳	(주)NE능률

개 발 책 임	김지현
영 문 교 열	Curtis Thompson, Alison Li, Courtenay Parker
디자인책임	오영숙
디 자 인	안훈정, 오솔길
제 작 책 임	한성일

등 록 번 호	제1-68호
I S B N	979-11-253-4961-7

대 표 전 화	02 2014 7114
홈 페 이 지	www.neungyule.com
주 소	서울시 마포구 월드컵북로 396(상암동) 누리꿈스퀘어 비즈니스타워 10층